The Postmodern Chronotype

Postmodern Studies 30

Series
edited by
Theo D'haen
and
Hans Bertens

Postmodern Studies 30

The Postmodern Chronotype

Reading Space and Time in Contemporary Fiction

Paul Smethurst

The paper on which this book is printed meets the requirements of "ISO 9706:1994, Information and documentation - Paper for documents - Requirements for permanence".

ISBN: 90-420-1513-6
Editions Rodopi B.V., Amsterdam - Atlanta, GA 2000
Printed in The Netherlands

Part I
The Postmodern Chronotope

1	Introduction and Preliminaries on Postmodernism	1
2	Postmodernism's Spatial Turn: From Spatialisation to the Production of Space	31
3	The Chronotope as Idea, Optic and *Weltanschauung*	65

Part II
Reading Space and Time in Contemporary Fiction

4	The City in Late Capitalist Fantasy Alasdair Gray, *Lanark*	115
5	Spatial Historiographies Graham Swift, *Waterland*	145
6	Chronotopes of Reversible Time Peter Ackroyd, *Hawksmoor* and *First Light* Ian McEwan, *The Child in Time*	173
7	Post-colonial Island Chronotopes: Michel Tournier, *Friday* J. M. Coetzee, *Foe* Caryl Phillips, *Cambridge* Marina Warner, *Indigo*	219
8	The Trope of Placelessness: Graham Swift, *Out of this World* Don DeLillo, *Ratner's Star* and *The Names*	267
	Notes	311
	List of Novels	319
	Bibliography	321
	Index	331

Acknowledgements

Much of the research for this book was completed during the term of a PhD studentship at Birkbeck College, London between 1991 and 1995. I am grateful to the British Academy for providing funds. I must also thank Steven Connor for his expert guidance, and his encouragement to turn this into a book. I would also like to thank Doreen Massey and Paul Kenny for valuable criticism of my thesis, criticism that I have tried to address in the book.

The book was completed during my term at The University of Hong Kong, and I would like to thank the University Committee for Research Grants for funds to help complete the project. I would also like to thank staff and students at HKU for valuable comments and criticism. In particular, thanks are due to Ackbar Abbas, Jeremy Tambling, Douglas Kerr and to students of the Postmodernism module in the MA in English Studies.

I am indebted to Madeline Weston for editing the book and expunging as many slips as she has. I take full responsibility for those that remain.

PART I

THE POSTMODERN CHRONOTOPE

CHAPTER 1

Introduction and Preliminaries on Postmodernism

Postmodernism is conceived here as a significant and far-reaching shift in the indicators of space and time, affecting areas of life as far apart as cosmology and comic books, economics and ecology, architecture and archaeology, mysticism and history, cyberspace and cinema. All of these areas and more are considered in the present work, first to establish the case for the postmodern chronotope as a way of seeing the postmodern world out of kilter with a modern consciousness of space and time, and then as subjects and themes explored in the postmodern novel.

I begin with the premise that postmodernism has changed the way the past is re-presented, the contemporary apprehended and the future envisioned, and it has changed fundamentally perceptions of space and place. There are specific postmodern concerns, like what happens to the nation state in postmodern consciousness, and how will this be affected by globalisation, but I am presenting postmodernism as a more general and fundamental shift than this.

In *The Postmodern Chronotope*, I will argue that simple operations in the phenomenal world that require differentiation, between for example, past and present, inside and outside, real and representational, and space and place, have become problematic. As for postmodernism's relations with modernism, postmodernism is mostly considered as a continuation of modernism, but a continuation that might eventually seek to transform it and to take it off in other directions. Rather than a decisive break with modernism, postmodernism is a re-engagement and a reworking of all that might be considered modern, and at the same time, it is engagement with the material conditions of postmodernity.

Although postmodernism as a set of cultural and artistic practices is the main concern of this work, I begin with a synopsis of postmodernity within and across a range of disciplines. I will be shuffling back and forth between what might initially be distinguished as material postmodernity, theoretical postmodernity and cultural and artistic postmodernity. Such distinctions are not easily made in the postmodernity I present, and a good deal of my approach is distinctly un-postmodern as I move to differentiate, integrate, synthesise and analyse. I trust that readers will appreciate this temporary shift of register out of the postmodern, and accept that it is done knowingly and largely with their interest in mind.

To suggest, as I do, that postmodernism can be conceived as a shift in the indicators of space and time will likely raise the question that surely modernism could also be so conceived. This is true, but I believe there is a difference in that the time–spaces of modernism are rather more transparently linked with the artistic, cultural and material projects of modernity. The postmodern shift is less driven by projects and material conditions, with the one major exception of globalisation, through which the time–spaces of postmodernity certainly follow on from modernity. But in other respects, the postmodern is affected more by lack of development, loss of direction, and ambivalent approaches towards the past and the future.

For modernism, the speed of change in the age of machines inevitably affects the way we live, think about, and represent the world and our place in it. This has a lot to do with space and time, whether in the design of modern cities and individual buildings, abstract form in modern art and literature, the sense of the shrinking globe, the rise and fall of imperialist geographies, the centrality of science and technology (and a corresponding fear of a lesser humanity). Time here is predominately, although not exclusively, future-oriented, and space is predominately abstract, homogeneous and expansive (although geographical space is a barrier to time and to be reduced or passed over).

Even in high modernism at its most solipsistic, thinking and artistic representation reflect material changes in a real world. And this real world can be detached from the world of art and representation that in turn seeks to reflect or act upon that world with the intention, sometimes, of changing it. Postmodernism, on the other hand, is haunted by the sceptre of self-consciousness and the idea that representations of the world more likely form the world (or rather worlds) rather than take their form from it.

Here then is the first significant shift that can be conceived as a spatial and temporal change in the way we see the world: postmodernism signals a radical loss of differentiation between the real world as historical and geographical referent, and representations of the real world. And the second significant shift is that this loss of the real occurs not in the age of machines that were visible and palpable, but in the age of information, where so much is invisible and falsifiable. If the time–spaces of modernism were constituted in cities and suburbia, and traversed by motor vehicles, aeroplanes, electromagnetic devices and the cinema, postmodernism is constituted in cyberspace and transmitted through electronic media. The real world, as a visible world in which things could be seen to be happening, work could be seen to be getting done, and people and objects moved around in physical space, is gradually effaced, leaving its traces on the surfaces of the new 'real' world of electronic simulacra.

This Baudrillardian sketch does not refer to a completed process, only to a direction, and a transformation in the real that I suspect will turn out to be rather less alarming than some would predict. Nevertheless, there is a perceived loss of the real in postmodernism, and there is a major question hanging over relations between such perceptions and the cultural and artistic practices that seek to reflect and effect change both in the perception of the real and the real itself, wherever and whatever that might now be.

There are two principal and fundamentally different approaches we might take:

1. like modernism, postmodernism has a material base, which is now determined by the interconnected developments of advanced capitalism (exemplified by derivatives trading and other indirect and contrived forms of investment), and by the domination of visual media and information technology as our major conduit to reality;

2. postmodernism emerges out of the failure of the projects of modernity, which have run aground on the rocks of historical materialism and wrecked the idea that there is any discernible pattern in the traces of history enabling us to be masters of our own destiny.

In either case, postmodernism is a slippery character, at home either in deep cyberspace or the flickering of TV monitors, or in the lofty and esoteric towers of the academy that invented and institutionalised it. There is limited scope for thinking through postmodernity and envisaging the future, because, in a material sense, the present seems already to be the future, constantly shocking us with its science fiction turned fact, in areas such as cloning, genetic engineering, cybernetics, and information technology. And, down the other path, a loss of a sense of historicity is confirmed by a stream of events unforeseen by the world's pundits, such as the fall of the Iron Curtain, and dramatic shifts in financial markets.

Not wishing simply to add to the proliferation of accounts of an indeterminate postmodernism, it is my aim to focus on a particular aspect of the postmodern, namely the more or less technical relations of time and space. The plan of the present work is to begin by highlighting time–space relations as a recurring and interdisciplinary theme in recent studies of the postmodern. Then comes the formulation of the generalised postmodern chronotope; the idea being that certain features of time–space relations, such as de-centring, de-differentiation[1], non-linearity, are sufficiently prevalent across a range of disciplines to warrant being drawn together into the general case of the postmodern chronotope. From here, the postmodern chronotope is considered briefly as an optic and *Weltanschauung* for seeing and reading the contemporary. I propose to raise these common features of the postmodern above the level of style, which often has negative connotations when, for example, comparing postmodern art with modern art, and to take them seriously as an integral part of the postmodern world and therefore a necessary element in the way we read that world. Having arrived at the general shape and theory of the postmodern chronotope, the major portion of the work considers a selection of postmodern novels through the general chronotope, and also examines whatever particular chronotopes the novels use.

I hope that this approach, as well as offering some interesting new readings of important contemporary fiction, will go some way towards identifying a version of postmodernism that is equally valid in, and disrespectful to, the boundaries between formal aspects of literature and its own history, and between literature and the 'real' world of contemporary cultural and social life.

Having set out my stall, it is time to say a little about what is meant by the chronotope. A chronotope is a time–space in which the conscious mind frames and organises the real, but it can also be the time–space where it disorganises and re-presents the real. The emphasis in this work is on representational chronotopes, and in particular, novelistic chronotopes. Importantly, neither time nor space is a privileged category in the novelistic chronotope, where space and time sometimes swap axes, so for example, distance might signify time passing, proximity the present, and the past might be presented as wilderness. Novelistic chronotopes are representational chronotopes that convey worlds both real and unreal.

In realist novels, the mimetic function seems to draw the representational chronotope close to actual historical and geographical realities to present models or microcosms of the real world. Yet, even in a classic realist text like *Middlemarch*, there are artistic chronotopes in which history is assimilated and re-presented as metaphor. The constraining image of provincial life represented by the 'dull brown pond', and the crushing weight of history contained in Dorothea's vision of the 'ruined basilica and colossi of Rome', are both examples of a shift in the register of seeing through the novelistic chronotope (Eliot [1871] 1987: 1, 227–8). Here, the shift is from the general chronotope of Victorian reality, found elsewhere in this and other Victorian novels, of the deep, well-fenced historical reality, to an individualised and specifically female response to that historical reality.

One of the hallmarks of postmodernity, many say, is a failure to conceive of, or a loss of faith in (it is not clear which), such deep and well-fenced historical reality. Indeed, it is true that the postmodern novel often lacks that fixed pole of representation offered by historical reality, and so lacks a backcloth across which other representational chronotopes might play. In postmodern novelistic chronotopes, history slips its anchor, the fixed pole moves, and the backcloth shifts, and so the play of representation extends from the fictional into the historical. Furthermore, in the postmodern novelistic chronotope, the loss of privilege suffered in the historical dimension is also felt in the geographical plane, where space and place cannot always be relied upon to determine exactly where we are. The conditions that lead to this are complex: part historical, part conceptual, part technological, part philosophical and a large part representational. These contributing factors are summarised in Chapter 3. The postmodern novel gives a good indication of this complexity with its self-conscious presentations of complex and conflicting worlds careless of, although conscious of, the mimetic function. The degree to which the postmodern novel reflects such postmodernity, for example by problematising modern developmental ways of seeing the world, or to which it presents creative tension in the conflicts between different modes of representation, are the chief concerns of the present work. The methodology is to analyse spatio-temporal aspects of postmodernity and to see how and in what ways the postmodern novel as an artistic form responds to these.

The idea of the postmodern chronotope is put forward as an attempt to organise and articulate the main features of the shift in time–space relations that gives rise to postmodern ways of seeing. Importantly, the chronotope, as a binding of space and time into time–space, has applications beyond the literary and aesthetic. It is equally useful in analysing scientific and cultural models of space and time, so that we can talk of the chronotopes of black holes, chaos theory, financial models, music videos and TV advertisements, and possibly find some connections between these.

I wish to demonstrate, first, that it is possible to define the general properties and attributes of postmodern chronotopes; second, that these can be drawn from both the material conditions of postmodernity and the abstract and conceptual content of recent scientific and philosophical discourse; and, third, and most important, that representational chronotopes (similar to Bakhtin's novelistic chronotopes) in the postmodern novel are neither simply anti-representational (presenting 'unrepresentability' in representation, e.g. in impossible worlds) nor are they neo-realist, reflecting the seemingly unreal nature of space and time in postmodernity.

I must accept straight away that there are exceptions that prove this rule. Some postmodern novels, are properly postmodern(ist) in my definition because they are clearly organised around anti-representational chronotopes that deconstruct the mimetic function, through metafictional 'play', self-reflexivity and so on. Also quite a few are neo-realist in retaining the mimetic function to present postmodern worlds in the popular sense of perplexing but 'real' worlds dominated by advanced capitalism and information technology. In between, I think, lie the majority of what might be usefully called postmodern (although perhaps not postmodernist) novels.

In *Novel Arguments: Reading Innovative American Fiction*, Richard Walsh uses the term 'innovative' while trying to steer a line between a solipsistic experimental 'literature of exhaustion' pointed up by John Barth (Barth 1967: 29–34) and a 'capacious realism' that precedes and post-dates it. The 'literature of replenishment' called for by Barth as the project for postmodernist fiction (Barth 1988: 65–71), is dismissed by Walsh as a 'synthesis of the dualism of innovation and realism' which falls back into a concern for form and technique (Walsh 1995: 16). Whether or not innovative American fiction is postmodernist seems to rely, for Walsh, on a definition entirely within a literary-artistic sphere, as though the business and history of literary production is divorced from cultural production and the 'real' world. In my formulation of the postmodern novel, I aim to link some innovative British and American fiction to postmodernity through the idea of the chronotope, and in the process demonstrate that the postmodern novel continues to represent real worlds, and to imagine alternative worlds, and it does so by both using and abusing realist conventions.

A key feature of materialist accounts of postmodernity to which the literary chronotope of postmodern fiction refers is the so-called 'spatial turn', as a number of postmodernist geographers would have it. Here, the emphasis on time and materialist accounts of history which characterised many accounts of modernity are countered by a 'reassertion of the dialectics of space' in postmodernity.[2] In *The Condition of Postmodernity*, David Harvey does much to bring the materiality of spatial as well as temporal conditions to our attention through his account of the economically determined time–space compression in postmodernity. And Henri Lefebvre, who I am sure inspired many to shift their concerns to space and so started much of this with *The Production of Space*, gives a firm nudge towards spatial concerns when he calls for a 'history of space'.[3] It is I think, after Lefebvre, that Foucault turns to space:

> The present epoch will perhaps be above all the epoch of space. We are in the epoch of simultaneity: we are in the epoch of juxtaposition, the epoch of the near and far, of the side-by-side, of the dispersed. We are at the moment, I believe, when our experience of the world is less that of a long life developing through time than that of a network that connects

points and intersects with its own skein.
(Foucault 1986: 22)

Fredric Jameson's account of postmodernism also emphasises the spatial dimension of human affairs, connecting spatialisation in cultural and aesthetic forms to economic factors operating in an era of global capitalism. But unlike Foucault and Lefebvre and the postmodern geographers, who seem to be calling for an emphasis on the spatial, Jameson tends to regard the shift as largely negative, lamenting a loss of historicity, loss of depth models, as though the postmodern signalled a falling off of critical distance. Jameson, I think, gets rather entangled in his metaphors here, denigrating the spatial by associating it with superficiality, as though critical distance is necessarily maintained by the depth of historical conceptualisation, and the loss of historicity necessarily leads to a failure to 'map' contemporary forms. In this respect, Jameson is still with the moderns in wishing to frame the contemporary and to frame it within some privileged order of historical development. For Jameson then, postmodern forms signal a surrender to the economically determined order, and postmodernist culture is both the sign and affirmation of the present phase of late capitalism, a phase that has slipped the anchors of history and ideology.

There are a number of ways in which the postmodern condition has been presented and interpreted, but there is, I think, a commonality in many of the spatio-temporal characteristics of postmodernism, and there is, in this, the basis for establishing the general model for the postmodern chronotope. This, I will attempt to set out in Chapter 3. Without ignoring the important issues of value, truth and meaning, which circulate within discourses on postmodernism, my emphasis is on the nature of space and time in the postmodern, its immediate effects on everyday life, and responses to and engagements with it in the artistic chronotopes of postmodern novels.

Readings of postmodern literature are frequently concerned with literary-historical issues of form (McHale 1987), narrative structure (Currie 1998, Francese 1997), realism (Lee 1990, Versluys 1992), and relations between fiction and history (Hutcheon 1988). There are also a number of works on postmodernism in which postmodern novels are presented as examples to support general theories of the postmodern (Connor 1989, Huyssen 1988, Jameson 1991, Bertens 1995).

In the present work, readings of postmodern novels are informed by the routine assimilation of postmodern chronotopes into the form of the novel, so they are neither restricted to commentary on literature as a special literary-historical category, nor are they required to demonstrate a wide-ranging theory that encompasses cultural and artistic production as a whole. The link between the postmodern novel and other aspects of postmodern life is through the *shape* of the postmodern chronotope. By extending the general case of the postmodern chronotope into forms of chronotope found in the postmodern novel, attention shifts between the materiality of the postmodern condition to the representational chronotope and its artistic and aesthetic relevance in the more abstract postmodernism of cultural production and artistic creation.

I make this distinction between art and culture because I would like to use the postmodern chronotope as a weapon against those theorists of postmodernism (I have Fredric Jameson in my sights) who draw attention to a loss of depth and affect in postmodernism, and an associated loss of resistance and loss of vision within artistic activity. For Lyotard, this postmodernism, the postmodernism that talks of a shift in cultural dominant, presents, and in the case of Jameson contributes to, a conflation of artistic activity with the overlapping, but ideally separate, order of cultural activity which in postmodernity (both the historical and cultural condition) is led by consumer demand and the culture-industry and inevitably shaped by the new technologies which distribute, mediate, consume and diffuse it (Lyotard 1991: 34).

Increasingly, I see the postmodern chronotope as an important intervention in Lyotard's idea of postmodernity as the 'rewriting of modernity', the working through in the Freudian sense of the unpresentable in the past, hidden in this case not so much by the repression of memories too painful to bring to consciousness, but hidden by their future-directedness which makes them unavailable to the present, as they are always projected into an unrealised future (Lyotard 1991: 22–35).

Postmodernity is not modernity's future, and so does not mark the end of the history of modernity. Rather it is a phase of modernity in which modern temporality, and the legitimation of that temporality's processes of development in goals of human emancipation through science and cognitive reasoning, are for the time being suspended. As Lyotard puts it, 'Postmodernity is not a new age, but the rewriting of some of the features claimed by modernity, and first of all modernity's claim to ground its legitimacy on the project of liberating humanity as a whole through science and technology' (Lyotard 1991: 34). The 'now' of postmodernity is not after modernity, but a moment in modernity where the temporality that sustained it has stalled. This places us in a phase of radical reflectivity.

Reflection on modernity, new perspectives on the spatial and temporal conditions of modernity – this is the postmodernity I would like to concentrate on, attaching it where necessary to the more popular, and populist cultural postmodernism, but ultimately seeking some signs of artistic activity that might resist this postmodernism's fall from the sublime to the ridiculous, from beauty and form to the counterfeit and banal.

In this case, the chronotope takes on far more import as a carrier of the spatio-temporal characteristics of a modernity governed by temporality, but variously skewed by the working through of modernity, not simply the remembering or repeating of modernity. In the postmodern chronotope, there is far more emphasis on the dynamics of space, which is not the same as modernist spatialisation (essentially a temporal concern not a spatial one) and is certainly not to be confused with Jameson's emphasis on the spatial as superficiality, loss of depth models and so on.

My attention was drawn to postmodernism and relations between postmodernity and the form of the novel in the 1980s. Then I was concerned with questions of poetics and form in postmodernism, and in particular, with reading space and time structures, or more properly, after Bakhtin, reading the time–space structures (chronotopes) of postmodern novels. The main thrust of my argument was that postmodernism, at least as far as the postmodern novel was concerned, marked a shift in sensibilities from a predominantly temporal and historical imagination that had informed, and in part constituted, modernity, to a more geographical and spatial imagination shaping many aspects of postmodernity, not least the means of both economic and cultural production in a world dominated by global capitalism. That this shift might be 'mapped', to use the (spatial) jargon of the day, to the spatio-temporal conditions of a historical, material, and everyday postmodernity was perhaps not as obvious in the 1980s as it has become in the late 1990s. I am aware that perhaps too naïve a relationship might be forged between an artistic postmodern chronotope within the postmodern novel, and a generalised postmodern chronotope through which the material conditions of postmodernism might usefully be glimpsed. In other words, postmodernity might become too much of a determining factor in the reception of postmodern art, and then there would be too little appreciation of what postmodern art might be *doing* with postmodernity besides reflecting and re-representing its forces and forms.

So, while the core of the present work is still concerned with the spatial turn in various realms of postmodernity, and with its relationship with postmodern chronotopes within the novel, I am also keen to explore the nature of that spatial turn more systematically, and highlight a recent tendency to naïve realism in reading the postmodern novel. This, I hope, will balance an otherwise too materialist approach to the postmodern chronotope, and will proceed, by using the chronotope to re-differentiate an actual reality of postmodernity from worlds of representation in examples of postmodern novels, returning in the process to postmodernism's relations with the sublime, aesthetic forms, and the unpresentable.

I have felt uncomfortable for some time that postmodernism is losing its power to worry, to provoke and to question, especially to question its own nature and origins. The emergence of an unlikely hegemonic postmodernism can be detected: a postmodernism which is hopelessly imbricated in consumer capitalism and paradoxically acknowledging the failure of art to represent an unrepresentable world, while at the same time, in its mainstream form, representing the collusion of art in cultural production dominated by capitalism. I find myself strongly resisting recent trends in criticism that see the postmodern novel as simply a mirror to postmodern, post-industrial societies typically depicted as multicultural, global, politically and ethically indeterminate, capitalist, consumerist, media-driven, and impossibly, wallowing in the loss of referents: worlds of signification in which the 'real' (that such a representation depends on) has itself been 'lost'.

We must remind ourselves here of the methodological dangers of a naïve realism which confuses the represented world with the world outside the text. But if the neo-conservative view of postmodernism is one of affirmative 'dirty realism', the Left's is no less troubling. This either leads to a selective blindness to postmodernism as a legitimate contemporary phenomenon (e.g. in Eagleton, Norris and Giddens), or, in the case of Jameson, what begins as a complaint against loss of affect, loss of critical reason, implosion of economically-dominated cultural forces into art, and so on, ends up with fascination and guilty pleasure at the new aesthetic forms of spaces and surfaces through which it operates.

My particular interest, then, is in the gap between the postmodern chronotope as an active and creative aesthetic form, and a more material and generalised postmodern chronotope acting as a kind of postmodern *Weltanschauung*, or mode of seeing and showing the world, dominated by the much trumpeted 'conditions of postmodernity' proclaimed by David Harvey and Fredric Jameson, for example, and containing the usual suspects – time–space compression, globalisation, spatialisation, depthlessness, placelessness, loss of historicity etc. Overly materialistic accounts of postmodernism are in danger of cancelling out the 'differend'[4] separating the realms of science and reason (the theoretical), the material realms of the everyday (the practical) which might include cultural production and criticism, and the realm of creation and imagination (the artistic). The gap or differend that I would like to see maintained between the world of the text and an actual reality is, as Bakhtin suggests a gap between differentiated chronotopes:

> Out of the actual chronotopes of our world [theoretical and practical] (which serve as the source of representation) emerge the reflected and *created* chronotopes of the world represented in the work (in the text).
> (Bakhtin 1981: 253)

The boundary line is not absolute, of course, but postmodernity cannot dissolve the separation of categories by which the historical world is kept distinct from a representational world. As Bakhtin has put it, 'A literary work's artistic unity in relationship to an actual reality is defined by its chronotope' (Bakhtin 1981: 243), and it is precisely the nature of this chronotope in the postmodern novel, the creation of temporal and spatial unities (and sometimes disunities) and their chronotopic relationship with the real world, that is the subject of the present work.

The argument that I would like to make here is that the boundary line between an actual world and the world as represented in the text is maintained, even if it is has become, or perhaps always was, a very soft and permeable boundary. We hear a great deal from the Left and from the so-called neo-conservatives about loss of critical distance in postmodernity, the end of history and reason, legitimation crisis, and the domination of the arts by a predominantly capitalist mode of cultural production. All of which may point to a postmodern implosion into undifferentiated worlds dominated by the structural function assigned to cultural production in a capitalist world (Jameson 1991: 4). Or to a world in which the mode of production has become irrelevant in a world dominated by a general political economy of the sign, and where commodity and sign are virtually interchangeable (Baudrillard 1983a).

Of course, it would be dogmatic to insist on the total separation of these realms and disingenuous not to acknowledge that postmodernism itself questions and subverts borders and deconstructs boundary conditions. This is especially true of those boundaries installed by high modernism between art and life – the 'great divide' as Andreas Huyssen puts it, which avant-gardism sought to erode before it became assimilated into the 'affirmative culture' of pop culture, one of postmodernism's precursors (Huyssen 1988: 196).

The idea of postmodernism as an 'anything goes' dispersal of art into life is a depressing prospect, and does not do justice to those practitioners of postmodern art who, I am pleased to say, continue to re-imagine the world in whatever forms are appropriate and available to them.

Clearly, there is constant traffic between theoretical, practical and artistic realms and these relationships are complex. As Henri Lefebvre has suggested, the category of space, is an example of the intrinsic relatedness of the abstract, the representational, and the actual (and representations of the actual) through a number of primarily social activities, which include, but are not limited to, economic production, and verge on organic interdependency (Lefebvre 1991: 32–3). But postmodernism only ever puts borders under erasure, their traces remain, and sometimes the attention given them causes such a reaction that they are, for a time, reinforced. The conflation of history and fiction in postmodernism is clearly a case in point, and one which we will return to often in considering the postmodern chronotope both as an optic for examining time–space relations in postmodernity generally, and as the means for relating the artistic unity of particular postmodern novels to such actual reality we might salvage from a Baudrillardian world of pure signification – the self-referring textuality of our world(s).

The abstract, the material and the artistic seep into and contaminate each other, but it would be naïve and eventually catastrophic to yoke cultural and artistic production to the beast of late-capitalist means of production. And yet a not too careful reading of

The Postmodern Chronotope

Jameson's hefty tome on postmodernism might lead to this. An example, briefly: Jameson's reading of Doctorow's *Ragtime*, is determined by its status as a postmodern artefact (Jameson 1991: 22) which, he suggests, removes political import from a text whose author, he insists, has impeccable (leftist) political credentials. This is not a reading that emerges from the text in relation to the various conditions of its production and all available means of interpretation. Rather, it is a reading determined by Jameson's relentless application of a cultural logic that insinuates itself into his reading to effect an a priori removal of the historical referent, leaving us – 'condemned to seek history by way of our own pop images and simulacra of that history, which itself remains forever out of reach' (Jameson 1991: 25). The loss of historicity, the loss of depth models, an intense and pervasive superficiality, are all, for Jameson, givens governing our reception of anything, cultural or artistic that happens to be produced in postmodernity. Most readers, he suggests, would fail to read any political import into this text, and even if they did, as Linda Hutcheon does, they are wrong, because this is a postmodern text and therefore has predetermined readings.

An alternative reading of the text, and one closer to Linda Hutcheon's,[5] is that the novel does indeed succeed in presenting an off-centre American history, a history of the development of immigrant, working class aesthetic forms essentialised in the motif of syncopated ragtime music, and, importantly in the novel, a development in spite of dominant capitalist economic and political pressures, and even perhaps because of them. (And I suspect it is the apparent failure of the novel to express sufficient class consciousness here that really troubles Jameson.)

Both readings are possible it seems, and, I would suggest, anticipated by the author, and perhaps more controversially they are complementary. I see no reason why the novel cannot both make reference to a reduced historical past and at the same time present an unpresentability in the larger concept of the history of events and processes. And in its presentation of the unpresentable-ness of history it not only registers a loss of historicity in postmodernity but, at the same time, also a struggle to overcome the signs of history, for the characters in the novel to transcend the times and fail, and for the author (and readers) to re-present a plausible slice of connected history and succeed in failing to do just this. But it succeeds instead in presenting an imaginative chronotope in which fact and fiction are confounded to produce a tableau vivant: not history as such, but intense enough in its presentation to ask questions of the past, to invoke the curiosity that is the lifeblood of history.

The postmodern chronotope, as it appears in a number of postmodern novels, registers a shift in sensibilities from a predominantly temporal and historiographic imagination to one much more concerned with the spatial and the geographic, as categories in their own right rather than as spatialised histories. The clearest evidence for this can be found in the number of texts concerning problematic approaches to history and narrative, which at the same time explore the nature of space, and place and placelessness. Most of the novels explored in the present work fall into this category, but these are by no means odd examples. Indeed, I would suggest that the novel of place and placelessness is as important in considering postmodernism as that of historiographic metafiction. The endemic loss of historicity in many accounts of postmodernity might usefully be linked to a material and conceptual loss of place, confirming Lefebvre's argument that places contain the traces of the historical events that have shaped them, and so the effacement of history is never complete.[6]

So the novelistic chronotope, which is first and foremost, even in the postmodern novel, an artistic chronotope, must be separated from the simple cultural mapping of the material conditions of postmodernity so easily reflected in the chronotope of cultural activity. My aim is to re-situate and reconsider the artistic chronotope in postmodernism as an attempt to reconnect with an aesthetics of space and time which is not dominated by post-structuralist anti-representationalism. In such chronotopes, space is not merely in the service of time, but has a poetics of its own, which reveals itself through a geographical or topological imagination rather than a historical one.

The selection of novels used in Part II of the present work involves a kind of a spatial logic of its own, the focus opening out from the localised chronotope of a post-industrial city in Alasdair Gray's *Lanark*, to global and cosmic chronotopes in works by Peter Ackroyd, Graham Swift and Don DeLillo. An extensive range of postmodern chronotopes is used to illustrate different aspects of the experience and representation of space and time in postmodernity.

We begin with an exploration of localism as an aesthetic project to restore the identity of post-industrial Glasgow in Alasdair Gray's

Lanark. This novel marks a transition in Glasgow's history, as the city changes from a confident modern industrial city to an uncertain, post-industrial, postmodern city struggling to find an identity, and to resist being 'consumed' by global economic forces. In this vision and re-vision of Glasgow, Gray searches for an identity for the city which acknowledges, but moves away from, the standard vision of Glasgow's industrial past, with its slums and exploitation of the working classes. *Lanark* flirts with fantasy to present a vision of late capitalism in its all-powerful and all-consuming glory; and it sets this fantasy against a realist and historical account of Glasgow which is contained within the fantasy. The novel introduces complex chronotopes that include grotesque parodies of the city in postmodernity, mixed with representations of the industrial city and its geographical context of the Scottish landscape, with its lochs, glens and mountains.

In this novel, earlier realist accounts of Glasgow's history, in which the city is depicted as a modern industrial dystopia, are alluded to and then joined with the late capitalist fantasy of the city's post-industrial demise. On the one hand, the novel represents the failure of local, separatist action to resist the strange hegemony of postmodern globalisation, but on the other it uses postmodern chronotopes to re-imagine and rewrite the city. Paradoxically, the novel, while presenting the destruction of Glasgow through its post-industrial loss of identity, can be linked with other cultural activities taking place in Glasgow in the 1980s which have injected new life and new identity into what has become one of Europe's least likely cultural centres. So the late capitalist fantasy, in this case, does not record the demise of a city, but is itself part of its rebirth.

By contrast, Paul Auster's *New York Trilogy* belongs to another tradition of city writing altogether. The narratives here are also intertextual, but the city here eludes representation. In an all-encompassing world of signification the subject, the city and writing are reduced to a common denominator of codes and texts. Both Auster and Gray use the city as a site for exploring subjectivity and authorship, both invoke the modernist dirge for the death of the subject, and both, in different ways, seek to counter it. But in Auster's work, the play of codes would seem to be the only matter of the text, and the matter of who is speaking is indeed made irrelevant (it is, after all, in Auster always another Auster, but Auster all the same).

Introduction and Preliminaries

The chronotope of *New York Trilogy* is predominantly spatial, and space here is a place for signs, texts and images; the subject is left to decipher this and is seemingly uninvolved in constituting this space. Gray's postmodern vision of the post-industrial city installs and then subverts the artist's attempts to represent the city in text and image, but at the same time, it installs a further and more radical (futurist) aesthetic of creative destruction, the phoenix of a new Glasgow emerging from the ashes of both the left-wing cooperatives and the all-consuming creature that is the conspiracy of late capitalism. The chronotopes of *Lanark* are not dominated by a space of codes, images and texts, because history does intervene (through fantasy) and human agency would seem, in the end (or perhaps after 'The End') to win through. Clearly in Gray's highly politicised postmodern text, 'it *does* matter who is speaking'.[7]

Graham Swift's *Waterland*, at one level a continuation of the realist tradition in the English regional novel, creates a self-enclosed world, clearly connected with real geography and history, and it explores the social life of families and communities rooted there. In this respect, Swift uses a chronotope familiar to English novel writing, and used by a long tradition of writers, including Jane Austen, Anthony Trollope and Thomas Hardy. Like earlier regional novels, *Waterland* explores the relationship between a society and its history, but the crucial difference between *Waterland* and, for example, *Middlemarch* is in how they conceptualise an idea of historical progress, and how they reconcile the life and history of family and community with the big historical events on the world stage.

Swift problematises history through recognisably postmodernist narrative technique and through direct appeals to the reader (we have become the children in his history class), but of more interest to the present work, Swift constructs postmodern chronotopes out of the metaphorical possibilities of the very landscape and the local history of the novel's setting: the indeterminate space of water–land, neither entirely solid nor entirely liquid, constantly shifting, being reformed and reclaimed. Swift uses metaphors drawn from nature, and in particular the idea of reclamation, as metaphor for the constant process of man/nature interaction out of which a postmodern idea of progress emerges. He also privileges a vaguely romantic notion of *natural history* as opposed to the *artificial history* characterised by modern obsessions with progressive development based on the domination of

17

nature. However, this is not to promote an anti-modern return to nature, rather *natural history* is a metaphor for delimiting the progress of man through history.

Two other novels directly concerned with history and the postmodern – E.R. Doctorow's *Ragtime* and Italo Calvino's *Invisible Cities* – are briefly considered here for comparison. As mentioned earlier, *Ragtime* is chosen by Jameson as an example of a right-thinking novelist (and so of the Left) falling foul of 'the aesthetic situation engendered by the disappearance of the historical referent' (Jameson 1991: 25). The historical novel can no longer re-present history as an actual series of events, but can only register our ideas and responses to a past that is always out of reach. As usual, Jameson's magisterial vision rests on his particular interpretation of a single text or work (later in the same work he will do likewise with Edward Munch's *The Scream*, and the Westin Bonaventure Hotel), and while this has the advantage of presenting a broad sweep of theory unhampered by conflicting evidence, it does rather encourage simplified and sensationalised readings of postmodern texts. Jameson's reading of *Ragtime* rests largely on narrative style and language, and what he seems to consider as the postmodern tone in the writing. But there is nothing in the novel itself that interferes with re-establishing a historical referent.

Indeed, it seems to me that the novel has a very good sense of the past and of a particular period in American history. The novel connects centres and margins, those making history and those suffering history, the real becomes fictional and the fictional becomes 'real'. It seems to me to be an important reflection on one of America's myths of origin, and a fascinating study of history as journalism: a particular selection of events and stories which are to form a history. In terms of the novel's chronotopes, the novel sticks fairly closely to realist conventions, and it is only postmodern in its de-differentiation of real and fictional worlds. In the temporal direction, the chronotope is linear and historical. What the novel does not do, is try to establish any particular interpretation of this period and connect this with a grand theory of history. The novel's chronotope stays firmly in the past that it re-presents, and so it is never linked with history as a series of events. It is in this sense a spatialised historiography, history outside the streams of cause and effect. Most importantly for Jameson, it does not find causes and consequences in this history from which a critique of capitalism must ensue.

In Calvino's *Invisible Cities*, the spatiality of history has a material as well as a representational basis. In other words, history is governed by proximity, contingency and distance, and so is determined by geographical factors such as the fear and desire created by borders, dreams of elsewhere, dislocation, and the power and decay of unimaginable empires. In this novel, discussed in more detail in Chapter 3, the historical referent is taken apart through a dialogue between Kublai Khan and Marco Polo, itself a dubious historical event. In this dialogue, the allegedly real geography and history presented in Marco Polo's *Travels* is re-presented as fiction, indulging the fantasies of the teller and the listener.

There are several other aspects of the postmodern, aside from history, which impact on the nature of space and time in postmodernity, and so influence the shape and characteristics of the postmodern chronotope. In postmodernity, as in modernity, science has had considerable influence on how space and time are conceived. Where Einstein's Theory of Relativity had considerable impact on modern chronotopes, postmodern chronotopes are influenced by chaos theory and ideas from theoretical physics concerning non-directional, non-linear and reversible time.

In Peter Ackroyd's *Hawksmoor*, modern and non-modern concepts of space and time are set against each other when a chronotope of seventeenth century London interpenetrates a chronotope of late twentieth century London. If we think of a postmodern chronotope somehow overarching these separate worlds, this is doubly complex because it includes not only different space–times, but also different concepts of space and time governing those space–times. The interwoven histories show how space and time have been conceived differently in pre-modern, modern, and postmodern societies, and how these different conceptions are inscribed and spatialised in architectural and textual forms. Using two transitional periods (the late seventeenth and late twentieth century), the novel presents a double critique (from the past and the present) of the dominant modern concept of time. This idea of time, with its ideology of development, is linear, quantifiable and progressive. The novel tests this idea of time by entertaining alternative non-directional forms of time, displaced by modern scientific method, but never entirely driven underground, and which re-emerge to confound the modern detective. Non-directional time is also explored in the chronotopes of Ackroyd's *First Light*, and Ian

McEwan's *The Child in Time*, two very different novels, but both to a large extent influenced by concepts borrowed from theoretical physics.

Postmodern chronotopes also play a role in post-colonial literature, where they disrupt and sometimes reconstruct the space–times of colonialist world views presented in literatures which are now realised to have been colonialist. A common feature of such colonialist literature is the representational power of spatial differentiations such as centre/periphery, mainland/island, and island/sea. Space, and to an extent time, are used in colonialist literature to demarcate racial, ethnic and master/slave relations. I have selected a number of postmodern novels here which refer back to the colonialist representations of the Caribbean island in *The Tempest* and *Robinson Crusoe*, these are Michel Tournier's *Friday, or The Other Island*, J.M. Coetzee's *Foe*, Caryl Phillips' *Cambridge*, and Marina Warner's *Indigo: Or, Mapping the Waters*. The Caribbean island has a complex spatial and representational history, existing first as the home of Carib Indians, second as the prison/home of African slaves, third as the *unheimlich* abode of the coloniser, and fourth as the exotic 'other' place that differentiated it from the British 'homeland'. The postmodern chronotopes in the novels here generally work through a procedure of de-differentiation.

The final chapter deals with novels in which placelessness is the main theme. A postmodern idea of de-differentiation contributes to placelessness, but so too do the material conditions of postmodernity, the so-called postmodernisation of the world and the actualisation of the 'global village' anticipated in modernity. Graham Swift's *Out of this World*, and Don DeLillo's *The Names* both deal with the lives of characters who for one reason or another are placeless, or seeking some kind of grounding. They are not placed in a traditional sense of being rooted in a town, city or region that is in some way associated with their identity and their being. This sense of a 'placeless' existence in a geographical sense is linked then to a placeless existence in the sense of lives that cannot be put in order, given value, or tied to some purpose.

There is a trope of placelessness to be explored here in which placelessness stands for dysfunctional postmodern lives, an extension perhaps to the city chronotope as a metaphor for dysfunctional modern lives. But a question is raised here about how far the placelessness of postmodernity really gives rise to a sense of being removed from local geographical and historical context, even within western society. To the extent that Graham Swift's novels might be representative of British postmodern fiction and Don DeLillo's representative of American postmodern fiction, there seems to be a clear distinction in approaches to placelessness. Swift's characters have usually not lost their sense of history and tradition, even though they recognise its constructedness and unrepresentability, but DeLillo's characters are much more at sea. Here, there is a nostalgia, not so much for history and tradition, but for the systems and certainties brought by modern science and technology.

In DeLillo's *Ratner's Star*, the task of communicating to another form of life immediately puts into question the systems of symbolic representation, such as language and mathematics, which modernity has trusted with conferring meaning on the world and the place of humans within it. Here is another, most extreme, form of placelessness where our conventional systems of grounding human experience are exposed when the history of human existence on earth is bent back on itself revealing a mirror civilisation existing billions of years ago regressing backwards to meet our year zero. The characters in these novels seek some form of grounding, occasionally finding it in human bonding within family and other relationships. But these novels also present passive acceptance of placelessness as an inevitable, and perhaps not so disastrous, postmodern condition. Indeed, perhaps there are some advantages in not being grounded in history, and not being tied to rational systems of symbolic representation.

THE SHAPE OF THINGS GONE BY – PRELIMINARIES ON POSTMODERNISM

Postmodernism's heyday was surely the 1980s when postmodernism was a fertile ground for research, bringing forth responses in disciplines as far apart as dance and architecture, anthropology and history, geography and law. Postmodernism sprang from a Western (American) *zeitgeist* and promised new forms in which to articulate the 'post' world order (post-imperial, post-colonial, post-détente, post Soviet, postmodern). Postmodernist forms, attitudes and fashion were transmitted unevenly but globally, through the mass communication and modes of diffusion that were part of postmodernism and help characterise this era of postmodernity. But postmodernism refuses to settle down into a clearly definable and welcome '–ism'.

Despite finding its way on to the syllabus in many Western universities, postmodernism and postmodernity are routinely dismissed as negative developments in the mostly left-leaning academic institutions. Postmodernism is often regarded as a phenomenon rather than a 'worked out' set of artistic and cultural practices, and a symptom of the ills of society, a falling away from ideology. Rather than ushering in the new, postmodernism quickly became associated with disruptive and decentring theories and practices, and with the sign of 'end of era' exhaustion, occasionally Saturnalian perhaps, not without humour, and yet flippant, without direction, without focus, and without goals. Of course, for supporters of postmodernism (rather rare and shy beasts these days), such features might have seemed justified response to a bankrupt and discredited modernity obsessed with history, projects and ideology. And postmodernism might also have injected a little levity and scepticism into what for some had become an elitist modernism, taking itself too seriously and too far divorced from everyday life.

In a more political vein, postmodernism might also have intervened in the troublesome alliances of art and power in the West, to counter the 'perversion of modernism into a form of affirmative culture' (Huyssen 1988: 190). For a post-détente Soviet Union, postmodernism might have countered the Socialist Realism that grew up with the totalitarian regime: an odd alliance here between art and politics. As Tristan Tzara puts it in Tom Stoppard's *Travesties*: 'As a Dadaist, I am the natural enemy of bourgeois art and the natural ally of the political left, but the odd thing about revolution is that the further left you go politically the more bourgeois they like their art'.[8] In the culture wars that shadowed the Cold War of the 1950s and 1960s, the liberal democracies of the West fielded, of all things, Abstract Expressionism as the polar opposite of a state-controlled realism, as if this somehow expressed the individual freedom enjoyed by the Western subject.

I think we can see postmodernism as a transformation in the ideology of *development* across most realms of contemporary life: cultural, political, sociological, aesthetic, historical, scientific, philosophical and material. The idea of development, the ideology of the contemporary, is itself in question. Hence the 'ends of' discourses in postmodernism (with a deliberate pun on 'ends') which are auto-suggested by the 'post' prefix: the ends of ideology, ends of history, ends of 'the real', ends of scientism, and so on.

Postmodernism also problematises the differentiation and periodisation through which modern development marks its progress. And postmodernism explores the boundaries surrounding discourses, or 'phrase-regimes' separated by a gulf or differend, to use Lyotard's terminology (Lyotard 1988). For Lyotard, a postmodern desire to suppress the differend brings realms of scientific and historical fact into the realms of fictional narrative and the realms of ethical and moral judgement. Postmodernism, has an odd role to play here, first it allows for such heterogeneous discourse across phrase-regimes, but it also underlines the differences that mark this heterogeneity. Postmodernism, at least in Lyotard's view, should be above all against totalising narratives: 'Let us wage a war on totality . . . let us activate the differences' (Lyotard 1983: 82). This has become one of the most influential markers of the postmodern, and has to some extent become the peg on which diverse postmodernisms have been hung.

So the appearance of postmodernism in the late twentieth century might be seen as a symptom of the contemporary, a sign of the times perhaps rather than the shaping force of the times. For the Left, this is symptomatic of the sickness at the heart of the contemporary (following on from the 'something rotten at the core of the empire') and the triumph of capitalistic modes of production. The dangers of postmodernism are evident in the proclamation that it signals an end to histories and an end to ideologies, replacing both with simulacra and the image-as-truth. For example, in Britain, Christopher Norris has blamed the demise of left-wing politics there on a postmodernist plot to manufacture and manipulate public opinion through the displacement of ideology into images of power (Norris 1993: 8–14).

Another version of this, and one which, I would suggest, is closer to the truth as most British voters were to see it, was that the Left lost power, and any chance of returning to power, not because of postmodernism's cancelling out of ideology and false consciousness but because they suspected that the Left were inept and incompetent. They later chose pragmatic New Labour, a party apparently without ideology, but it would be naïve to assume that the British public did not realise this. To suggest, as I think Norris does, that the British voters have been seduced by New Labour's honeyed words is to underestimate the ability of the public to detect a false note.

But the Left is surely right (as it were) to be concerned with an apparent absence of political will or direction in postmodernism, and especially with what it regards as a falling off, a failure to conceive of the totalising politics that might frame the economic forces of a postmodernity dominated by the flows and fluctuations of global capitalism and information. This, together with Lyotard's once provocative but now clichéd headline regarding postmodernism's incredulity towards all metanarratives, absolutes and truths, leads to postmodernism being cast in a neo-conservative role, affirming a dominant capitalist culture with which it is allied, and fracturing politics and history into single-issue and local concerns, the provisional and limited truths of Lyotard's *petits récits* (Lyotard 1984: xxiv, 20–3) and bereft of the totalising vision that has been the *sine qua non* of both left and right politics in the twentieth century.[9]

But it is not only the Left and the Right who have cause to worry about postmodernism, it would seem to be no friend of a centre occupied by humanists and liberals. Postmodernism gives short shrift to the autonomy of the subject in history. This is how postmodernism is often constructed, but in postmodern novels, humanist impulses frequently resurface and the human condition is still a concern, notwithstanding the very real and postmodern bind of representing this outside totalisation and sometimes outside representation itself.

It is one of the key concerns in the present work to draw attention to the degree to which the postmodern novel has in many cases stayed ahead of its own language games, stepping outside the self-reflection that threatens to sever the link between the text and its referents in worlds of human activity. Indeed, I would argue that few texts are truly postmodern*ist* in the limited sense that they surrender to a world of pure signification. At some point the frame of interpretation returns and the text is re-differentiated from the world of human and social history, and this is probably a consequence of postmodern reading. Postmodern novels may draw attention to their own status as fiction and even indulge in some tail-chasing, self-reflexive metafiction that characterises a number of formulations of postmodernist fiction, but paradoxically, the exposure of fiction's reality-making devices often confirms the reader's appetite for stories, which metafiction leaves intact.[10]

In Italo Calvino's *If On a Winter's Night a Traveller*, this is taken a stage further, exploiting that very demand for stories within the text itself, a demand which the author's ironic interventions and deferrals fail to exhaust. The story of the story, of the story . . . , eventually resolves into story, and does not entirely break through into some other phrase-regime of criticism or literary theory. The representational status of this overtly anti-representational text remains intact, and the illusory referent is restored to us. So it is time, I think, to break up that generalised model of what postmodernism might have been in its early constructions, and to begin to regard postmodern fiction in the 1990s as finding responses to the abyss, in other words, doing things with the postmodern as well as simply regarding it.

Postmodernism, in cahoots with post-structuralism, subverts received ideas and beliefs, and questions established truths and norms, especially where these are associated with the progressive, positivist and emancipatory impulses of modernity. Much less clearly, postmodernism can also be presented as a reaction to modernism, but this is a complex and slippery relationship redefining modernism as much as defining postmodernism. Postmodernism can certainly not be regarded as simply the antithesis of a modernism, as modernism was never simply the antithesis of realism. In his essay 'The Painter of Modern Life' (1863) Baudelaire draws attention to the two halves of modern art, on the one hand, the transient, fleeting and contingent and, on the other, the eternal and immutable.

Likewise, postmodernism might be seen as a complex arrangement of contradictory strands, with the further complication that this is all contained within an intense self-consciousness of its own contradictions. Hassan's much-cited binary list of modernism versus postmodernism has done much to reinforce the view that postmodernism is a simple inversion of modernist features and attributes, but it would be wrong to attribute postmodernism's energy to a simple reaction to modernism, and wrong to rest a definition of postmodernism on such an un-postmodern binary schema (Hassan 1982: 267–8). But perhaps it is postmodernism's function ultimately to rework, as Lyotard has put it, modernist theories and practices (Lyotard 1991: 34). Perhaps in future history books, postmodernism will be seen less as a break with modernism than as an evolution and reconstruction of it in response to the material changes of the late twentieth century.

This, I think, is how recent postmodern novels have dealt with the otherwise stultifying discourse of postmodernism in its purely anti-representational guise. But this does not mean that postmodernism is folded back into modernism, because there is certainly a historical and material condition of postmodernity, sufficiently different from modernity to warrant the prefix, and requiring a cultural and aesthetic response. Even if this material postmodernity of post-industrial, media-driven, information-saturated, globalised communities is considered as just more modernity, there is a sufficient shift in pace, a change of gear, to bring the postmodern to bear on things.

Back in the realms of the academy, postmodernism has secreted itself into many disciplines and caused a certain degree of soul-searching, especially regarding critical practices that seek to establish truth and meaning within a discipline. Straw people have been put up on both sides of the divide, with phantom 'postmodernists' and 'scientists' accused of all kinds of crimes against reason and humanity. Any initial enthusiasm for postmodernism was quick to dissipate, partly, I believe, because although there were many profiting from explaining, criticising, or constructing their own versions of postmodernism, few were involved in producing anything like a manifesto for postmodernism, or even admitting to being postmodernists, least of all artists and writers.[11]

In the 1980s, publishers were persuading us to put the word 'postmodernism' in the title of our books, but by the 1990s the 'p' word was losing its appeal. After its launch in the 1970s, most people were continuing to ask the question 'What is postmodernism?' And indeed, in the 1980s we were falling over each other trying to put our spin on exactly what postmodernism was or wasn't while, true to its own form, a postmodernism industry emerged within the academy as a major branch of the theory industry, and closely related to the American deconstruction industry and the European cultural theory industry.

If postmodernism has been fertile but problematic ground for theorists and critics, how have the practitioners of postmodernist culture fared – the film makers, writers, artists, architects and so on? For a while, there seemed to be something that was recognisably postmodernist architecture, thanks largely to Charles Jencks, Robert Venturi, Denise Scott Brown and Steven Izenour. This has had a grain to work against, the institutionalisation of International Style against which popular and leftist opinion might be ranged. Postmodernist architecture was populist and ironic, it toyed with modern and pre-modern styles, and revelled in commercialised kitsch. In Jencks' 'double-coding', postmodernist architecture sought not to displace modernist architecture but to continue it in juxtaposition with non-modernist forms (Jencks 1984: 8).

But postmodernist architecture has generally become diluted, driven by fashion and economic forces rather than design principles. It has become uniform in its throwbacks, in its ornamentation, in its 'other-directedness', and even in its contextualisations. In Hong Kong, we have the clearest example of this, where postmodern architecture has been installed not to serve the immediate demands of the local community, but, as always in this high-tech market place, to serve the global business community. This city of all cities is without history, its existence seeming to depend on being 'up to date', and fashionable at all visible levels. In this increasingly competitive role, Hong Kong thrives on reconstructing itself every ten to twenty years, each time looking more and more like recent developments in New York and European capitals, as though architecturally it were trying to simulate these places.

However, these are largely signs of somewhere else, elements of other-directedness in place, and no matter how carefully these are eased into the impressive natural topology of Hong Kong, the city, from an outsider's point of view (and I stress that this is not necessarily how local residents regard their city, which is perhaps in the end more important) the city is inauthentic, a pseudo place with no possible association with local context, unless the local context is this very emphasis on other-directedness.

In the last decade or so, postmodernism has undergone a number of reinterpretations, dilutions, appropriations and re-engineering, but still we encounter it as a curious or infuriating phenomenon, rather than a directed or systematic mode of thinking. Indeed, one of postmodernism's main features is its subversion of system, a feature which it frequently turns on its many selves. Terry Eagleton refers to the 'illusions of postmodernism', as an aberration of this age, a further capitalistic plot to divert us from political and social realities (Eagleton 1996). This does not dismiss postmodernism, rather it imbues it with a sinister intent and far more agency than I think it deserves. I fail to see such political agenda within postmodernism, although various political activities have made use of the waves made by it.

In a very general and loose definition of postmodernism, it is generally accepted (to the point of cliché) that it has various stylistic features of play, pluralism, anti-history, anti-structure, and is loosely attached to poststructuralism. But it cannot really be said to have a poetics as such. Much of what is associated with postmodernism is either negative, relativistic, or more simply, indeterminate. Indeed indeterminacy at various levels: artistic, historical, sociological and philosophical, is the one hallmark of postmodernism that most would agree on. This indeterminacy flows from a connection with modernism in which the impetus of the parent movement is both carried forward and reversed. For some this is no more than a trick, a sleight of hand, but for others, this simultaneous faring forward and faring backwards, like the double helix which underwrites the building blocks of life itself, signals new directions in the structure of space and time with far reaching impact on how we come to read and write history, and construct the human subject. At the sociological level, this indeterminacy reflects a failure to conceive of and represent subjectivity in postmodern societies, unable as yet to integrate the less rigid constructions of gender and ethnicity that identity politics in the 1990s brings them to.

There is another kind of indeterminacy inherent in postmodernism, and that is concerned with the movement itself, or rather the many movements that never cohere into a definable '-ism'. Postmodernism is essentially undirected, a driverless car, which since the 1980s, has lurched onwards not through any particular driving force, but through an antithetical relation, initially to modernism and the project of modernity, but then to virtually any systematic ordering of human affairs. Postmodernism became a byword for anti-system, and this move prevented it from making true claims about the 'real' world. Here I am simplifying enormously, and in the late 1990s, there are, in fact, versions of postmodernism that do indeed make claims to map postmodern reality, having arrived at a point where the anti-system and radical indeterminacy of postmodernism are found as material fact in postmodern societies. This is a move of which we should, I think, be highly suspicious.

Postmodernism has its many authors, but they are nearly all of the disappearing kind. Although postmodernism through the 1980s was being identified in its many forms in various disciplines, those who advocated it as an artistic movement, a cultural trend or as a school of thinking were rather thin on the ground. Indeed, much of the attention paid to postmodernism in the 1980s was sceptical or even negative and hostile. Postmodernism seemed to emerge out of popular culture, out of disrespect for the ideas of the past and out of some alliance with global capitalism. Within universities, postmodernism has often been introduced by the same individuals who had campaigned for 'theory' to be introduced into English and cultural studies. This has caused something of a conflict, and has led initially to the very guarded reception of postmodernism into the academy, and this is, I suspect, because cultural and literary theory deals with ideologies, and a fairly clear-cut politics of the Left. But postmodernism does not sit well with Marxism, and there is little in postmodernism to encourage the politics of the Left, other than as a sign of a rising decadence in Western culture and philosophy that signals the end to capitalism. But the 'late capitalism' version of postmodernism does not anticipate the glorious revolution of socialism: far from it, because this essentially apocalyptic view of postmodernism takes the project of modernity to its zenith, only to see it accelerate out of its own planetary system and into some as yet uncharted territory, where the basic parameters of up and down, left and right, are still to be defined.

CHAPTER 2

Postmodernism's Spatial Turn: From Spatialisation to the Production of Space

THE MODERNISATION OF TIME

Conceptualisation of time has exercised philosophers for hundreds of years. In the fourth century, Saint Augustine, is said to have remarked 'I know what time is if one does not ask me', and so encapsulated the problem of representing the experience of time in narrative.[1] But in the late nineteenth century and early twentieth century, there was a sharp rise of interest in the subject of time in western society.

As Stephen Kern notes in *The Culture of Time and Space 1880–1918*, there were contrasting views about the number, texture, and direction of time(s), and this was complicated by the fact that two types of time were often being confused: public time and private time. The general idea of a public time related to the rotation of the earth around the sun, and the moon around the earth, was not challenged, but arguments for the plurality of private times, and the multiplicity of social times were posited.

The introduction of world standard time created greater uniformity of shared public time, and according to Kern:

The Postmodern Chronotope

> triggered theorising about a multiplicity of private times that may vary from moment to moment in the individual, from one individual to another according to personality, and among different groups as a function of social organisation.
>
> (Kern 1983: 33-4)

In physics, Einstein noted in his General Theory of Relativity (1916) that a sequence of events in one reference system, when viewed from a differently moving reference system, may not hold to the same sequence. There could therefore be no absolutes in time and space, only positions relative to a given reference system. In psychology, Henri Bergson insisted that the division of time into standard units was contrary to experience, as Zeno's paradox had demonstrated.[2] As Bergson puts it 'The most we can say about it [the arrow, or time] is that it might be there, that it passes there and might stop there.' (Bergson 1911: 325). Emile Durkheim emphasised the social nature of time, in much the same way as Lefebvre emphasised the social nature of space, noting that in many non-western societies, the experience of 'public time', or rather 'social time', is more qualitative than quantitative, and is ordered around a framework of special occasions and seasons, ensuring a heterogeneous and discontinuous time. In such societies, says Durkheim, 'a calendar expresses the rhythm of the collective activities, while at the same time its function is to assure their regularity' (Durkheim 1915: 22, 32).

Nevertheless, the intrusion of public time into the private experience of time in western society was widespread, and many modernist writers turned to the plurality of private times, where the private experience of time flows freely in a 'stream of consciousness' unbridled by the order of public time or traditional narratival time. Novelists such as Proust, Joyce and Woolf, with their stream of consciousness narrative style, seem to free private time from the strict sequence and division imposed by public time, and separate the experience of time for the individual from an increasingly universal public time which marches inexorably, and ever faster, into the future.

THE POSTMODERNISATION OF SPACE

The experience of private time was a major theme in early twentieth century writing, with writers reacting to radical changes in public time, such as the standardisation of time and new social divisions of time in the workplace. But at the close of the twentieth century, writers seemed exercised more by the problems of space and place, problems arising partly from a perceived homogenisation of space under global capitalism and by a shift from industrial to information-based societies in the west.[3]

Such material changes as the grip of multinational corporations on world trade, the use of the world wide web, the emergence of an abstract international community in post-détente politics, the migrations of post-coloniality, postmodern simulation of places and the growth of non-places such as airports, holiday villages, theme parks etc., all help to bring about a particular postmodern spatiality in which the modern nation state is less sovereign than it was.

More fundamentally, the spatial indicators of inside/outside, cease to have quite the distinction they did in the abstract and sharply delineated spaces of modernity. Even the cardinal points are not as cardinal as they used to be: east is east and west is west does not have quite the same currency in a lumpy and misshapen postmodern world. All of which leads to a focus on spatial relations that is related to, and in some ways an extension of, the focus on temporal relations engendered by modern industrial-based capitalism and mass production, in which the urge was, as Harvey puts it, 'to annihilate space through time' (Harvey 1990a: 306–7).

One effect of the postmodernisation of space can be seen in placelessness, as places are less easily differentiated from each other and from their surroundings. Cities and towns appear more uniform because the same signs, shops, building styles etc., can be found almost everywhere, and the spaces around them are gradually filled by a flat, undifferentiated suburbia. There is also a growth in the presence of utterly uniform 'pseudo places' such as petrol stations, shopping malls, and international restaurant chains. These often emulate place-bound familiarity, but in fact undermine the essential characteristics of place. The dominant architectural form in world cities still conforms to an international style, and even where postmodernist architecture seeks to reassert difference and contextuality, the effects are often a different kind of sameness, rather than true variety. There is a recognisable 'spatial syntax' in towns and cities which is mostly bent to the demands of global capitalism, and facilitates the efficient and uninterrupted movement of materials, goods, money, information and people between places.

Globalisation is one of the hallmarks of postmodernity, and yet the urge to break down spatial barriers has not led to a general and even homogenisation of space, as might have been expected. If we look more closely at spatial relations, *beneath* public space, *in* social space and representational space, and at the links between individuals, social groups and the places they inhabit, space often becomes very conflictual and heterogeneous. The absence of certain spatial boundaries, worn down by globalisation, seems merely to shift emphasis to other boundaries and divides. Cities fragment here into thousands of pockets, divided by boundaries of class, race, ethnicity, and gender. As Edward Soja has pointed out, Los Angeles is a hotchpotch of social spaces mainly defined by ethnic and socio-economic categories that overlap each other within the same physical space (Soja 1988). Such divisions are not obvious unless the city is 'taken apart' in a spatial sense, and then we uncover the many conflicts and tensions at the boundaries of these spaces. Cities like Los Angeles lack a centre or 'heart' where different groups might share space and develop a common identity. Los Angeles is a city composed of a number of transposed groups, brought together almost entirely for the purpose of providing labour at a given time, and when that need no longer exists they have little or no attachment to the place. As the riots of 1992 demonstrated, Los Angeles provides little social coherence, or shared identity, and the apparent sprawling mass of uniformity hides an underground social world of conflict, resentment, and insecurity.

Abodetion can also increase the frustration of those who are connected with the global village through television, but are unable to participate in the world presented to them. Culture may be exported from the slums of South America in the form of music, dance and football, but the street boy from São Paulo who sees his world reappear translated onto the screens of MTV and CNN, sees a world he has no access to. Clearly we do not all live in the same world.

For postmodern writers, this gap between an apparently homogenised space and the experience of social space – fractured, dislocated and displaced – is a particular concern. In postmodern literature, the organisation of multiple, seemingly disconnected worlds might be read as reaction to globalisation, deliberately resisting it through a process of re-differentiation. It might also be read as a neo-realist representation of tensions and conflicts in social space, and the experience confronting the individual as s/he encounters postmodern placelessness.

THE SPACE VERSUS TIME DEBATE

In recent times, coinciding with the emergence of postmodernity, there has been a trend among writers and theorists to shift attention from time and history towards space and geography. In 1980, Foucault registered the famous complaint that space was largely ignored in the nineteenth and early twentieth centuries, when time and history were the primary concerns:

> Did it start with Bergson or before? Space was treated as the dead, the fixed, the undialectical, the immobile. Time, on the contrary was richness, fecundity, life, dialectic.
> (Foucault 1980: 70)

Fredric Jameson has drawn attention to the 'spatial turn' in cultural theory, claiming that contemporary culture is 'increasingly dominated by space and spatial logic', and suggesting that 'a model of political culture appropriate for our own situation will necessarily have to raise spatial issues as its fundamental organising concern' (Jameson 1991: 154, 364).

In postmodernist theory, recent works by Linda Hutcheon, Brian McHale, Steven Connor, Jon Stratton *et al.*, all point to the importance of spatial relations. It seems that we can now recognise a postmodern perspective of space and time that differs significantly from a modern perspective, and the key to this shift is the growing importance of space and spatial issues in postmodernity. Foucault goes as far as to suggest that this epoch (the late twentieth century), 'will perhaps be above all the epoch of space'; this he compares with the previous epoch, the nineteenth and early twentieth centuries, when our experience of the world was more like 'a long life developing over time' (Foucault 1986: 22). Foucault suggests that late twentieth century polemics are animated by an ideological conflict between 'the pious descendants of time and the determined inhabitants of space' (Foucault 1986: 22). It is tempting now to link this shift from time to space, to the shift from modern to postmodern, but this would be a gross simplification.

As far as the shift from modern to postmodern is concerned, it is more helpful to conceive of this in terms of a change in 'cultural dominant'. This would then imply the presence of other cultural impulses in the postmodern, especially those coming from residual modern forms. The cultural dominant in postmodernity is essentially a resisting impulse, and so requires the modern to rub against. This shift in cultural dominant, as the modern gives way to the postmodern, is coincident with an increased awareness of spatial issues, but the nineteenth century problems of time and history are still with us, and the spirit of the 'modern', characterised by a Faustian soul, restless, striving and inherently temporal, is not anachronistic, although his 'unsurpassably intense Will to the Future' might be rather less driven now (Kern 1983: 105); and we cannot expect the postmodern to take us in a circle back to a pre-modern classical Euclidean world, 'spatially extended, atemporal, centred in the polis, visibly symbolised by monumental architecture' (Kern 1983: 33–4). Similarly, the spatial turn should not be seen as a simple shift from time to space, but rather a shift in spatio-temporal relations. In the postmodern, the categories of space and time are more fluid, and so the space versus time debate is in a sense already an anachronism and a hangover from modern binarist thinking.

The space versus time debate is still useful, however, in comparing modernist and postmodernist thinking, even if this is not as polemic as Foucault has suggested. Time, in one form or another, was a major preoccupation of modernist thinking. Modernism, in particular modernist literature and art, frequently attempts either to capture a sense of the ephemeral and fragmentary, or to resist it. The main problem for modern art, and for theorising modernity, suggests David Harvey, is, as Baudelaire pointed out, to tie its two incompatible strands: one, 'the transient, the fleeting, the contingent', and the other, 'the eternal and the immutable' (Harvey 1989a: 10). The problem of bringing these two strands together is essentially a 'temporal' one, although the lack of grounding and orientation, and the sense of fragmentation and dislocation resulting from modernist impulses are sometimes represented in spatial terms. If the Faustian spirit that characterises the temporality of the modern suffers from a failure to position itself in time, caught between the eternal and immutable earth and a transient and airy future, it is also existentially homeless and, by that token, a yet more tragic figure.

Modernist writers mostly engaged with the problems of time, and space was regarded in the abstract sense as a container in which to represent time, arrested and frozen into disconnected frames or moments, as suggested by Cubists and put into practice in emerging cinematic form. It was the problem of time rather than space which gave rise to theories of flux and stream of consciousness developed by Henri

Bergson and William James, and later practised in literary form by Virginia Woolf and James Joyce. This attempt to capture the passing of time is sometimes referred to as the spatialisation of time.

Henri Lefebvre has suggested that physical space in modernity is detached from history and social space, and that in modern urban planning there has been a concretisation of 'professional' definitions of abstract space. This was a time when grand city plans could be realised. The tyranny of the straight line, introduced by Haussmann into Paris, for example, resulted in the zoning of urban spaces, and introduced modern clean spaces, emptied of everyday bustle and conflict (Lefebvre 1991: 312). These became the dead and silent spaces of the modern, spaces purged of their dialectical moments. In older pre-modern spaces, such as the market place and the street, different classes and groups were brought together much more by everyday spatial practice.

It is such concretisation of abstract spaces that Dostoyevsky brings to life in *Notes From Underground*. In the Nevsky Prospect, to which the underground man is constantly drawn, different social classes no longer meet and renegotiate social space, but charge at great speed down the wide pavements, refusing to give ground, constantly rushing onward in undeviating lines (Berman 1983: 226–8). The efficiency of the modern city as a machine for producing goods, and moving goods, people, and at times armies and the police, demands the dispersal of the social space by which individuals previously claimed attachment to their city. Space is, as it were, 'ironed out' in order to speed things up. Time is of the essence here because industrial capitalism demands ever-increasing and faster returns. The machine must be more efficient to do more work in less time.

In the modern city, abstract plans are informed by an ethos of machine-like efficiency, and there is no time or space for the apparent clutter of traditional market places that might interrupt the traffic flows. The associations which constituted older spatial constructs, and through which people knew themselves and the identity of the social group to which they belonged, were destroyed by some of these developments.

In modernist culture, it seems that social space was sidelined by more pressing problems of time, and place was regarded as an historical and possibly regressive construct, and therefore a hindrance to progress. In postmodernity, social space and place are the subject of renewed interest, and the spatial turn here signals a reassertion of space in contemporary social and cultural theory. According to Edward Soja, we are witnessing a change from an essentially historical epistemology, born out of nineteenth century obsessions with the emplacement of social being and becoming in the contexts of time, to:

> a critical sensibility to the spatiality of social life, . . . a consciousness that sees the lifeworld of being creatively located not only in the making of history but also in the construction of human geographies, the social production of space and the restless formation and reformation of geographical landscapes: social being actively emplaced in space and time in an explicitly historical and geographical contextualisation.
> (Soja 1988: 11)

The space versus time debate is obviously much less polemic if the indicators of space and time cannot be separated. In the early twentieth century, Bergson was criticised by Wyndham Lewis for first 'putting the hyphen between space and time', and confusing distinctions in his 'romance with flux' (Kern 1983: 26). But in cultural and scientific theory, space and time are increasingly dealt with as a single property, or as two aspects of the same thing. In theory of the novel, Bakhtin draws our attention to the artistic chronotope in which time and space assume materiality as a whole:

> Time, as it were, thickens, takes on flesh, becomes artistically visible; likewise, space becomes charged and responsive to the movements of plot and history. The intersection of axes and fusion of indicators characterises the artistic chronotope.
> (Bakhtin 1981: 84)

In social theory, space and time should also be bracketed together, according to Anthony Giddens, who refers to the generation of power in a social system through structures of domination that stretch across time and space, and are retained in 'storage containers' that bracket time–space (Giddens 1981: 4–5). He gives the term 'time–space distanciation' to the mode in which such stretching takes place, and suggests that in pre-modern societies, this distanciation takes place with a high degree of 'presence', and the principal 'storage container' which brackets time–space is the human memory (expressed in knowledge of tradition, and in story-telling and myth) (Giddens 1981: 4–5). In modern societies, this time–space distanciation is extended, and 'storage containers' are no longer visible or easily accessed through human memory. In postmodern society this perhaps reaches a limit where the structures of power are so 'unseen' and 'absent', as to appear metaphysical, chaotic and random.

This theme of the lack of visibility of power structures is often taken up in postmodern literature. In *Libra*, for example, Don DeLillo shows the state taking advantage of its control, and the 'invisibility' of its power across time–space, to engage in widespread conspiracy; and in *The Names*, which we will examine in Chapter 8 below, postmodern American society is stretched across the globe, detached from any visible or rational power structures, and seemingly at the mercy of unseen forces that connect individuals in bizarre naming rituals. *The Names*, in a similar manner to Dickens' *Bleak House*, makes odd connections between apparently unconnected elements of a society, but the law suit at the centre of Dickens' novel represents a visible link between them, even if it is occasionally hidden or satirised by the narrator. In *The Names*, power is so stretched across space and time that there is no rational system underlying its mysterious dispersal, and the fog of unreason that occasionally connects characters never clears to reveal who or what controls society.

Where time and space are bracketed together, it is less a question of the ascendancy of space over time, and more a question of deciphering space–time. In postmodernity, it seems particularly important to try to map the heterogeneous time–spaces that society has produced. In comparing modern and postmodern approaches to space and time, it seems as though modernist culture was more concerned with the individual experience of 'private' time, and escape from 'public' time. In postmodern culture the emphasis is more on the spatial component of spatio-temporal relations. In the postmodern novel, this change of emphasis entails a different organisation of the novel's chronotope, and this, I will argue, has considerable impact on the space and time of narrative as well as the construction of worlds as representations of multiple time–spaces.

In postmodernity, there are parallels between the theory of space and time in cultural and in scientific spheres. In both, the intrinsic inseparability of the indicators of space and time is emphasised. Space and time are combined, and space is no longer regarded as a static container in which events occur, nor is it entirely shaped by events. Rather it affects, and is affected by, events. Events produce space–time as well as occur in space–time.

Spatialisation

Spatialisation (of time in particular) is associated with both modernity and postmodernity, and making clear distinctions between modern and postmodern spatialisation in thought, and cultural and aesthetic practices is crucial in defining the postmodern chronotope. As Stephen Kern claims in *The Culture of Time and Space 1880–1918*, technological innovation in this period of industrial modernisation radically affected the experience of space and time in the late nineteenth and early twentieth centuries, leading to a 'transformation of the dimensions of life and thought' (Kern 1983: 1–2).

Marshall Berman suggests that experience of the individual during this transformation is that of an alienated soul, driven by an intense will to the future, torn out of history, and adrift in a Bergsonian flux of time. The emergence of this modern 'anomie' as a symbol of the modern condition, is symptomatic of a failure of the individual to bond in the disparate and complex communities of industrial cities. In the economically-driven placelessness of the modern city, Berman likens the condition of modern man to that of a weightless and ungrounded Faustian spirit, taking to the air in anticipation of fulfilment of economic desires, but then left hovering in a netherland between present and future.[4]

Disconnected from history, adrift in space and time, clearly these are not problems to emerge suddenly in the late twentieth century. But there is a crucial difference between the modern and postmodern chronotope in this respect. Modernity, while it emphasises individual angst, at the same time seems to press on with deterministic and materialist accounts of history and with the aspirations of modern utopian thinkers on the left and on the right. In postmodernity, those aspirations are largely discredited and associated now with totalitarian regimes and prescriptive and elitist attitudes to art. So where modernist spatialisation might have tried to capture time and represent the passing of time in various spatial forms (and so signal the onward rush of the present), postmodernist spatialisation is without that rush, without any pretence of being able to visualise time, or to see into the entrails of time to prophesy. We might say that the postmodern chronotope is without any sense of the historical, alternatively we might say that the postmodern chronotope marks a shift in emphasis from a historical to a geographical imagination, from the dialectics of time to the dialectics of space. The emphasis is spatial, the orientation is spatial, but not exclusively spatial.

In a lecture given in 1967, Michel Foucault suggests that space, rather than time, is now the major concern for contemporary thinkers.[5] He claims that 'The present epoch will perhaps be above all the epoch of space . . . the anxiety of our era has to do fundamentally with space, no doubt a great deal more than time' (Foucault 1986: 22–4). Foucault signals a postmodern interest in space here as a rethinking of modernist spatialisation, the control and domination of public and social space by utopian planners. Such modern spaces are fundamentally unreal and inauthentic because they are detached from the actual wishes and needs of the societies that inhabit them, and are used to reflect either a perfect version of society or society as radically other than it really is, a cleaned up and homogenised social order. Such spaces are:

> sites with no real place . . . sites that have a general relation of direct or inverted analogy with the real space of society. They present society itself in a perfected form, or else society turned upside down, but in any case, these utopias are fundamentally unreal spaces.
> (Foucault 1986: 22–4)

The modern utopia is imposed upon social space severing its links with history, tradition, and the disorderly patterns of the everyday – the utopia is abstracted, essentially a non-place.

As a postmodern counter to the modern utopia, Foucault introduces a concept of 'heterotopia', as the 'real' places produced by society as part of its continuous coming into being. But oddly, Foucault does not develop the heterotopia as a general model for social space in towns and cities, restricting his attention to particular kinds of sites, or containers within social space where the spatial dynamics are rather detached from history. His examples include: cemeteries, fairgrounds, libraries, museums, cinemas, theatres, and gardens, their principal properties being:

- they are capable of juxtaposing in a single real space, several spaces that are in themselves incompatible
- they are linked to particular slices of time, such as the duration of a performance, or the accumulation of historic time, or the continual re-enactment of a past time
- they presuppose a system for opening or closing (entering or

leaving) them, and this presupposes a relation between themselves and the space around them, from which they are constituted.

In choosing to develop the idea of heterotopia with specialised sites in mind, Foucault avoids dealing with postmodern spaces as responses to modern utopian spaces. The spatial turn here expresses a change in interest but hardly a shift in approach to contemporary social and political issues, even though the heterotopia might be a useful model for understanding certain changes and tensions specific to postmodernity, and especially the failure to produce traditional place-bound communities. Foucault distinguishes between heterotopia and utopian, or 'unreal' space, but this is still a modern approach to the abstraction and division of space. Surely the lesson to be learned from disastrous modern utopian spaces is to treat social space as multi-form and multi-functional: the harsh, concrete public square and the shopping mall can be transformed by different social uses – they too can become theatres, gardens and fairgrounds. The utopian spaces imposed by modern planners have too often become dead space, empty of social life and abstracted from the everyday.

Having introduced the very interesting concept of the heterotopia in the context of social space here, Foucault seems to deal quite separately in his major works with the spaces of institutions, the control and surveillance within institutionalised spaces (such as prisons), the space of the body, and epistemological space. Foucault always seems to deal with the dynamics of particular isolated sites, as though these are unconnected with the space around them. He divides and categorises space, as the title of his lecture 'Des Espaces Autres' implies. Foucault deals with abstract space, not with the dynamics of its production.

For Henri Lefebvre, the continuous production of space by society is crucial, as is recognition of the different but inter-related kinds of space that contribute to this production. As Lefebvre argues in *The Production of Space*, Foucault never really distinguishes between the different kinds of space to which he refers. For example, in *The Archaeology of Knowledge*, Foucault asserts that 'knowledge [*savoir*] is also the *space* in which the subject may take up a position and speak of the objects with which he deals in his discourse' (Foucault 1972: 182).[6] But he never explains how the space he refers to is able to bridge a theoretical (epistemological) realm with a material one.

Lefebvre thinks Foucault's use of space is 'casual', and more fundamentally (and this is really the main theme of Lefebvre's study of social space in *The Production of Space*), he argues that such a focus on the 'thinking subject' and his/her space, as opposed to the space out there in the world of objects, creates an opposition between 'space' and the 'thinking subject', and between the thinking subject and 'objects in space'. It is Lefebvre's general complaint that much discourse on space fails to take account of the position of the 'collective subject', and therefore fails to conceptualise social space (Lefebvre 1991: 4).

In *The Production of Space*, Lefebvre calls for an assessment of time and space which traces a 'long history' of space. This history is to be more than an inventory of things in space, and geographical descriptions of natural space:

> It [the history of space] must account for both representational spaces and representations of space, but above all for their interrelationships and their links with social practice. The history of space thus has its place between anthropology and political economy.
> (Lefebvre 1991: 116)

Lefebvre's project is not simply to substitute for traditional history, a geographical description of the changes to physical space over time, but to study the social structures and processes that interact with, and modify, 'natural' rhythms, and inscribe themselves in space. This involves the analysis of such traces within physical space, ranging from the near incomprehensible scribbling in the networks and paths formed by people traversing rural space, to the complex structures imposed on urban space by work-related activities, such as the construction of specific work-places, and the means of transporting materials and goods.

Of particular interest to the present work, is Lefebvre's recognition of the influence of representational space, and representations of space on this history of space, because here representational arts such as literature are clearly implicated in passive and sometimes active roles. In one of his main examples of the dynamics of social space, and its inscription in physical space, he looks at the development of Italian Renaissance cities, such as Florence, and their relationship with the Tuscan countryside. The design for rebuilding the city in the twelfth century needed to balance economic demands for expansion, with demands for security, and a new economic relationship with the countryside around it. But these demands and changes in social practices were woven into a configuration that also corresponded to representational spaces, such as the *imago mundi* and *rose des vents* or compass-card designs. These designs helped place the city symbolically in the world and the cosmos, and also reflected artistic and philosophical conceptions of space (Lefebvre 1991: 119).

So social space is linked through spatial practice to representational space, and to symbolic, sacred and quasi-religious space, but it is also linked to subjective and phenomenological space. In this respect, social space spans the dichotomy between 'public' and 'private' space evident in the modern functional division of space, and in cultural and aesthetic responses to this. The dichotomy between public and private has been reinforced in modernity, a time in which the social space of older communal traditions and religious ceremonies is disappearing and a public world gradually encroaches on the private.

As Stephen Kern has noted, the intrusion of the public world into the private at the beginning of the twentieth century, largely as a result of technological innovation, gave rise to increased privacy laws, planning regulations and a fear of intrusion into individual space. Such penetration of the private world and efforts to protect it were also evident in psychology and the literature of the time (Kern 1983: 190).[7] When the shell-like space of home is under threat, it takes on increasing significance as refuge, and it and the spaces within it are imbued with symbolic meaning. In Gaston Bachelard's *The Poetics of Space*, houses and their rooms, drawers and chests are elevated from their status of everyday objects to become externalised representations of human space, with their analogues in natural space, and connected to a cosmic whole (Bachelard 1969: xxxiv). Lefebvre refers to Bachelard's reading of the house in *The Production of Space*:

> The house is as much cosmic as it is human. From cellar to attic, from foundations to roof, it has a destiny at once dreamy and rational, earthly and celestial. The relationship between Home and Ego, meanwhile, borders on identity. The shell, a secret and directly experienced space, for Bachelard epitomizes the virtues of human 'space'.
> (Lefebvre 1991:121)

While recognising this individual and universal identity lodged in the shell-like house, Lefebvre wants to reassert a notion of the collective subject through social space, and to promote this over both private and public spaces. In this respect, Lefebvre's approach to space is analogous to Bakhtin's approach to language (dialogism) which insists on the social nature of language, and both might be read as a critique of hegemony, the monologic/monolithic, public/official and at the same time, the individualistic/bourgeois. The figurative site of exchange for Lefebvre and Bakhtin is the traditional market place, the social hub of communities, a place of business, performance, entertainment, recreation and gossip.

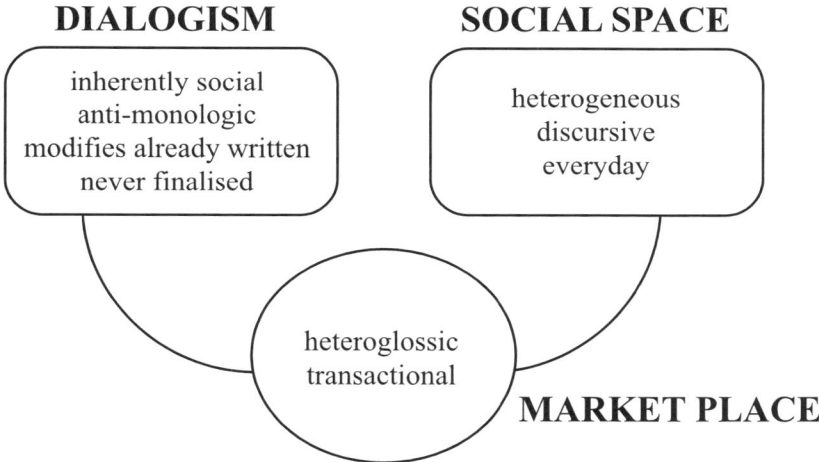

Figure 1. An analogy between dialogism and social space

    Bakhtin argues that language is produced through social discourse (dialogue) between subject–objects. It does not (should not) emanate from the individual subject or authoritative sources. In dialogue, meaning is continuously renegotiated in the space the utterance creates between speaker and listener. Of course, such unhindered social interaction would require the absence of overriding, monologic forces, and that all individuals are heard in the market place, and permitted to enter it. Also, the market place is the traditional site for the lower classes to exercise their limited freedom. The ruling classes are immune from having to negotiate here.

In modern and postmodern societies, the market place is relocated into shopping malls and electronic spaces, where the space between subject–objects is differently mediated, and meaning is no longer negotiated in the space opened up by the utterance. Rather meaning is predetermined as subject–objects are themselves absent from the space of the utterance and communicate through already written sets of codes. But in a less literal sense, the market place is still a useful site for conceiving of language and space in their 'ideal' social form. In modern and postmodern society we perhaps need to find new ways of simulating that 'ideal' situation. The market place is a sign of the 'everyday', and this is as important for Bakhtin's philosophy of language, as it is for Lefebvre's philosophy of space, as language (and space) here are never fixed, but renegotiated on a daily basis. As Bakhtin puts it 'each day has its own slogan, its own vocabulary, its own emphases' (Bakhtin 1981: 263).

Social space is of course more than just 'doing things' in space. Institutions, religious authorities, ethnic groups, and individuals themselves, tend to reserve space, peg out an exclusive patch, removing it from the processes of social production. Conflicts arise, especially at significant boundaries between reserved and occupied space, and in postmodern, multicultural societies the open social space of the market place is often removed and different social groups are more confined in delineated areas with limited freedom to wander elsewhere, so social space becomes fragmented, owned and sometimes barricaded.

There are also external, mainly economic forces shaping social space. In postmodernity, global capitalism has its own spatial dynamics, operating through social space and shaping it. Where economies are especially sensitive to land prices, social groups, and sometimes the state itself, find they are unable to intervene in capitalism's slicing and re-slicing of the cake. Exceptions prove the rule, but are nonetheless encouraging. For example, London's Docklands, which was for decades an unloved and largely derelict riverside site, was developed in the 1980s into desirable warehouse apartments fronting the river. These private developments meant that public access to the riverside was denied, but various groups, helped by left-wing councils, campaigned for and succeeded in getting a riverside walkway, giving back the Thames to local people. In some cases, private developers built walkways in front of their developments because they realised that this added value to the site, increasing property prices. The argument previously put forward by the developers that there would be security problems if they created a walkway were shown to be fallacious, and both the public and occupants have mostly gained from the increased use of the space.

Indeed, it can now be seen that London Docklands suffered a major setback in the late 1980s because there was too little public space. The traditional market places and public houses of London's East End were displaced by deliberately but disastrously exclusive spaces of private developments. Slowly more public space is being created, not necessarily by a benevolent state, but by a slightly more enlightened property industry. And these are not public spaces simply to be seen, but spaces for people to do things in. An awareness of the need for social space is, I think, evident now in postmodern developments, and this is an awareness that has been long absent. Since the clearing of Paris by Haussmann in the nineteenth century, space had been subject to the tyranny of the straight line, the abstract and empty spaces of modernist planners.

David Harvey argues that capitalism reaches across all social spaces, compressing both space and time to meet capitalism's own demands to increase continuously production and supply (Harvey 1990a).[8] We can also see that when capital is switched from one region to another, it must drastically alter the social fabric of two places at once, and that it suits global capitalism to create homogenised market places to unify production and demand. But I believe Harvey overstates the influence of global capitalism on the production of social space, partly because, in practice, capitalism's own internal conflicts such as competition between suppliers, ensure that the market is never entirely homogenised, and that it must, to a degree, remain open to individual and social demands. The forces of global capitalism are not constantly at odds with the production of social space, and it seems to me to be dangerous to assume that we are powerless in the wake of economic forces. Certainly capitalism is a major shaping force on social space, but it does not entirely take away our freedom to act within it.

Lefebvre's splendid analysis of the production of social space suggests a rather more complex interaction between the spatial practices of capitalism and space as it is conceived and realised by the subject. This analysis proceeds from the identification of a triad of spatial moments constituting social space, and is arranged as follows (Lefebvre 1991: 38–9)[9]:

1. *spatial practice* of a society is perceived through the deciphering of that society's material organisation of space, and can be empirically evaluated in the 'daily round' of subjects in and in between distinct sites of home, work, leisure, shopping, travel etc. In modern societies, this might typically be described as so many journeys to and from the workplace, shops, etc., and enclosure within the so-called private space of an apartment. Increasingly in modern societies, and very much in postmodern societies, perception of social space is determined by electronic spaces, first and foremost the space of the television screen, now expanded and spatially extended by mobile phones, VCRs, portable computers and the internet. Moving from an analogue (representation) to a digital (simulation) culture creates an extraordinary sense of mobility that pervades postmodern social space, and yet much of this is mediated through virtual travel and simulations of other places by electronic and physical means. A corresponding decrease in bodily mobility can be experienced as journeys themselves become less imperative.

2. *representations of space* are the conceptualised spaces of planners, architects and scientists which tend to dominate and impose themselves on the lived space of the everyday. The production of space in modern societies proceeds largely from the materialisation of such intellectual and systematic concepts of space. In postmodernity, space is reckoned to be far more heterogeneous, although perhaps the postmodern age merely imposes its own concepts on to lived space. We are perhaps able to discern in postmodern social space the traces of a nostalgic return to some pre-modern ideal, but now without reference to some higher cosmic order such as that which organised the spaces of mediaeval and classical cities. The representations of space that inform today's lived space are muddled simulations of a past order which cannot be recovered. Such nostalgic seeking after the past only emphasises the loss of an order representing itself in space.

3. *representational spaces* are the symbolic and metaphorical mental maps by which we experience physical space. We live by representational spaces, reading signs and symbols as our reality, but this is also a poetic space which writers and artists may appropriate and seek to change.

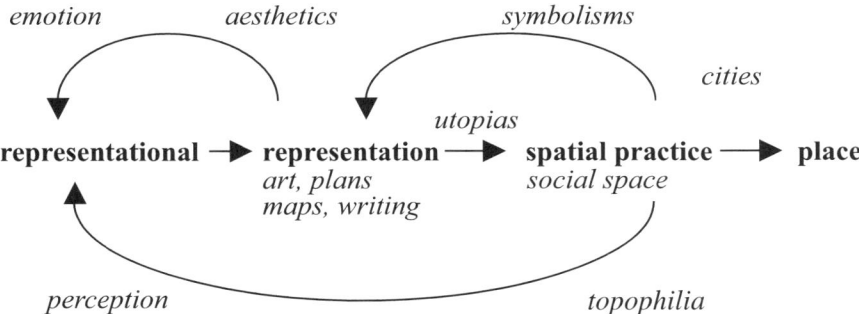

Figure 2. Interdependency of representational space, representations of space and spatial practice (after Lefebvre)

The plan that Lefebvre posits for interactions between different kinds or different orders of space and spatial activity is, of course, in danger of itself becoming a representation, an abstract design which he is imposing on an actual reality. To be fair to Lefebvre, the diagram is mine not his, yet a diagram or map of the production of space is implicit in Lefebvre's distinction between the different realms of his conceptual triad. Indeed, cognitive reasoning inevitably tends towards spatial representation in verbal and figurative form. As reason presents itself, it differentiates, orders, integrates and systematises, so although the idea itself may have lodged itself in non-verbal, intuitive space of 'pure' imagination (and so, in Lefebvre's schema, in representational space), at the moment it comes to presentation it is organised into a representation of space and, in this way, capable of being transmitted either into the actual reality of spatial practice, or re-appropriated back into representational space. But Lefebvre's model is not designed as a perfect rational system organised around self-evident and demonstrable proofs, and so it does not conceive of a philosophical truth, but rather it attempts to describe a process by which space is perceived, conceived and lived.

The idea that perception and lived experience is somehow received through representational space is in itself arresting and highly relevant for literary studies. But Lefebvre also puts great faith in the body and in the everyday, and his concerns for the processes by which every society produces its space, the traces of which can be perceived, deciphered and felt long after the events that produced them, is an idea with repercussions in psychology, the social sciences, architecture and the arts generally. The challenge for the present work is to project Lefebvre's idea of a history of spatial process, of the production of social space by different societies at different times, into a discussion of modern and postmodern representation.

As mentioned earlier, Lefebvre's approach differs from that of Foucault, in that Foucault establishes an opposition between the thinking subject and space, a boundary between external space and internal space. Lefebvre sees the distinction as rather more fluid than this, as representational space conditions our perception of external space, as much as external space reflects a society's representations of space. There is a dynamic and dialectic relation between the perception and production of space, as particular readings of space are in themselves constitutive of space. To conceive of social space, it is necessary to suspend the idea that space is absolute and measurable, as in the 'billiard board' idea of Euclidean geometry which only operates within the realm of particular representations of space. But if social space cannot be measured, like external space, it is nevertheless present, affecting, describing and forming traces of our daily movements.

To further emphasise the distinction between absolute space and social space, Lefebvre considers its production as the effects of various energies and events rather than their container. Fred Hoyle's somewhat dated theory of cosmological space–time in which he suggests that events produce energy which in turn *produces* space–time, rather than *filling* the space of the universe in a universal time scheme, is used more or less as metaphor by Lefebvre.[10] Of course, as Lefebvre points out 'There is no reason to assume an isomorphism between social energies and physical energies, or between "human" and physical fields of force' (Lefebvre 1991: 14). This would be to confuse the conceptual with the practical, extending scientific thinking beyond its reach and giving rise to the kind of scientism which was the bane of some modernist utopian projects. On the other hand, to dismiss all of this simply as metaphor would be to ignore the potential of social space as a way of seeing a transition from modern to postmodern space.

Lefebvre introduces into social theory an idea of social space that is not pre-formed or static, but produced by the energies of social interaction. Traces of past events may be left in that space but, as with Hoyle's theory of physical energies, these traces may appear in different places at different times because the energies were not uniformly distributed. This has always made large scale histories difficult, because the 'fall out' of major social events occurring in one place will occur elsewhere in the world at a different time. This plays havoc with grand historical narratives and prophesies that depend on historical evidence. Making social space the product of spatial practice, rather than an arena for historical events, is at the core of Lefebvre's thesis, and this has major implications for social theory. It calls for a closer analysis of spatial practice, and changes the focus of attention from grand unified theories to more local and 'contextual' approaches.

Social space provides a writing tablet of history, because major events will tend to leave traces across landscapes, and register themselves in significant public sites such as churches, monuments and public squares. But this history must be read critically as there is a danger that major public spaces controlled by the state will contain the 'official' writing of history, rather than a trace of the event itself. The event to note and criticise would be that official writing of history by the prevailing order. Other histories of space may leave some trace in the shanty towns and ghettos of the homeless and dispossessed, for example, while still others remain apparently invisible, unless some record remains in a representational form, such as those recorded in literature.

To summarise, in Lefebvre's theory of social space, space becomes rich and dialectic because we learn to 'read' space, not in its separate compartments of natural space, absolute space, and imagined space, but as a space that links all of these and contains within it the inscriptions of human activity as social structures and processes. Representations of space (the absolute space of scientists, architects and planners) and representational space (symbolic space, and the space of writers and artists), are linked to these structures and processes, and it is the particular relationship between writing and social space that we will explore further now.

Social Space and Literature

For too long, Lefebvre insists, there has been a schism between knowledge of subjective space (the space of the individual), and objective space (the space of the physical world), and this is where social space is intended to overlap and bring these two categories together again. But how do we come to know social space? Lefebvre proposes, and then rejects, first philosophy, because it seems to have introduced this schism in the first place and is too abstract; and second literature, because of the difficulty in choosing a text that gives a 'true' account of space. Architecture is also rejected as this depends on prior analysis and understanding of the concept of space informing it, and general scientific notions are dismissed as being too enclosed and specialised. Returning to philosophy, Lefebvre then considers the Hegelian concept of the concrete universal, and suggests that *production* and the *act of producing*, as universal concepts, might be recovered from the realm of political economy and applied to spatial relations (Lefebvre 1991:14–15).

In the present work, I would like to explore relations between literature and the production of social space in literature, not to demonstrate that literature presents 'true' pictures of that social space, but that the representational space of the postmodern novel registers shifts in the perception of space specific to postmodernity. If we regard social space as a kind of writing produced by dialogic process, it would leave marks in physical space that could subsequently be read and interpreted as signs of the social processes that produced them. But as with writing, space can also embody complex symbolisms, or be written in ancient 'languages' and inscribed in sacred spaces, such as churches and temples. These are what Lefebvre refers to as *representational spaces*, less the everyday 'surface' activities of spatial practice, and linked more to the 'clandestine or underground side of social life, as also to art.' (Lefebvre 1991: 33).

Representational space is of course a specialism of literature, and here Lefebvre suggests that art may come to be defined 'less as a code of space than as a code of representational spaces' (Lefebvre 1991: 33). In literature, as in social space, complex symbolisms are often linked to the 'underground side of social life', where contemporary space is resisted, or re-imagined. Although, paradoxically, in *Notes from Underground* Dostoyevsky's hero struggles against what he perceives as a dysfunctional modern social space contained within a monologic urban landscape. The Nevsky Prospect epitomises the spatial practice of a harsh modernity, which seems to have purged itself of a social underground, of an ulterior space in which art might flourish, and the hero is increasingly alienated. The social space of the modern city seems to exclude the hero and he is forced to retreat into his own world. Unable to decipher the new symbolisms of modern space, he constructs his own paranoiac 'underground' world, but this is a prison, a representational space inhabited by an abject solitary hero.

In postmodern society, however, spatial practice is less directed and less concretised than it was in modernity. The 'soft city' of late modernity (Raban 1974) allows for multiple interpretations, multiple representation of space in the same site. In this heterogeneity, the production of space is not only more diverse and more plural (and so potentially more accommodating, reflecting multicultural social needs and outputs) it is also more resistant to domination by the totalising forces of utopian planners – to the imposition of the abstract and conceptual space of planners.

But postmodern social space perhaps goes to the other extreme, to the point where no new concepts are applied, no vision of the city as a whole is produced. Added to this, postmodern social space reflects a failure of representation and so space repeats itself, recycles the codes and symbols of past spaces, without the concepts or spatial practices in place that gave rise to such places. In this age of simulation, social space is in danger of becoming an outmoded concept itself. We are at a time when Lefebvre's concept of social space needs also to take account of the production of the 'virtual spaces' produced by electronic means. The idea of a spatial practice divorced from conceptual space, and yet taking signs willy-nilly out of representational space, has the hallmark of postmodernism, as it shows both a failure of representation and the rise of simulacra, simulations of other spaces.

This is to have a profound effect on the idea of place in postmodernity, as places constructed out of postmodern spatial practice lack the differentiation that gave identity to traditional and even to modern places. Although modern cities began to resemble each other because of shared utopian visions and the advent of a common international style in architecture, they often retained identity in the integrity of their conceptualisation, even if the realisation of such dream was a disaster, because at least this gave the place a name. For example, the English city of Birmingham is well-known as an example of modern planning gone wrong, in a place where modernity was hardly welcomed anyway. The result is that even though I have never been to the city, it presents a clear image to me in a way that postmodernised spaces never can.

The provincial English high street is a prime example of postmodern spatial practice, identical facades of national and international enterprises erasing any local character. 'Character' is then reintroduced in the form of identical iron lampposts, hanging baskets of flowers, benches and paved pedestrian areas, frequently now sponsored by the same enterprises whose facades destroyed the identity of the place. What remains is the sign – the identity of an English provincial town or city is now provided by a proliferation of welcome signs that substitute for the concrete differentiation of traditional places more secure in their outward signs of difference and identity.

FROM SPACE TO PLACE (AND TEXT)

Concern for place in postmodernity is associated with a sense of the loss of traditional place already found in modernity, but exacerbated by post-colonial migrations forming multicultural societies in previously mono-cultural sites, and by a postmodern proliferation of signs as places. Postmodern place, suffers from (is enabled by) post-structuralist thinking. As with texts, places no longer have referents, only further signifiers, and texts and places both register, and show signs of a nostalgia for, the values or transcendent signifiers which would provide meaning in texts, and roots and belonging in places. The similarities between place and text from a post-structuralist standpoint might be summarised as follows:

- dialectical relationships between absence (space, writing) and presence (place, speech, performance)
- deciphering of spatial practice (life) into the symbols and images of representational space (reading)
- historical referents, and attempts to inscribe or capture time (spatialisation)
- meaning mediated through other places (intertextuality)
- polymorphic, heterotopic.

As with texts, places are complex constructions which do not reveal some intended meaning, but enable various possible readings. Both refer beyond their own internal design and construction to other sites, and to a geographical and historical context: the larger chronotope. Like a text, place is never a 'finished' construction, but reaches backwards and forwards in time, and the experience/reading is a subjective, cultural and historical activity.

Common sense tells us that the difference between space and place is one of nothing and something, absence and presence. For Yi-Fu Tuan, it begins like this:

> Space is more abstract than place. What begins as undifferentiated space becomes place as we get to know it better (experience it) and endow it with value . . . space and place require each other to define themselves . . . from the security and stability of place, we are aware of the openness and threat of space.
>
> (Tuan 1977: 6)

Place never has complete presence, both because it is always disappearing and being reproduced, and also because much of its presence is conditioned by representational spaces which are properly absent from the concrete structures and spaces that constitute physical place, and so are hidden, not available to a superficial survey. Representational space, in Lefebvre's scheme, is where we decipher and sometimes reinterpret spatial practice and where we experience lived space. But, as we have seen already, in postmodern place there is no deciphering of spatial practice in the traditional sense, there is no need to look beyond the signs of spatial practice because spatial practice in postmodernity is, in effect, simply the arrangement of signs which point only to other signs and not to a referent lodged in some 'higher' order or value system. And this arrangement of signs is, we are told by all sides, determined by the play of economics, and in particular that of a pervasive, global capitalism in which the very signs of authenticity in place, historical sites, sites of great events, ancient stones, palaces and temples and ruins, have themselves become signs of something else, of a heritage industry. So, very little decoding is required of postmodern spatial practice, it would seem, because postmodern spaces are already representational spaces reflecting the dominant practice of late capitalist production of signs, and little else. And where spaces already contain representational spaces, and there is no referent beyond these signs, they are, as Baudrillard has noted, pure simulacra (Baudrillard 1983a: 2).

Here we are describing a postmodern placelessness related to what Edward Relph calls 'inauthenticity' in place, caused by modernisation initially, but later by the 'Disneyfication' of old cities and the production of new pseudo places, and where capitalist means of production displace an 'authentic' development where place grows organically according to changing social needs and desires (Relph 1976: 95).

The 'authentic' and 'inauthentic' are two extremes of course, and even in America the idea if not the practice of authentic place has not entirely disappeared. Although, as Jan Morris has noted, in a place like Vermont, it is very difficult to tell the 'real' New England, itself already a kind of counterfeit, from copies of it (Morris 1992: 1–14). In Vermont today, new homes are indistinguishable from the old buildings they seek to simulate, and this would seem to signify a nostalgia for an oxymoronic 'old' New England, where the sign of America was of a pure and wholesome kind, unsullied by the corrupt old Europe from which it distanced itself. But as Morris records, Vermont does still retain, underneath all of this, a belief in its own authenticity. It is easy to be cynical but, despite the tourism and the influx of foreigners, Vermont people still believe in this 'old' New England, a space–time capsule in which the original ideals of America are somehow preserved.

Postmodernity may go some way to effacing place, but the symbolic power of place can resist this disappearance. It is largely a matter of faith in what the place might signify. In a east European mediaeval city like Tallinn in Estonia, McDonalds, Benetton and Body Shop have moved into the mediaeval square, and there has been an unseemly rush to 'tart up' the city. Here the fresh paint, gilded roofs, covered-over cracks in the walls, the new-old lamp posts, hanging baskets and benches sponsored by McDonalds, are all for the benefit of western tourists, consumers and investors. And yet beneath all of that, Tallinn still signifies, for local Estonians, a site of resistance and rich cultural heritage retained through fifty years of German and Soviet occupation.[11]

Postmodern effacement of place is also resisted by everyday life. In the many picturesque English villages that provided the *mise en scène* for countless film and TV productions of period dramas, everyday life goes on as it has for centuries, the little dramas of ordinary life in a village that the movie never shows. So, we might conclude that 1) one person's simulacra might well be another's real place, 2) spatial practice continues to produce place, and 3) representational space is not entirely overwhelmed by the symbols and images of a capitalist mode of production. These are important points for place and for representational forms such as the novel. As with place, the postmodern novel reflects the dominant forms of capitalist production but it also resists them by reasserting ideals and faith in human values, love, family and so on. There is a conceptual space between the postmodern novel's representational spaces (poetic form and the chronotope as imaginative decoding of spatial practice) and its representations of space (content as presentation of contemporary spatial practice).

Apart from the seemingly genuine retention of faith in place as the sign of something beyond itself, there are also spurious and unconscious associations made in places, and these are often seeded by powerful representational spaces occurring in literature, dreams, myths and so on. For example, Yi-Fu Tuan refers to a visit by the physicist Werner Heisenberg to Kronberg Castle, Denmark, where Heisenberg is given to associate Hamlet with the castle, although there is no historical or circumstantial evidence that links the two. But having made this entirely spurious association, the castle produces a very different experience. It becomes very difficult to resist such associations once a link with a particularly strong external representation, in this case the text of Shakespeare's *Hamlet*, has been made (Tuan 1977). It is just as difficult, of course, to do the reverse, that is to avoid making associations with 'real' places, or physical places already experienced, when reading a literary text.

For Tuan, place is a kind of object that consists of valued space and physical objects, but it is not the sort of object that can be picked up and carried around – place is essentially an object to be *occupied* (Tuan 1977: 12). Place is always at odds with the space around it, like a city walled off from the potentially threatening space around it. Man inscribes physical space and gives it a name in the same way, according to legend, that Romulus and Remus drew a circle in the earth with a stick and named it Rome. But place is never neutral in human affairs. The walled city serves as an example of place, but the experience of place and the relationship to the surrounding space can be ambiguous. For a slave in the city, the wall encloses and keeps him from the freedom of the borderlands, whereas for the ruling class, the wall is protection from a real or perceived enemy in the space outside.

Geographical, historical and other quantitative analyses of place can never render the whole story of a place: place is always partially subjective, and it is literature, personal memories, myths and local histories that tend to give place its true character by bringing out the richness of its multiple meanings/readings. Traditionally, place has been a social construction where people act in concert, or in conflict, to establish a configuration of objects and spaces in a place, and bestow on objects and spaces particular values. It is this attachment of value which makes place out of the undifferentiated space around it, and a crucial aspect of this attachment of value seems to be the inscription of *time* in place.

In the construction of early religious and symbolic places – in temples and stone circles – a value of timelessness, or eternity, or connection with an ancient past was important in establishing a 'zero' time: a time of creation, before which there was a void. This 'zero' time is then celebrated and re-invoked in religious ceremony as a way of 'fixing' human existence in a planned cosmological scheme. This 'fixing' through creation myths can allow society to transcend its own little history when visions of its future begin to look apocalyptic. This could be read in a modern context as an attempt by man to escape the arrow of (thermodynamic) time, which points toward increasing disorder.[12]

The value of time inscribed in place was also present in the concept of the Grand Tour, which was part of the education of Europe's young aristocrats in the seventeenth and eighteenth century. But although they visited the 'honeypots' of antiquity in Europe's cities, this early form of tourism was not intended merely to broaden or refresh parochial minds. The Grand Tour was intended to reinforce the conviction that European history was richer and her culture superior to others. As Jon Stratton has written, it was intended to supply a retrospective pattern in which Europe was destined to be superior:

> This journey became known as the Grand Tour. It became important for young aristocrats and later the bourgeoisie, and was undertaken in a very specific context. This kind of travel was not the travel of exploration but the productive travel of established difference. It was the travel for which guidebooks were written.
> (Stratton 1990: 69)

It has always seemed slightly odd to me that part of the established difference which supposedly articulated a European superiority was the inscription of past greatness in ruins. These ruins could easily have been read as a lesson in mutability and the destructive power of time, rather than as a sign of European greatness. The antithetical quality of ruins is a common theme in English literature. It is present in Anglo-Saxon elegiac poetry such as *The Ruin* and *The Wanderer*, where poets wonder at the power of the 'giants' (Romans) who built these structures, and compare this past greatness with the ineptitude of contemporary Anglo-Saxon leaders. It is also present in Shakespeare's *Sonnet 55*: 'Not marble nor the gilded monuments/Of princes shall outlive . . .' (ll.1–2), and in the poetry of the English Romantics: Byron, Keats and Shelley.

But the story of European greatness was presented as *already written*. The ruin, as a sign of a great imperial past and destiny, was a *donnée* in the prehistory of colonisation by the emerging modern European nation states (Janowitz 1990). Rome, above all, epitomised this placement of value for European ruling classes in its celebratory 'park' of triumphal arches: each a testimony to lands conquered and then inscribed in the representational centre of the Empire. For Victorian writers who visited Rome there must have been a familiar aspect to the triumphalism and inscription of imperial greatness, as the buildings and monuments in London became etched with references to Victoria's 'possessions' and 'protectorates'.

Although a time of creation may be inscribed in sacred places, and times of imperial and national glory may be inscribed in cultural epicentres, the experience of place for most people, was, and still is, the random bustle of the everyday. In secular places, such as market places, halls, public squares, and streets, time does not stand still. In fact, time has always been critical to secular activities centred around the provision of, and exploitation of, labour. As David Harvey notes:

> Mediaeval merchants . . . in constructing a better measure of time 'for the orderly conduct of business' promoted a 'fundamental change in the measurement of time which was indeed a change in time itself'. Symbolised by clocks and bells that called workers to labour and merchants to market, separated from the 'natural' rhythms of agrarian life, and divorced from religious signification, merchants and masters created a new 'chronological net' in which daily life was caught.
> (Harvey 1990a: 228)[13]

Clocks appeared in public spaces as capitalist enterprise recognised the need to maximise labour, and reduce 'wasted time'. Clocks were used to synchronise meetings, transactions, and to measure 'free time' and 'working time'. Clocks in the eighteenth and nineteenth centuries are like the maps of the seventeenth century, they redefine the world symbolically by dividing it up into governable, exchangeable, exploitable segments. As David Landes puts it: 'Time measurement was at once a sign of new-found creativity and an agent and catalyst in the use of knowledge for wealth and power' (Landes 1983: 12).

In complex mental transactions between the internal and external world a cognitive structuring of space occurs that maps our own version of the material world. These 'mental maps' are often at odds with Euclidean or Cartesian space, ignoring distance, geometry and proportion. Mental maps are bent to our individual perception, desires and needs, so they sometimes shorten distances of frequently travelled journeys, enlarge 'home' territories, and shrink areas of little interest. But as Gould and White discover in their classic study of British mental maps, these tend not to be very individualistic, and we can find broad similarities between the mental maps of individuals from similar social groups and from the same regions (Gould and White 1974).

This structuration of space has further significance when we construct logico-mathematical spaces based on direct sensory experience of the environment, and then 'map' these to concepts and theories. Mark Johnson's work on the theory of the imagination suggests that metaphor, especially spatial metaphor, might be the means by which the mind transfers information between the synthesising, reproductive and creative faculties of the imagination. Johnson suggests that narrative, image-schemata (or large-scale spatial metaphor), metaphor and metonymy are a fundamental component in the cognitive process (Johnson 1987: 233). Without going too far into these interesting areas of research in the present work, we can nevertheless recognise the importance of spatial metaphor and its role in mediating between the perception and imagination of space, our cognitive and conceptual apparatus, and the process of representing and constructing space and place.

Whenever we voice, draw or otherwise illustrate concepts, our language inclines toward spatial metaphor, and this is true whether we are explaining thought or feeling. For example, we tend to rank properties according to a vertical bias, privileging high over low, so that we 'reach for the sky', 'plumb the depths' etc., although we must be careful about where we draw the line between universal human tendencies and cultural differences. It seems probable that if Johnson's image-schemata are fundamental parts of human cognition and they are based on sensory experience, different social groups in different landscapes may nevertheless construct different forms and shapes, and translate these into different ways of thinking, and different faiths and beliefs. Certain cultural conflicts may indeed come down to a misunderstanding of one group's spatial metaphors, by another.

To summarise the properties of place, we can say that it has subjective, cultural and physical dimensions, and is associated with individual and cultural identity not only in terms of the physical occupation of a given locality, but as 'a focus where we experience the meaningful events of our existence' (Norberg-Schultz 1971: 19). Places are therefore incorporated into all the structures of human consciousness and experience, and consciousness includes an awareness of objects in their place. In the imagination we use a spatial 'syntax' to read the environmental world, construct value systems, and conceptualise. Place is the foundation of our experience in the world, serves as a site for national and imperial placing and indoctrination of value, and can be a testing ground for new possibilities.

But of more significance to the individual subject perhaps is the way place plays a central role in the imagination as a 'home' for fleeting memories, moments of crisis, feelings of existential 'insideness' and 'outsideness', constraint and freedom, the security and constraint of home, and the freedom and dangers of exile. In between the internalised spaces that map our world and give expression to our private and received thoughts and feelings and the material world itself, lie the representational spaces and places we find in the literary/artistic realm, especially in the novel. It is to the construction of the novel itself, or rather its use of space and time to create fictional worlds, that we move now.

SPATIAL FORM

Clearly, as Lefebvre has pointed out, we cannot rely on literature to provide 'true pictures' of the world. But the form of space and time in the novel, the chronotope, can tell us something about how an author has arranged representational space to convey conceptions and anxieties about space and time in society. In the case of the modern novel, contemporary concerns about the 'modernisation of time' in western society is evident in the content, but also in the chronotopic structure of the novel. The fragmentation of space and time in the modern novel has been interpreted by some, rather dramatically, as a 'crisis' in a realism. For John Berger, this 'crisis' can also be regarded as a response to a material condition of simultaneity in modern life:

> We hear a lot about the crisis of the modern novel. What this involves fundamentally is a change in the mode of narration. It is scarcely any longer possible to tell a straight story sequentially unfolding in time. And this is because we are too aware of what is continually traversing the storyline laterally (the diachronic in other words). Such awareness is the result of our having to take into account the simultaneity and extension of events and possibilities.
> (Berger 1974: 40)

The 'simultaneity and extension of events' refers directly to the modernisation of time, and to various fundamental changes in the conception of time in the late nineteenth and early twentieth century, to which I will return later. But there is another way of seeing this change in the modern novel. Joseph Frank has argued that the modern novel often shows signs of resisting modernisation and claims that 'spatial form', or the spatialisation of time in the modern novel, reveals an inclination to resist changes in space–time relations inherent in modernisation. Although Frank's theory of spatial form is not an integral part of my methodology here, it will become important to differentiate between spatial form in the modern novel and the geographical imagination in the postmodern novel, because both seem to emphasise the spatial dimension of the chronotope.

Joseph Frank's essay 'Spatial Form in Modern Literature' of 1945 is concerned with establishing the generic significance of spatial form in modern literature (Frank 1991: 17). Frank argues that spatial form in modern(ist) literature opposes the dominant modernist concept of time as *becoming*, with its insistent will to the future. For Frank, modern literature breaks with traditional form, and especially with traditional space–time structures, to create works the reader might apprehend spatially, *in a moment of time*, rather than encounter *sequentially* through conventional plot narrative.

Frank's idea of spatial form is derived from Pound's idea of Imagism: 'An 'Image' is that which presents an intellectual and emotional complex in an instant of time' (Pound 1934: 336). But this instant of time can only exist in abstract analysis, removed from the experience of reading. Imagism is problematic to the reader because it demands transcendence of the sequentiality of narrative. The *clock time* of reading can never be entirely avoided in reality because it is fundamental to the consciousness of reading, and therefore always intrudes on the theoretically timeless reconstruction of images in the imagination. Nevertheless, Frank applies the idea of spatial form to the works of T.S. Eliot and Flaubert. Eliot, he says, fragments images, doing violence to sequence to force the reader to unify the text into a new whole. In which case, modernist fragmentation presents an absence but refers to complete presence. This holism is a triumph of space over time: the reader is forced outside time, as it were, to comprehend a space–time wholeness, in other words, *transcendence*.

In Flaubert's *Madame Bovary*, Frank notes the fragmentation of narrative sequence where the author cuts back and forth in cinematic fashion between apparently unconnected scenes occurring at the same moment in time. For Frank, this represents a halt in the narrative, creating an 'immobilised time-area' (Frank 1991: 17) in which relationships are highlighted and differences magnified. This 'time-area' or gap creates a discriminating moment – a hiatus in the novel – which draws the reader in. In Joyce's *Ulysses*, we are presented with an excess of simultaneous images, and for Frank this indicates an attempt to reproduce a unified spatial apprehension of the whole work. Historical time, and the time experienced by the characters in the novel are displaced by the subjective instant of time: the time when all the threads and fragments cohere in an instant of understanding.

Recently, there has been some debate about the idea of spatial form, and Frank has answered criticism from Frank Kermode and others, who claim that modern literature is mainly concerned with two entirely different forms of time, one cyclic and enduring, and the other linear and progressive (Frank 1991: 67–106). But both seem to agree that whether space or another form of time is used, the tendency in modernist literature is to question modernisation of time and its emphasis on linearity and progress. In so far as this idea of spatialisation exists to such a degree in anything other than a handful of experimental novels, the idea of spatial form in modernist literature is still a subordination of space to the indicators of time and is careless of representational space in its own right. The modernist obsession with time *wastes* space, as it were, reducing it to blankness and silence.

In Bakhtin's essay 'Forms of Time and Chronotope in the Novel' time is also regarded as the 'dominant principle', but we should allow here that Bakhtin is mainly concerned with modern and pre-modern chronotopes, and within the chronotope, space and time fuse and swap sides, creating a time–space of mutual dependence, in other words, space cannot exist without time, and vice versa (Bakhtin 1981: 86).

In my adaptation and extension of the novelistic chronotope as a means of reading the time–spaces of the postmodern novel the dominant principle is, I would argue, more likely to be space than time. Italo Calvino's *Invisible Cities*, briefly discussed below, is an example of how space can dominate time in the chronotope. We cannot claim that this is a typical postmodern novel but it does illustrate a shift, less prominent but nevertheless present elsewhere. This shift in dominant can be read as another twist in Bakhtin's historical poetics, his charting of the forms of time and space in the novel, but it seems to me that there are wider implications beyond the literary-historical. I think that shifts in conceptualising, cogitating about and representing space and time can be found across other artistic and practical realms as a signature of the postmodern. This is the hypothesis I now want to test through a synoptic survey across various realms of the contemporary to see if any general theories and shapes for postmodern chronotopes emerge. The plan for Part II is then to examine ways in which any such general theory of the postmodern chronotope might be assimilated into artistic chronotopes and manipulated within the form of the postmodern novel.

CHAPTER 3

The Chronotope as Idea, Optic and *Weltanschauung*

One of the most productive ways of approaching postmodernism is to examine its peculiar arrangements of space and time and consider the chronotopes (time–spaces) it produces as ways of seeing and ways of responding to the contemporary world. The present work is primarily concerned with the chronotopes of narrative art (representational chronotopes), and those of the postmodern novel (literary chronotopes) in particular, but the methodology also requires that postmodern literary chronotopes are related to a historical development of the novel (itself a kind of chronotope), to representational chronotopes in other art forms, and to the *practical* chronotopes that describe the material conditions and cultural forces of postmodernity. My thesis is that we can gather together general observations from various sources about the characteristics and shape of the postmodern chronotope as a way of seeing contemporary culture.

The idea of the postmodern chronotope is initially to present a reasonably coherent way of seeing and representing the contemporary world. Of course, representation is problematic here; the postmodern chronotope is not a magic lantern through which the contemporary suddenly becomes imaginable and presentable, but it can reveal an understanding of the contemporary as a temporal and spatial situation.

The Postmodern Chronotope

Such understanding may be limited to either recognising the unpresentability of the present moment (which is of course well on the way to presenting it), or the continuing struggle to bring forth representation of the past, however informed or constrained by contemporary thinking. So the postmodern chronotope is first considered in the context of the ideas that can be said to produce it under the separate conditions of particular forms and disciplines. Then it can be used as an optic, ranged back on to contemporary culture, here in the form of the postmodern novel. In the end, the plan is that the postmodern chronotope acts as a kind of *Weltanschauung* – a time–space map of the contemporary world.

To begin, it is important to recognise that the postmodern chronotope, as an attempt to isolate general spatio-temporal conditions of the times, will have been shaped by developments in a number of disciplines. In most cases, these developments arise from rethinking and reworking modernity. In this chapter, we will consider briefly some of those disciplines in which time and space relations have been of prime importance in theorising the postmodern (and to an extent re-theorising the modern), and so are prime contributors to the postmodern chronotope. The postmodern chronotope marks a significant shift in spatio-temporal relations in the postmodern, but this is a shift that needs to be traced through the modern chronotope to realise its full import and complex nature. This chapter attempts to summarise the spatio-temporal relations that characterise the postmodern and differentiate it from the modern. There is a discernible shift in such relations across a range of disciplines, even though these disciplines (science, architecture, economics etc.) belong to different realms of knowledge, result from different historical and cultural forces, and so require different responses and levels of understandings. We must be reminded that some realms are still centred in logic, fact and causality, while the aesthetic and representational realms that concern us most are more speculative, reflective, disruptive and even anti-representational.

Of course, one mark of the postmodern, a particularly spatial one, is that the boundaries between realms and disciplines is not as clearly delineated as in modernity. The rise of interdisciplinary studies (and anti-disciplinary studies) is a result of this postmodern lessening of differentiation within the knowledge business: postmodernism by the back door. Postmodern knowledge is already itself a suitable subject for considering spatio-temporal relations, as it requires that we return to and rework distinctions between conceptual neo-Kantian divides, and this has a profound impact on how we treat representation, the unpresentable and the sublime in the postmodern.[1] We will return to this later, but this is really only background to the present work: one more area in which the spatio-temporal relations that characterise the postmodern can be discovered. The main focus is the chronotope of the postmodern novel, and here we will find that there are many technical chronotopes (constructions of time–spaces within the narrative) that need to be related to the general case of the postmodern chronotope (optic and *Weltanschauung*). To complicate matters slightly, this range and diversity of technical chronotopes within postmodern novels is itself an important feature of the postmodern. This can be related to the sheer eclecticism of times and spaces that is itself a feature of the general postmodern chronotope, with particular instances in architecture and history. But also the wide variety of technical chronotopes and the imaginative potential of these in postmodern novels suggest something other than the simple affirmative response to postmodernist culture that some commentators, both on the left and on the right, have asserted.[2]

This chapter will proceed by introducing the technical chronotope as defined by Bakhtin, and then gather together characteristics of a general postmodern chronotope from a variety of disciplines. In this general postmodern chronotope, we expect to see general characteristics of spatio-temporal relations in the postmodern. The chapter closes with an example of a particular technical chronotope in Italo Calvino's *Invisible Cities*. This discussion is a precursor of the more detailed analyses of literary chronotopes in Part II.

BAKHTIN AND THE TECHNICAL (LITERARY) CHRONOTOPE

The literary chronotope suggested by Bakhtin treats time and space as twin axes of fictional worlds in the novel. Bakhtin uses the chronotope as a generic signifier, differentiating between, for example, the Rabelasian folkloric chronotope of 'collective' time, and the 'biographical' time of Dostoyevsky's novels. But Bakhtin also notes how the chronotope can function as the 'primary means of materialising time in space' and can become 'a centre for concretising representation' (Bakhtin 1981: 250). In the literary chronotope, time and space can sometimes turn through ninety degrees, as it were, and act as indicators on the other axis. Here, the indicators of time and space tend to fuse, allowing different spaces to be represented by different times, and different times to be represented by different spaces. Modernist literature, in attempting to represent a modern consciousness of time, tends to use space in the service of time, translating temporal indicators into spatial ones in an attempt to 'freeze' moments of time along a horizontal axis of space, like the still frames of a cinema film.

The use of the chronotope as an optic makes it clearer to see those moments when time as a vertical force and space as a horizontal one seem to slew through ninety degrees. For example, the chronotope of the road in a Hardy novel often turns the space of the road into a place for meetings and a division between social groups, but it also transforms it into a duration, and Hardy often uses this temporal quality of the road to organise his plots.[3] The literary chronotope allows the indicators of time and space to fuse into the road, which becomes a visible and concrete representation of that time–space. In modernist literature, the fusion of space and time in the novel's chronotope is sometimes designed to represent the experience of time passing as a 'thickened present'. In other modernist literature, chronotopes of particular places sometimes invoke other times, translating space and place into historical time, or the enduring time of nature.[4]

In further examples used by Bakhtin – the visions of Dante (*Divine Comedy*) and William Langland (*Piers Plowman*) – a conceptualisation of space and time specific to the Middle Ages is noted. In these pre-modern chronotopes, Bakhtin describes the characters' attempt to escape into historical time along the horizontal axis of the chronotope, but instead find themselves displaced on to the spatial and otherworldly vertical axis. This, suggests Bakhtin, is an attempt on the part of the author to deny 'the essential thought-shaping power of "earlier" or "later", that is, to deny temporal divisions and linkages' and to 'lay open the world as cross-section of pure simultaneity and coexistence (a rejection of the inability to see the whole of time that is implicit in any *historical* interpretation).' (Bakhtin 1981: 158).

There is a clash here, suggests Bakhtin, between the historical, willing itself forward, and the extra-temporal in which all is contained within the aesthetic form of the whole. The Dantesque world is a triumph of form over history, of the spatial over the temporal, and it captures a particular moment between two epochs, the Middle Ages and the modern age. 'In the subsequent history of literature', claims Bakhtin, 'the Dantesque vertical chronotope never again appears with such rigor and internal consistency' (Bakhtin 1981: 158). Dostoyevsky comes close to this in the modern age, but it is not until postmodernist literature arrives that the vertical chronotope re-emerges as a force, certainly not the same force or in the same form as that of Dante's, but an emphasis on otherworldliness (or multiple worldliness) and a thwarted historicity is common to both.

Bakhtin's theory of the chronotope is a way of visualising and conceptualising spatio-temporal relations in literature, privileging neither the indicators of time nor those of space. The chronotope is defined as a 'unit of analysis for studying texts according to the nature and ratio of the temporal and spatial categories represented'; chronotopes are 'places of intersection of temporal and spatial sequences' (Folch-Serra 1990: 281–2). By concentrating on these intersections, rather than seeking to draw conclusions about temporal or spatial form, space and time are less differentiated than in other approaches (see section on Spatial Form above, pages 62–4 for example), and the indicators of space and time within the novel are treated more or less as two sides of the same coin. So, in some chronotopes, 'a locality is the trace of an event, a trace of what had shaped it. Such is the logic of all local myths and legends that attempt, through history to make sense out of space' (Bakhtin 1981: 189). Whereas in other chronotopes, 'the contingency that governs events is inseparably tied up with space, measured primarily by distance on the one hand and by proximity on the other' (Bakhtin 1981: 99).

Here are two kinds of chronotopes, one in which locality or place is defined by its history, and the other in which events, or history, are governed by the relationships between things and people in space. Both chronotopes coordinate time and space, but in one, many events are used to define an object or point in space, whereas in the other, spatial properties determine a moment in time by producing an event. This distinction of Bakhtin's allows for a shift in dominant from the first (event-driven) to the second (contingency-driven) kind of chronotope coincidental with a shift in dominant from modernist to postmodernist in the narrative arts and a corresponding shift towards spatial concerns more widely in postmodernist culture. Of course, such a shift in dominant and its consequences still remains to be demonstrated and explained, but this is, in a nutshell, the trajectory of the present work.

The chronotope as a method for perceiving relations between the cultural and literary-artistic sphere has already been foreseen by Bakhtin, and although his work applies to classical and early modern literature, the idea that the chronotope might be an 'optic for reading texts as x-rays of the forces at work in the culture system from which they spring' (Bakhtin 1981: 425–6), is surely no less valid in the literature of any period. Indeed, it seems to me that Bakhtin chooses a history of time–space relations in literature as optic for reading the cultural systems that produced it because time–space relations are always present in literature and are reliable indicators of time–space relations in the cultural sphere. Narrative art is always chronotopic, and the chronotope is always sensitive to larger cultural shifts. Bakhtin's metaphor of the x-ray suggests that forces within the cultural system can be directly perceived within the literary text, but there is no reason to expect a direct correlation between art and culture, and the optic must take account of the filtering, refraction, and inversion through which literature renders cultural systems.

This reminder of the function of art to misread and misrepresent the real world is particularly relevant when considering claims that postmodernist art either gives up on representation entirely, or conversely, affirms the postmodernist culture that produces it. I fear that some commentators on postmodernism fail to differentiate between the representational chronotopes of postmodern fiction and the practical chronotopes of postmodern culture.

1) Literary-Artistic Developments in Space and Time

In the arts, a number of sub-movements, such as anti-modernism, neo-realism, anti-realism, and 'new' avant-gardism, have all, at various times, and by various critics been associated with postmodernism. Such diverse and conflicting flows and eddies muddy the waters of postmodernism, and turn it into a rather appropriating rag bag of rejoinders to, or re-inscriptions of, modernism. The only common ground here seems to be that all of this coincides with a historical postmodernity in which particular cultural changes are assumed to have ushered in a new era. With artistic theories and practices that are on the face of it so contradictory, can postmodernism be construed as a 'shift in sensibility' (Huyssen 1988: 181), or is it a catch-all for differently conceived responses to the postmodern condition?

In the course of the present work, I will be seeking to demonstrate that there is indeed a shift in sensibility and a transformation in cultural practices that combine to produce aesthetic forms sufficiently different from those of the preceding period to warrant the label 'postmodern'. In particular, I will seek to demonstrate that these aesthetic forms can be read through the organisation of the indicators of space and time in the postmodern novelistic chronotope. But there is also a chronotope that encompasses the work of art itself and the world of art and its history, and this intersects with popular culture and the everyday. This aesthetic-cultural chronotope, if we can call it that, articulates postmodernism's shifting relations between art and mass culture. It is here that we can test the theory put forward by Andreas Huyssen that in postmodernism's attempt to collapse the boundaries between high and low art, we can detect a return to an avant-gardism where lines between art, life and culture are redrawn (Huyssen 1988: 188–95).

Looking back at modernism, it is clear that a spatial divide between high art and mass culture was already tested by avant-gardism in the late nineteenth and early twentieth centuries. This historical avant-garde sought to redefine the distinction between high art and mass culture by embracing modernity and especially its technological innovations. The movements, which included expressionism, Dada, constructivism, futurism, and French surrealism, were revolutionary because they connected iconoclasm and de-traditionalisation with a conflation of high and low art. Later, during the 1930s, a return to the distinction between high and low was seen as necessary by Adorno, to protect art from Fascism and socialist realism.

In the pop art of Andy Warhol in the 1960s, with its recycled images of Marilyn Monroe, soup cans and soap powder boxes, Andreas Huyssen recognises a return to the ready-mades of Marcel Duchamp. It was Duchamp who had produced a copy of Leonardo's *Mona Lisa* with moustache and beard back in 1919, and yet he never recognised Warhol's work as carrying forward the spirit of avant-gardism from the early twentieth century (Huyssen 1988: 146–8). Pop art introduces art as cliché, the kitsch art movement, and art as mass-produced for mass consumption, although paradoxically, Warhol's art became collectable, and the 'originals', if they can be so called, are returned to the exclusive realm of high modernism. Here, mass culture is the inspiration for an art form that is developed, discussed and appreciated outside of the popular culture it pretends to be part of.

DE-DIFFERENTIATION

Modernism's urge to differentiate conceptually, representationally and practically between high and low art is opposed by both avant-gardism and postmodernism which have in common the process of cultural *de-differentiation*.⁵ De-differentiation is essentially a spatial practice and a key element in the postmodern chronotope. The boundary between high and low art is only one such division under erasure in the postmodern chronotope. Another is the de-differentiation between author, author-figure and text, famously differentiated by Roland Barthes and Foucault in the 1960s.⁶ The ironic re-appearance of the author or author-figure in postmodernist fiction signals a de-differentiation of author and text. In a post-structuralist sense, the author disintegrates, pulled apart by the presence of the text at the moment of reading, and the trace of the text that marks his absence.

In Paul Auster's *New York Trilogy*, and Italo Calvino's *If On a Winter's Night a Traveller* this presence/absence of the text/author is a major theme, and we might regard such strategies as Derridean in their play of writing and authorship. But the return of the author in postmodern texts has another, less lofty reading: is it perhaps instead (or also) 'the merging of the author into the cultural product' as Scott Lash suggests (Lash 1989).⁷ This is clearly the case in Alasdair Gray's *Lanark* and Martin Amis' *Money*, where the postmodern author, for very different reasons, places himself in his work, coexists with the work, and appears to rather enjoy being part of the cultural product. In Amis' case, there is a certain merging of author and cultural product, although I suspect he is consciously creating himself as a character in his own fiction to highlight the commodification of writing. Both he and Will Self, who also appears in *Money*, are in this sense commenting on and theorising that commodification (Amis 1984 and Self 1994). In Gray's case, the self-conscious intrusion of the author into the text attaches the text and Gray to a cultural project rather more than to a cultural product. For Gray is engaged in an imaginative reconstruction of Glasgow through aesthetic and political means, as I will seek to prove in Chapter 4.

The chronotopes of postmodernist art frequently problematise differentiation, especially where this involves value judgements, propositions and absolutes that can be imagined as spatio-temporal divides. Part II includes many examples of the collapsing and blurring of spatio-temporal division, but here is a short example to illustrate the idea. In Angela Carter's novel *Wise Children*, cultural de-differentiation of high and low art is brought within the artistic chronotope to create an aesthetic form in which various other problems of differentiation are played out, including child/parent, male/female and north/south.

The novel is narrated by two sisters born into a world of music hall, or vaudeville: a world of bawdy gags, popular song and dance, illusions and showmanship. They have relations with high art through their father, an ageing Shakespearean actor, Melchoir Hazard, but they are his *illegitimate* daughters. Geographically, generically and artistically speaking, they are from the wrong side of town, from the 'bastard side of Father Thames', that is south London, Bermondsey, very close, incidentally, to the playhouses where many of Shakespeare's plays were first performed (Carter 1991: 1). But in the course of the novel, high and low, north and south, music hall and Shakespeare, father and daughters, young and old, all refuse to stay on the 'right' side of the imaginary divide. This raises questions about the implicit value systems and moral order associated with the differentiation. The moral seriousness of high art, into which Shakespeare's plays have, in modern times, been elevated, is debased through assimilation (arguably re-assimilation) into mass culture, when the action shifts to the set of a kitsch Hollywood production of *A Midsummer Night's Dream*. This may indeed signify a collapse of art into commodified capitalist culture, but it also serves to close the gap between high and low art. In this novel, a re-invigorating and re-humanising of high art is revealed through its common relations (in both senses of the word) with the humour, vitality and potency (especially sexual) of low art. Shakespeare's comedies are replayed as postmodern romp, but the postmodern novel remains in tact, commenting on its own status as a novel while bridging an artificial divide between literary culture and the mass culture of movies and television.

This is by no means the only example in this novel of the postmodern chronotope being used to de-differentiate hierarchies and other spatial or temporal delineation associated with a modern rationalisation of time–space. Indeed, the whole novel depends on space and time being stretched beyond the bounds of credulity, to question various cultural constructions regarding art, gender, sexuality, class and ageing. But this does not head towards the arrangement of new social and moral codes, partly because the process of de-differentiation, like deconstruction, does not proceed towards a new construction, and partly because the community concerned is in no sense typical. In *Wise Children*, Angela Carter creates a 're-enchanted world', using the motif of the music hall as both a *re-singing of the world* and a challenge to legitimated reason and morality.[8] Within this eccentric society of music hall artistes, the novel creates a complex chronotope in which social codes are ignored or dismantled.

Wise Children is an example of the postmodern novel as anti-realist, neo-realist, and anti-modernist, and in the sense that it is engaged in questioning the bounds between high and low art, it is avant-garde. Although, as a work of art itself, the novel is hardly innovative, its realism just about keeping the lid on the subversive illusions it borrows from the music hall, and perhaps also from *A Midsummer Night's Dream*. Modernist avant-gardism as a mode of representation embracing new technologies is perhaps not evident here then, although it could be argued the novel does incorporate a fascination, if not exactly a love affair, with a Baudrillardian world of simulation, the 'bastard show' of the mass media (Carter 1991: 41). To some extent, this is a postmodern equivalent of the modern fascination with machines, but here the machine produces realities through the electronic processing of information, signs and images, rather than using mechanical and electrical energy to transform a material reality.

DE-*FORM*ATION AND THE CINEMATIC

In trying to configure a general case for the shift in sensibility in postmodernist art, shifts in the perception of time and space and an awareness of the socially constructed nature of space and time are especially helpful and insightful, and this remains true for narrative and non-narrative art forms. Beginning with visual and performing arts, the organisation of space and time is critical and always constrained by particular limitations of form, mostly spatial, but sometimes temporal as well. The spatial limitations of the two-dimensional canvas and the three-dimensional solid, can become the subject (form into content) of the work of art itself and this is true of much modernist art.

In Cubism, which is typical of one major strand of modernist art, we can see that the innovative break with linear perspective as the dominating principle of figurative art since the Renaissance, and the introduction of spatial form containing multiple spaces, are signs of a reaction to the limitations of spatial form and a desire to transcend temporal limitations. Cubism is an attempt to produce, as Roger Allard has said of the painting of Jean Metzinger, 'elements of a synthesis situated in time' (Allard [1910] 1966: 62). Such modernist experimentation has clear relations with the many scientific, technological and cultural changes at the beginning of the twentieth century – although Picasso seems to have denied this, and complained that such materialist theories of art were 'blinding people with theories' (Picasso [1923]1966: 168).

Cubism is a clear response to cultural changes in modernity pertinent to changes in space–time relations, and this is an example of an artistic chronotope responding to and registering a shift in cultural and scientific chronotopes. The unpresentability in static form of multiple (more than three) dimensions or multiple (more than one) perspectives is indicative of a modern cinematic consciousness influenced by such inventions as the x-ray, which could see inside solid objects, and the conceptual shift in understanding of time as the 'fourth dimension', as suggested in Einstein's General Theory of Relativity. But ultimately, where a modern consciousness of time and space takes hold, traditional art forms such as painting, sculpture and literature are, as it were, left standing.

From a postmodern perspective, Cubism seems to have been a case of a move forward that was also something of a retreat: into art and away from engagement in culture in the wider sense. It may have offered a new way of seeing the world, unconstrained by rules of perspective in art, but it also registers something of a failure in form and a failure to connect a world of aesthetics influenced by new scientific concepts to the world of everyday experience. Gleizes and Metzinger, in an essay of 1912, claimed that modernist art's break from linear perspective enabled the artist to share with the spectator a subjective space that becomes pictorial space when the spectator fully engages with all his faculties and personality.[9] Such claims for modernist art, in retrospect, seem to indicate exclusion rather than inclusion of the spectator. The intended shared space of artist and spectator turns out to be a rather private and 'in' space, and not one that an uninformed spectator can easily enter.

Postmodernist artists such as Hans Haacke clearly intend to share the *physical* and *representational* space of the work of art with the audience, not the subjective or imaginative space. His installations draw the space of the galleries that contain them, into their subject matter and into their form. This attempt to merge the chronotope of the work of art with that of the postmodern world outside it has at least two consequences. One is Jameson's conclusion that this is indicative of a loss of cognitive mapping in postmodernity, and all that is left for postmodernism to do is register the implosion of simulacra, the undermining of the image by the image itself (Jameson 1991: 409). Another is that the artist is really seeking to make the work of art radically accessible to the audience in another case of de-differentiation between high art and popular culture. Far from setting up discursive barriers between the art and the public, postmodernist installation art positively invites the audience to join in, by de-forming the work of art.

A further sense of failure hangs over Cubism, again from a postmodern perspective, and this is the sign of the impending dominance of cinema, a sign that cinematic form is about to detract from that of traditional painting and sculpture. This is evident in Cubism where the form of speed and movement that the cinema was able to represent successfully can only be presented through its absence in the static forms of painting and sculpture. The absence is registered in the traces of events that escape representation. It is sometimes claimed that Cubists were able to transcend the limitations of temporality by presenting multiple perspectives in multiple spaces. But surely Picasso's *Les Demoiselles d'Avignon* (1907), where the figures of two women are shown in frontal pose but with their noses in profile, only draws attention to the static form of painting, and is rather grotesque in its 'unnatural' presentation of time–space.

Unnatural that is, once cinema arrived to arrange and manipulate time–space so convincingly that art, for the first time in its history, really did seem to have the potential to share the same representational space as the everyday world. In several senses, the gap between cinema and the 'real' world in the mid to late twentieth century is *filmic*: it is thin, more or less transparent, and increasingly mediated by the time–space of the moving image. Whereas the Cubists relied on a small, informed circle to see the world of experience through its abstract and intellectual form, cinema, at least in its now dominant Hollywood narrative form, is the reverse, offering immediate accessibility through a representational form virtually indistinguishable from the everyday. Indeed, this has become so much the case, that the moving images of the cinema and TV have begun to displace 'real' experience of the world by confirming reality rather than recording or re-presenting it. In this reverse mimesis, life would seem to imitate art. A goal for postmodernist cinema might then be to problematise this 'real', to draw attention to the reality-making devices of cinematic form, perhaps by exaggeration, excess and overt self-reflexivity.

PROBLEMATISING REALITY

The problematisation of reality appears to give postmodernism critical potential by inserting distance between postmodernist culture on the one hand, and a postmodernist art concerned with destabilising the real. Scott Lash describes such potential in *Sociology of Postmodernism* (1989) where he suggests, in somewhat simpler terms than others, that the main difference between modernism and postmodernism is that '*modernism conceives of representations as problematic whereas postmodernism problematizes reality*' (Lash 1989: 13).[10]

Lash distinguishes between a mainstream postmodernism which is similar to the consumer postmodernism recognised by Fredric Jameson, Mike Featherstone *et al.* and an anti-representational postmodernism (Jameson 1991 and Featherstone 1991). This oppositional postmodernism somehow operates within and against the culture that produces it, and it comes into being not as a discursive response to the loss of the real but rather more as an unconscious desire to break with the formal representation of classical and modernist art and literature and connect with a 'real' real (or is that real 'real'?) beneath the signifier. So, this postmodernist art is designed to appeal to the sensations, to be directly experienced rather than intellectually received.

Here then is another position in which the chronotope of the reception of the work of art is reconfigured with a conflation of audience time–space and performance time–space. For Lash this is conceived as a shift from a 'discursive' (literary) sensibility to a 'figural' (visual) one, from emphasis on mediated and rationalist readings to emphasis on the emotional and sensuous impact of the work, a shift from formalist and didactic views of culture to an immersion in the spectacle of signifiers derived from the banal and the everyday (Lash 1989: 175). But although this seems to work well enough in theories of postmodern culture generally, and corresponds to postmodernist shifts from text to image detected by Jameson among others, there seems little evidence to suggest that postmodern novels are in themselves more figural than discursive. It is hard to see how we could approach any of the novels discussed in the present work without reading them first as discursive structures, not least because of their ironic intertextualisation and revisiting of earlier texts.

From De-traditionalisation to De-framing

In modernist art, representation is problematised through the de-traditionalisation of artistic form, partly for its own sake to exercise artistic freedom, and partly in response to the confusing experience of the modern age which traditional forms seemed unable to render. In postmodernist art, modernism's problematisation of representation is itself problematised and re-evaluated. Such adventures in aesthetics are now regarded as part of modernity, but on the whole they distanced art from modern life. In postmodernism, all representation can do is to confirm the unpresentability of the real and to do so self-consciously, so as not to be compromised by its own pretence at representation.

In postmodern visual and performing arts, the work's spatial and temporal form and its siting (spatial positioning) are often problematised. Here, attention is drawn to the spatial distinction between the abstract art form as a self-contained abstract thing, and the space beyond itself. This can be done by drawing attention to the gallery space beyond the 'frame', as in works by Hans Haacke mentioned earlier, or by moving outside gallery space altogether as in the wrap-up projects of Christo. The installation works of postmodern art signal an urge to relocate art, physically and conceptually outside itself and outside the institutionalised spaces that still contain the inward-looking forms of modernist art.

This radical and often ironic re-contextualisation of art extends the context whereby meaning is found for the work to a space beyond the frame of object–subject, or creator–work–audience. The performance art of Laurie Anderson and Bruce Maclean likewise can be seen as examples of a move back into public space and a move to bring art closer to the public, to re-integrate art into life in an accessible and participatory manner. In the chronotope of postmodern installation and street performance art, the spectacle of the work of art is brought into real time as well as real space, as the audience experiences the work in the normal course of events, a momentary pause perhaps in the chronotope of everyday life.

In the chronotopes of postmodern metafiction such as Italo Calvino's *If On a Winter's Night a Traveller*, the frame of the story is constantly broken, or rather deferred, in a game that teases the reader into a text where authors and readers appear to share the same subjective space. Not so much characters in search of an author, as in Pirandello's modernist play *Six Characters in Search of an Author* (1920), but rather characters and authors in search of a text. The story of the search for the text, and the ironic intrusions of the several authors and readers *is* the text the reader ends up with, as the frame-breaking dissolves into the mechanics of a clever plot contained and resolved within the structure of the novel. Once more, the novel's status as representation is confirmed, even if the process of reading defers this representation as long as possible. Calvino's metafiction, because it resolves itself eventually, hardly troubles the reader's sense of a divide between fiction and reality. In other postmodern novels the reader is challenged to make connections across multiple and conflicting chronotopes that are not given away in the narrative itself.

The juxtaposition of seemingly irreconcilable 'worlds' or world-views is a common feature of postmodernist fiction, as Brian McHale has pointed out, but McHale's conclusion that this signals a shift from epistemological to ontological concerns, neat as it is, does not really connect with areas of postmodernism in which a conceptual divide between epistemological and ontological hardly seems to be a determining factor, or even a major influence (McHale 1987). We might challenge this assumption by turning it on its head.

Imagine that a re-thinking of space–time relations supported in a number of disciplines and backed by simultaneous shifts of an everyday–practical–cultural kind, theoretical–conceptual kind and representational–artistic kind – an unholy and almost unthinkable alliance to be sure – but imagine all of this to be *causal*, leading to this shift from epistemological to ontological concerns. My point really is that a consideration of postmodernism, in which shifts in space and time relations is key, demands an inter-disciplinary approach because, as studies such as Stephen Kern's excellent analysis of modernism reveal, when changes in the way we think space and time enter a culture, it is 'all change' in philosophy, architecture, social sciences, the arts, technology, science and politics. Postmodernism, as with modernism before it, signals such a change.

2) *Postmodernist Architecture as Chronotope*

In its simplest formulation, postmodernist architecture is, or rather was, a direct response to a late modern International Style and to some of the precepts of modernist architecture. In this formulation, postmodernist architecture responds to a unified, technology-led mission to transform the built environment through abstract and systematic organisations of space. Postmodernist architecture, in some cases, reverses modernist moves towards unity, transparency and integrity. Commonly, postmodernist architecture is conceived as a 'mish-mash' of styles from different historical periods, flying in the face of modernist utopian architects, such as Henri Le Corbusier, Frank Lloyd Wright and Walter Gropius. For these modernist visionaries, the ideal of architecture was the outward expression of an inner meaning or essential truth, or of form determined by function (Connor 1989: 66–8). Frank Lloyd Wright wrote in 1910 that modern architecture would be 'one great thing instead of a quarrelling collection of so many little things' (Conrads 1970: 75). From a postmodern perspective, this seems like an attempt to prescribe and impose an abstract and *monologic* spatiality on the organic and historical space of American and European cities.

Postmodernist architecture responds to what it sees as the unifying, monologic and decontextualised 'truths' of a form that set out to impose itself on and transform the environment with a manifesto of abstract demands. On the face of it, postmodernist architecture is more sensitive to context and sets up *dialogic* spaces within the city. As Fredric Jameson puts it, these newer buildings 'respect the vernacular of the American city fabric . . . they seek to speak that very language' (Jameson 1991: 39). Charles Jencks, Jane Jacobs and Robert Venturi, in different ways and for different reasons, have called for a more plural, heterogeneous use of space, with buildings offering a range of connections, or 'dialogues', with the landscape around them and with buildings from earlier periods.[11] In this case, we could say that the use of space in the postmodern is rich, dialectical, questioning and self-questioning, although critics of postmodernist architecture could equally well say that it demonstrates indeterminacy, lack of vision and purpose, and lack of integrity.

There are points of resistance in postmodernist urban design where a modern tendency to sweep away the spatial clutter accumulated through history is questioned. Where modernism sought to zone and divide space along functional lines, largely ignoring the complex social, symbolic and sacred spaces of the European city for example, postmodernist approaches try to draw attention once more to the social, historical and representational aspects of space. This shift inevitably leads to a more heterogeneous and plural approach to space and design that might provide the opportunities for social space to be produced more freely.

But the residuality of modernism continues to exert an influence on space–time relations, and modernist or 'late modernist' architecture continues to appear. Economic demands still prevail, of course, and the need for functional buildings to perform in a difficult economic period is bound to influence design, and determine the amount of public space in cities available for social interaction. Postmodernist approaches can therefore lead to a superficial 'dressing' of what is essentially modernist space underneath. Postmodernist architecture loses its critical capacity and becomes trivialised when it offers no more than ornamental afterthoughts – sops to fashion.

Despite these complications and antithetical strands, postmodernist architecture does make concrete some of the theoretical impulses of postmodernism. The visibility and accessibility of postmodern architecture and its physical presence provide us with visual cues and icons of the postmodern, although there are obvious limitations as to how far we can read the postmodern through architecture. The chronotopes of postmodernist architecture are highly visible, but compared with the chronotopes of postmodern novels, which are the main subject of this work, they operate through a rather limited language.

The chronotope of postmodernist architecture could be regarded as a banner headline of the postmodern, whereas that of the novel is the inside story. Like postmodernist architecture, the postmodern novel resists some of the moves of its modernist counterpart. Where the modern(ist) novel strove for a new kind of realism, and took seriously the pretensions of artistic endeavour, the postmodern novel is much more ambivalent and, unsure of any objective reality, it often questions any claims to access a reality beyond the text itself. The postmodern novel also tends not to project itself into the future as the modern(ist) novel often does, and it is not, in that sense, predictive or futuristic; again like postmodernist architecture, the postmodern novel often surrounds itself with the clutter of history and contexts. But the postmodern novel also retains many of the characteristics of the modern(ist) novel and, as with postmodernist architecture, the postmodern form is sometimes a superficial attachment to its modernist antecedent. Postmodernist architecture and the postmodern novel both mix styles from different periods and revisit earlier 'texts' in an overtly 'intertextual' way. A disregard, or distrust, of (temporal) direction seems to be a strong feature of the postmodern, and this is evident in the construction and representation of postmodern place, as we will see in later chapters.

3) *History and Prophesy, Time and Narrative*

So far we have dealt mainly with the spatial dimensions of the chronotope, but of course the temporal is at least as important, and postmodernism's relations with history, time and narrative are crucial to an understanding of the postmodern chronotope. One idea commonly attached to the postmodern is that history as a form of time that takes a line from the past through the present into some determinate future, is somehow severed, or stalled. The clocks still run, calibrating the constancy of the earth, sun and moon, and although the approaching millennium has caused some to consider the apocalypse or some other catastrophic intervention, most assume that life will continue (or perhaps as you read this, has continued).[12] But while the calibration of time continues, something seems to have happened to its representation or mapping.

 A modern approach to the mapping of time might be summarised as the sequencing and plotting of events that is designed to give shape and direction to history. But to orientate ourselves in history we need to make certain assumptions about the form of time. A modern approach to history makes certain demands on the form of time it uses to construct its charts and narratives, and these are that time is essentially linear, progressive and homogeneous. Such a form of time is necessary to draw a line towards the future horizons on which modern eyes are generally cast. In imperialist histories the domination of this one form of time subsumes the different experiences of time of diverse peoples into grand narratives. A postmodern approach to history would have to begin by recognising that to construct such narratives is to erase the myths, traditions and cultural memories of subjugated people. Indeed time itself is part of this subjugation. History as a collection of diverse personal memories, each with their own organisation of time, is perhaps closer to a postmodern history. This then resists history as the larger narrative in which individual stories cohere into a pattern and begin to conform to a grand unified theory.

Materialist accounts of history attempt to draw conclusions from 'what is really happening' in the world, rather than what the individual is obliged to see through the masks of unreason, superstition and ideology. Marxists are therefore resistant to the postmodern because in it they see the curtain finally falling on a particular grand theory of time and history. Other prophets and seers have come and gone, but the most enduring are those whose predictions are couched in the most ambiguous terms, leaving the actual playing out of their visions in history to the reader's imagination. Symptoms of postmodern approaches to history can be seen in post-colonial revisitings, but also in reinterpretations of ancient prophesies, such as those of Nostradamus, the Maya and Mother Shipton in which visions of the millennium are supposed to have been foreseen.[13]

Modernist extrapolation of the past continues in, for example, predictions of world population, the exhaustion of natural reserves and global warming, but most effort is reserved for predicting economic indices. Here, prophesy is not an art or a science, but an industry. Economic pundits and prophets are especially aware that past results give little clue to future performance, and most rely on financial models to simulate complex economic systems, aware, in a most postmodern fashion, that these models themselves contribute to the results. Like economic systems, weather systems are also too complex to grasp in the present moment and these too are modelled.

In postmodernity, extrapolation as a means of understanding the present and predicting the future is replaced by *simulation*. This is what the revolution in information has given us: the end of history as written narrative and the beginning of history as simulation. An almost unseen, but very significant moment occurred in the 1970s within information technology, and this was the shift from analogue to digital control systems. Modernity was based on analogue technology, and so it was an age of representation through direct calibration, plotting and measurement. The digital age of computational models has been capable of assimilating so much data that these construct alternative realities. It is through such simulation that surgeons can carry out remote operations, lifts can search for passengers, and cars can tell us when they are due for a service.

The postmodern world is guided by simulacra, and sometimes this becomes a substitute for measurement and extrapolation. One effect of this is that we suffer from an excess of information, and the more information we have about the status quo, the harder it becomes to establish precisely where we are and where we might be heading. This has been one of the most surprising discoveries of postmodern science, so much so that we might regard the defining moment of the postmodern as that moment, whenever and wherever it was, that scientists in various fields realised they could never absolutely define a moment in time or a position in space. And furthermore, that small inaccuracies are multiplied exponentially during mathematical procedures giving entirely *unpredictable* results. This is the basis of what we are coming to understand as Chaos theory (Hawking 1988).

Not the end of history, but the end of history as a map: in the modern chronotope, history may be used as a map and a compass for divining the future, but in postmodernity, such future-oriented approaches are dissipated. This does not mean that the postmodern chronotope is entirely retrospective, nor does it signal a return to something like the walled garden of mediaeval time containing an already completed and static cosmos. It is more an eclectic mix of times and spaces in which an unfinalised modernity continues to loop back on itself.

A figure in which such a time–space could be conceived would be the double helix where movement appears to lack direction, and yet twists and turns back on itself in a loop. Although, of course, such a representation would be distinctly un-postmodern, because to conceive of such a model would require an abstract space outside the model, and as Brenda Marshall maintains, the postmodern is marked by an existential insideness: 'The postmodern moment is an awareness of being-within, first, a language, and second, a particular historical, social, cultural framework' (Marshall 1992: 3).

SCHIZOPHRENIA AS PRESENT-FILLED PAST AND LOSS OF LINEARITY

In Jameson's extension of Lacan's account of schizophrenia as linguistic disorder, he relates psychic and linguistic malfunction to a breakdown in temporal unity:

> The connection . . . may then be grasped by way of a twofold proposition: first, that personal identity is itself the effect of a certain temporal unification of past and future with one's present; and second, that such active temporal unification is itself a function of language, or better still of the sentence, as it moves along its hermeneutic circle through time.
>
> (Jameson 1991: 26–7)

The sentence is then reduced to a heap of signifiers unable to follow the trajectory of meaning conditioned by temporality, 'just as' (?) the individual is condemned to a series of unrelated presents, unable to locate himself in historical time.

This all sounds as though it might connect neatly with post-structuralist and postmodern thinking, and David Harvey does rather too neat a job of pasting Lacan, Jameson, Derrida and Deleuze and Guattari together on this subject (Harvey 1990a: 53). The idea of the perpetual present as a condition of postmodernity does seem to have stuck, although for Mark Currie, the metaphor of schizophrenia (for we should be clear that we are using the psychic condition figuratively), becomes a 'flight from the present' rather than a perpetual present when it is applied to postmodern culture (Currie 1998).

Currie links schizophrenia with postmodern culture because this is a condition in which the subject loses sense of himself in time, and is unable to ground his identity in a stable passage of time from past into future.[14] If postmodernity is to be construed in this way, then it would seem that postmodern culture is condemned to representing this series of unrelated presents, which, as Jameson would admit, then becomes a very intense present, charged with energy and manifesting itself as 'a rush of filmic images', sensationalism and the rise of the spectacle.

We are back then to a loss of depth models, and the general superficiality of the postmodern, both arising out of and also eerily bringing about a loss of historicity. I have more to say about these readily received headline features of the postmodern elsewhere but no doubt *superficiality* and *loss of linearity* do need to be incorporated into the postmodern chronotope. My arguments later will centre on the degree to which we can claim that there is any direct correspondence between various overlapping theories of postmodern culture and postmodern cultural practices and forms such as the novel. It seems to me that Jameson is always constructing grand theories and then fitting them to examples of postmodern culture rather than surveying and commenting on postmodern culture as it arises.

But there is more to say here about the loss of linearity and postmodern narrative in both history and fiction. In schizophrenia, the failure of the subject to experience linearity, to recognise a gap between the 'I' that speaks and the 'I' that is spoken about, causes an abnormal secondary identity coexisting with and engaged with the first. Continuing with the metaphor of schizophrenia applied to postmodern culture, we might think of the postmodern as a cultural phenomenon unattached to tradition and history, and so constructing an *alter ego* by which it simulates a critical distance between itself and the real.

However, the 'real' thus seen in the distorted mirror of this other self has no grounding, no origin and no centre, it is only real by virtue of its distance from what is not real: its ironic *recontextualisation*. In narrative, this recontextualisation appears as the metafictional play we get between fiction and history, or between author-figure, author and reader, or between the text being read and already written texts. In such metafictional play, grounding is always sought and withdrawn, as the real is always turned into a construction of the 'real' in a continual installing and subverting of authority.

Historical linearity, as a fixed pole of representation, is generally absent from the postmodern chronotope, except where it is used for ironic subversion. This occurs particularly where postmodern narrative engages in a critique of origins and positivist history, as in Graham Swift's *Waterland* (Currie 1998: 81–2). But there is another reason why linearity is absent from postmodern narrative, and this is because of its tendency to subsume the differends, or the gaps between different realms of knowledge (Currie 1998: 111). Postmodern narrative re-inscribes difference by reinserting the gaps and silences between different histories and forms of knowledge, and a linear narrative would suppress these breaks and intrusions.

TIME–SPACE COMPRESSION AND NARRATIVE

An account of David Harvey's theory of time–space compression as an economic condition of postmodernity is given below. This is clearly an important input into the general postmodern chronotope, but Mark Currie, in a clever move, has linked economic theory with postmodern narrative theory. He remarks on how time–space compression speeds up the cycle that consigns events to the past. In economics, production cycles demand ever-faster renewal of products to feed a consumerism hooked on the (re-)new. And in narrative, this might be reflected in a re-writing and re-telling which eventually overtakes the story (Currie 1998: 111).

4) *Economics, Time–Space Compression and the Runaway World*

We saw earlier how the spatial turn in the postmodern is related to problems in time–space relations reaching back into the late nineteenth and early twentieth century. Some commentators believe we are now at a moment of 'crisis' in the economic and political spheres of postmodernity. For Tony Giddens, globalisation has led not only to change, but also to a significant acceleration in the rate of change, the speed of the new (Giddens 1999). This crisis, according to David Harvey, is precipitated by an acceleration in the process of 'time–space compression' (Harvey 1990a: 240–2), which has been taking place since the Enlightenment (early modern) period, but which moved up several gears in the 'high modern' period of the late nineteenth century and early twentieth century.

    Modernity here is marked by a sense of becoming and an intense will to the future, which engendered a sense of the ephemeral and fragmentation; and modernisation, as a process, relied on the destruction of the past (sometimes given the antithetical label of 'creative destruction' because it enabled the new to come into existence), and a constant reproduction of the new. This reproduction of the new is then fuelled and intensified by a capitalist mode of production which over-accumulates through increased efficiency and expansion. With capitalism now the driving force, the goal is to overcome distance continually through speed, eroding spatial boundaries. This process is often seen as an attempt to 'annihilate space through time'. Time and space are compressed until a crisis looms: a crisis in which normal sequences of time and measurements of space no longer apply.

But does this conceptual crisis have any material consequences, and if so, do these impact on everyday life in postmodernity? A 'crisis' in space–time relations could occur conceivably in the economic sphere as a result of the acceleration in modern capitalist economics. In the space–time of the dominant economic systems of the world, capital moves from place to place according to that which is most likely to provide a higher return on capital over the shortest period. This global, and sometimes 'virtual', market place is inherently unstable and unpredictable because each movement in capital has secondary and tertiary (and so on . . .) effects on the prevailing economic conditions in that place and elsewhere. This market is a system with feedback loops and with incremental shifts in its time parameters, and it might therefore behave randomly or, rather, like the non-linear mathematics found in Chaos theory.

The system is difficult to monitor or control because of the volume and speed with which transactions move within computerised dealing systems linked by global communications systems. Dealers can connect to computer systems in almost any country in the world and buy or sell 'units' to and from any other country. But this speeding up and globalisation of transfer of capital is not only a terrestrial acceleration because, in postmodernity, capital also moves into virtual space. Derivative deals can be struck within the cyberspace of computer systems and projected into the future, so capital begins to move outside the world and outside the present. So far, these systems have managed to remain fairly stable, and nobody can really predict whether the inherently unstable aspects of the global market are what gives it an overall equilibrium (as Chaos does in biological systems) or whether they will eventually lead to the nightmare scenario of a global crash.

In *The Condition of Postmodernity*, David Harvey illustrates how capitalist economics has tended to shape the modern world. In the postmodern period he points to the drive towards time–space compression inherent in capitalist accumulation, and to the global impact of this on postmodern culture. Postmodern culture does indeed seem to refer to this economic model, and I am persuaded by Harvey's argument that economics does have a material effect on real space–time relations, and does indeed shape the world through its impact on culture. But space–time compression is not the only shaping force on the real world, or on postmodern culture, and Harvey sometimes seems to concentrate on economic forces in the postmodern to the exclusion of others.

As Doreen Massey has suggested, gender and class differences prevail in postmodernity, and at a local scale, in the realm of everyday life, the power structures that operate across space and time have changed very little for the less privileged members of the global society (Massey 1993: 60). Life for the abandoned children on the streets of Peru's cities may seem distant from the world economic markets, and they are of course powerless to influence those markets, although their future will almost certainly depend on how the unstable systems underpinning those markets behave in the future.

Because of its apparent ambivalence to, and uncritical mirroring of, the 'crisis' in space–time relations, postmodernist culture is sometimes accused of surrendering to the forces of capitalism, and being complicit in the phase of historical development that Marxists like Fredric Jameson and David Harvey optimistically call 'late capitalism'. The debate between different postmodernities and postmodernisms incorporates a number of academic debates which are beyond the scope of this study into the postmodern novel. But it should be noted that any crisis in space–time relations, although it can be helpful in conceiving of change, also leads to a general lack of direction and orientation. Postmodernist culture has this mixed reputation of helping to create a 'space' for new theories and movements, but then denying them a solid platform: taking the carpet away from under their feet.

Economic development in postmodernity is global in the sense that investment capital, labour and the production of goods are rarely located in the same country or even the same continent. Development such as this certainly leads to the erosion of a traditional sense of rootedness in place, with postmodern industrial towns growing out of 'green field' sites, almost overnight, maintaining only superficial links with surrounding landscapes and community. In itself, such development is not critical. It is when material changes such as these are abstracted and conceptualised that the transformation becomes a 'crisis'. In this crisis, these material changes are only the outward signs of a general failure to conceive of development through a planned, progressive and mappable future.

Fredric Jameson speaks of the use of deliberately disorganising space in postmodernist architecture, in which the body can no longer map itself, or find its 'place'. This is where Jameson finds his 'postmodern hyperspace' (Jameson 1991: 43–4; 115–18). For Jameson, the confusing spaces that make up the interior of the Westin Bonaventure Hotel in Los Angeles provide a rich metaphor for a postmodern condition in which we are no longer able as a society to place ourselves or know where we stand. Unlike the utopian modernist architecture of Le Corbusier, such architecture does not refer to a pre-existing 'grand plan' or 'narrative', and it does not attempt to transform its surroundings.

Some postmodernist architecture does attempt to reflect its surroundings however, as we saw earlier, and Jameson's example is located in Los Angeles, hardly the kind of place produced by a society at ease with itself and confident of its direction. We might therefore read the confusing spaces of the Westin Bonaventure Hotel as a reflection of the confusing spaces of Los Angeles, making it a fine example of contextual architecture.

5) *Postmodern Geographies as Chronotope*

The concept of social space adds considerable complexity to the problems of mapping space, and in geography it has been recognised that mapping social space demands a different approach to the mathematical and quantitative disciplines normally associated with cartography. Geographers such as Edward Soja, Neil Smith, James Duncan, John Agnew, David Ley, and Edward Relph have suggested that modern geography ignored the fluidity and qualitative aspects of social space, and new theoretical approaches in geography and anthropology are being worked out which attempt to bring together sociological and geographical imagination (Smith and Katz 1993: 67–83; Agnew and Duncan 1989).

These new approaches are sometimes given the label 'postmodern geographies', although a number of geographers working in these areas would deny categorically that they are *postmodernists*.[15] The local politics of academic life aside, many geographers are looking at social space and place, and in the present work, it is the relationship between social space and configurations of place in a postmodern context that is relevant. In particular, it is the idea of placelessness as a sociological and geographical condition within postmodernity that is of most interest here.

Place has often been treated as the preserve of the geographical imagination because it commonly is locatable and we can make quantitative assessments of actual places. But place is also deep-rooted in our cultural life, and the spaces that constitute a place are produced by sociological interaction. Place is also important as representational space, and it is connected therefore with artistic, literary and aesthetic aspects of human activity. Place is clearly the foci for a number of human, social and material activities, and any transformation of place in the material, or geographical sense is bound to affect these social and cultural activities.

If a 'crisis in time–space relations' is widespread in the material world, then we might expect radical changes to our cultural life. One of the questions the present work will be asking is, if there really is a crisis in time–space relations as Harvey and Jameson insist, and if time–space relations are fundamental to all levels of human activity from imaginative to mundane everyday activity, as Lefebvre suggests, why is it that life seems to carry on in postmodernity without massive social unrest? In the study of postmodern novels in subsequent chapters, we will perhaps find some clue to how humanity, as represented in literature, manages to adapt to far-reaching geographical and sociological changes, or perhaps we will find that the changes were not so far-reaching for most people in the first place.

In nineteenth and twentieth century modernisation it seems that there was always a conflict between, on the one hand, futurist aspirations for environments that cut across geographical and other boundaries to create a modern utopia, and on the other, a desire for difference and identity frequently rooted in pre-modern myths and histories concretised in particular places, and symbolising regional, national and cultural identity.

In postmodernity, this conflict is not so easy to visualise because space and place have generally become more mixed and more heterogeneous, and it is difficult to see how either modernist utopias, or homogenised national, regional or cultural identities can ever emerge from single, well-defined places in the future. People everywhere are moving into closer physical proximity with those from other social groups, and in the 'cyberspace' produced electronically and experienced by every computer user, people are beginning to share virtual space, and create virtual communities across and between physical place.

In Place and Placelessness, Edward Relph draws attention to a lack of 'significant places', the erosion of a sense of place and of authentic place-making, and highlights the 'Disneyfication' of place that creates synthetic and absurd pseudo places made up of 'surrealistic combinations of history, myth, reality and fantasy that have little relationship with particular geographical setting' (Relph 1976: 95). The placelessness that Relph describes has the following manifestations (Relph 1976: 119–21):

Manifestations of placelessness

- <u>Other-directedness in places</u>
  Landscape made for tourists
  Entertainment districts
  Commercial strips
  Synthetic or pseudo places:
  – museumised places
  – Disneyfied places
  – futurist places

- <u>Uniformity and standardisation in places</u>
  Instant new towns and suburbs
  Industrial commercial developments
  New roads and airports, etc.
  International styles in design and architecture

- <u>Formlessness and lack of human scale and order in places</u>
  Subtopias
  Gigantism (skyscrapers, megalopi)
  Individual features unrelated to cultural or physical setting

- <u>Place destruction</u>
  Impersonal destruction in war
  Destruction by excavation, burial

Destruction by expropriation and redevelopment by outsiders
(e.g. urban expansion)

- Impermanence and instability in places
Places undergoing continuous redevelopment
Abandoned places

These manifestations of placelessness are not all specifically postmodern, because they are mostly derived from the impulses of modernisation begun in the late nineteenth and early twentieth centuries in North America and Europe. But the spread of this placelessness, to the point where it encompasses global space and reduces the prospects for authentic place and place-bound community everywhere, is a late twentieth century manifestation and a postmodern phenomenon. The degree to which this placelessness has spread is partly the result of economic forces, as Harvey argues, and the means for broadcasting it in the late twentieth century is mostly down to mass media systems, as Relph shows (Relph 1976: 119–21.):

Media and systems transmitting placelessness

- Mass communication and modes of diffusion of mass attitudes and fashions of kitsch.

- Mass culture of dictated and standardised values; maintained by but making possible mass communications.

- Big business and multinational corporations: these encourage standardisation of products and needs to ensure economic survival, and they supply objects of kitsch through the application of technique.

- Central authorities: these encourage uniformity of places in the interests of efficiency and through the exercise of uniform power.

- The economic system: the abstract system, dominated by technique, which underlies and embraces all of the above.

These media directly influence landscapes, but also act as channels for what Relph calls fundamental 'inauthentic attitudes to place', relating to what he calls 'technique', in which places are understood to be manipulable in the public interest, and relating to attitudes to kitsch, in which places are only created and experienced in terms of stereotypical and superficial mass values. We arrive then at the idea of inauthentic existence, which is, for Relph, 'the very root and essence of placelessness' (Relph 1976: 121).

We should recognise, however, that Relph's seminal work on place and placelessness was accomplished in the 1970s, and the complaint registered against inauthentic place is beginning to sound a little forlorn twenty years later. We should also recognise that in the postmodern, any attempt to re-instate authentic place would be viewed very suspiciously, and would get dangerously close to being another form of what Relph calls the 'other-directness' in place, which includes 'museumisation' and 'Disneyfication'. We must be careful therefore not to make a simple opposition between 'authentic place', and 'placelessness'.

Relph registers the loss of authentic place, with its connotations of organic community and a traditional sense of place, but this postmodern perspective is perhaps something of a luxury enjoyed by the west. In other parts of the world, where the benefits of modernisation are still anticipated, the loss of old communities may seem a price worth paying. It is easy to become nostalgic for 'authentic places', but the idea of returning to live in rural villages, for example, which once grew unwittingly according to the needs of a community rooted in the landscape, is no longer possible given present economic conditions and population numbers in the west, and given the desire to modernise in Asia, Africa, South America etc. Nostalgia leads only to the construction of pseudo places, such as Prince Charles' re-invented rural community, Poundbury, near Dorchester, England. Here, a new model village constructed on Prince Charles' rural estate is occupied mainly by outsiders with one foot lightly touching on the past.

There seems to be an inevitability to the spread of placelessness in postmodernity, so how do we cope with this fundamental change in our environment? The postmodern novel is often concerned with place, placelessness and a sense of belonging, and so it seems to address the problem of how to satisfy what seems to be a human universal: the need to belong in some place. Brian McHale suggests that postmodernist fiction is directed towards these problems of belonging, but rather than providing us with some kind of grounding, it presents us with an array of choices, suggesting that the process of *being* in a postmodern world is not grounded, but neither is it as airy as in the modern world. He suggests that the 'dominant of postmodernist fiction is *ontological*', and it poses questions such as 'Which world is this?', 'What kinds of world are there . . . and how do they differ?' (McHale 1987: 9–10). If this is the case, the postmodern novel would seem to suggest that placelessness also offers opportunities to redefine and reconfigure place, and perhaps to belong only in a provisional and partial sense to 'real' places.

6) Cogitative Chronotopes

In forming some idea of the postmodern chronotope, we need to explore practical, representational and abstract realms, and we also need to examine relations *between* such realms as spatio-temporal conditions in themselves. We also need to consider the spatial positioning of the thinking subject as s/he cogitates about such relations. In this way, isolated 'breakthroughs', such as McHale's shift in cultural dominant from the epistemological, and Jameson's loss of depth models, and so on, are seen as having some basis in a general shift in relations between space and time.

Although the same conditions and determinants are not in play in different realms of science, arts, culture and so on, we can begin to see that there are similar shifts in spatio-temporal conditions that make feasible the conceptualisation of a general case for the postmodern chronotope. Cultural historians might try to solve the chicken-and-egg problem of which comes first in guiding such shifts: philosophy, arts, science, culture. But the answer probably requires an anti-historical and an anti-disciplinary approach, as there are surely linear and non-linear currents seeping across these artificial spatial and temporal boundaries we set up between areas of knowledge.

This brings us to several key spatio-temporal concerns that directly affect *thought* itself in the postmodern. The first of these is Lyotard's working of Kant's theory of the sublime into his own theories of postmodernism. For Kant, there are two principal realms of thought, one of historical and factual knowledge, and one of speculative and pure reason. Theoretical understanding requires that phenomenal intuition be brought under control through, for example, the ordering of the senses and the construction of histories. But there are clearly limits to the degree to which reflective judgements, ideas, intuition, creative thought etc. can and should be reduced to fact and logic. And, going the other way, science and cognitive disciplines, if not partially restrained to particular fields of endeavour, are in danger of running their heads against some hard walls and ending up bruised with scepticism and doubt. Through a misreading of Lyotard, it is often assumed that the postmodern would gleefully remove the boundaries between realms, but in fact Lyotard insists on the absolute heterogeneity that exists between different *phrase-regimes*. For example, he insists on the gap or 'differend' that exists between judgements in the abstract cognitive mode, and practical judgements of a political or ethical nature.

The Kantian sublime is a name for that which 'presents the unpresentable' and here is a space between imagination and theoretical understanding, a place for the 'beautiful', where aesthetic pleasure is derived from a free rein given to the elements provided by sensibility, and not subject to reasoning. For Kant, the imagination gives the mind a lot to think, but Lyotard argues that it is not a matter of recognition of what is given in a moment of time, but the ability 'to let things come as they present themselves' (Lyotard 1991: 32)

Christopher Norris has attacked Lyotard over what he sees as his over-emphasis of the Kantian sublime in the postmodern, and what he sees as the logic of Lyotard's argument which leads to a multiplicity of language games (phrase-regimes) each with its own self-generating criteria of meaning, validity or truth. In this situation, claims Norris, the cognitive phrase-regime must give up its privileged truth-telling role, because to assert truths in the matter of ethical or political justice would be to suppress Lyotard's precious narrative differend (Norris 1993: 15–16).

The point of this discussion is not to enter the well-rehearsed debates over truth, ethics and Nazi death camps, which seem to proceed from the setting up of straw-men on either side of an artificial pro/anti-postmodernist divide, but to register the importance of shifts in conceiving of space and time in the postmodern. However one takes Lyotard's reworking of the Kantian sublime, there are clearly important issues of spatiality and temporality concerned with heterogeneous realms, the differend and a postmodern consciousness. These spatio-temporal concerns feed into the postmodern chronotope and inform many debates about the postmodern and postmodern culture.

Another spatio-temporal concern which emerges here is the removal of the human subject from an assumed centre ground. The fragmentation and dispersal of the subject profoundly affects both space and time in the postmodern. It is often associated with drawing distinctions between modern and postmodern, and it leads to a repositioning in centre–periphery debates. The removal of the human subject from the centre of his (deliberate use of male gender) universe was described by Leonard B. Meyer, writing in 1963:

> Man is no longer to be the measure of all things, the center of the universe. He has been measured and found to be an undistinguished bit of matter different in no essential way from bacteria, stones, and trees. His goals and purposes; his egocentric notions of past, present, and future; his faith in his power to predict and, through prediction, to control his destiny – all these are called into question, considered irrelevant, or deemed trivial.
>
> (Meyer 1963: 186)

As Bertens notes, Meyer, Charles Olson and Ihab Hassan belong to an anti-modernist movement that is to bring forth an idea of postmodern literature in which indeterminacy and silence are foregrounded. For Hassan, this 'Literature of Silence' extends to the world of Henry Miller and Samuel Beckett (Bertens 1995: 23–6).

The decentring of the human subject is not only a spatial phenomenon however. It is also a temporal one, as William Spanos claims. For Spanos, the postmodern ushers in, or rather should usher in, a new existentialism, and the job of postmodern literature is to engage in the radical temporality of the times, a temporality which modernist literature largely avoided through a spatialisation which was, at the same time, a shot at timelessness (Bertens 1995: 47–8).

Elsewhere, I have been emphasising the spatial turn in the postmodern, a shift from a historical imagination to a geographical one, and a reassertion of the dialects of space after a modernist downgrading of space into the service of time. Here, with Spanos, there is another direction that does not necessarily preclude the spatial turn. For Spanos is also concerned with using the postmodern to make differences and to make a difference, and to engage in questioning the problematic historicity of the modern subject. This is entirely counter to a spatialisation that removes difference *from* time and *in* space. The postmodern chronotope must allow for engagement with a historicity which is heterogeneous and decentred, neither the flight from history into space, nor the construction of narratives of history which subsume the individual's historicity.

But perhaps the most significant and far-reaching spatio-temporal concern in thinking about the postmodern is the very process of thinking about the contemporary itself. As Steven Connor puts it: 'We are in and out of the moment we are attempting to analyse, in and out of the structures we employ to analyse it. One might almost say that this terminal self-consciousness . . . is what characterizes our contemporary or "postmodern" moment' (Connor 1989: 5). Whereas modernism attempted to register the passing moment and find the form to render transience of the present, the postmodern has somehow become conscious of a gap between experience and knowledge: a gap that means knowledge always comes too late to explain the present moment, because it was always formed out of those older experiences.

7) IT, Digital Culture, TV, Video: Surfaces and Loss of the Real

A crucial sign of the postmodern, and for some its essence, can be found in a post-industrial age of information, largely made possible by the spread of information technology. Attached to capitalism and the immense power and wealth of the global market a digital culture has emerged, and this seems to be recognised as a culture of surfaces, signs and images, an intensely superficial world, and a spatially extended world. Here, superficiality is etched into the ubiquitous screen of TV, video and PC, where sounds, images, texts are remixed and recycled daily. On the surface of the screen, geographically and historically diverse content is flattened into a grotesque simultaneity of seemingly equally important and uniform phenomena. Here, then, is an idea of the postmodern chronotope that I am sorry to say has become all too portable and influential. Largely through this metaphor of a ubiquitous screen, the postmodern has come to equal surface, loss of depth, loss of differentiation and loss of historicity.

In 'The Ecstasy of Communication' Baudrillard argues that advertising and television have destroyed both public and private space, reducing both to 'transparence and immediate visibility' (Baudrillard 1983b: 130). The intense proximity of everything leads to a crisis in representation, to the 'loss of the real'. This is both a temporal and a spatial condition, a loss of both geographical and historical distance, which leads to the figuration of collapsed perspective and collapsed critical distance. After the loss of the real, we live in Baudrillard's most famous formulation and most dubious contribution to the postmodern, 'the image as pure simulacrum'. In the 'hyperreal', the real is no longer re-presented, but reproduced or simulated, largely by digital means: a constant flickering of an artificial world that has displaced the real. And this exists not only on the billions of electronic screens around the world, but materialises in the market places, shopping malls, and public spaces in which an older real was once enacted. The hyperreal is thereby extended into the fabric of the world, and cannot be avoided by adopting a three monkeys' approach to digital culture (hear no TV, see no TV, speak no TV).

In such a spatially-extended world in which time seems to be reduced to a series of perpetual presents, what is the effect on consciousness? Is the mind equally extended and flattened by the experience? For Jameson, this postmodern version of the sublime takes the body to the limits of itself, to the point of losing itself in uncoordinated hyperspace. And again, such experience is both temporal and spatial, especially when we consider video and other more recent forms of digitally-coded images, which we watch in a curiously removed time. This is neither the real-time of watching, nor the time of the image-narrative, if it has one, but is rather a programmed stream of time detached from any other reference points but the play of images and sound itself.

I have mentioned earlier that the postmodern marks a shift from an analogue to a digital age. The earlier analogue age of representation kept some distance between the world and representations of it, and this was recognised in the technical remove of the analogue. For example, in analogue computers, the real world measurement is presented to a device that converts units of this measurement into an electrical impulse, and so will translate the real world into a representation of it. In digital computers, the real world feeds directly into the computer as a series of 0s and 1s, and joins with a constantly updated model of the world within the computer. There is no translation, just the easy flow of data, and there is no real boundary between the simulated world within the computer and the 'real' world outside.

A further extension of digital culture is the predominance of networks. Here, the old spatial boundaries marked by, for example, local, regional and international telephone exchanges, are replaced by networks in which the route between any two points is never fixed, but dynamic, tracing different, unpredictable paths through networks of participating *nodes*. The internet depends on such networks, as do mobile phones and, increasingly, international telecommunications of all kinds. The network is a reality in postmodern culture, but it is also a metaphor for postmodern space–time. It breaks with the linearity of the modern and with the kinds of spatial distinctions that kept local and global apart. Local and global are made irrelevant in a network of constantly chattering links criss-crossing the globe. We may never know by what route an e-mail message travels from London to Hong Kong, and we never need know, because when connected to the network, modern conceptions of time and geography are swept away.

8) *Science and Science Fictions: Through Metaphor to Chronotope*

The identification and development of a postmodern chronotope in which postmodern theory and practice might be cast is the foundation, premise and atrium of the present work. As we have already seen, the idea of the chronotope as a way of considering space–time relations comes from Bakhtin, who uses it to construct a historical poetics of forms of time and space in the novel. The principles of this representational chronotope, which is attached to aesthetic form, have already been outlined, and I have also attempted to gather up the threads of a generalised postmodern chronotope, based on various discussions of space and time that have become associated with postmodernism.

But I have already hinted at the dangers of making too simplistic a link between chronotopes in different realms, an all too common error in discussions of the postmodern. So I want to maintain a semblance of difference here, while allowing that my thesis does in fact require such boundaries to be crossed. Some distinction must exist between the realms of the novelistic (artistic/imaginative) chronotope and those of the everyday (practical/cultural) and the scientific (conceptual/abstract). Some readings of the postmodern collapse the boundaries between the 'material conditions' of postmodernity and the aesthetics of postmodernism, and these go too far I think towards making postmodernism affirmative and uncritical of postmodernist culture.

We have only to review the assimilation of scientific theories of space and time in nineteenth and early twentieth century literature to see how influential science has been on the representational chronotopes of the English novel. Clearly science does not operate in a closed regime, but affects representational and practical chronotopes through which we perceive the world and our place in it. Scientific theory and its conceptual chronotopes not only feed into material changes through the practical chronotopes of technology and culture, but also change our perception of the shape of the world, and its place and ours in the cosmos. All of this has a marked effect on how we imagine and represent space and time in representational chronotopes. This is complicated by extreme and emotional reactions to what might be perceived as de-humanising or de-deifying, detracting from religious and other traditional beliefs in space and time.

As Stephen Hawking has noted, at the beginning of the nineteenth century when Marquis de Laplace claimed that he could predict the state of the solar system, given accurate starting positions and velocities, this doctrine of 'scientific determinism' as it was to become, was resisted on the basis that it 'infringed God's freedom to intervene in the world' (Hawking 1988: 53).

But, despite these objections, scientific determinism, and Darwinism to give another example, greatly influenced Victorian thought. Both provided a model for individual and social development in which destiny was without the intervention of God or nature. The deterministic model was particularly important to nineteenth century social and economic progress. In science, it remained the standard assumption until early in the twentieth century (Hawking 1988: 53). Human perception of the universe changed dramatically in the nineteenth century, and prediction was no longer a matter of star-gazing in the romantic sense of looking for celestial patterns, signs and inspiration. Astronomy, not astrology, was a popular science for Victorians, who put scientific determinism into practice to predict the movements of stars and comets, and many watched the much-publicised appearances of new comets. Thomas Hardy had the idea for an 'astronomical novel' after observing Tebbut's comet over Dorset in 1881 (Ahmed 1993: xii), and in *Two on a Tower* (1882) Hardy refers to a tension between pre-modern ideas of the celestial sphere set in a fixed cosmos with destiny already inscribed in its patterns, and a modern idea of an impersonal and unbounded universe. Levelling his 'achromatic' at Sirius, Hardy's young astronomer tells Lady Constantine "'Though called a fixed star it is, like all fixed stars, moving with inconceivable velocity'" (Hardy (1882] 1993: 31). Then, linking the 'arrow of cosmological time' with the 'arrow of thermodynamic time',[16] he goes on to explain: "'there is involved the quality of decay. For all the wonder of these everlasting stars, eternal spheres, . . . they are not everlasting, they are not eternal; they burn out like candles'"(Hardy [1882] 1993: 34).

Determinism and Darwinism were not only very common themes in the Victorian novel, they also influenced the form and structure of these novels. There is a particular chronotope, in the *Bildungsroman* novels of Dickens, Hardy and Eliot, for example, which owes much to a deterministic approach. Heroes and heroines are given their starting points and then become established in their environment or milieu, which is shot through with the inherited standards and values of family, class and gender, and other socio-historical factors that we take to be real. They then travel, literally or figuratively, through life, informed and constrained by their environment and character. There are choices to make, branches and deviations to take on their road, but the journey's end is often *predictable*, and reassuringly so. We can deduce it in scientific terms from 'starting position' and 'velocity', and in terms of the novel, from character, environment, and the particular road the author sets the characters on.

There are other factors here of course, such as the constraints of artistic convention and readers' expectations, which determine the author's hand as much as the lot of the characters in the novel. Also, the novelist's art is concerned here with a tension between dramatic interest through suspense, and adherence to the verisimilitude of realist fiction. Chance encounters help achieve this, and the chronotope of the road is often used within the larger chronotope of the *Bildungsroman*. As Bakhtin has noted 'The road is a particularly good place for random encounters. On the road ("the high road"), the spatial and temporal paths of the most varied people – representatives of all social classes, estates, religions, nationalities, ages – intersect at one spatial and temporal point' (Bakhtin 1981: 244, 243).

The introduction of chance into the Victorian novel also suggests Darwinian interjection into the deterministic schema. In Hardy's novels the fate of individual characters sometimes seems to be determined by running into some highly improbable bad luck, given an unrealistically poor starting position. But if Hardy is assimilating scientific models into his fiction, this might explain (though not necessarily excuse) some of the awkwardness in his plots. In a number of his novels, Hardy attempts to use a model of Darwinian evolution with its slow process of change, occasionally interrupted by the 'blip' of a random mutation. To effect this within his fiction, he introduces characters with distinguishing marks that set them apart from the norm, and, by implication, from the *species* they are born into.

The distinction may occur as a small visual cue, like Eustacia's blue garb in *The Return of the Native* but this is enough to mark her out for a completely different track when this slight mutation is set within the slow, cyclical and timeless rhythms of Egdon Heath. In *The Return of the Native*, the timeless and as yet unchanging qualities of Egdon, trap Eustacia in a closed microcosm, cut off from the modern world that she senses is just beyond her in space and time if only she can escape into it. She is trapped in a world that is destined to become extinct, but she lacks the means to launch herself into a new world; so Hardy presents us with one of his infamous 'accidents'. Within the ancient heath – this massive self-sustaining organism of inter-related species – a moth flies into a candle, setting off a chain of events in this natural world that leads to death (and a kind of escape) for Eustacia. The heath rids itself of this alien creature in her blue garb, and reverts to its timeless existence, containing within its borders the heath dwellers – the 'natives' who merge easily into the heath, barely distinguishable from it, in their brown and dark green clothes. A chronotope of Darwinian science is appropriated, quite consciously I think, by Hardy into this novel.

Scientific determinism was displaced in the early twentieth century, when Laplace's dream of predicting the state of the solar system was shattered by Heisenberg's Uncertainty Principle and the birth of quantum mechanics (Hawking 1988: 54–5). This undermined Laplatian determinism by demonstrating the impossibility of accurately measuring both the position and speed of a particle: the more accurate the measurement of speed, the less accurate becomes the position, and vice versa. Combined with the General Theory of Relativity, and the theory that the universe as a whole was expanding, the Uncertainty Principle turned the universe into a far less predictable place than Laplace conceived. Absolute prediction became impossible and quantum mechanics learned to deal in spectra of probability rather than certainty. This was to have a profound effect on twentieth century thinking and aesthetics, although arguably this could be expressed the other way around.

RELATIVITY AND REALISM IN THE MODERN NOVEL

When Einstein's Theory of Relativity was announced in 1915, the conventional sense of the stability of the entire material universe, already subject to some preliminary blows from scientists working on electromagnetic and radiation theory, was finally demolished (Kern 1983: 183–5). It was no longer possible, based on scientific theory, to conceive of space as separate from matter, or conceive of space as a fixed quantity in the universe, disconnected from time. This sense of breakdown in the primary form of the universe was not confined to scientific theory, but reverberated throughout cultural and artistic spheres as well. Bold claims were made at the beginning of the twentieth century, as the world seemed to be on the verge of release from 'fixed frames' of Victorian thought in which there was 'a place for everything, and everything in its place'.

In her essay, 'Mr Bennett and Mrs Brown', Virginia Woolf asserts that 'on or about December, 1910, human character changed' (Woolf 1971: 320), and she goes on to refer to changes in cultural, domestic and social life and the break-up of conventional narrative in modern literature, especially in Joyce's *Ulysses*, as evidence of the destruction of old forms. Woolf was to find these changes 'vigorous and stimulating', but, as Stephen Kern records, others would find them troubling (Kern 1983: 183).

There was a general sense of breakdown in structures, frameworks and order, and diminished faith in the existence of a definite, objective, 'outer-reality', in early twentieth century thought, and this was probably directly related (certainly indirectly related) to the Relativity proposition and to a new scientific concept of the universe expanding in space–time. Certainly early modernist literature responded to this fundamental change in thought with an urge to abandon conventional forms and realistic representational style in favour of a style that examined the process of realistic representation itself.

After the modernist experimentation in form in the early twentieth century, the modern novel perhaps became more concerned with political and social reality than the processes of artistic representation. The chronotope of the modern novel (as opposed to the modernist novel) returns to more conventional space–time organisation, and scientific theory has little impact on the 'new realism' either thematically or structurally. After the assimilation of relativity into the modernist novel, scientific theory tends to be concentrated into a sub-genre of literature: science fiction. So although science had a fundamental impact on modernist thought and artistic representation for a while, by the 1930s Aldous Huxley and George Orwell, for example, moved on to the political and social implications of modernism. A new form of realism dominated British literature in the 1930s and 1950s, and further significant experimentation with the form of the novel was to wait until the 1960s and 1970s. In the postmodern, scientific theory seems to influence social and cultural theory again, with the Big Bang theory, Chaos theory, and the possibility of non-directional (non-linear) time exercising the imagination of the authors of postmodern novels, leading them to experiment with form again.

There are other factors affecting this later stage of experimentation in form, such as developments in structuralism and post-structuralism, and I would not attempt to argue that the space–time structures of the experimental novels of Alain Robbe-Grillet, for example, are directly informed by scientific theories of space–time. Nevertheless, I would argue that the use of space and time in the postmodern novel could be linked to certain changes in scientific thought. The postmodern novel also recovers some of the themes of space–time that had previously been the preserve of science fiction, and perhaps this is partly because the boundaries between culture, literature and science are less differentiated than they have been for some time. At the end of the twentieth century the world seems even more unpredictable than at the beginning. We always knew it was difficult to predict the weather, but now science has attached respectability to the ineptitude of forecasters by recognising the chaotic element inherent in weather systems. The problematic status of reality is a concern in science as well as in representational forms like the novel. As B.S. Johnson remarks, 'Present-day reality is markedly different from say nineteenth-century reality. Then it was possible to believe in pattern and eternity, but today what characterises our reality is the probability that chaos is the most likely explanation'

(Johnson 1973: 17).

The Uncertainty Principle and Postmodern Literature

In the late twentieth century, a modern scientific and rational approach to human affairs prevails in most secular societies. But theoretical science is itself no longer still governed by the laws of thermodynamics, causality and motion on which rational thought, governance and ethics are sometimes thought to rest. Scientists today come up with worrying laws that formalise uncertainty and chaos as inescapable properties of the world and, rather than offer mathematical models for determining ethical solutions, they create ethical problems of their own in genetic engineering for example.

In twentieth century science, Heisenberg's Uncertainty Principle, which Stephen Hawking calls 'a fundamental, inescapable property of the world' (Hawking 1988: 55), underlies the theory of space–time relations, and this principle seems to undermine a whole raft of scientific proofs and validations. We must be very careful, however, not to misappropriate the Uncertainty Principle and apply it too widely in cultural theory, remembering how scientific determinism has often been misapplied in human and social affairs. Science only uses uncertainty and chaos in certain specialised systems, such as the behaviour of elementary particles. The remainder of scientific research still relies on traditional certainties like scientific determinism, so if we are going to appropriate scientific theory for social and cultural theory, we should add uncertainty and chaos to the standard theory of quantitative time and deterministic approaches, not simply move from one fashion to another. We might consider then the concept of the 'spectra of probability', which is used in physics to allow a range of likely outcomes, accepting a degree of uncertainty, but attempting to quantify and put a fence around the uncertainty.

Some contemporary scientific theory of space–time is difficult to transfer to social and cultural theory, although Lefebvre's concept of the production of social space comes close to it. In cosmology, space–time allows the possibility of 'hyperspace' (a multidimensional universe), and the expanding universe theory does not disprove that the universe might begin to contract again, at which moment, life as we know it would cease. Space–time theory does not preclude this possibility because it does not currently distinguish between forward and backward directions of time. In particle physics, it is possible in a particle accelerator for elementary particles to travel into 'the future', but we should not take this as evidence that humans could ever travel in space–time except in the imagination, and in fiction. In the work of Peter Ackroyd, we can see the influence of contemporary scientific theory, which seems to allow the possibility of time travel, but we must recognise that this is stretching science. Ackroyd uses the possibility of non-directional time in *Hawksmoor* and in *First Light*, both examined in detail later.

USES AND ABUSES OF SCIENTIFIC METAPHOR

Relationships between science and social and cultural theory have often been fraught, and 'science' has often been opposed for not being directed by philosophical or human demands. But in the twentieth century, science has provided us with a number of developments that have enormous potential to improve life materially, and science has also provided social and cultural theory with much of its conceptual apparatus, especially with respect to conceptions of space and time. We should perhaps not blame science, then, if its material and conceptual developments are inappropriately used.

Within the novel, science is often appropriated, extended and abused, and this is acceptable provided that we recognise that once appropriated, science no longer offers 'proofs' but offers imaginative capability. There is a danger of being seduced by science in the novel, because science is associated with realism, and can easily assume the novel's realistic pole of representation. For instance, there is a danger that Peter Ackroyd's *Hawksmoor* might be taken as a 'scientific' rejection of the mathematical, the logical and the rational, as defined by modern science. It is in some ways a contemporary ghost story travelling backwards from an excessively rational age into a pre-modern world of metaphysics, but it might also suggest the emergence of a new science in which the possibility of multiple universes exists, with the possibilities of 'travel' between them only now beginning to be seen.

The postmodern novel often entertains such non-realist readings but, as I hope to demonstrate in subsequent chapters, the relationship between fictional space–time, scientific theory, and the space–time of everyday experience is quite subtle in the postmodern novel, and the art of representation as a means of bringing the complexities of human experience to light, and of suggesting new possibilities, is frequently overlooked.

The possibility of particles shifting into another space–time, while not making a practical difference to our lives, does present a model that might change the way we conceptualise space–time relations. If we look back at the modern concept of space–time, it seems to be firmly built on a deterministic model that can be traced to a Newtonian concept of a fixed universe with immutable laws of energy and motion. The laws of cause and effect emerge from this model, as did the ideas of a number of Utopian thinkers in the nineteenth and twentieth centuries who developed historical models which analysed the past and projected a certain future.

The deterministic approach is a powerful organising metaphor, which had considerable influence on nineteenth century thinking, as Foucault puts it:

> The great obsession of the nineteenth century was, as we know, history: with its themes of development and of suspension, of crisis and cycle, themes of the ever-accumulating past, with its great preponderance of dead men and the menacing glaciation of the world. The nineteenth century found its essential mythological resources in the second principle of thermodynamics.
> (Foucault 1986: 22)

It is not that we are finding flaws in the second principle of thermodynamics in the late twentieth century, but we are finding limitations in its application. Whereas many Victorians might have dreamt of quantifying and explaining all natural phenomena, and containing nature within verifiable and universal laws, we are now finding that there are elements in nature and in the cosmos that seem to defy measurement and prediction.

In the nineteenth century, Darwin introduced the deep history of evolution, and this was surely a major influence on Victorian thought: at least as important within the 'mythological resources' of nineteenth century thinking as the second principle of thermodynamics. Darwin's evolutionary models had a major impact on concepts of time, vastly extending the age of the Earth, and throwing doubt over religious myths of creation.

The model was also, it would seem, largely misappropriated in cultural and social spheres, as Gillian Beer points out in *Darwin's Plots* (Beer 1983). It was used as a metaphor for hierarchy, progress and development; in the Victorian novel, the individual's progress is hindered or helped by her family and environment, and society seems to have a sense of itself moving forwards in time. The stronger, fitter and better-adapted survived, and society evolves forwards and upwards. But Darwin's model for evolution was far less *directed* than this implies. He never suggested that evolution had any purpose or direction, but that any change came about by 'pure accident', and evolution therefore 'progresses' through chaotic impulses that produce mutations. In the late twentieth century, science is turning its attention more to 'chaotic' components in biology, physics and cosmology and, at the same time, we can see in social and cultural spheres a less formulaic approach to history, progress and social development as though, here too, the chaotic and mutating component of Darwin's schema is being reasserted.

FROM LINEAR TO NETWORK NARRATIVE – A CASE IN POINT

Modernist literature, either in its attempts to ground the experience of modernity through connection with a past, or in its attempts to connect with a visitable future, or in its attempts to freeze the present or grasp a moment from the flux, can be considered as a literature reflecting or reacting against linearity. Positioning the present moment, historical or experiential, within the passing of time requires a particular narrative form which may not always be linear in terms of plot, but which assumes an arrow of historical time against which experience might be measured. In other words, modern experience of time may be fragmentary, but this does not preclude, indeed it probably confirms, the supposition that there is a historical time maintaining its measured pace and synchronising historical events on the world stage.

In the postmodern, not only is private time fragmentary and non-linear but the historical time, which supposedly fragments through individual consciousness, is itself fragmentary and heterogeneous in nature. Here, the past is more contingent with the present, not only through individual memory, but also through the non-linear properties of historical time. This uneven proximity and nebulous contingency of history can be imagined through the postmodern chronotope as a kind of levelling, a flattening of the axis of historical time: history as a

The Postmodern Chronotope

superficial phenomenon, rather than a vertical structure, or depth model. For Foucault, this chronotope is arranged such that the present is like 'a network that connects points and intersects with its own skein' (Foucault 1986: 22).

In the chronotope of the postmodern novel, the sense of the present as a network connecting points across historical time is commonplace. In this chronotope, spatial separation, or rather topographical separation to be more precise, can substitute for the temporal contingency in which past, present and future exist as a network within the present. Where such a chronotope is used to organise the narrative of the postmodern novel, it inevitably incorporates what might usually be thought of (in the modern depth models of linear time) as non-directional time, that is, time that is not predisposed to travel in only one direction. And such non-directional time is no longer restricted to the realm of subjective experience, in the subconscious, in dream or in flashbacks, but can also be found in historical and narratival time.

Such a narrative form is used by Peter Ackroyd in *Hawksmoor*, which juxtaposes two 'stories', or time-directed narrative sequences, separated by two hundred years, and yet remains connected through spatial proximity. In this chronotope, spatial proximity alone connects narratives that are separated by historical time. It is in particular historical sites in London, the real churches of Nicholas Hawksmoor, that time appears to become flattened, to shift from a vertical degree of separation to a horizontal contingency based on complex time-altering symbolisms.

Perhaps the best example of network narrative I can think of is to be found in Italo Calvino's *Invisible Cities*. This is an example of a postmodern novel that relies almost entirely on such narrative. It takes Venice as a representational site containing complex symbolisms, which it attempts to decipher in order to disclose its 'will to be produced'. The development of Venice starts with a challenge to nature and to enemies, in a settlement on the lagoon, but that space cannot be separated from the other spaces, such as the vast space of commercial exchange extending through the Mediterranean and the Orient. Nor can it be separated from the grand design of the merchant oligarchy that dominated the political space.

The symbolism of Venice incorporates a sense of history as an impenetrable container of the past, and a sense of time as a destructive force, reducing the created monuments and palaces to a decaying heap, where rats and termites thrive. But it also hides the many spaces which the tourist does not see, and it is a 'history of space' that Italo Calvino attempts to describe in *Invisible Cities*. Here there is no temporal continuum, either in the fictional sense (there is no plot development in the narrative: in a way nothing *happens*), or in the historical sense, through which past events might be measured or reconstituted to determine their causes and consequences. In terms of the novel's chronotope, the vertical dimension of time barely registers against the horizontality of space. But these spaces do not cohere. Calvino's strategy is to create many conflicting worlds co-existing across time in one heterogeneous version of Venice. This challenges a conventional historiographic approach to Venice, by collapsing all possible spaces of the past into one. These spaces include the practical, the ideal and the imaginary, and all of the spaces produced by Venice's challenge to nature, and nature's resistance which continues to threaten it from the sea. It also includes the spaces produced by the merchant classes in their grand architectural designs, and the conflicts hidden by the unitary design, such as the 'alternative' designs stored in the museums of Fedora and, finally, the spaces produced by a great sea port exchanging goods and *signs* with the Orient.

In *Invisible Cities*, space is rich and dialectical. The dead space of Venice as a work of art, or as a spectacle, is denied by Marco Polo in Calvino's fiction:

> 'Did you ever happen to see a city resembling this one?' Kublai asked Marco Polo, extending his beringed hand from beneath the silken canopy of the imperial barge, to point to the bridges arching over the canals, the princely palaces whose marble doorsteps were immersed in the water, the bustle of light craft zigzagging, driven by long oars, the boats unloading baskets of vegetables at the market squares, the balconies, platforms, domes, campaniles, island gardens growing green in the lagoon's greyness.
> 'No, sire', Marco answered, 'I should never have imagined a city like this could exist'.
>
> (Calvino 1979: 68)

When the Kublai Khan finally asks Marco Polo why he has never mentioned Venice among all the various cities he has described to Kublai, he replies that they have all been Venice, or some aspect of it: 'Every time I describe a city I am saying something about Venice' (Calvino 1979: 69).

Calvino almost rules history and the experience of time out of the narrative but even its representational mode tries to suppress them: as we will see in later chapters, although postmodern novels emphasise the problems of space and place, they never escape traditional problems of time and history which are perhaps any novel's *sine qua non*. In *Invisible Cities* it is the arrow of time which converts future-directed desires of empire into fading memories of the past, and which ultimately hands empires over to the termites. Kublai Khan is obsessed with loss of empire, and so he instructs Marco Polo to keep recounting and 'making real' the spaces of his empire. But Marco Polo is merely the story teller who brings the empire into existence through his imagination, and his elaborate descriptions merely postpone the inevitable:

> Only in Marco Polo's accounts was Kublai Khan able to discern, through the walls and towers destined to crumble, the tracery of a pattern so subtle it could escape the termite's gnawing.
> (Calvino 1979: 10)

Storytelling is Kublai Khan's defence against time, but when he asks Marco Polo about the spaces of the future, Polo insists that such a journey is 'discontinuous in space and time', because the future is already 'rising scattered within the confines of your empire'. Polo suggests that history and the future are contained in the spaces of the present, and Kublai Khan's ultimate destination is already prefigured in the crumbling cities of his fading empire. Kublai sees in his maps only the 'infernal city', the city of destruction, as his 'last landing-place', but Marco Polo points to the presence of that inferno within the present: 'where we live every day, that we form by being together'. The answer to the future, insists Marco Polo, exists in the present, where it is possible to discern the inferno, exclude it, and reshape the spaces of the present:

> seek and learn to recognise who and what, in the midst of the inferno, are not inferno, then make them endure, give them space.
> (Calvino 1979: 127)

It is space here that is revolutionary, and time reactionary and conservative, inverting futurist concepts of space and time. In Marco Polo's advice to Kublai Khan, we can see how Lefebvre's idea of a history of space differs from a materialist view of history. Marco Polo suggests that we can prophesy and change things in the present, rather than waiting for the crumbling and regeneration in historical time. This is to be achieved, it would seem, by looking around us now at the non-destructive elements in society, and ensuring that they are given space to endure. This perhaps is a reversal of Darwinian notions of survival in which the more destructive elements of society might be expected to win the 'trial by space', and it is also brings to the surface the non-destructive elements within society which might previously have been lost or marginalised by the totalising impact of imperial histories.

In the following chapters we will explore the time–space structures and narrative structures of postmodern novels in detail and we will see that, although the postmodern novel has many similarities with modern(ist) forms, there is this change of emphasis, not from history to geography or time to space *per se*, but from a historical imagination to a geographical imagination. This allows the problems of history to be examined, but the mode of examination is *geographical*. This shift could be described as a move away from the *spatialisation of time* which Joseph Frank and Frank Kermode highlighted as the mark of the modern(ist) text, and a move towards Henri Lefebvre's *history of space*, in which space and place are the focus of experience, and exist *across* and *through* time.

PART II

READING SPACE AND TIME IN CONTEMPORARY FICTION

CHAPTER 4

The City in Late Capitalist Fantasy: Alasdair Gray, *Lanark*

THE CITY AS HETEROTOPIA

Earlier I referred to an emphasis in contemporary social and cultural theory on the spatial dimension of human affairs, and to an underlying tension between residual centralising and homogenising forces of modernity, and postmodernist moves to assert difference through plurality and heterogeneity. Alasdair Gray's *Lanark* is, I think, a good example of how such tension can be represented in the postmodern novel. Here, a reassertion and reinscription of local and peripheral forms of representation is pitched against dominant capitalist forces of globalisation.

In *Lanark*, Gray presents the power of multinational corporations in postmodernity, as they homogenise and command economic space which then subsumes other spaces: social, political and cultural. In the novel, the city of Glasgow, Scotland's second city and at one time a major industrial city of the British Empire, is threatened both by a dominant (within Britain) English culture and by a conspiracy of multinational businesses and central government. The notion of place with a distinct identity, history and culture seems about to be blown away by these external colonising forces.

This is in some respects a 'condition of Scotland' novel which acts as a complaint against, and a rallying cry to, local writers and artists. 'We' writers and novelists of Scotland, Gray seems to suggest, have failed to create rich representational spaces and invest the city with the power of representation to counter economic, cultural and political colonisation. Where a place is undervalued imaginatively and representationally it loses its potential for differentiation, leaving it exposed to the homogenising forces that will prey on it and eventually subsume it. Paradoxically, while Gray depicts Glasgow exploited, subsumed and eventually 'swallowed' by external forces, he simultaneously rewrites the city, reasserts its uniqueness and difference and reinvests the place with representational power.

The imaginative re-creation of Glasgow begins with earlier literary representations of the city through a harsh, gritty realism concentrating on the inescapable and unrelenting hardship of life for the working classes. Gray reinstalls this historical reality of Glasgow, but he recontextualises it in the natural beauty of its topography: the lochs, mountains and sea that surround it. But more than this, he transforms the harsh realism of traditional Scottish urban writing by recontextualising it in the rich literary landscapes usually associated with cities like London, Paris, New York, or even Edinburgh. The urban spaces of Glasgow are transformed and extended into an extravagant literary 'park', a representational space in which the inhabitants of Glasgow might take their imaginations for a walk.

The multi-layered and variform structure of this postmodern novel is able to accommodate the juxtaposition here of the urban, natural, literary and fantastic. All these landscapes are somehow rolled into the representational space of Glasgow, through the manipulation of a variety of separate but connected chronotopes. The arrangement of these chronotopes brings the customarily gritty experience of 'real' Glasgow life, as presented in a tradition of Scottish urban writing, into the rich literary spaces and visionary writing of Dante, William Blake, Shakespeare, H.G. Wells and many others.

The object of all of this literary and geographical play is to create a rich contemporary identity for Glasgow that incorporates the past, but does not attempt to recapture or dwell on it. There is space in this new Glasgow for the future, and there is a sense of transcendence from the dismal life endured by the alienated and suicidal artist hero in the loosely autobiographical sections of the novel. The idea for the book is hinted at by the author/narrator in the novel:

> Perhaps the best thing I could do is write a story in which adjectives like *commonplace* and *ordinary* have the significance which *glorious* and *divine* carried in earlier comedies. What do you think?
> (*Lanark*: 494)

Thaw, the young artist trying to succeed in the 'ordinary and commonplace' Glasgow, attempts to achieve this transformation in his art school project: 'Washing Day', which contains the figures of three women hanging out their washing in the tenement backs of Sauchiehall Lane, juxtaposed with a leafless tree, its top branch crossing the sky line. The shape of this tree in Thaw's picture is informed by an engraving by William Blake, which Thaw recalls as a grey ocean with an arm 'sticking out of a wave, the hand clutching at the empty sky' (L: 236). Blake and Dante are evoked a number of times in the novel, and this does at times seem a little pretentious, especially when Thaw explains that his ambition and by implication the ambition of the author, is 'to write a modern Divine Comedy with illustrations in the style of William Blake' (L: 204). Gray can be excused this little fantasy, I think, because this is a very knowing inflation of the status of his own novel, and the purpose is not to emulate such works but to evoke them and to connect with them. The novel borrows from Blake and Dante the idea of connecting the 'hell' of contemporary life with other religious and imagined spaces that might not only transcend, but also help transform them. It also borrows from a wide range of other literary sources, mostly attributed in the 'Index of Plagiarisms' (L: 485–99).

In *Lanark*, Gray does not present a future utopian Glasgow, a city of dreams, but rather he constructs the city as 'heterotopia': a city of oddly connected, confusing, chaotic and fantastic chronotopes. The form of the novel might suggest a literary *tour de force* or disengaged experimentation with postmodernist form. But Gray is very much engaged in the cultural and political life of Glasgow both within and outside the novel, and the chronotopes of the novel are all in some way connected with the city itself. The appropriation of many literary monuments into a text firmly set in Glasgow foresees a cultural rebirth for the city. Even where the novel seems to descend into fantasy or science fiction (as though these were automatically not politically or culturally engaged, although of course they often are) direct reference to Glasgow can be found. Everywhere is 'very like Glasgow', whether it is named Unthank, Provan or Glasgow, and although places sometimes seem fantastic, each place is a rejigging of a 'real' place. Glasgow is indeed turned into a monster, loosely based on Hobbes' *Leviathan*, but this monster is formed out of what Gray sees as late twentieth century capitalism, a monster whose belly is the market.[1]

On the face of it, *Lanark* looks like two separate novels, and it is tempting to divide it into separate sections of realism and fantasy. But as heterotopia, the interplay between realism and fantasy represents the postmodern experience of interleaved spaces, neither quite real nor simply unreal. The postmodern city commonly has a sense of unreality when disconnected from its historical moorings, its cultural memory, and the tradition that forged its earlier identity. A point of focus for this slide into postmodern unreality in the case of Glasgow can be found in an earlier erosion of place during industrial modernisation.

Modernity versus Community

As discussed in Chapter 2, postmodern placelessness can be traced back to some of the effects of industrial modernisation in the late nineteenth and early twentieth centuries. Such developments led to new monotonous landscapes geared to industrial production, and the physical placelessness was compounded by a lessening of belonging in communities, which were often dispersed to meet labour requirements. Industrial towns sucked people into newly formed and uniform urban environments, such as the tenement blocks of Sauchiehall Lane featured in *Lanark*. In the nineteenth century, the decline in traditional rural communities, the large scale migration to industrial cities, and the intricacies of the experience of life in these cities is a common theme for writers such as Dickens and Elizabeth Gaskell. These writers often set up a dichotomy between nature and humanity, and the mechanisation demanded by industrial production, and imply that life in cities, which is so closely geared to industrial production, must by definition be 'inhuman'.

After this attack on traditional place-bound community in the nineteenth century, modernity then seems to launch a second wave attack to destroy those communities established within the formerly 'placeless' urban environments of industrial cities. In the twentieth century, modern, post-war urban development and 'renewal' often seems to destroy the urban 'villages' that once centred around workplaces, and were inhabited by the newly rooted urban communities. During this second attack, the shared and plural space of urban communities became more homogenised and sanitised as this space was divided into residential, industrial, commercial and recreational zones, and workers migrated to suburbia where zoning of a different kind takes place, based on divisions of class and income. In this twentieth century placelessness, it has proven more difficult to re-form the plural, social spaces that were found either in traditional rural communities or within nineteenth century urban communities.

The culture of urban planning in Britain for much of the twentieth century privileged the abstract and geometric spaces of modernist aesthetics where form follows function. This homogenisation of space has a detrimental effect on place as a social construct. Rather than bringing elements of a community together in social space, where they might continuously and locally produce their own place to inhabit, this homogenisation imposes divisions that prevent it. Place as an authentic locus for a community is undermined by the imposition of these planned and designed divisions.

POST-INDUSTRIAL CITIES

A sense of community has been reduced by the material changes of modernity, and the identity of modern industrial cities has become centred round their exchange value rather than any intrinsic character or context. For example, Sheffield and cutlery were synonymous, until its decline as an industrial city in the late twentieth century. Then a new set of problems began: how does the city and its inhabitants whose identity and place in the community had been forged by steel and its products recreate itself? The movie *The Full Monty* (1997) explores some painful lessons in reconstructing this traditionally masculine identity in post-industrial Sheffield. In this post-industrial phase, the once model industrial cities like Glasgow enter a critical phase. There is a question mark over the identity of Glasgow in postmodernity, and *Lanark* captures this sense of an entire place alienated and unrooted. As modernity created the alienated individual soul, figured here in the failing artist/writer, postmodernity creates a whole alienated place, unloved and redundant. Glasgow loses even its poor and gloomy identity gained through the 'standard vision' of its slums and deprived working-classes. The original reason for the city's existence is gone, and the post-industrial city loses its place in the world. An industrial city disconnected from production is a strange, fantastic place, with its once smoking chimneys and massive iron structures a reminder of past glories. As its industrial spaces fall empty and silent, the whole city might despatialise and disappear.

In *Lanark*, multinational corporations subsume the unproductive space of Glasgow. Unthank, the fantastic vision of post-industrial Glasgow set in the near future, is eventually swallowed *en bloc* by a multinational economic and political conspiracy: Gray's Leviathan. The metaphor of swallowing is represented as the actual consumption of the whole city, complete with inhabitants, as and when they reach the end of their usefulness. As the city fails, it surrenders to the all-powerful, all-consuming 'creature'. But unlike science fiction, this 'creature' is no visitor from another planet, or an escapee from a mad scientist's laboratory: this is the mundane logic of multinational capitalism, operating under the auspices of national governments, councils and institutions – it is 'A conspiracy which owns and manipulates everything for profit' (L. 410). The omnipotence, ubiquity, and seemingly inescapable logic of multinational capitalism, combined with a failed aesthetic and cultural project, is what brings Glasgow to its perilous state in the novel. But this Frankenstein/Leviathan-like 'creature' is not of the visible, modern kind. This creature is more conspiratorial and has the power to transform as well as consume.

Philip Cooke argues that although local communities still appear in postmodernity, such communities often exist to serve multinational corporations, and this is their only grounding. For example, a new community has been created in northern England around the new production facilities of the Nissan car plant (Cooke 1990: 147–8). This post-industrial community is created around a local web of businesses involved in the production process. Such a community is fragile: rooted in the profitability of the car plant at its centre. It is also superficial and inauthentic, bearing the signs of community, shops, schools etc., but the whole community can be regarded as part of a mobile production process which would operate anywhere the right economic conditions prevail. The identity of the workplace itself, and its internal sense of community may be very strong, but this is not shared with the community outside. And as this identity is transplanted from Japanese culture, it is hardly likely to take root in a community in northern England. The power of multinational corporations to appropriate place and create inauthentic places and 'pseudo places' is a manifestation of postmodern placelessness. This power is more pervasive and more pernicious in its attacks on traditional place-bound community because it transforms real places into simulacra. It is this kind of power that Gray represents in his vision of Unthank, where the simulacrum is a grotesque parody of post-industrial Glasgow.

Localism and Postmodern Theory

In postmodern theory, valuing the local and the peripheral seems to offer a challenge to some of the universalising centralist influences attributed to modernity. As Philip Cooke points out, the privileging of local discourse by Foucault, and the highlighting of local narratives by Lyotard, for example, seem to indicate general agreement that 'the local dimension has been for too long neglected by an overcentralized, dominating and exclusive modernist culture' (Cooke 1990: 115). The local and the peripheral promise resistance to the abstract and homogeneous spaces of modernity, but the places created by postmodern culture may only differ on the surface. The postmodern 'business park' replaces modern office blocks, and the modern shopping precinct is transformed into a 'shopping village'; but it is perhaps only the signs that change, to accommodate a nostalgia for some lost real world. A mixing of signs that confuses concrete shopping complexes with rural villages, and in which reproductions of architectural styles from earlier periods suggest connections with the past and with long-displaced rural communities, is part of the language of postmodern architecture. A new kind of homogeneity grows up in postmodern places, in this strange world of Sainsbury's and Tesco's superstores simulating the barns and granaries of countries estates.

The massive homogenising forces of multinational capital can roam freely, locust-like, across the globe. Indeed it must do so to survive, and its appetite is never satiated:

> Industrially speaking, you see, Unthank is no longer profitable, so it is going to be scrapped and swallowed. In a piecemeal way we've been doing that for years, but now we can take it *en bloc* and I don't mind

> telling you we're rather excited. We're used to eating towns and villages but this will be the first big city since Carthage and the energy gain will be enormous . . .
>
> (L: 369)

THE POLITICAL DIMENSION OF *LANARK*

Although the novel indulges itself in literary pyrotechnics, and seems more concerned with Glasgow as an aesthetic and cultural project, there are socio-political strategies in *Lanark* which are explicitly localist and separatist. Gray has stated that the failure of Scots to vote for independence from Britain in the Home Rule referendum of 1979 removed a writer's block that had afflicted him for years.[2] Clearly, there is a local political dimension to Gray's work, and although this novel is particular to Glasgow and Scotland, the issues of devolution, local autonomy and the disappearance of post-industrial cities are prevalent in postmodernity.

In the novel, the demise of community in this once great industrial city is presented partly as social realism, or at least that sub-genre of social realism in which the working class artist fails both to climb out of his class and to stay in it. He fails to bond in his community, becomes alienated both as an individual and an artist, and finally commits suicide. But the realistic sections of the novel are connected to displaced and fantastic worlds where the episodes and settings are grotesquely distorted. In this re-projection, that local tragedy, which could easily be the failure of a single individual, is turned into the failure of a whole city, and this gives it another dimension. Furthermore, the demise of Glasgow is universalised through the 'fantasy' sections of the novel, even though the novel as a whole still draws heavily on the fate of this particular locality. In the 'Epilogue', the 'conjuror' (who is one of several versions of Alasdair Gray) suggests to Thaw (who is another) that when he arrives at the assembly in Provan to lobby for action to prevent the deliberate wasting of Unthank, he will represent Scotland and Glasgow, but he will be:

> speaking for a majority of lands and cities everywhere, all of which are suffering at the hands of the great corporations [that] are wasting the earth. They have turned the wealth of nations into weapons and poison, while ignoring mankind's most essential needs.
>
> (L: 491)

The lord president director (suggests the conjuror) might then express 'full-hearted agreement', and announce immediate action on breaking up the states so that 'no state will be bigger than a Swiss canton', wages will be equalised, and all work that kills people or damages the environment will be stopped (L: 491). But the conjuror raises Lanark's expectations only to dash them immediately: 'Nobody who knows a thing about life or politics would believe me for a minute' (L: 492). There is a ring of authenticity as well as a touch of postmodernist irony in the conjuror's sardonic reference to the aspirations of the 'Scottish Wholesale Republic' in 1950; he believed himself that such things might happen then, and that Scotland would be one of many 'small peaceful socialist republics which would emerge . . . when all the big empires and corporations crumbled' (L: 493). Now, in the 1980s, he just admits that the 'world model' he must work with is essentially a 'hopeless one' (L: 493). In terms of direct action, the novel not only fails within itself, but the novel's architect seems to have lost faith in the possibility of history and politics to bring about a socialist world.

A question of localism in postmodernity hangs over the novel. Gray's politics, as presented in the novel, point towards the desire for a bottom-up kind of socialism: localist rather than state-controlled. Using Glasgow and Scotland as particular but also typical examples, the failure of such local politics in the face of global capitalism and multinational power structures is presented with crushing effect. How then does this at once historical and imaginative failure of localism gel with Philip Cooke's emphasis on the local in postmodernism? Is Gray the realist, and Cooke the idealist, or is Gray overly pessimistic in his vision?

Cooke suggests that postmodernism puts back into modernity what was deliberately left out or undervalued; postmodernism, he argues, is an 'internal critique of modernism', and an 'interpretation of the reason embodied in modernity', and its objective is to reassert 'the concerns of minorities, local identities, non-western thinking, a capacity to deal with difference, the pluralist culture, and the cosmopolitanism of modern life' (Cooke 1990: x). How can this be done? Given the awesome power and vested interests of multinational capitalism and the governments that support it, what action can be taken in either the political or cultural sphere? The argument that seems to follow from Gray's novel, and from the work of Henri Lefebvre discussed earlier, is that while recognising the need for some kind of localism within postmodernism, direct political action is in itself largely ineffectual. However, within postmodern culture, a reassertion of local space in the arts, in architecture and design, in other words in *representational* space, can lead to changes in spatial practice, the production of social space and to more far-reaching political changes. The local and the peripheral are important in helping to resist homogenisation, but postmodernist approaches fail where the heterogeneous spaces they produce are superficial, as is the case where they are simply rearranging disconnected signifiers in the postmodern spaces of shopping villages, heritage sites, theme parks etc. There is a need to create *and maintain* plurality and heterogeneity in place, and to resist its appropriation by multinational forces. For this, connections are necessary between imagined space, social space, built space, and political space; in other words, the realms of culture and aesthetics need to be reconnected with the practical and theoretical realms. As Philip Cooke rightly points out 'community has actively and consciously to be created anew in defence of a sphere vulnerable to colonisation by the [im]morality of the market place' (Cooke 1990: 52).[3]

A key element in Gray's strategy in *Lanark* is the association between the individual and the place – the place as self, and the self as place. The subtitle of the book, 'A Life in 4 Books', suggests not only the life of the protagonist, a composite self based on a number of real and fictional characters, including Gray himself, but also the life of Glasgow. A quasi-religious concept of *continuous creation*, with cycles of death, going down to hell, redemption and rebirth, organises the imaginative re-creation not only of the artist/hero, but also of the *place* Glasgow. Glasgow undergoes a process of creative destruction before dawn finally breaks and it re-emerges from the sea.

Writing Glasgow: From Standard Vision to Postmodern Vision: Life into Art into Life

Alasdair Gray's *Lanark* can be read in the context of postmodernist resistance to the combined forces of multinational capitalism and centralist government, but his strategy is not obvious, as the novel seems to portray little but crises for its hero(es) and for Glasgow. The multinational corporations ultimately bring destruction to the city, and the hero 'dies' in Books 2 and 4. Nevertheless, *Lanark* recreates an imaginative space and a placeable identity for Glasgow that overshadows, or rather *outshines* previous representations in Scottish urban writing. This can be seen in the move from darkness to light, with its allusions to passages from hell to heaven, from unconsciousness (or false consciousness) to full consciousness which are all part of the novel's imaginative structure. Indeed, the tradition of Scottish urban writing is something that Gray needs to install and subvert, as it is the collective representations of dark industrial wastelands and grim toil in poor housing conditions that need to be cleared away if the city is to be born again. Although the tradition of Scottish urban writing was realistic, it left a dark and heavy legacy for post-industrial Glasgow. Using postmodern strategies, such as the postmodern chronotopes, *Lanark* does not dismiss earlier representations of Glasgow, but incorporates, transforms, subverts them, and juxtaposes them with other representations, realistic and fantastic, but always connecting with the 'real' place.

Postmodern chronotopes are always complex, enabling connections and disjunction in space and time not possible in realistic chronotopes. They are designed to bring a multiplicity of forms, as well as space–times into the novel, and this is consistent with a postmodernist strategy to assert plurality, indeterminacy, and positionality over the ordering structuring and generalising chronotopes of realist fictions. In *Lanark*, we could describe the structure of the novel as a hybrid of realistic chronotopes in Books One and Two, enclosed within the postmodern chronotopes in Books Three and Four, with an especially 'tricksy' and self-reflexive chronotope in the Epilogue that tries to take us outside the space and time of the novel altogether. But the novel is really a whole, and the connections between its parts are the imaginative strength of the novel.

It is significant that Books One and Two are enclosed by Three and Four, because this disrupts the narrative sequence, preventing the sudden shift from realism into fantasy which would indeed divide the novel into two halves. All of the chronotopes are constructed around the heterotopia of Glasgow, so the city is never reduced to a single point of view. The standard vision of Glasgow as a deprived post-industrial city is imaginatively extended here. Gray connects his reconfigured Glasgow with many literary texts, and advertises these other texts, offering footnotes for his plagiarism in the Epilogue. This Epilogue is designed to disrupt the fiction, forcing the reader to recognise the fictionality of the text, and the world of print that s/he has been seduced into, but also, if we excuse the alleged 'narcissism' and 'self-indulgence' of Gray,[4] the connections with other texts generates in its intertextuality a far richer version of the place Glasgow. By pointing to his borrowings, which is itself a borrowing from classical literature, he asks the reader to connect his text to these other texts, and his space of Glasgow to these other spaces.

Historically, Glasgow has undergone massive disruptions in the last two hundred years. From a small rural community in western Scotland in the eighteenth century, it became one of the British Empire's premier commercial centres and ports. As a pre-industrial city, the ancient Gaelic name for Glasgow, *Gles Chu*, meant 'Dear Green Place', and Scottish urban writing has traditionally depicted the corruption of this 'dear green place' by the forces of industrialisation (Witschi 1991: 37). In modern times, it was these forces that shaped Scotland's cities, especially in the case of Glasgow which was constructed specifically to serve the industrial needs of the British Empire. In the design of the city, people were fitted into the spaces between the factories, railways, canals and docks. The lack of sunlight in Gray's grotesque parody of Glasgow is to some extent metaphorical, suggesting Dante's Inferno, and other representations of hell, but the lack of sunlight was also a reality within the tenements of Glasgow in the 1930s. This triangular extension of space–time, which takes 'real' historical place, redraws it in the spaces of present and near-future fantasy, and through metaphor extends it into the literary spaces of Dante, Blake *et al.*, is one of Gray's main strategies for extending Glasgow as an imaginative space.

As Beat Witschi has noted, Archie Hind's *Dear Green Place* is concerned with 'telling the truth' about Glasgow, and in the social realist novel of the twentieth century this involves 'preaching' the '*experience* of Glasgow working class life' (Witschi 1991: 37). In postmodernity, this idea of 'telling the truth' seems rather quaint, and suspect. Gray's vision of Glasgow is more concerned with boundaries between truth and fiction, than in knowing and telling the truth *per se*. This is perhaps another reason for *Lanark*'s shifts between realism and fantasy. In the frontispiece to Book One of *Lanark*, Gray includes the motto 'Let Glasgow Flourish by Telling the Truth' (L: 119). This refers both to the inscription on Glasgow's coat of arms 'Let Glasgow Flourish', and, ironically, to the naive intentions of social realist fiction, such as that of Archie Hind's, to 'tell the truth'. Claims to 'tell the truth' are already questioned in the Prologue, which precedes Book One (but follows Book Three), and here it is the position of the 'oracle', and his ability to tell the truth about the hero Duncan Thaw that is under scrutiny (L: 108–17). The placement of this motto also questions the meaning of 'flourishing' with respect to Glasgow as a place. The novel as a whole seems to be aimed more at enabling Glasgow to flourish as a rich representational and imaginative space, rather than as an economically successful industrial city, which was presumably the intent written into Glasgow's coat of arms.

In the early twentieth century, post-war recession struck Glasgow and it is out of this period of Glasgow's history that the 'standard vision' of the Scottish urban novel comes. This is the vision of the Glasgow tenements 'a world of bad housing, extortionate rents, unemployment, alcoholism, and violence' (Witschi 1991: 48). One of the clearest examples of this vision can be found in Edward Gaitkens' novel *Dance of the Apprentices* (1948), which I quote at length here because we will later find that it has a number of echoes and resonances in Gray's novel:

> The close known as 150 South Wellington Street was like thousands of other Glasgow slum closes, a short, narrow walled-in passage leading up to three landings and through to a grassless earthen or broken-bricked backcourt, with its small, mean communal washhouse and open, insanitary midden. In such backcourts the women of the tenements, after taking their weekly turn in the washhouse, hang out the family washing and take it in dried with sunshine or strong seawind and half-dirtied with industrial smoke and grime. They are the only playground of the thousands of the city's children, where the youngsters play football and children's games, climb on the midden and washhouse roofs and escape death or injury from the perilous traffic on the streets.
>
> They look like tunnels cut through solid cliffs of masonry, these closes, . . . There are often great holes in the walls, left unplastered or, if filled in, left unpainted and presenting unsightly daubs of crudely plastered cement. . . Many tenement dwellers live indifferent to all this ugliness and those with some spirit, who are angered by it all, lose heart in their long, unequal struggle against the tight-fistedness of factors, and live on and die in homes too narrow for fuller life, from which it seems there is no escape. These closes, badly lit, with their dangerous broken-stepped stairs, often filthy and mal-odorous, smelling of catpiss and drunkard's spew, have been for generations of Glaswegians the favourite, and for thousands, the only, courting-place, and many hurried, unhappy marriages have originated there. 'Stonnin' at the close' or 'closemooth' is a social habit of tenement dwellers and at all hours lone individuals lounge, staring vacantly.
>
> (Gaitkens 1948: 87–8)[5]

A similar vision is present in *Lanark*, but the chronotope of the 'standard vision' is extended here into a postmodern chronotope. In Books One and Two, the 'standard vision' forms much of the realistic chronotope in which Thaw grows and dies, but through the eyes of Thaw, we see a distorted version of it as it becomes warped by his physical and emotional failings, and his development as an artist. As compensation for his failure to bond with the society around him, Thaw tries to transform his environment and his own context into art, and so find a place for himself in the imaginative world he constructs for himself. Child-like, he extends the grim, grown-up reality of the Glasgow tenements described by Gaitkens into a rich world of play:

> Thaw found it a foreign kind of street. The tenements were faced with grey stone instead of red, landing windows had broken glass in them, or no glass, or even no window frames, being oblong holes half bricked up to stop children falling out . . . the spaces between pavement and tenement (neat gardens in Riddrie [where Thaw lived]) were spaces of flattened earth where children too young to walk scratched the ground with bent spoons or floated bits of wood in puddles left from last week's rain. In the middle of the street a pale lipless smiling young man sat on a donkey cart with a bugle on his knees. His cart held boxes of coloured toys which could be bought with rags, bottles and jam jars, and already a crowd of children surrounded him wearing cardboard sombreros, whooping on whistles or waving bright flags and windmills.
> (L: 126)

Thaw sees children transform the grown-up, 'standard vision' of tenement slums into a creative space for play, and the world of bad housing and deprivation is temporally displaced. The 'standard vision' is also extended laterally into other social areas, as the children run through nearby middle-class housing, and reveal that not everyone in Glasgow lived in tenements. Some live in 'semi-detached villas with privet hedges', and there is 'a small power station humming behind aspen trees' and 'allotments with beds of lettuce like green roses and glasshouses glittering in the late sunshine' (L: 125).

When Thaw attends art college he expects to find the warmth of human fellowship, but on his first day 'Nothing had enriched or warmed except the sight of a certain girl, and that had less warmed than scorched him into a different kind of unease' (L: 226). Now he reassesses the 'standard vision' of unloved tenement spaces, extending this drab landscape into the stuff of art – Sauchiehall Lane as a romantic space:

> ... now he began to relax, feeling (in that obscure channel between tenement backs) a comfort he sometimes found in graveyards, the canal and other neglected parts of the city. The stone walls, stapled over with iron pipes, seemed to hold something grander and stranger than the builders knew. He looked through a doorway and saw a huge unhealthy tree. It grew in a patch of bare earth among pale-green rhubarb-shaped weeds; it divided at the roots into scaly limbs, one twisting along the ground, the other shooting up to the height of the third-storey windows; each limb, almost naked of branches, supported at the end a bush of withered leaves. Thaw stared and munched for several minutes then moved away feeling triumphant. It was not a feeling he understood. It might have come from identifying with the tree, with the confining walls or with both.
>
> (L: 227)

Gray portrays the artist responding to the spaces around him, building up the imaginative resources for the later fantastic versions of Glasgow: Unthank and Provan. As Thaw shrinks away from the real world into a world of his own imagining, this world begins to accommodate him, so that eventually Thaw/Lanark exists in an in-between world: between that of the alienated art student, an emotionally distorted version of a past real world, and the imaginative spaces constructed by the writer from various literary sources.

As an art student in Glasgow, Thaw wants to 'grip' the people of the city, but finds himself limited by the constraints of the art college syllabus. He wants to show the people of Glasgow that 'the universe is bigger, stranger, more sombre, colourful and distinct than they know'. His unpromising project is to produce a picture called, 'Washing Day' (L: 236). And yet when begins to draw the tree he saw earlier in Sauchiehall Lane, he finds himself transforming a simple image of washing day into an allusion to Blake:

> Around it three dwarfish housewives were stretching ropes between iron clothes-poles. They wore headscarves, men's boots, and big aprons covering their chests and skirts giving them a sexless, surgical look. At the top of the picture the tree's highest branch stuck into a strip of sky among the tenement chimneys. He remembered a Blake engraving of a grey ocean with an arm sticking out of a wave, the hand clutching at the empty sky.
>
> (L: 236)

But identifying his own condition with objects and places in this bleak landscape, and transcending them through art, takes Thaw further and further from the community, love and human warmth he seeks. This has tragic consequences, when working on the Creation mural for Cowlairs Church, he enters a neurotic phase which will end in his suicide. He slowly merges with the imaginative world he creates around himself, losing himself in his art:

> 'Here it is: land, sky and sunlight,' he said to God his father as they strolled round the bramble bush, the serpent wagging its tail behind them.
>
> (L: 338)

In this postmodern novel complex chronotopes organise different space–times that then leak into each other, testing boundaries between reality and representation. The Thaw narrative, according to the character of the author in the Epilogue, 'shows a man dying because he is bad at loving', and the *Lanark* narrative that encloses it 'shows a civilisation collapsing for the same reason' (L: 484). The destruction of Unthank is blamed on an incapacity to love, which could be interpreted as a failure for communities to bond in and sustain place. Similarly, Thaw's failure to orientate himself in the real world, and negotiate boundaries between the real world and an imaginary world, might also be extended to Unthank's failure: the *Lanark* narrative shows a civilisation collapsing because it is unable to differentiate between what is real, and what is not – a commonplace in the postmodern. The novel presents not only the failure of a neurotic artist/writer to bond in his community, but also a general failure of communities to bond. In *Lanark*, the general form of the tragedy of the modern artist in the city is turned into a postmodern tragedy affecting the whole city. Thaw goes down to hell in Books One and Two, but the whole of Glasgow goes down to hell in Books Three and Four.

The imaginative and 'unreal' spaces in Unthank are extensions and distortions of the 'standard vision' of Glasgow described earlier, but in the chronotopes of Books Three and Four, those imaginative spaces suggested by Thaw in Books One and Two, are reassembled into a futuristic nightmare of a city, a grotesque parody of the 'real' Glasgow. Thaw arrives in Unthank for the first time after committing suicide at the end of Book Two, and here he is reborn as Lanark. Lanark is a transformation of Thaw, but much of Thaw's interior world, in which there is a collision of images of the real Glasgow, the 'standard vision', and artistic representations of it, is transformed into Lanark's exterior world. Lanark inherits Thaw's imagination, and then inhabits it as it becomes externalised in landscapes; and because he can externalise and objectify, even though the world he inhabits is 'unreal', Lanark is more capable of action, and 'slightly more capable of love' (L: 493). Lanark is told that he is 'Thaw with the neurotic imagination trimmed off and built into the furniture of the world you occupy' (L: 493).

We can read Unthank as some kind of 'after-life' experience for Thaw in a displaced world – a kind of hell. Passing from the 'real world' to hell, heaven, or some 'other place', has many literary precedents which are alluded to in the novel, including Dante's *Divine Comedy*, Milton's *Paradise Lost*, the 'Dream Visions' of Chaucer (especially *The House of Fame*),[6] and Virgil's *Ovid*. By alluding to these literary classics, Gray connects the 'real' Glasgow to the representational spaces of literature, enhancing and then transcending the standard vision of Glasgow and seeking to establish a new and richer space for the city.

The landscape of Unthank is based on Glasgow, but it is a darker version, lacking sunlight, and with little to occupy its inhabitants. This version of Glasgow is not just a personal hell for Lanark, it is a dark vision of what Glasgow could become as a post-industrial city: dysfunctional, devoid of meaning and identity, and no longer capable of producing anything, or maintaining itself as a significant place. It is also a city that is 'bad at loving'. This is a dark and cold city where the lack of sunlight experienced in unlit tenements in the 'real' city, is now a permanent feature:

> The city did not seem a thriving place. Groups of adolescents or old men stood in occasional close mouths, but many closes were empty and unlit. The shops not boarded up were small stores selling newspapers, sweets, cigarettes and contraceptives. After a while we came to a large square with tramcars clanging around in it. The street lamps only lit the lowest storeys of the surrounding buildings. . . Some soot-black statues were arranged around a central pillar whose top I couldn't see in the black sky.
> (L. 19)

Lanark is lured away from the city to the Necropolis on a surrounding hill, and here he escapes from 'the city more sterile and lonely than anything a pit could hold' (L: 47). He escapes through a three feet wide mouth that appears in a monument, and like the close mouths that connect the street to the tenement backs, this mouth transports him to another place – the Institute. Here, the darkness of a hell-like Unthank is contrasted with the brightness of this heaven-like place. In this floating hospital, bathed in light, Lanark finds it impossible to orientate or ground himself. The light seems to obscure rather than illuminate and the horizon has disappeared:

> The institute seemed drifting toward the sun between the precipices of a canyon and he peered forward and down, trying to catch sight of the bottom, but when the mist below the window thinned and parted he saw a violet space containing stars and a sickle moon. Feeling dizzy he looked back at the sun for reassurance, for though dimmed by haze it shone solidly in the centre of the scene, illuminating and uniting it; but now he wondered if the sun was maybe far overhead and this a reflection in the sea, or perhaps it was behind him and he was seeing it mirrored in a glacier among the mountains in front. Nothing was visible now but sunlight and milky cloud with a single peak rising from it.
> (L: 57)

This bright vision from the Institute seems 'unreal' and unplaceable, but it is clearly drawn from Thaw's experiences of climbing to the summit of Ben Rua (L: 142). However, the mountain is not a fixed point of reference here: the clouds and mists around its summit, and the bright sunlight, are merged in Thaw's imagination with the visions of William Blake. The Institute itself is not grounded in the 'real' Glasgow, unlike Unthank, which includes the material of the buildings, streets, and characters that Lanark recognises from his previous existence, even though they are transformed and distorted.

So the space of the Institute disorientates Lanark, and he is unable to position himself inside, or place the Institute in the world outside. There seems to be no perspective or fixed horizon, and what he sees seems to be dependent on the direction in which he views it. This disorientating space, which makes all views positional and indeterminate, is rather like the 'hyperspace' that Fredric Jameson finds in the Westin Bonaventure Hotel, and which symbolises for him the indeterminacy of the postmodern.[7]

The Institute is sinister and confusing, but it seems to offer light, and bright images that contrast with the dark and gloomy prospect of Unthank. Although the light is too bright, and the space is too 'open' and undifferentiated, the Institute offers imaginative space out of which new visions of the city might be formed. These contrasting imaginative spaces suggest the possibility of creating something new out of the city that the straightforward images of the 'real' Glasgow found in the social realist novels of Archie Hind perhaps never could. Yet Gray's vision is clearly not a modernist utopia. The confusing and multiple spaces of this imaginative Glasgow seem deliberately not to cohere into a single place, as though it is Gray's intention not to tie Glasgow down into a single blueprint for the future. In this heterotopian chronotope, imaginative spaces drawn from landscapes of the real city are unanchored and disorganised, wafting around within literary space.

CITIES OF DARKNESS AND LIGHT

When Gray transforms Glasgow into culturally and aesthetically rich representational space, he does not so much move away from the social realist tradition as extend it into other imaginative spaces. The use of light is important here, because the lack of sunlight in Glasgow is a major feature in the standard vision of the city, and it is this lack of light, and lack of representations of the city in light, that have contributed to Glasgow's poor self-image. Glasgow is deprived of the real and metaphorical 'lightness' found in major modern cities such as London, New York and Paris. These 'Cities of Darkness and Light', as Raymond Williams calls them, have benefited from alternating visions of brightness and gloom, signifying the grand utopian projects of modernity as well as registering a harsh underground reality (Williams 1993: 215–32). Gray presents Glasgow in chronotopes that combine the light and dark, the utopian and dystopian.

The chronotopes of *Lanark* combine allusions to literary representations of other cities with a phenomenological account drawn from first-hand experience of Glasgow. Parallels are drawn here between its tragic hero and other literary heroes. In literature, the modern 'hero' in the city is depicted as a shadowy figure, lonely and alienated, and failing to bond with others in a seemingly unknowable mass of individuals. Thomas Hardy, describing London in 1887, noted that it appeared 'unable to see *itself*. . . Each individual is conscious of *himself*, but nobody conscious of themselves collectively' (Hardy 1928: 271). But one of the darkest representations of London can be found in James Thomson's vision of the city in *The City of Dreadful Night* (1857). Here, the darkness is pervasive and all-encompassing, resembling the permanent gloom of Unthank in *Lanark*:

> Although lamps burn along the silent streets,
> Even when moonlight silvers empty squares
> The dark holds countless lanes and close retreats;

> But when the night its sphereless mantle wears
> The open spaces yawn with gloom abysmal,
> The sombre mansions loom immense and dismal,
> The lanes are black as subterranean lairs.
>
> (Thomson [1857] 1963: 137–65, III: ll.1-8)

Thomson finds no joy in the artificial light of the city, which for him, paradoxically, obscures the 'truth'. The truth he tries to reveal is the 'bitter old and wrinkled truth/Stripped naked of all vesture that beguiles,/False dreams, false hopes, false masks and modes of youth' (Thomson [1857] 1963: Proem: ll 9–11). Thomson tells us that he writes not for the 'hopeful young', or those who 'pasture and grow fat', or those 'who foresee a heaven on earth' (Thomson [1857] 1963: Proem: ll 15–21). But other writers were more optimistic in their portrayal of the metropolis and, for some, the artificial light provided by widespread street-lighting in the late nineteenth century was a cause for wonderment, and a symbol of man's ingenuity and enterprise in countering the natural gloom of the night (Williams 1993: 228). The modern city, bathed in light might also represent a visionary landscape and suggest new horizons.

Unthank is a city of perpetual night like Thomson's London, with the hero, Lanark, cast in the mould of the tragic lonely figure, trapped in an underground hell-like place, with only the slightest hint of light on the horizon:

> . . . where the streets reached the crest of a wide shallow hill, each was silhouetted against a pearly paleness. Most of the sky was still black for the paleness did not reach above the tenement roofs, so it seemed that two little days were starting, one at each end of the street. Rima said again, 'Look at what?'
> 'Can't you see it? Can't you see that . . . what's the word? There was a special word for it. . .'
> 'Dawn. That's what it was called. Dawn.'
> 'Isn't that a rather sentimental word? It's fading already.'
>
> (L: 11)

The gloom of Unthank is alleviated in Books One and Two by the real life of Duncan Thaw. Here, night follows day in a realistic chronotope, and hell is only an idea, beyond representation. As Thaw begins to believe in this idea, as predicted by the minister on the summit of Ben Rua, then hell turns from an unpresentable sublime to the 'reality' of Unthank. Although for the minister, the real Glasgow was already a hell:

he tells Thaw 'I was six years a student of divinity in that city. It made hell very real to me' (L: 144).

The gloom of Unthank is also alleviated by two very unlikely and reality-breaking events. One is the intrusion of the character of the author, who breaks the frame of the 'real', by collapsing real and unreal, heaven and hell into the representational chronotope, the 'world of print'. The other is the flight of Lanark to Provan, where a seemingly ideal city is spread out below him. Finally, the gloom is completely lifted at the end of the novel, when Lanark returns from Provan (which was not an ideal city at all) to Unthank, which is about to be completely destroyed. As the city collapses and slides into the sea, Lanark sees the full light of day for the first time since his 'death' as Duncan Thaw, and the last time before his death which ends the novel:

> He looked sideways and saw the sun coming up golden behind a laurel bush, light blinking, space dancing among the shifting leaves. Drunk with spaciousness he turned every way, gazing with wide-open mouth and eyes as light created colours, clouds, distances and solid, graspable things close at hand.
>
> (L: 558)

Gray links his representation of Glasgow with more optimistic and imaginative writing about the modern city, giving it both light and shade. But he goes much further than this, because in the end Glasgow seems to enjoy a new dawn, in full, natural sunlight rather than the visionary, transcendent brightness of the Institute. In this renewed Glasgow, the landscape has a tangible quality again, the hand is no longer clutching at an empty sky, like in an engraving by William Blake, everything is now real, 'solid', and 'graspable', and real space is being created again.

IDEAL CITIES

There is no ideal version of Glasgow in *Lanark*, and there is no political blueprint for rebuilding the city. Gray promotes the city, drawing attention to its social and geographical richness and variety, yet it is never romanticised or sentimentalised. When Lanark travels to Provan, the author-figure tells him that he has 'come here from my city of destruction, which is rather like Glasgow, to plead before some sort of world parliament in an ideal city based on Edinburgh, or London, or perhaps Paris' (L: 483). But the city that Lanark has seen from the air, which the author-figure tells him is an 'ideal city', is of course none of these, but Glasgow, as Lanark tries to argue. When Lanark is asked 'when you were landing this morning, did you see the Eiffel Tower? Or Big Ben? Or a rock with a castle on it?' Lanark answers, 'No. Provan is very like –' (L: 483), but he is cut off by the author-figure before he can say 'Glasgow'. Glasgow is not allowed to become 'idealised' or Utopian, because this would make it unreal. This postmodern novel does not imagine ideal cities in sunlight, but presents the city as a plurality of time–spaces, in turn utopian and dystopian, and in turn in light and dark and shade.

Modern representations of the city typically focus on prominent buildings, offering a unified image, spatially extended, as though the city sees itself from the air. The modern city is perhaps best seen from the air, it is from such distance that it seems to cohere into the designed, ideal place. From such distance, the city seems like the models, the abstract spaces of planners from which it grew. The view of Glasgow that presents itself to Lanark when he flies to Provan is such a view. The city is laid out before him as though it were a child's model, and from this perspective it all looks 'splendid' and 'familiar':

> On the left were mountain ridges and high bens silvered with snow, the sun striking gold sparkles off bits of sea loch between them. On both shores he saw summer resorts with shops, church spires and crowded esplanades, and clanging ports with harbours full of shipping. . . a paddle steamer churning with audible chunking sounds toward an island big enough to hold a grouse moor . . . This island looked like a bright toy he could lift up . . . Then the high land sloped away left and right and he came to a valley, a broad basin of land filled by a city with the river gleaming toward a centre of spires, towers and high white blocks. . . tenements of clean stone enclosing gardens where children played and lines of washing flapped in a slow breeze. . . The width and beauty of the view, its clearness under the sun seemed not only splendid but familiar. He thought, 'All my life, yes, all my life I've wanted this, yet I seem to know it well. Not the names, no the names have gone, but I recognize the places.'
>
> (L: 470–1)

When Lanark lands here and meets the inhabitants of Provan, he complains about the dangerous sanitary problem in Unthank that threatens to destroy the city. He tells the inhabitants of Provan how lucky they are to be living here (although in fact, they are both

Glasgow). He is soon disillusioned of his 'splendid' impression of the city, when he is told that he suffers from a 'Gulliver complex', having, like Gulliver, who recorded the first aerial survey in Lilliput, fallen into the trap of mistaking distance for brightness. From the air, Gulliver saw enterprise and ingenuity in 'the homes, streets, public buildings of a very busy people': it took him two or three months to discover 'their stupidity, greed, corruption, envy, cruelty' (L: 477). And so it is for Lanark in Provan, only it takes him much less time to realise that the ideal city of Provan, and the assembly gathering there, is a sham. The assembly attempts to unite nations in global brotherhood and sisterhood, but in fact papers over their huge differences and, despite the political rhetoric, is clearly continuing to support dreadful regimes while multinational corporations continue to grow. After the assembly, Lanark prefers to return to Unthank although its destruction is imminent.

Monboddo's speech at the assembly refers to the growth of multinational capitalism in the twentieth century, and its homogenising effect on world space: 'wealth has engrossed the whole globe, which now revolves in a tightening net of thought and transport woven round it by trade and science. The world is enclosed in a single living city' (L: 543). But this 'single living city' is not utopian, because it is split by the forces of capitalism that only appear to unite it. Although Monboddo, in this parody of world economic summits, puts a gloss on the world city, suggesting that the world is a well-ordered and flourishing city, what *Lanark* as a whole presents is a picture of multinational capitalism, in which one half feeds off the other. Capitalism is intrinsically divisive, depending on a division between producer and consumer, as Ritchie Smollet, the left-wing leader of Unthank's ineffective council puts it: 'The efficient half eats the less efficient half and grows stronger. . . Man is the pie that bakes and eats himself, and the recipe is separation' (L: 411). Gray's vision of Unthank, about to be consumed by multinational corporations, suggests that Glasgow is in the less efficient half of the divided world. But Provan is also a representation of Glasgow, so the city has divided itself into dystopia and utopia, both failing, one because of lack of political will, and the other because it has come to believe in an idealised version of itself and the world. The real is about to become consumed by its own simulacrum.

THE GEOLOGICAL CHRONOTOPE, LANDSCAPE AND RE-CREATION

Problems of time and the concept of creation occupy Thaw in Books One and Two, and as with other concerns in Thaw's life, these are externalised, i.e. they are extended to the material of the fantasy worlds, in Books Three and Four. The organisation of time in Books Three and Four is very complex, and in common with postmodern chronotopes in general, a number of conflicting forms of time are used. The natural landscapes of Scotland, with their highly visible geological structures, signify a deep and enduring time. This geological chronotope presents a very obvious deep verticality reducing human activity to a scratch barely penetrating its surface.[8] And this verticality leads inevitably to an origin, where the time of creation itself is inscribed, the zero-time of planet earth.

In *Lanark*, the natural beauty of the west of Scotland offsets the novel's mostly urban representational spaces. As well as relieving the dour images of Glasgow in Books One and Two, the patterns and surfaces of Scottish hills, glens and lochs help to furnish some of the fantastic spaces in Books Three and Four. The novel exploits this scenery for the simple aesthetic pleasure it offers, and also for its associations with a romantic sublime. But it is the visualisation of geological time through the Scottish landscape that is the most striking, and helps organise the chronotope of the novel's grand finale. The mountains around Glasgow are particularly fine for revealing geological time; this is where we see what the geographer Yi-Fu Tuan describes as:

> not just an attractive pattern, but the yawning of geologic time and the violence of geologic forces. In the stratified and folded beds, time becomes visible and tectonic violence, though long dead in fact, is vividly alive as image.
> (Tuan 1989)

In this geological chronotope, the time horizon stretches way in front of and beyond the creation and destruction of Glasgow and the life and death of Thaw/Lanark. So this chronotope contains the disorientating placelessness of Unthank, where time is non-synchronous and space discontinuous, and it contains the realistic chronotopes of Thaw's life, which is of course fictional. The geological chronotope would seem to offer a stable frame of reference for the whole novel, but there is a further twist in the tail (tale). Ironically, the geology on which this geological chronotope is based, with its extensive and deep time, contains not only evidence of *past* tectonic violence, but also of a violence about to happen in the present. The immediate cause of Unthank's final destruction is a shift in the Merovicnic Discontinuity, the huge fault line between shifting tectonic plates, and this is enough to tip the whole city and all its inhabitants into the sea.[9]

Gray uses natural landscape in *Lanark* to give a firm geographical context to a city that in economic, political and cultural terms is subsumed, consumed, and then destroyed by fire and flood. This destruction seems to signify the *death* of a modern industrial city, very like Glasgow, as it fails to find the means to sustain itself. But the city's death does not seem to be final, as Thaw's and Lanark's death are not final. As Lanark watches the destruction of his city from a nearby hill, the natural landscape persists, and the sunlight reappears, signifying a dawn of re-creation for the city.

Within *Lanark*, the geological chronotope operates as a realistic pole of representation, the fixed time–space overarching other artistic chronotopes. There is no historical chronotope as the realistic pole of representation, and this is consistent with the postmodern novel, in which historical chronotopes interplay with fictional ones. The geological chronotope as such is quite un-postmodern as a beacon of aesthetic pleasure, value and constancy. It contains primary reference sites, such as the triangulation point on the summit of Ben Rua, which acts as a threshold between man and nature, and between father and son. Here, Thaw and his father, and Lanark and his son experience the sublime. Here they are close to nature, close to each other, and seemingly outside time (L: 142–3, 514–5).

As well as extending time horizons, natural landscape is also used to register memories and emotions, turning it into a map of psychological interiors, and providing further escape hatches between the separate halves of the novel, the realistic and the fantastic. When Lanark flies to the assembly at Provan, he surveys the familiar scenery below and drifts into a reverie of the world that 'could-have-been':

> The width and beauty of the view, its clearness under the sun seemed not only splendid but familiar. He thought, 'All my life, yes, all my life I've wanted this, yet I seem to know it well. Not the names, no, the names have gone, but I recognize the places. And if I really lived here once, and was happy, how did I lose it? Why am I only returning now?'
>
> (L: 471)

This sense of return through a familiar landscape of the past is a fantasy of renewal, a fantasy of escaping time. But at the end of the novel, Lanark, or possibly the author, adds a postscript about maps and time which withdraws the fantasy of return, the bastard time of nostalgia:

> I STARTED MAKING MAPS WHEN I WAS SMALL
> SHOWING PLACE, RESOURCES, WHERE THE ENEMY
> AND WHERE LOVE LAY. I DID NOT KNOW
> TIME ADDS TO LAND. EVENTS DRIFT CONTINUALLY DOWN,
> EFFACING LANDMARKS, RAISING THE LEVEL, LIKE SNOW.
>
> I HAVE GROWN UP, MY MAPS ARE OUT OF DATE.
> THE LAND LIES OVER ME NOW.
> I CANNOT MOVE. IT IS TIME TO GO.
>
> (L: 560)

Lanark plays with romantic and fantastic concepts of escaping time, of rebirth, of return and renewal, and these are always implicitly concerning both life and *place*. The novel is of place more than of character, of Glasgow more than of Gray, Thaw or Lanark. The rebirth of Thaw into Lanark is significant as it signifies a merging of character with place, and here the real places of 'Lanark' and 'New Lanark' in the Clyde valley in Scotland close to Glasgow, are especially significant. New Lanark was a model community run by the social pioneer Robert Owen from 1800–1825, it was, if there can be such a thing, an industrial utopia, and it is now a World Heritage site. Lanark is an ancient town and site of the first Scottish parliament in 978. Although Glasgow is portrayed as dystopian in the novel, it seems that there is a socialist utopian undertow and an attempt to reconnect the city with past ideals. But this is not to suggest the novel is optimistic; it is still primarily a dark postmodern fantasy of dystopia, of place in its death throes.

The representation of return and renewal in the novel seems to borrow from Fred Hoyle's theory of continuous creation, which is explicitly referred to in the text. Gray uses Hoyle, as does Lefebvre, to conceive of both time and space as uncontained and continuously produced in an ever expanding universe.[10] As Thaw explains to the minister: 'hydrogen atoms are continually coming into existence in the increasing spaces between the stars [space created because the universe is expanding] and forming new stars and galaxies and things.' (L: 182) But a world of continuous creation is inconsistent with Christian mythology, as Thaw realises when he fails to complete the Creation mural on a church wall. Within the realist form of Book One, the scientific chronotope of an expanding universe producing space and time is irreconcilable with the time–space of Creation which Thaw is trying to represent in a two-dimensional and bounded artistic chronotope in the church wall mural. Thaw, in himself, and through his art form, seems unable to cope with apparently conflicting concepts of space and time. God is supposed to have created a perfect universe at one time, and only since then has history intervened in the shape of man to turn it into hell. But in the mural, although the moment of creation is successfully negotiated, with 'just enough killing to keep predators alive and the herbivores jumpy' (L: 320), trouble is always brewing in the background, where 'history was acted in the loops and delta of the river on the way to the ocean'. The river is evidence to Thaw that there must have been a time before the moment of creation, that history precedes creation and there is no point of origin: 'history was an infinitely diseased worm without head or tail, beginning or end' (L: 160), and the rot was already there in Genesis, with God popping up all over the place:

> driving out Adam and Eve for learning to tell right from wrong . . . God fouling up language to prevent the united nations reaching him at Babel . . . God telling a people to invade, exterminate and enslave for him, then letting other people do the same back. Disaster followed disaster to the horizon . . .
>
> (L: 321)

The revelation of the church wall mural destroys any faith Thaw might have had in a benign God, and it also destroys his faith in an art form that he finds unable to represent the different forms of space and time. He finds himself attempting to illustrate 'God's discredited first chapter' through 'an obsolete art form on a threatened building in a poor province of a collapsing empire' (L: 321). It is not until Thaw's after-life *alter ego* Lanark appears in Books Three and Four that we find artistic chronotopes flexible enough to handle multiple time–spaces. These chronotopes will range across geological time, mythological time and biological time, and interface with chronotopes from other literary texts and the chronotope of the real world of the artist's study, that of the book's creation.

Relations between life, place and book are crucial here, as the novel is designed to report on and intervene in the destruction of

Glasgow. Gray's declared project is to rebuild an imaginative, representational city, something sadly lacking in the past, as Thaw points out in the novel:

> Imaginatively Glasgow exists as a music-hall song and a few bad novels. That's all we've given to the world outside. It's all we've given to ourselves.
>
> (L: 243)

Beat Witschi explores a number of novels in his study of Scottish urban writing, and he concludes that Glasgow has continued to produce the same novel of crisis which perpetrates the standard vision of a miserable and poor place (Witschi 1991: 48–9). This standard vision in isolation is a mean-spirited representation of the city, bogged down in a dour realism, lacking vision beyond present misery and in the end stifling its creative energies. So the standard vision becomes a barrier to the re-creation of place in literature, for as V.S. Naipaul has written 'No city or landscape is truly rich unless it has been given the quality of myth by writers, painters, or by association with great events'.[11] This point is emphasised in *Lanark* when Thaw draws attention to the physical spaces of Glasgow in which the inhabitants live and work, and contrasts these with the representational spaces of other cities that are found in books and films:

> if a city hasn't been used by an artist not even the inhabitants live there imaginatively. What is Glasgow to most of us? A house, the place we work, a football park or golf course, some pubs and connecting streets. That's all. No, I'm wrong, there's also the cinema and library, and when our imagination needs exercise we use these to visit London, Paris, Rome under the Caesars, the American West at the turn of the century, anywhere but here and now.
>
> (L: 243)

The chronotopes of the city itself repress the imagination which must find its exercise in other representational sites via the heterotopia of the cinema. In a sense, *Lanark* offers imaginative exercise within the recognisable, but altered spaces of the city, collapsing the heterotopia of the cinema into the city's representational space.

The defence of Glasgow is thus an imaginative and cultural assault on its standard vision, not displacing it, but transforming it into art. Gray demonstrates that the production of representational space in art, such as the writing of *Lanark*, and the various other artistic projects in which Gray has been involved in Glasgow, can help enrich place and strengthen its sense of itself. By using postmodern form in this novel, with its multiplicity of views, styles, times and spaces, Gray shows how it is possible to produce a plural vision and a new identity for the post-industrial city. This new identity includes the industrial history and the standard vision, but it also takes the city outside itself into the natural beauty of its surroundings, which has always been its geographical context. Further out, the identity of Glasgow is extended to Lanark and New Lanark, where it connects with ancient Scottish history and utopian projects, and further still, into the imaginative spaces of a considerable number of literary texts.

In the context of postmodernism, it is a novel about late capitalist economic forces subsuming the local, but as a cultural project with such local emphasis, it revalues the local and recharges it. In the novel, the city is destroyed, unable to resist globalising and homogenising forces. There is a sense of impending doom in the novel, but this is gently undercut with a creative tension between apocalypse and creation. Perhaps Gray's hopes and aspirations for the emergence of a new Glaswegian and Scottish identity, politically separate from Britain and the homogenising influence of multinational capital, never quite overcome his doubts and fears about the continuing power of multinational capital. Nevertheless, Glasgow is today something of a success story in economic and cultural terms; it has been voted European city of culture and it has now firmly on today's cultural map. Gray's novel was undoubtedly part of a renaissance in arts and culture in the city in the 1980s and 1990s. And this year (1999), the Scottish parliament sat for the first time in centuries, albeit in Edinburgh and not in Lanark – the seat of the first Scottish parliament.

CHAPTER 5

Spatial Historiographies:
Graham Swift, *Waterland*

In the last chapter I suggested that Alasdair Gray's *Lanark* enriches and extends the representational spaces of Glasgow to give the city a breadth, colour and complexity more often associated with major writerly sites like London and Paris. Such enhancement of a post-industrial city's sense of itself is consistent with postmodernist strategies to value the local and peripheral. And in this postmodern novel, Gray makes use of non-realist forms of representation to re-imagine and re-present the city beyond the limitations of traditional Scottish urban writing. The use of natural landscapes is a small but important part of this part-real, part-fantastic re-presentation of the city.

But we move on now to a postmodern novel in which natural landscapes are central to a conceptual schemata in which history and historical process are re-envisaged and re-formed in the context of postmodernism. The main part of this chapter is devoted to Graham Swift's use of natural landscape and natural processes in *Waterland*, and a case is made for *spatial historiographies* as disordered and *deranged* historical narratives in which the temporal logic of causality and the timing chain of grand narratives is absent.

Traditional Historiography: A Parody of the Moment in History in J.G. Farrell's *The Singapore Grip*

As a precursor to exploring the treatment of history in Graham Swift's postmodern novel, *Waterland*, here is a very brief account of traditional historiography at work in the novel. This is intended to illustrate the intrinsic problem of using static or linear form to plot dynamic and diachronic events, and to illustrate the dangers of trying to ascribe meaning to a truncated and artificially isolated set of contingent historical events – the so-called moment in history represented as monumental past.

An assumption in traditional historiography is that we can arrest the flow of history and analyse a moment as if it were a cross section extracted from this flow. *The Singapore Grip* by J.G. Farrell could be described as a 'limit text' of traditional historiography. It threads together into a variform text, historical records, diaries, newspaper cuttings, fictionalised histories and stories. As a whole, the text seems designed to explore that particular moment in history when the Japanese invaded Singapore in the Second World War, and to explore this moment as widely and from as many points of view as possible. Characterisation is mostly restricted to functional and typical caricatures whose personal histories are truncated to fit the moment of history. In other words, we see only as much of the characters before the Japanese invasion as an analysis of the invasion seems to demand, and nothing at all afterwards that is not formulaic. The novel's chronotopes are synchronised with the historical moment, so the chief interest in the novel is the question of how this defining moment in history came about, and what it might have seemed like to have been within it while it was unfolding.

The novel is a 'limit text' in traditional historiography and its association literary form, the realist novel, because even this baggy form is stretched to breaking point by multiple and conflicting points of view and by the introduction of different kinds of historical data. It attempts to rationalise and comprehend data belonging to different realms of knowledge – attempts to weigh up the evidence. But there is no scale, no imperial system of measurement into which diverse facts, rumours and intelligence might be resolved. Walter Blackett is the novel's main character, a British plantation owner and rubber exporter in colonial Singapore. In Blackett, the failure to see what has been happening, and so to anticipate the Japanese invasion of Singapore, is dramatised. Instead of the organising, omniscient, helicopter view that could attach some meaning to what may or may not have been an avoidable tragedy, we are given Walter's limited perspective from within the historical moment. And we are given the whimsical and ambiguous voice of the narrator looking back, safely distant in time and space in his garden in England, musing over history's many ironies.

There were, it would seem from the historical research that lies beneath the novel's surface, many seemingly unconnected events, many random, absurd and even comic goings on that preceded the invasion of Singapore at the crux of the novel. To organise all of this data into some form of conclusion, revelation or charge is not the function of the novel, as it might be the function of traditional historiography. In other words, if Farrell were writing an historical account of the invasion, he might be expected to come up with some new evidence confirming or disproving other narratives. But writing a historical novel, he only gives a sense of what it might have been like for some people to experience the moment. The reader is none the wiser as to whether the invasion resulted from unpreparedness and a series of military blunders, whether it was an inevitable consequence of world events, or whether it was a symptom of the spirit of the times, or a combination of these.

The novel makes no claim to understand root causes, rather it seems to suggest that such things are, by their nature, unknowable and unpresentable. The novel might therefore be described as verging on the anti-historical, not yet the problematisation of historiography that characterises much postmodern fiction, but definitely showing signs of worrying about historical analysis. In the novel, Walter Blackett is a businessman on the verge of a nervous breakdown as he desperately tries to hang on to his little bit of Empire. It is he who, in a passage undercut with delightful irony, suggests that it is indeed possible to find meaning in the millions of events crossing a particular moment in history.

The problem, he suggests is only one of finding the right perspective, the right distance, which will presumably take many of these events out of the frame. Walter believes he could have foreseen the moment from the changes taking place around him. He muses then on how we might visualise a moment of history. Here is his naive and myopic attempt to spatialise the historical process:

'What was all this, anyway,' mused Walter grimly, 'but the physical evidence of all the more fundamental changes that had taken place in Singapore the last two decades?'... He found himself now brooding on what makes up a moment of history; if you took a knife and chopped cleanly through a moment of history what would it look like in cross section? Would it be like chopping through a leg of lamb where you see the ends of the muscles, nerves, sinews and bone of one piece matching a similar arrangement in the other? Walter thought that it would, on the whole. A moment of history would be composed of countless millions of events of varying degrees of importance, some of them independent, other associated with each other. And since all these events would have both causes and consequences they would certainly match each other where they were divided, just like the leg of lamb. But did all these events collectively have a meaning?

... Perhaps sometimes, in retrospect, we may stick a label on a whole stretch of events and call it, say, 'The Age of Enlightenment' the way we might call a long hank of muscle a fillet steak, but we are simply imposing a meaning on what was, unlike the fillet steak whose cells are organised to some purpose, essentially random. Well, if that was what most people thought, Walter did not agree with them.

Certainly it was not easy to see a common principle in the great mass of events occurring at any moment far and near. But Walter believed that was because you were too near to them. It was like being a single gymnast in a vast stadium with several thousand other gymnasts; your movements and theirs might seem quite baffling from where you stand whereas viewed from an aeroplane, collectively you are forming a letters which spell out 'God Save The King' in a pattern of delightful colours.

(Farrell 1984: 434–5)

The point that Walter is missing is that history is never afforded that aeroplane view. If we cannot see what is up close because we are still experiencing the moment, equally we cannot see the moment as it recedes into the past because we no longer experience it. What appears as the advantage of hindsight is the privilege of reordering the past to spell out the message the present wants to hear. Although a realist novel, *The Singapore Grip*, presents a plurality of textual evidence and turns analysis of the historical moment into parody. The train of events as represented in the novel, has an absurd, comic twist, always threatening to wriggle away from the grip of rational explanation. The narrator suggests that if there were an organising principle that explained events leading to the invasion – a spirit of the times – it would need to modify subtly each individual event in an historical moment, to ensure that:

If a Japanese bomber had opened its doors over Singapore in the year 1920 no bomb would have struck the city. Its bombs would have been

> lodged in the transparent roof that covered Singapore like a bubble, or bounced off it into the sea. This transparent roof was 'the spirit of those times'.
>
> (Farrell 1984.: 435)

The attempt to visualise a moment in time and give a label to a set of historical conditions is, according to Henri Lefebvre, a feature of traditional historiography:

> Traditional historiography assumes thought can perform cross-sections upon time, arresting its flow without too much difficulty; its analysis thus tends to fragment and segment temporality. In the history of space as such, on the other hand, the historical and the diachronic realms and the generative past are forever leaving their inscriptions upon the writing-tablet, so to speak, of space.
>
> (Lefebvre 1991: 110)

Lefebvre's answer is to conceive of a *history of space*, as a history of events traced in space, and as the representation, production, commodification and everyday use of space inextricably linked to the historical process. In the example of the invasion of Singapore, this would involve focusing on the geopolitical situation, that is Singapore's position in the organisation of world trade, and the many local conflicts within this 'pseudo place', i.e. not a place built up organically over time and inhabited by a local population, but created at once for commercial and political ends. Its inhabitants were all outsiders: economic refugees of one kind or another.

Singapore was also a representational site, standing at once for the colonial power and prestige of the British Empire. It seems significant that such a site should pass between imperial powers, one asserting itself as a new regional power, and the other showing that it is no longer a global force. Farrell does refer to such histories of space in *The Singapore Grip*, but his representational model follows the form of the realist novel and so is subject to the framing and linearity of realistic chronotopes. To present spatially organised historiographies, in a form more appropriate to the concept, postmodern novels like *Waterland* and *Ragtime* must break with some of the conventions of the realist novel.

In *Waterland*, Graham Swift uses a different narrative form to organise a Lefebvrian 'history of space'. This accounts for a continuum of events reaching back and forth through history, and conceived through metaphors drawn from landscapes no longer mere historical stage and backcloth, but active in the process of representation. Drawing from the particular landscapes of the Fens, Swift presents an alternative, postmodern model for time and historical progress. In this model, the historical moment does not drop on to the dry land ripe for dissection or the building of futures, rather it remains connected to the flows of history. The flows of history are likened to the flows of the River Ouse, present in the landscape since the beginning of history, meandering on towards the sea, although in another sense, returning to where they begin.

THE WATER–LAND CHRONOTOPE AS HISTORY

The main argument pursued in this chapter is that in *Waterland*, landscapes, and the natural processes that interact with them, are used metaphorically to question traditional models of historical development. Although the novel questions certain forms of history, it also launches itself into various histories of its own, some real, some fictional, and some on the margins of reality and fiction. The novel presents an exposition of the real geography and history of the Fens and its relations with the rest of the world, including the natural history of this particular ecosystem, and the history of the region's commercial exploitation.

But intertwined with this is the story of the history teacher, Crick, his wife and their families. Crick's narrative is both a personal tale and a reflection on the form and processes of history, a reflection partly initiated by the closure of the history department at his school and partly by the arrest of his wife for stealing a baby. This last momentous and significant event has a history itself reaching back through family history and it is this history, insinuated in hitherto unconnected memories, that orders the complex narrative of the novel as it weaves back and forth across historical time. The form for telling stories here is clearly different from that for telling histories of the kind previously related by the schoolteacher. In the process of telling these local and personal histories, the schoolteacher's narrative presents an alternative conceptual model of history and the historical process that is both explicitly discussed and traced in the narrative.

A conceptual model for time and history emerges from metaphors drawn from natural landscapes and so cast in geographical terms. In such artistic time–spaces or chronotopes, temporal codes are translated into spatial terms, for example: time as the course of a river; nothing happening as a flat empty landscape; historical perspective and prophesy in the vantage point of high ground. Such chronotopes derive from a *geographical*, more than a *historical* imagination (or a historical imagination seeded with strong geographical imagery). In such chronotopes, the rush of history is somehow curtailed and the temporal drive towards some ultimate goal is diminished. Similarly, the idea of history progressing through time, a nostalgic reversal of time, or a linking of time with tradition are all less significant than the idea of histories traced in space. The ideological implications of such spatialisation are on the face of it anti-revolutionary and conservative, and the choice of a rural site like the Fens seems particularly conservative. There is a strong sense in this landscape that nothing much happens for real, and so stories, myths and histories are constructed to substitute for an actual loss of history as reality.

The value of historical enquiry itself is never in doubt though, and I am not claiming that this novel marks a simple shift from historical and temporal concerns to the spatial and geographical.[1] In the novel, the teacher, Crick, claims that history, story-telling and historical inquiry are part of the human condition. We have an innate sense of curiosity, he suggests to the troublesome pupil Price, and the historical process, however we construe it, is therefore indispensable:

> What is the point of history? Why history? Why the past? . . . But your 'Why?' gives the answer. Your demand for explanation provides an explanation. Isn't the seeking of reasons itself inevitably an historical process, since it must always work backwards from what came after to what came before? And so long as we have this itch for explanations, must we not also carry round with us this cumbersome but precious bag of clues called History? Another definition, children: Man, the animal which demands an explanation, the animal which asks Why.
>
> (W: 92)

This curiosity attaches itself to a unique capacity in humans for language, memory and an instinct to represent the past and anticipate the future (and sometimes the reverse of this, to disremember, suppress memories and misrepresent the past). History, in this sense of enquiry and questioning, is used in the novel 'to disentangle history from fairy-tale' and retrieve the history teacher's own past from the 'old swamps of myth' (W: 74). It is not historical enquiry that the novel opposes, nor is it the content of history, which is after all the stuff of stories. Rather it is the *form* of traditional historiography, what Crick calls that *dry* history, or that 'artificial history', which is critiqued. Throughout the novel, oppositions appear to be set up between natural/artificial, water/land, story/history, and these seem to privilege the first term: natural, water, story. But really, these pairs of opposites are always held in a creative tension, the point being precisely not to exclude either term.

Crick abandons the curriculum with its grand sweep of history and embarks on a different kind of history lesson. In Crick's new history lessons, history is not presented as sequential narrative organising the past into a procession of events. The model of events proceeding in a causal chain was there in Crick's now abandoned history lessons which trawled through the master narratives of modern European history. These were the dry, artificial histories from which myths, stories and so on had been expurgated, and into which an order had been insinuated: an order of human progress based on reason, rational thought and science. But these lessons are interrupted and gradually displaced by local histories and personal memories as the history teacher is forced to reflect on his own past. The narrative path of the novel traces the deviations, returns and odd connections of Crick's memory of past events, stumbling from time to time across a 'golden nugget' of knowledge whose light illuminates the past for a moment. If there is a logic or order to the narrative, and by extension to Crick's 're-memories', it takes a geographical course, metaphorically at least, as time is compared to the twists and turns of the River Ouse flowing through the landscape of the Fens. There is a fluid and sometimes cyclic form to the narrative suggesting not only spatialised history, that is history without direction or order, but also history somehow conforming to *natural* form. This is further reinforced in Crick's explicit denouncement of the *artificial* form of deterministic and foundationalist concepts of history.

This seems consistent with postmodern critiques of historical materialism and of modern narratives of progress, and is consistent with the renewed emphasis on the spatial and geographical dimensions of life discussed earlier in this work. But the use of 'natural' in this context is rather odd, as this seems to displace one kind of metanarrative (broadly based on Enlightenment thinking) with another (with its connotations of natural religion, nature worship and so on). In another context, 'natural' might suggest non-ideological approaches to history, *pure* value-free interpretations of events, but this is not Swift's purpose. Here, nature is clearly used as metaphor, not as an absolute. Forms and processes present in nature are used primarily as sources for the imaginative and cognitive schemata behind the novel's representation of history, rather than to underlie any ideological, mystical or quasi-religious message.

Swift's masterstroke is not to rely simply on nature as a whole for his model, but on particular aspects of the actual geography of the Fens, a place where land and water are constantly at odds. So, history is not expected to follow any particular course or direction, but to issue forth as unpredictably as the results of a battle between two fundamentally incommensurable elements: land and water. The chronotopes of *Waterland* are especially complex as they are called upon to frame and organise not only different periods of history, but different kinds of history and different forms of time, and this is managed through metaphors drawn from the very region that is the subject of the history. In the geological chronotope of enduring time discussed at the end of the previous chapter on *Lanark*, a zero time is preserved as history's bedrock. But the water–land chronotopes of *Waterland* turn history into a kind of structured chaos, a continuing dialectic between surface and depth, movement and stasis, flux and concretisation.

THE FLOWS OF HISTORY AND THE TEXTUALITY OF LANDSCAPE

Waterland theorises another aspect of postmodern historiography, which is the idea that the past can only be accessed via texts, none of which has any privileged claim to truth. History fragments into variform and never finalised assemblages of texts, resisting the closure offered by the selective ordering of events into smooth explanatory narratives. Such grand narratives of history, by their very form, demand omissions and reductions, and lead to the 'natural' hotchpotch of history masquerading as consommé. There is an authentic-looking dictionary definition of History included as an epigraph to the novel –

> *Historia, ae* f. **1**. inquiry, investigation and learning. **2**. a) a narrative of past events, history. b) any kind of narrative: account, tale or story.

This definition uses apparent contradictions of terms (for example, investigation and tale) and a short-circuit back to its own signifier –

history. Presumably this definition is used here to support the history teacher's view in the novel that history is as much about the myths, fairy tales, family legends, and natural histories of a place and its people, as about the learned and institutionalised accumulation and ordering of knowledge that passes for 'official history'. The novel itself interweaves supposedly factual accounts with myths and stories, partly to question or problematise the 'truth' value of official history, but also to show how, in the everyday, stories and myths may have as much currency in human relations as facts gleaned from official history.

One further postmodernist component in the novel, which has already been discussed in the preceding chapter on *Lanark*, is the centre–periphery question and the reassertion of the local. *Waterland* shifts the emphasis in historical enquiry to local detail and local history, pushing world history enacted on the centre stages of London and Paris into the wings. This study of the complexities and mysteries of the Fens – a tiny backwater in the history of the wide world – reveals the rich and subtle texture of local history. But it is not disconnected from the world stage. The history of the rise and fall of the British Empire is here, and the history of two world wars, but these are told from a local perspective and only so far as they intersect with local history. World history is perceived and understood through metaphors drawn from local landscapes and nature, and it is this localised perspective, imagination and cognition that makes the explanatory narratives of myth and history seem at times interchangeable.

Of the novels covered in this study, *Waterland* is the most obvious example of what Linda Hutcheon has called 'historiographic metafiction'. It is a self-reflexive, self-aware narrative that refers to historical events, but simultaneously questions the way we conceive of and represent history. In particular, it questions the means by which historical inquiry sifts historical fact from fiction, and the tendency for the accumulation of historical 'evidence' to be given meaning retrospectively. Implied in all of this is the idea that history, as knowledge, is not objective truth, but a set of narratives or 'texts' which are open to interpretation and reinterpretation, and that fiction, fairy-tale and myth can never be entirely excluded from this. As Linda Hutcheon points out, there is a view (not shared by her, or me) that postmodernism 'relegates history to the dustbin of an obsolete episteme, arguing gleefully that history does not exist except as text'.[2] Obviously, this is not to deny that the past ever existed, only that access to it is 'now entirely conditioned by textuality', and that in terms of knowledge one kind of text has no intrinsic privilege or truth claim over another kind of text (Hutcheon 1988: 16). Textuality is not necessarily limited to writing, of course, and we can also speak of the textuality of images, sounds, memories, buildings, cities and landscapes. It might be more helpful to suggest that the *signified* of history has been relegated, but the discipline of historical enquiry continues, and the many *signifiers* through which the past is traced, including the signifiers of space, still demand to be read. And here we can mark a return to Lefebvre's call for a history of space.

Official history, recorded in text books, might seem to have a prior claim over history recorded in landscape, but when history is inscribed in the 'writing tablet of space', it may be more visible and more apparent. In *Lanark*, Gray draws attention to the textual conditionality of access to the past, first by offering the hero (a figure very like the author) an archival voice which is capable of relating his official history since he arrived in Unthank (L: 103). But to access his deeper past he also needs the Oracle: another storyteller within the text of *Lanark*, released from the hell of his own past by relating the Thaw/Lanark history, as though this process of telling is in itself liberating: 'By describing your life I will escape from the trap of my own.' (L: 116).

The Oracle is beyond the official history in the archive, and beyond the 'water' which represents the threshold of Lanark/Thaw's unconscious. The archive tells Lanark: 'You reached Unthank through water, which is outwith the jurisdiction of the council.' (L: 104). In other words, official history is unable to penetrate beyond the biographical detail of Lanark. To do this he needs another kind of storyteller, one with access to his inner life. Of course, all of this relates to Gray's insistence on being present and not present in the novel. He invents various personae for himself in the novel, and here he tries to explain the writer's paradox of trying to escape the text, while simultaneously trying to discover himself in it. Ultimately, the novel demonstrates that there is no access to the past, especially to the author's own past, which is not conditioned by its own textuality.

This emphasis on the textuality of history in the postmodern undermines the role of history as a firm context for other forms of enquiry. In literature, it relegates history from its position as a realistic pole of representation. In postmodern novels like *Waterland* there is no clear distinction between text (or story) and historical context, but rather a rich surface of intertextuality. Here a dialogic imagination appears to disrupt traditional historiography, allowing diachronic exchange between and across text. In other words, history as a programmatic method of enquiry and univocal account of the past is disrupted by an intertextuality that reopens 'already written' official histories. Rather than letting these histories of place rest as unchallenged and closed metanarratives, they are re-presented together with previously excluded local histories, personal accounts, myths and stories.

In *Waterland*, the retelling of the history of the French Revolution to a class of schoolchildren in the 1970s is interrupted by meandering local and natural histories of the Fens, and by family histories spiralling away from the history teacher, Crick. In several respects, the novel is about the end of history, as Crick's departure from the curriculum partly results from the impending merger of the history department in the school into general studies, making Crick redundant. The end of history is also proclaimed by one of Crick's pupils whose apocalyptic visions of the future unnerve the teacher. If this child has already lost faith in humanity, where is the hope for the future? In this case, perhaps Price's vision of the future will become self-fulfilling: a postmodern generation turning its back on the lessons of the Enlightenment and standing by while the world ends in a 'gigantic traffic jam'.

The novel is also about the ends of history, in the sense of history's function and value, and here it seems to affirm the value of storytelling. For Crick, the human animal is the storytelling animal and retains a basic need for histories to persuade us that things are happening. So, when the grand histories of the world pass us by or when we stop listening to them we produce stories:

> So there's no escaping it: even if we miss the grand repertoire of history, we yet imitate it in miniature and endorse, in miniature, its longing for presence, for feature, for purpose, for content. And there's no saying what consequences we won't risk, what reactions to our actions, what repercussions, what brick towers built to be knocked down, what chasings of our own tails, what chaos we won't assent to in order to assure ourselves that, nonetheless, things are happening.
> (Waterland: 35)

Linda Hutcheon suggests that the postmodern, 'if it is anything', is a 'problematizing force', which 'raises questions about (or renders problematic) the common-sensical and the "natural". But it never offers answers that are anything but provisional and contextually determined (and limited)'.³ We might begin to question this definition in the case of *Waterland*, which Hutcheon includes in her canon of postmodern works, if, as it seems possible, *Waterland* begins to privilege nature and natural history. *Waterland* also refers to essential and natural human traits, like curiosity, as the basis for storytelling and history. It would be wrong to assume that Swift uses nature as a kind of metanarrative in itself. But there is no doubt that he uses nature as the source domain for metaphors targeted at history and the concept of *cultural process*, and there is a structure of opposition between natural process and artificial or cultural process.

Waterland is unusual among British novels set in the countryside, in that it does not allude to the natural beauty of landscape or to any intrinsic value in it. The Fens are not an area usually associated with the literary imagination. They lack the mountains, the wooded hills, and the deep river valleys associated with pastoral and romantic landscapes in literature, and they generally lack the variety in landscape that might contain novels of rural life. The landscape is chosen because of the almost equal presence of water and land, the interaction and interchangeability of these, and the metaphors that can be drawn from this, and it is chosen because it is flat, dull and monotonous.

The text of this landscape does not have a pre-coded romantic or nostalgic signified. It is either used metaphorically, as already discussed, or literally as the context for mundane human and social history. This is not quite the same as the very localised historical accounts and ethnographies of the English countryside found, for example, in Ronald Blythe's *Akenfield*, also set in East Anglia. In Swift's history of the Fens, the narrative is not foreshortened, but stretches back and forth historically and geographically, keying events on the small stage into big events on the world stage. In *Akenfield*, the landscape contains a 'hidden language' or 'convention' that gives it a clear underlying pattern, what Raymond Williams has called 'A critique of a whole dimension of modern life' (Williams 1993: 261). Here, the small sequestered spot, apart in time and space, is revered for its immunity from history, and so a refuge from the modern.

Connected to the critique of modern life in depictions of the countryside, there is also an implicit nostalgia figured in the adult's return to the landscapes of youth. But the landscape of the Fens does not provide the history teacher with cover in which to hide from the present. In a sense, the landscape of the Fens, with its wide-open spaces, denies the psychological hiding places Crick might be searching for. Rather than childhood innocence, he finds guilt and suppressed memories lurking in the unvoiced landscapes of the past. *Waterland* records not only the material and imaginative interaction between the landscape and its inhabitants, it also shows how the recorder, or history teacher, is implicated in the telling of history. He places himself within this history of the Fens, so his own history is bound up in a landscape that maps his imaginative and real life. We are privy to the 'truth' about the storyteller as he uncovers the 'truth' about the Fens its people, and his family.

WATERLAND AS GEOGRAPHICAL IMAGINATION

In *Waterland*, the landscape of the Fens, which is the main setting for the novel, could hardly be more different from that of the Scottish hills used in *Lanark*. Both novels incorporate a 'geographical imagination', in which the world tends to be conceptualised more in a spatial sense than a temporal one, and this use of a geographical imagination is consistent with a general reassertion of spatial concerns within postmodern social and cultural theory, as already discussed.

For Gray, the imaginative reconstruction of Glasgow is a 'real' project, referring to 'real' places and 'real' people, even though the form of the novel often seems 'fantastic'. He uses the imaginative space of the novel to help establish a new representational space for Glasgow. Whereas in *Waterland*, Swift chooses the natural landscapes of the Fens for their metaphorical properties, suggesting, as they do, models of space and time that gel with postmodernist approaches to space, time and history. The water–land chronotope, is derived from the Fens, and the landscape is therefore integral to *Waterland*'s postmodern representation.

The spatial indicators in this water–land chronotope are mainly linked to the flatness, monotony and emptiness of the landscape, and this flatness is used to signify a kind of vacuous reality, a nothingness:

> To live in the Fens is to receive strong doses of reality. The great, flat monotony of reality; the wide, empty spaces of reality. Melancholia and self-murder are not unknown in the Fens. Heavy drinking, madness and sudden acts of violence are not uncommon.
>
> (W: 15)

Spatial Historiographies

The vacancy of this 'reality' demands action of some kind to fill it, even destructive action, just so long as things are happening. In this model, open space signifies timelessness, or prehistory waiting for events to flesh it out. In a textual sense, this aspect of the Fenland landscape provides the blank pages of its history: an unchanging context without a primary text. But such spaces are soon filled, the history teacher suggests, by creating our own fictions:

> I present to you History, the fabrication, the diversion, the reality-obscuring drama. . . for each protagonist who once stepped onto the stage of so-called historical events, there were thousands, millions, who never entered the theatre – who never knew that the show was running – who got on with the donkey-work of coping with reality . . . each one of those numberless non-participants was doubtless concerned with raising in the flatness of his unsung existence his own personal stage, his props and scenery – for there are very few of us who can be, for any length of time, merely realistic.
>
> (W: 34)

Reality here is signified by absence, existence is 'flat' and 'unsung'. To give reality the presence it demands, history appears, rising up as temporal verticality from the flatness of space. And if history cannot bring reality into presence, then either things must be made to happen through plans and schemes, or existence is sung into being through stories and yarns:

> If you are an Atkinson it is not difficult. If you have become prosperous by selling fine quality barley, if you can look down from your Norfolk uplands and see in these level Fens – this nothing-landscape – an Idea, a drawing-board for your plans, you can outwit reality. But if you are born in the middle of that flatness, fixed in it . . .?
> How did the Cricks outwit reality? By telling stories . . . While the Atkinsons made history, the Cricks spun yarns.
>
> (W: 15)

So the Fens were drained and cultivated by the Atkinsons who wrote history, etching it deep into the fabric of the landscape while engaging in local and global geopolitics. But at the same time, alternative realities were written into the landscape as it became 'peopled with ghosts and earnestly recounted legends', such as 'The Singing Swans of Wash Fen Mere, the Monk of Sudchurch, the Headless Ferryman of Staithe' (W: 15). This is the milieu the future history teacher Tom Crick was born into, a landscape in which generations of Cricks and Atkinsons had installed stories and histories side by side. From this same landscape – this metaphorical textbook/storybook – the history teacher from a family of storytellers himself, relates the official history of the Fens interlaced with the yarn of his own childhood. This yarn in turn is inscribed in the landscape, becomes part of the fabric of the Fens, just as the stories of Thomas Hardy map a fictional Wessex on to the counties of Dorset and Wiltshire.

Flatness as temporal vacancy is one quality of the Fens used in the novel's geographical imagination: water is the other. The Fens contain large expanses of water with temporal and spatial implications for the water–land chronotope, but more than this, the Fens are a region in which the interaction between land and water is crucial to the identity of the place. The transparency of water, which lacks colour, taste and odour, suggests non-tactile and non-sensuous 'nothingness' when static and merely lying across the land. According to Crick, the watery Fenlands 'of all landscapes, most approximates to Nothing' (W: 11). This watery flatness has an illusory quality, as well – 'Every Fenman secretly concedes this; every Fenman suffers now and then from the illusion that the land he walks over is *not there*, is floating' (W: 11).

For the adolescent history teacher, exploring his sexuality for the first time with his future wife Mary, in the 'shell of the old windmill by the Hockwell Lode', the 'empty stage' of the Fens beyond with the presence of water, has a dramatic potency, and the dull, flat monotony becomes magical: 'the flat, empty Fens all around us became, too, a miraculous land, became an expectant stage on which magical things could happen' (W: 101). Here, the absence signified by the watery flatness is not history as such, but sex. Sexual desire is written into the expectant stage.

In *Waterland*, landscape is 'both palpable and real' (W: 6), it contains real places represented on maps, but it is also a place that lends itself easily to fairy-tales: 'in misty Fenland settings . . . history merges with fiction, fact gets blurred with fable' (W: 180). In textual terms, it is an ambiguous landscape, one that is 'so regular, so tamed and cultivated', yet one that, for the history teacher, 'would transform itself in my five- or six-year-old mind, into an empty wilderness' (W: 2). In this part-real, part-imaginary, watery landscape, the history teacher learns to 'jump from one realm to another, . . . to live an amphibious life' (W: 180). This is evidence of the metaphorical structure of the novel, the pairing of opposites, here real and imaginary, through a water–land opposition that is in truth not an opposition at all. It is porous boundary across which an 'amphibious life' learns to jump.

The deconstruction of water–land oppositions is particularly suitable in a postmodern context, suggesting indeterminacy and ambivalence at a metaphorical, but also at a natural, elementary level. Through a geographical imagination, various kinds of texts are juxtaposed, removed from their different contexts and superimposed truth regimes. The flatness and emptiness that signifies an empty page; the tamed and cultivated 'dry' history books; the misty, watery myths and legends, interact in the interconnected water-landscape. There is no textual dichotomy here with, on the one hand, verifiable facts and history signified by land, and on the other, myths, legends and fictions signified by water, because the water-landscape signifies constant interaction and exchange between the two. In the Fens, land and water, like fact and fiction are never finally differentiated.

Similarly, in the water–land chronotope, in which land might signify space, and water, time, the interaction and interchangeability denies differentiation. In a simple, non-dynamic analogy, land might stand for the spatial, and the flows of water running through it, might stand for temporality. But land is gradually eroded by the water and deposited elsewhere as silt. Siltation restricts the flows of water and changes its course, and so by analogy, space has an effect on the flow of time, or temporality. Similarly, the temporal flow alters the space through which it passes. Nothing on earth escapes the hand of time, but in this analogy, time likewise cannot escape the presence, or absence of space. And then, of course, the space–time model must be extended to allow for the hand of man.

The interference of man in nature has a long history, as the history teacher tells us in the novel, beginning, in the case of the Fens, in the seventeenth century when the water-logged land was first systematically drained. So, to the natural processes of erosion and siltation, can be added the human process of land reclamation, draining, dredging and pumping; an artificial process, and one which, while sometimes working with nature and sometimes against, never dominates nature.

In the water–land chronotope, water signifies both space and time. It is time when flowing and returning but space when lying across the landscape. Land also shifts between signifieds. It is space when cultivated and built upon, but time when siltation (the interaction of water and land) shifts its matter, unmaking it and making it again in some other place. There is no deep, vertical time here, as there is in the geological chronotope of *Lanark*. The horizontal nature of the water–land chronotope is crucial to what it is being asked to convey regarding the passing and accumulation of historical time, progress and development.

In *Waterland*, the chronotope of water–land is key to the novel's postmodernist strategy, because in incorporating the flows and returns of the water, the time horizon of the chronotope cannot be linear or progressive. If the water simply kept moving in cycles in an uninterrupted and eternal return, time would be revolutionary in one sense, but it would not move on, it could not produce the giant ruptures in history that social revolution requires, and it would be predictable. The River Ouse suggests return:

> So that while the Ouse flows to the sea, it flows, in reality, like all rivers, only back to itself, to its own source; and that impression that a river moves only one way is an illusion. And it is also an illusion that what you throw (or push) into a river will be carried away, swallowed for ever, and never return. Because it will return. And that remark first put about, two and a half thousand years ago, by Heraclitus of Epheseus, that we cannot step twice into the same river, is not to be trusted. Because we are always stepping into the same river.
>
> (W: 127)

But in the water–land chronotope time is not cyclic, even without the hand of man, nature is already a flux of making and unmaking. So, the cyclic time figured in the return of the River Ouse to its source is complicated by the micro-geography of meanders, erosion and siltation. And the hand of man is unable entirely to transform this geography into the straight lines or verticality of progress. In the water–land chronotope, a progressive linear time of materialist and deterministic histories is opposed by a twisting and a turning, and an urge for time and the river to repeat itself:

> How it repeats itself, how it goes back on itself, no matter how we try to straighten it out. How it twists, turns. How it goes in circles and brings us back to the same place . . .
>
> (W: 123)

This river, meandering through the Fenlands, has its origins in prehistory like the geological chronotope in *Lanark*, but time is not inscribed in a river, so it does not suggest a deep, enduring time, like a rock face. A river, by its very fluidity can have no time structure, or architectonics, and in this sense it has no history. The form of the river may suggest eternity and return, but the watery content of the river is a kind of anti-history, possessing 'a secret capacity to move yet remain' (W: 125). Time, as Crick suggests, has no direction and no structure:

> There are no compasses for journeying in time. As far as our sense of direction in this unchartable dimension is concerned, we are like lost travellers in a desert. We believe we are going forward, towards the oasis of Utopia. But how do we know . . . that we are not moving in a great circle?
>
> (W: 117)

Again we return to histories as a substitute for the missing structure in time. It is a basic human need, suggests Crick, not to leave behind us an empty space, a watery nothing. Somehow man needs to place markers in the past to trace his course:

> Wherever he goes he wants to leave behind not a chaotic wake, not an empty space, but the comforting marker-bouys and trail signs of stories.
>
> (W: 53)

The form of time suggested by the river, with its meandering and returns, is mirrored in the novel's narrative where deviation and a non-chronological presentation of events dominate the mode of telling. For example, the idea of return suggested by the River Ouse can be found in the storyline in the novel.

In this confessional novel, as Crick moves in cycles through his memory, objects with symbolic power keep returning. Events that have not been satisfactorily dealt with in the past cannot be flushed away in the river: they return to haunt. So, the beer bottle that dealt the fatal blow to Freddie Parr, and the eel that travels from the Ouse to the Sargasso Sea and back again, and most importantly, the foetus of Henry and Mary Crick's unborn child, all return as a recurring past that punctures the thin envelope of the here and now. The past rushes into the present, and the present connects with the past.

The time horizon of this water–land chronotope is not a constant reference point outwith a cycle of continuous creation, as it is in the 'geological' chronotope of *Lanark*. It is in this sense more concerned with the process of history than the structural accumulation of time. In *Waterland*, natural landscape suggests only provisional foundations, subject to being washed away. It is precisely because it has this quality of rootlessness and placelessness that Swift uses the landscape of the Fens as the main setting and chronotope of the novel. Here, place contains within itself the elements of change that allow it to transform itself, in a mutating, chaotic, evolutionary way; and then against this apparent chaos, man endeavours to build homes, and establish livelihood and commercial enterprise. Structure and chaos seem to coexist under the same roof. The process of land reclamation is a structural activity essential to man's continuing presence in this landscape, and it is, Crick suggests, a realistic model for human progress and modern civilisation:

> There's this thing called progress. But it doesn't progress. It doesn't go anywhere. Because as progress progresses the world can slip away. It's progress if you can stop the world slipping away. My humble model for progress is the reclamation of land. Which is repeatedly, never-endingly retrieving what is lost. A dogged and vigilant business. A dull yet valuable business. . . But you shouldn't go mistaking the reclamation of land for the building of empires.
>
> (W: 291)

This model of progress is clearly set against foundationalist and positivist models. In the water–land chronotope, the indicators of space and time, signified by land and water, constantly interact and undermine the building of futures through concrete and absolute principles.

A hero in this landscape is Dick, Tom Crick's half-brother: a 'natural', 'a fish of a man', who works the dredger and reclaims the land. Dick is unable to read or write, and so is disconnected from the text of his past. In contrast to his brother the history teacher, with his 'dry' history books, Dick is watery, and of the present – the 'Here and Now' – until the dreadful moment of realisation that places him in history, or rather misplaces him in a distorted and unnatural branch of the Crick family tree. For Dick is a short-circuit in history, the issue of a father and daughter incestuous relationship. Soon after opening the chest containing the signs of his past: the bottle that became a murder weapon, and the letter that spelt out his unnatural parentage, he is tracked down in the final scene of the narrative. His life ends as he plunges 'In a long, reaching, powerful arc' (W: 309) into the sea. This odd return of the fish-like Dick to the sea – 'He's on his way. Obeying instinct. Returning. The Ouse flows to the sea . . . ' (W: 310) – brings to an end the history teacher's narrative. It is a kind of sacrifice and it marks the end of Crick's confession, an end to delving into the detritus of the past to find the truth. Figuratively, Dick is the 'saviour of the world' because it is he who operates the dredger, he keeps scooping up the silt – the detritus of the past that time leaves behind but which can always be brought back into the present:

> And yet it has to be done. Because it won't go away. It gathers, congeals, no matter what's going on in the busy world above. Because silt, as we know, is the builder and destroyer of land, the subverter of rivers, the foe of drainage. There's no simple solution. We have to keep scooping, scooping up from the depths this remorseless stuff that time leaves behind.
> (W: 299)

Dick is also the saviour of the world, because he stops it sliding away; he keeps the water flowing, so time can move on and the dry land can be safe for habitation. In the land-reclamation model of progress, Dick is indispensable because he holds fast the present, bringing the past back into the present to shore it up against the vagaries of time. Dick's business is with the present, not with history:

> He's here. He knows his place. He knows his station. He keeps the ladders turning, the buckets scooping. The noise of the churning machinery drowns the fleeting aerial clamour of global strife. He hears no bombers, sees no bombers. And the smell of silt is the smell of sanctuary is the smell of amnesia. He's here, he's now. Not there or then. No past, no future. He's the mate of the *Rosa II*.
> And he's the saviour of the world . . .
> (W: 308)

NATURAL AND ARTIFICIAL

Although the Fens are the main locale for the stories and histories in *Waterland*, the classroom in Greenwich, from which Crick revisits his past and delivers his meandering history lesson, is another place used in the novel to signify a particular concept of space and time. The chronotope of this classroom spans the whole narrative, but is removed from the Fens, away from nature and natural processes, and Crick describes children in this artificial environment as 'suspended, encaged like animals removed from a natural habitat'(W: 51). It is from here that the history teacher looks out to the 'natural' landscapes of his childhood.

Where the Atkinson's looked down on the Fens from the relative high ground of the barley fields of Norfolk, and saw future opportunities in the 'drawing board' of empty space, the history teacher looks out to the Fens for the opportunity to unravel his past, and uncover the causes and consequence that might make sense of the here and now for him.

The classroom is located in Greenwich, near the Observatory where there are stored the 'antique chronometers, astrolabes, sextants, telescopes – instruments for measuring the universe' (W: 128). The site is significant as England's historical site for the scientific measurement of space and time. It was here that reference systems for dividing and bounding the world were developed, and here that the modern world was 'fixed' in a net of geographical coordinates, with Greenwich the zero space–time, from which the rest of the world was marked out.

When Crick describes the classroom in Greenwich as like a cage in which children are removed from their 'natural habitat', he suggests an opposition between the natural and the unnatural or artificial world, which is repeated elsewhere in the novel. The Fens are largely treated as a natural habitat in the novel, and the natural processes that are embedded in its (water-)landscapes are widely used as metaphor. But historically, the Fens also signify a raw and untamed nature, more water than land, and resistant to cultivation and occupation.

The water–land opposition is used in a conflict within this cultural history, between man's attempt to drain the land, and nature's insistent return of water and silt. The Fens are a marginal site between nature and culture, between those who live by water and those who live by land. There were the reactionaries, fowlers, fishermen and reedcutters, who were eventually ousted or marginalised by the modernisers as they set about draining the land. In this battle, Crick's ancestors were involved – they 'speared fish and netted ducks' and were found 'amongst the lists of those summarily dealt with for sabotaging drainage works' (W: 9). But the Cricks gave up the water and like most people, changed sides:

> They ceased to be water people and became land people; they ceased to fish and fowl and became plumbers of the land. They joined in the destiny of the Fens, which was to strive not for but against water.
>
> (W: 11)

Those who did not join the Cricks on the land were forced into a reclusive existence on the edge of the land. In the novel, Bill and Martha Clay still hold out on the margins of modern society, bypassed by history. Theirs is a watery life with few links to the land and fewer to modernity. Living entirely within a natural environment, self-sufficient, and immersed in natural processes, they are not rooted in solid ground, but eke out an existence from the water in a strange floating rootedness. But Bill and Martha Clay, although an oddity, have an important function in the novel, as it is they who perform the abortion of Mary's child, the rupture in the flow of human history which is at the heart and is the origin of the Crick's woes.

MODERNISATION AND GEOPOLITICS

In the cultural history of the Fens, the Atkinsons represent modernity. They are the modern architects of the future in the Fens as they drain the land for their own enterprises and connect them to the wide world via the waterways and railways they construct. The more the Atkinson enterprises become established, the more the land becomes developed and, in a sense, the further removed from nature its inhabitants become. For the modern, progressive businessmen of the Fens, imagination is fired by the potential of empty spaces in the natural landscape:

> The man who builds a malting house at Kessling and has the keys of the river will bring wealth to a wasteland. And himself.
>
> (W: 58)

Here the natural landscape is unexploited, and so a wasteland. But attempts to master the landscape and so control the future, although successful for a time, are limited. When the Atkinsons connect their local agri-ventures to the national interest and to international trade, they are, as Arthur Atkinson proclaims in 1874, 'not masters of the present, but servants of the future' (W: 81).

In Crick's history lesson, the 'Idea of Progress' that energised the Atkinson venture comes under scrutiny when 'land reclamation in the eastern Fens become[s] confused with the Empire of Great Britain' (W: 80). This is a lesson on the rise and fall of Empire, and it is being told through the rise and fall of a local enterprise connected to that larger history, and enacting it in miniature. This is a post-imperial perspective on history, the other end of the history that began with the French Revolution. And this is a view of history in which progress does not continue into the future, but reaches a zenith and declines. What begins as a simple domination of nature and the exploitation of the wastelands of the Fens moves out into the world at large as an imperial, capitalist and colonialist domination of space, which Crick seems to suggest could never be sustained. And so now he is standing in a history class trying to explain that a progressive idea of history was important to modernity, especially to the development of the British Empire, but that zenith is now long passed and so it is time for a new postmodern model of history.

In 1874, however, the Atkinsons had not yet reached their zenith, and world trade, capital and enterprise began to connect the Fens to the rest of the world, as though this region was a tiny river 'paying tribute' to the 'National Interest' (W: 80). The Fens are transformed from a natural place, 'a little Fenland outpost, once but a mud hump with a wattle chapel, once so removed from the wide world' (W: 80), into an important modern site, in which nature is dominated, and time marches on into the future. But as Crick asks, 'Is there no end to the advance of commerce?' (W: 79). Can it continue in a straight line through history, and if so, to what purpose? From a postmodern and post-imperial perspective, of course, there is an end to this particular advance, and it seems unlikely that such confidence in the future will re-establish itself for some time. A postmodern idea of progress is inevitably one in which foundations are shaky, and at best provisional, not a sound basis for building empires.

In the fate of the Atkinson enterprise and of the British Empire, Crick introduces an unpredictable, but ultimately inevitable, decline consistent with his model for progress figured in the water–land chronotope. It is this definitively postmodern chronotope that dictates that progress cannot continue as a straight line through history. Unpredictability is an integral part of the model, so there are only coarse probabilities and contingencies, no certainties and no absolutes.

NATURAL RETURNS

Old Crick is not always so postmodernist in appropriating nature for his analogies. Although the water–land model is mostly used as metaphor, there are times when Crick suggests that natural laws which govern the processes of nature, are also determining factors in human behaviour:

what water makes it also unmakes. Nothing moves far in this world. And whatever moves forward will also move back. It is the law of the natural world; and a law too of the human heart . . .

(W: 63)

We might wonder where such sympathies belong in a postmodern novel. Could it be that Crick, the unenlightened history teacher, is hankering for the pre-modern, an age before things all went wrong, not a time *without* history which might be found in postmodernity, but a time *before* history?:

> How we yearn . . . to return to that time before history claimed us, before things went wrong. How we yearn even for the gold of a July evening on which, though things had already gone wrong, things had not gone as wrong as they were going to. How we pine for Paradise. For mother's milk. To draw back the curtain of events that has fallen between us and the Golden Age.
>
> (W: 118)

In the *culs-de-sac* of modernity, where the regressions of a modern industrial and scientific age undermine its advances, it is hardly surprising that an 'insidious longing to go backwards . . . begets this pampered child, Nostalgia' (W: 118).

But this is of course a futile longing and, if anything, natural law precludes such returns; so why does the otherwise postmodern history teacher entertain such ideas? There would seem to be two likely reasons. First, Crick is at a moment of crisis in his life (although his wife is perhaps the one who deserves the more sympathy), and while he revisits the past to find the answer to his present woes, he cannot help finding a place back there free of present concerns. Second, and more worryingly, the patterning of modernity with the unnatural coupled with the privileging of the natural might suggest a anti-modern (as opposed to postmodern) flight from the present, based on some absolute truth offered by nature. In a world threatened by pollution and the exhaustion of natural resources, the troublesome pupil Price claims there is no point to history because it is all about to end in an apocalyptic 'traffic jam' (W: 256). But there is little evidence elsewhere in the novel to suggest that Swift is trying to promote any kind of anti-modern (or post-postmodern) ecologism or Green politics.

The two world wars are described as events that did not oppose nature in the Fens as the cultivation of the land did, but they perverted it. In the First World War, the men of the Fens swap the maintenance of the land in East Anglia for the digging of trenches in the muddy fields of Flanders, and in the Second, the Fens become home to 'V-forming squadrons' of 'twentieth-century skeins' heading for Hamburg with their 'explosive and inflammatory eggs' (W: 258). Here the perversion of nature is represented in the translation of V-shaped formations of wildfowl, naturally found in the Fens, to flights of bombers heading out to flatten German cities; and eggs that would normally carry new life are here the bombs destined to wreak destruction, and end it.

Chaos and Structure: Nature and the Postmodern

In *Waterland*, a model of natural processes involving the interaction of water and land in the Fens is a great source of metaphor for describing human and social affairs, especially those related to history, progress and the mapping of futures. If we examine this source domain in more detail, it seems to be based on a binary opposition between land and water, the one solid and structural, and the other chaotic and unstructured. But the land and water coexist and interact with each other in unpredictable and indeterminate ways, and they sometimes seem to be interchangeable, with silt being an intermediate state.

The results of the interaction of water and land are unpredictable, although in general, land is eroded by water, and carried to another place where it reforms as sediment into another structure. By using this tension between chaos and structure in the natural world, a model is introduced into the target domain of human and social affairs and history, in which there is no customary dialectic between progressive or revolutionary forces and reactionary forces, only a constant tension between the status quo and its undirected self-questioning. In the relativistic and differential model that emerges in the target domain, opposing forces are capable of mutating and turning back on themselves. This model is not directed by any particular goals or values, and it can easily unmake whatever it makes. It is, on all these counts, a postmodern model.

Using natural processes as the bases for his model, Swift enables chaos and structure to coexist, and this is different from the customary dichotomy in modernist thought of society as structure and nature as chaos (or vice versa in anti-modern thinking). This representation of nature and natural process, as I have already indicated, is consistent with postmodernist thinking, but it also has resonance in contemporary scientific thought. Since the 1970s, 'deterministic chaos', in which an object might behave randomly yet still operate within certain bounds, has become an established branch of mathematics, and is increasingly used in modelling weather systems and other 'natural' events and phenomena. Mathematical models and models of natural processes begin to share characteristics here rather than oppose each other, a theme explored by Tom Stoppard in his play *Arcadia* (1993).[4] In a postmodernist context, this seems to indicate a shift from the dynamics of development and modernisation, to the interrelationship of structure and chaos, like the 'chaotic equilibrium' recently discovered in the mathematics of natural processes.

CONCLUSION

The use of natural history and a geographical imagination in *Waterland* seems to have a dual function. Firstly, it questions or 'problematises' the chronotope of traditional historical narrative with its developmental and deterministic themes, which rely on the idea of progressive linear time and causality. In this function, *Waterland*, seems to conform to Linda Hutcheon's definition of 'historiographic metafiction'. But there is also a secondary role or effect when the organising chronotope of historical development is replaced by one of natural landscape, because this suggests a valuing of nature and natural processes over historical and deterministic process. This becomes apparent as the realistic pole of representation and the organising metaphor for the novel shifts from history, to nature and natural process (although history is still used to establish the local context). This might suggest a return to romantic, regressive or theistic elements inherent in English literary representations of nature, especially in the pastoral, where the natural world often promises a refuge from the ills of the world. But in the novel, although Crick's history lessons might take him back to the landscapes of his childhood, there is no refuge for him here. The landscape is punctuated by sharp reminders of the 'Here and Now', which emerge as he comes across suppressed memories and guilt.

Landscape is given a number of roles here: it is the 'real' stage for events; a psychological landscape in which the history teacher explores private histories and concealed guilt; a trace of the social history 'written' into its features; and by drawing on this particular landscape's interaction with land and water, a metaphor for visualising historical time and progress. Nature and natural processes are here promoted over civilisation and artificial processes as the novel draws on natural processes as a source of metaphor for questioning deterministic and foundationalist approaches to history. But one of the problems the novel has in its multiple use of landscape is restricting this privileging of nature and natural process to the metaphorical domain. It is difficult at times to see just how far Swift is taking the metaphor, and at times the novel seems to suggest that there really are universal natural laws, superior to those derived from rational thought, logic and scientific determinism, and these govern not only nature, but also human and social behaviour.

In the novel, Swift certainly undermines deterministic and progressive approaches to history and, using the water–land chronotope, he adopts a broadly postmodernist strategy, questioning assumptions about the direction and nature of time. But perhaps he also shows a desire to ground the postmodern fluidity that the water–land chronotope suggests, in something universal and dependable. It seems significant that he uses the River Ouse to represent an idea of 'return', governed by natural law, and this suggests a dependable, cyclic form of time, unlike both the linear time of deterministic history and the chaotic equilibrium suggested by the water–land chronotope. I would not like to overstate the significance of Swift's use of the river here though, because the river, and the 'return' it signifies has another function, which is to control narrative time, and bring together the many disparate strands of the plot. It would also be rather odd if Swift really did undermine his postmodernist water–land chronotope with an anachronistic faith in 'natural law'.

These 'problems' in *Waterland* are chiefly caused by the tendency in the postmodern novel to use several different forms of time. Here, different forms of time are used to order the narrative, to establish a conceptual model for progress, and to arrange the novel's argument about history. In the next chapter we find that the temporal axis of the postmodern chronotope is further complicated by the use of non-linear time, not only to order the narrative, but also to problematise reality.

CHAPTER 6

Chronotopes of Reversible Time:
Peter Ackroyd, *Hawskmoor* and *First Light*
Ian McEwan, *The Child in Time*

FORMS OF TIME AND THE POSTMODERN NOVEL

It is typical of postmodern novels to organise narrative time in non-linear fashion and to juxtapose disparate time–spaces. Story lines are fragmented, ruptured and reversed and, to some extent, this has become a matter of postmodern style, a fashion. Of course, there is nothing new in fragmented and disrupted story lines or temporal displacement in fiction. The epic begins in the middle, retraces the beginning and closes with the end, a convention self-consciously alluded to in Alasdair Gray in *Lanark*. And in modernist fiction especially, but not exclusively, narrative time often follows the non-linear logic of the conscious and unconscious mind, as in dreams or in the imagined private experience of time. In utopian fictions, temporal displacement occurs through the relocation of elements from present society into a nowhere place, a place outside time and space. But these are examples in which non-linear time and temporal displacement are more or less literary devices used to present imaginative extensions into internal or unreal time–spaces. They are, in other words, mainly examples of the use of non-linear time and temporal displacement as a matter of *form*. Reality itself is hardly troubled by such chronotopes, because these are distanced from the real.

But in the chronotopes of the postmodern novel, non-linear time and temporal displacement cannot be simply accounted for as literary device, here they seem to shake the very cornerstones of reality – linear time and extensive, contiguous space. Non-linear time and temporal displacement in postmodern novels problematise the real by calling into question scientific laws that govern the temporality of the modern world, and by questioning social and cultural constructions of time that underpin western versions of reality. The possibility of non-linear time, or the ability to travel back and forth within historical time, also exists in fiction before the postmodern novel, most notably in science fiction and in fantasy.

Non-linear time in the postmodern novel follows this tradition, and many postmodern novels could be classified as science fiction or fantasy. But in the postmodern novel, non-linear time is somehow incorporated into the fabric of the real rather than distanced from it, with the effect that reality is problematised rather more explicitly. In the non-linear time of postmodern novels, there may be no explanations as to how or why characters cross into different historical periods, or how time can seem to go backwards, or how a character can remember something that happened before he was born.

In postmodern science fiction, cyberspace is often the means by which alternative time–spaces are actualised and, in the tradition of science fiction, this offers technological explanations for things that have not yet happened, but which conceivably could in the future. But in postmodern novels such as Peter Ackroyd's *Hawksmoor*, there are no rational explanations for the time slips that occur between the eighteenth and twentieth centuries and, in some respects, the novel is a problematisation of that rational thinking that seeks causality and linearity.

In Ackroyd's *First Light*, there is half an explanation for the strange reversals of time based in the theory that an expanding universe that creates space–time cannot expand forever, and when it begins to contract, then time itself must go into reverse. It has been predicted that this moment will show itself to us on earth as a change in the wavelength of light (red–blue colour shift) received from the edge of the universe, and this 'first and last light' will be the signal that cosmological time is in reverse. But *First Light* uses an improbable version of this scientific theory to organise an imaginative return to prehistory, a return which is already suggested by the neolithic sites scattered around the region of southern England where the novel is set.

In the chronotopes of postmodern novels, non-linear time and temporal displacement are often integral to the thematic structure and *content* of the novel: they are not just sylistic elements of the novel. Although there are sometimes rational explanations for the reversals of time and time slips in these chronotopes, they are designed to problematise scientific, social and cultural constructions of time, constructions that are associated with western concepts of reality. Non-linear time in particular has a number of political and ideological implications in the postmodern novel. This is most clearly the case in Ian McEwan's, *The Child in Time*, where the time of childhood is becoming re-institutionalised as a political act, where one man regresses into childhood, and another man is able to enter a moment of time between his conception and his birth. This is a political novel, and one that recognises time as a persuasive social construction rather than the hard-edged and incontrovertible reality that supports the tyranny of the clock.

Although this chapter is mainly concerned with non-linear time and temporal displacement in the postmodern novel, it also contains some discussion about the nature of time and the many different forms that time can take. In the chronotopes of the postmodern novel it is common to find multiple forms of time being used, sometimes as metaphor, sometimes to organise the story-line, and sometimes as explicit problematisation of the real. This multiplicity of forms of time is consistent with postmodernist eclecticism in times and spaces, a common feature of the postmodern chronotope. To help clarify the terms used for different forms of time, I offer a brief summary of definitions:

- **ecological time** – cyclical and continuous, and corresponding to natural cycles, rhythms, and pulses; the time of nature

- **geological time** – long enduring time containing the complete span of earth's time as a base line, occasionally eruptions of the new, but mainly a time of endurance and very slow decay

- **biological time** – delimited by birth and death, a time of growth, but of eventual and inevitable decline in a short time-scale (relative to geological or cosmological time); in humans, the irreversible time of ageing that breeds nostalgia and fosters age-old dreams of reversing or halting the ageing process

- **historical time** – as chronology, elapsed and completed time, and records of the past, but chronological data is often reordered and reformed to suit demands of present-day society; as narrative, no longer the time of history, but of *writing* history – historiographic time

- **thermodynamic time** – an irreversible time of increasing disorder and decay; often associated, especially in nineteenth century thinking, with causality

- **cosmological time** – the time created by the universe expanding, and so inextricably linked to space; space and time are interchangeable here

- **social time** – the real time of a given social group, constituted and perpetuated by varying and conflicting requirements of members of that group; plural and like social space *produced* through social interaction; organised as embeddedness, stratification and synchronisation, which correspond to *place*, *class* and *technique*[1]

- **psychological time** – the *lived* time of experience, the time of being and becoming but also of memory; the time in which we remember the past, but not the future; dream time, imagination

- **clock time** – calibrates the passage of the earth around the sun; originally an analogue of the sun's passage reflected in sundials, and then in mechanical faces on which a hand depicts the hours of the day (and night); relative to longitudinal position and therefore used for calculating longitude; used for synchronising meetings, events, and communications of all kinds; clock time today is usually presented digitally (or in simulated clock faces) from electronically-generated pulses.

The form of time that dominates the chronotopes of *Waterland* is ecological time because the source domain for the novel's metaphorical structure is nature. Ecological time is used here to conceive of alternative forms of historical and social time, and especially to insinuate natural forms into modern constructions of historical time. The dominance of ecological time is evidence of a *geographical* imagination entering this reflection on history. This introduces an ambiguity into historical time. If it is like the River Ouse, as Crick suggests in *Waterland*, then it *both* progresses and returns. This insinuation of ecological time into historical time, in a postmodern context, is surely an attempt to question the hegemony of the future-directed, linear time perspective often associated with modern societies, and so inscribed as social time.

In anything other than a postmodern context, such insinuation of ecological time into historical time might look like a return to the time perspectives often found in pre-modern societies. In such societies, both social and historical time are based on myths of eternal return, grounded in the cycles and rhythms of nature and some understanding of cosmological time. A few pre-modern (or rather non-modern) societies can still be found living on into the twentieth century. Sociologists Pierre Bourdieu and Bronislaw Malinowski find that time in such societies is experienced in a less quantitative way. Historical time is only used for remembering a particularly good season, and so is qualitative rather than quantitative. There is no attempt here systematically to map or give meaning to the past, and no attempt to extrapolate into the future.[2]

In modern societies, social life has become severed from nature and the cosmos, and so social time has lost that simple order. As a result, modern man searches for alternative systems of belief, such as science and historical materialism, so that he might master history, rationalise it and bring it to a conclusion. As John Hassard puts it, 'Modern man seeks refuge in several forms of faith in order to rationalise a process that seems to have neither beginning or end' (Hassard 1990: 9).³ This rationalisation involves the analysis of time that has already elapsed and Gurvitch suggests that this process 'lures us into forecasting the past' and 'projecting this prediction into the future' (Gurvitch 1990: 74).

It seems reasonable to assume that in modernity it has been an attempt to rationalise the past and predict the future that gives rise to a linear time perspective. And, as John Hassard claims, a linear time perspective has been crucial to modern ideas of progress:

> ... it is during the evolution of industrial capitalism that the hegemony of a linear time perspective is cemented. For the industrial age, progress is the key. Here the past is unrepeatable, the present is transient, and the future is infinite and exploitable. Time is homogenous; it is objective, measurable, and infinitely divisible; it is related to change in the sense of motion and development; it is quantitative'.
>
> (Hassard, 1990: 12)

This is precisely the form of time challenged in the water–land chronotope of *Waterland*, where cyclic and chaotic elements of ecological time are introduced as metaphors. In this chapter, the emphasis is on the multiplicity of social time. For Georges Gurvitch, whose work has done much to reveal the complexities and plural nature of social time, the problems of historical time might be reduced to the fact that it has already *elapsed*, and is already *completed*. Historical time is a reconstructed time imposed on the past (Gurvitch 1990: 74). Social time, on the other hand, is 'in the process of happening', and constructed more in the present. It is more diverse than historical time, concerned more with everyday life and with the different experiences of time of different social groups.

The linear time perspective of industrial capitalism still dominates western society but, in postmodernity, other ways of seeing time are emerging from scientific, cultural and anthropological studies. In Stephen Hawking's *A Brief History of Time*, the assumption that time has a particular direction is challenged through various developments in cosmology and theoretical physics. In Bronislaw Malinowski's and Pierre Bourdieu's studies of the time perspectives of non-western cultures, the hegemony of western forms of time is challenged. New forms of capitalism in postmodernity rely less on the idea of progress demanded by industrial capitalism. Time in late capitalism is sometimes conceived as a perpetual present, so fast are the processes of production and exchange.

In the postmodern novel, the re-presentation of historical time is common, and this may be offered as a challenge to the imposition of a western historiography on events that might well have been experienced differently by the different participants in the historical moment. Re-presentation might also problematise the very assumptions of historiography to bring the past to a conclusion. But when the postmodern novel attempts to present alternative and irreconcilable versions of history through disruptive narrative procedures, it may run into problems with the modern sensibilities and perceptual apparatus of the modern reader who, detective-like, restores the fragments of narrative to a linear and casual sequence. When it is reassembled by the reader, the narrative of *Waterland* is like that of a traditional realist novel, with its detective work, suspense and disclosure, all of which still suggests a dominant linearity, despite all the questioning of linearity contained within the novel.

Postmodern novels that explore non-linear time as a reality, rather than use it metaphorically, are not so easy to reassemble into a linear narrative. Here, suspension, circularity and discontinuity is not just a narrative device, it also requires the reader to entertain non-directional time as a reality – i.e. to conceive of time not predisposed to travel in any particular direction. This is not so much a contemplation of historical time, as a way of evading it: a way of passing back and forth through history. The chronotopes of such novels either reverse the arrow of time, or juxtapose historically discontinuous time frames. The nature and direction of time is a major theme in these novels, and this is not only to look back to pre-modern concepts of cyclical time, whether magical, mythological or 'natural', but also to look to the present, especially to models of space–time developed in physics and cosmology.

This is very much the case in Peter Ackroyd's *First Light*, and Ian McEwan's *The Child in Time*. Peter Ackroyd's *Hawksmoor* does both, as a postmodern detective equipped with the latest techniques for reconstructing crime scenes is forced backwards in time to try to solve a series of murders. The particular period of time he needs to return to is significant because it marks the beginnings of modern science and an end to seventeenth century mysticism.

In postmodernity, scientific imagination is no longer steeped in the laws of thermodynamics, or informed by a thermodynamic arrow of time. Scientific imagination today is steeped in quantum theory, chaos theory, and Heisenberg's Uncertainty Principle, and as the terms suggest, these theories deal not in causality and certainty, but in spectra of probability, simultaneity and reversibility. As Thelma, the physicist in *The Child in Time*, tells Stephen when he is *lost in time*, contemporary physics offers much to help us re-imagine space and time and lift us out of the straitened causal perspective that has dominated western thought since the Enlightenment:

> 'Who do you want? Luther? Copernicus? Darwin? Marx? Freud? None of them has re-invented the world and our place in it as radically and bizarrely as the physicists of this century have. The measurers of the world can no longer detach themselves. They have to measure themselves too. Matter, time, space, forces – all beautiful and intricate illusions in which we must now collude. . . Shakespeare would have grasped wave functions, Donne would have understood complementarity and relative time. They would have been excited. What richness! They would have plundered this new science for their imagery. And they would have educated their audiences too.'
> (*A Child in Time*: 44–5)

Later in this chapter, *The Child in Time* is itself examined to see how it exploits this new science for its imagery, but I will begin this exploration of non-linear time and temporal displacement in the postmodern novel with *Hawksmoor*.

MAKING TIME: ARCHITECTURE AND THE BOOK IN *HAWKSMOOR*

Hawksmoor uses a double time-frame containing two more or less separate and interleaved narratives that share a common locale. Most of the crossover between the two narrative strands is achieved through a kind of literary deception that relies on echoes, repeating motifs, and casual coincidences. Clearly there are two worlds colliding here, and the reader is asked to find connections, partly for the pleasure of making a whole and partly to confront conflicting ideologies and concepts of space and time within and between the two worlds.

The two narratives are divided by three centuries of historical time and, in this complex chronotope, the mysticism that is being routed in the eighteenth century narrative by modern science and rational thinking seems to be necessary to allow the narratives to converge. In other words, the novel as a whole seems to depend on pre-modern concepts of time and space for it to work. At the same time, the modern science available to the detective, Hawksmoor is never going to solve the mystery. It is a trick then, because the postmodern reader's desire to bring the mystery to a conclusion, to close the text, is only to be satisfied by entertaining the non-linear time of a mysticism that was driven underground in the eighteenth century by modern science and rational thinking.

Hawksmoor has a self-conscious and playful approach to time and history, seeming to delight in its own trickery, allusions and word play. The sense is of lightly touching parallel worlds that the process of reading seems to connect. In some ways it is a ghost story, a chilling tale of existence outside the time–spaces of material worlds, and of irrational contingencies. But on another level it is a postmodern reworking of certain basic assumptions underlying modern thought, especially concerning the nature of space and time, and the emphasis in modernity on a material, phenomenal and quantifiable approach to existence.

The historical chronotope to which the novel returns – early eighteenth century London – is chosen because it marks a time and a place when the ascendancy of modern thought, as it emerges from Englightenment thinking, displaces earlier belief systems, marginalising and even criminalising them. The contemporary chronotope of London in the 1970s is chosen because it seems to mark the decline of that modern rationalist thinking championed by the Royal Society. Sir Christopher Wren, the architect of St Paul's Cathedral, and a leading figure in the Royal Society, appears in the novel as the butt of many of its time-slipping jokes. From a postmodern perspective, it is significant that both *Waterland* and *Hawksmoor* look critically at the Enlightenment as the beginning of a particular consciousness of time, and then revisit the time of its making to rework it. *Hawksmoor*, especially, questions the concept of quantitative and linear time arising out of Enlightenment thinking.

In *Hawksmoor*, Ackroyd uses a double time-frame to stage a conflict between different constructions of social time, and through these, the ideologies that underlie those constructions. The dual time consciousness in the novel raises a number of questions about the constitution of social time then and now. In the historical context of the eighteenth century, the novel also explores the inscription of social time within the church and its inscription within the book, drawing parallels between the writing of the book and the design of a church. In the novel, architecture and writing – the church and the text – are both attempts to produce spatial constructs outside time, to escape time or to merge with an enduring or cosmological form of time. They are attempts to transcend historical time by using these interstices in the matrix of the present almost as black holes – tears in the fabric of the universe through which time and space might slip. In the novel's somewhat muddled finale, there seems to be a suggestion that today's interstices in the present are to be found in the flickering surface of the TV screen, which, from a postmodern perspective, is more often associated with a perpetual present and a loss of historicity. Here the TV image seems to suggest an excess of historicity rather than an absence of it.[4] In Yi-Fu Tuan's terminology the church and the book are sites that might be 'pauses in the flow of time' (Tuan 1977: 198). Both provide the space for the author/architect to make symbolic inscriptions of time, and signify something of the nature of time itself.

In a postmodern context, the novel explores the limits of quantitative time as an analytical tool in the twentieth century, and questions the inviolable 'truth' of causality and rational science based on empirical method. From a twentieth century perspective, the dominant belief system for the last three centuries in the west has been that of rational and empirical science, which demands an unambiguous, unidirectional arrow of time. Within the novel, such a form of time, and the belief system associated with it, seems to be in question when the twentieth century detective, Hawksmoor, is faced with solving murders that seem to have been perpetrated, or are still being perpetrated, in the eighteenth century. So time in the eighteenth century seems to project itself forwards into the twentieth century, and for Hawksmoor to solve the murders, it seems he needs to travel back to the eighteenth century. What is asked of the reader here is to imagine that it is possible to pass between historical times, as though they were, under certain conditions, parallel. Events seem to resonate across historical time and manifest themselves in the traffic through time of voices, echoes, rhymes and symbolic designs in space.

Hawksmoor is a pastiche of eighteenth century writing strangely connected to a modern detective story. But the pastiche does contain a well-researched and persuasive historical reconstruction of part-historical and part-fictional events and meetings. This is the hallmark of much of Ackroyd's work, and he is very good at fictionalised histories. But *Hawksmoor* is more complicated than this because, as well as being a historical reconstruction on which the present looks back, it is also a fictionalisation of the near-present into which the past looks forward. The connection with seventeenth and eighteenth century mysticism is important here, because it is by legitimating the visionary possibilities of an underground and clandestine mysticism that the past is able to peer into the present. Meanwhile, the tools of twentieth century science are made available to reconstruct the past, and they fail to do so.

For the reader, the past, or rather the historical reconstruction, is perhaps more *real* than the present. The narrative of the detective in the twentieth century is tied to real places and real events, and yet the twentieth century, the present, is the time which has a ghostly quality about it. There is a pervasive vagueness and sense of indeterminacy here, of being *lost in time*, compared with the opposing certainties in the narrative of the eighteenth century world – the mystical and an emergent modern.

Both times are presented realistically and convincingly in the novel through the use of eighteenth century dialect and writing style, and through careful attention to the actual sites of the eighteenth and twentieth century. The use of the real Hawksmoor churches in London works particularly well because these churches are still present and still remarkable in their design. It is this continuing presence of the churches through history which is key to the temporal crossover in the novel, as though times converge in these symbolic sites. Through these sites, the novel flickers between historical times, splitting and then bringing together the double persona of Dyer/Hawksmoor. Another way of looking at it would be to see the chronotope of the whole as a thickened present similar to that sought by William James and Henri Bergson, but here extended into a thickening not of psychological time, but of social and historical time as well.[5] In a postmodern context, such thickening of the present makes the past available to the present – the presence of the past in the present.

Hawksmoor depicts an early eighteenth century London society constituting a form of time that would come to dominate other forms of time. The importance of the constitution of this particular social time cannot be underestimated because it underlies many of the major faiths of modern society (such as rational science and causality) and although *Hawksmoor* makes no direct reference to it as such, this form of time was a prerequisite for industrial capitalism. As Nigel Thrift argues, from the fourteenth to the late nineteenth century there was a change in time consciousness, and we can chart the 'gradual diffusion of a new type of time, based on calculative rationality' (Thrift 1980: 57). The application of this 'calculative rationality' to the 'productive order' was to be a crucial factor in the growth of industrial capitalism.

In the eighteenth century, this new conception of time was still emerging, and *Hawksmoor* refers to its crucial presence within the framework of new rational science at the Royal Society. But the novel also portrays the resistance and scepticism of a society which retained its attachment to residual belief systems, and the architect, Nicholas Dyer, is depicted as the retainer of the older faiths and metaphysical thinking. As faith in the new rational science, with its quantitative and linear forms of time, comes to dominate eighteenth century thinking, metaphysical thinkers like Dyer and his mentor Mirabilis are treated as subversive elements, forced into underground and clandestine meetings. Dyer sees beyond the new rational science and its depth models retaining faith in a 'Natural' time transcending the abstract 'Beginnings and Depths of Things' preached at the Royal Society:

> Then as he entered the main part of his discourse on Selenoscopes, Muscovy Glasses, Philosophical Scales, Circumferentors, Hydrostaticall Ballances, and the rest, my Mind wandred into the following Reflections: such vain Scrutinyes and Fruitless Labours are theirs, for they fondly beleeve that they can search out the Beginnings and Depths of Things. But Nature will not be so discover'd; it is better to essay to unwind the labyrinthine Thread than hope to puzzle out the Pattern of the World.
>
> (*Hawskmoor*: 139)

Eschewing science and modern religions that assimilated it, Dyer insists on upholding an older faith with a very different concept of time and remaining true to this faith in the design of his churches. To do this he must pay homage to the creator of death as well as life:

> I shall say only at this point that I, the Builder of Churches, am no Puritan nor Caveller, nor Reformed, nor Catholick, nor Jew, but of that older Faith which sets them dancing in Black Step Lane. And this is the Creed which Mirabilis school'd in me: He who made the World is also author of Death, nor can we but by doing Evil avoid the rage of evil Spirits.
>
> (H: 20–1)

This 'older faith', which Mirabilis teaches on the ancient Druid site in Black Step Lane, is based on a *mélange* of Druid and Old Testament teaching, with an emphasis on mythological, mystical and magical beliefs. It is the older faith that demands that Dyer includes the patterns, signs and sacrifices that designate eternity within the designs of his churches.

This older faith is very much opposed to Christian faith, which seems to 'move with the times', as it were, and fit rational science within its own schema. As Parson Priddon puts it '. . . we see how God guides the whole of his Creation in the wonted course of Cause and Effect which we may prove, Mr Dyer, by considering the unaffected Simplicity of Nature.' (H: 134). But Priddon's vision of God working in unison with rational science to the benefit of human society is not something Dyer sees all about him in the streets of Cheapside. Only in abstract space can Priddon imagine God and science hand-in-hand:

> . . . look you Heavenwards (and he raysed his Voice as he looked up at the Sky) and you will be pleased with a pleasing Astonishment if you could see with the aid of a telescope so many Worlds hanging above one another, moving peacefully and quietly round their Axles and yet shewing such an amazing Pomp and Solemnity.
> (H: 134)

Here, both science and religion share an abstract and theoretical space removed from the realities of the present day, and time is segmented into the causal chains of science, with many beginnings and endings, overseen and guided by an omnipresent God. In the older faith of the Druids, the emphasis is on the real space of the everyday, where the fallen world is essentially evil and people are full of sin, but where, in time, man can redeem himself, as Dyer tries to explain:

> What is Time? The Deliverance of Man. These are the ancient Teachings and I will not Trouble my self with a multiplicity of Commentators upon this place, since it is now in my churches that I will bring them once more into the Memory of this and future Ages. For when I became acquainted with Mirabilis and his Assembly I was uncovering the trew Musick of Time which, like the rowling of a Drum, can be heard from far off by those whose ears are prickt.
> (H: 21)

For the architect Nicholas Dyer, enduring time must be inscribed in the design and the fabric of his buildings, so that all time can be perceived, like the harmony of the spheres, echoing across a bounded cosmos in which all time is already completed and contained. It is easy to dismiss this as a mediaeval and unenlightened view of the cosmos but, from a postmodern perspective, it is in a sense true that the (expanding) universe does contain the traces of events from billions of years ago as they travel in light waves across the ether. And these waves are perceived as 'sounds' picked up by radio telescopes, so we do indeed listen to the past as it travels across space. Here is a postmodern author using the imagery of new science, and connecting it to the end of a period (late sixteenth, early seventeenth century) during which, according to the physicist in *The Child in Time*, poets and writers might have been more alert to its metaphorical possibilities.

Dyer's plan is to replicate ancient patterns in the layout of his churches, to use materials with time already inscribed in them, such as stone, and to follow certain rites and ceremonies in the construction, in particular the interment of a human sacrifice in the foundations of each church. In this, Dyer believes he is continuing the tradition of the Druids and the architects of Stonehenge. We should note at this point that in Dyer's time, the concept of 'eternity' was rather shorter than it is today. It was not until the advances in earth sciences in the nineteenth century that what we now refer to as prehistory was accepted as fact. In Dyer's time, the world was thought to be not much older than Stonehenge.

For Dyer, 'architecture aims at Eternity and must contain the Eternal Powers: not only our Altars and Sacrifices, but the forms of our Temples, must be mysticall,' (H: 9). But this is not the fashion of the time and, in the novel, Sir Christopher Wren, who is very much a 'Royal Society' man, believes that architecture should reflect the 'Harmony' and 'Rationall Beauty' of the world, as illuminated by science. A new aesthetics as well as a new science and new conception of space and time is emerging.

Wren oversees Dyer's work in the novel, but does not seem to realise just how subversive Dyer's churches are becoming. He incorporates references to older faiths through pyramids with ancient inscriptions and by encoding patterns to evoke ancient mythical characters, and he sacrifices boys and young men and buries them under the foundations. But this is not Wren's concern, he is interested in the phenomenal world, in the surfaces of things, and with appearance. What seems like a conflict in aesthetics between the two architects is also an ideological conflict. This comes to light in their trip to Stonehenge. For

Wren, the layout of the stones on the Druid site discloses an underlying aesthetic of harmony and rational beauty represented in pure geometric form; for Dyer the stones represent something far more sinister in human nature and history:

> Geometry, he called out, is the Key to this Majesty: if the Proportions are right, I calculate that the inner part is an Exagonall Figure raised upon the Bases of four Equilaterall Triangles! I went up to him saying, Some believe they are Men metamorphosised into Stone, but he payed no Heed to me and stood with his Head flung back as he continu'd: And you see, Nick, there is an Exactness of Placing them in regard to the Heavens, for they are so arranged to estimate the position of the Planets and the fixed Starres. From which I believe they had magneticall compass Boxes.
>
> (H: 61)

For Wren, the geometrical beauty of spatial constructs, such as the church, are to be found in their representation of a rational order which throws light on a mystical and unseen world. Science and mathematics are tools to reveal hidden truths about the world, bringing to the surface and exposing the mysticism of Dyer's older faith. At Stonehenge, Wren imposes this enlightened view retrospectively on the Druids, assuming that they too were concerned with geometry, and making the clearly false deduction that they possessed magnetic compasses.

Dyer is not detached and analytical like Wren, because for him Stonehenge still speaks to him of the past. He believes that like him the Druids were constructing, through a particular arrangement of stones, the means to communicate with their ancestors and future generations. The stones, like today's astral telescopes, transmit and receive messages to and from the deep past, and they also have inscribed in them some trace of the Druids who erected them:

> And when I lean'd my Back against that Stone I felt in the Fabrick the Labour and Agonie of those who erected it, the power of Him who enthrall'd them, and the marks of Eternity which had been placed there. I could here the Cryes and Voices of those long since gone.
>
> (H: 61)

Dyer's art is based on the 'art of Shaddowes' learnt from ancient books on the design of pyramids, where he finds that the hidden or shaded aspect of a structure is as important as its visible or illuminated dimension, because without shadow, nothing has substance:

> It is only the Darknesse that can give trew Forme to our work and trew Perspective to our Fabrick, for there is no Light without Darknesse and no Substance without Shaddowe.
>
> (H: 5)

Wren and Dyer both use mathematics and geometry in their designs, but to different ends: Wren uses them to enlighten and bring truth to the surface but Dyer uses them to encode and mystify the darkness. Yi-Fu Tuan suggests that such ambiguity in the use of mathematical language stems from its 'emergence in the quasi-mystical atmosphere of ancient times' (Tuan 1989: 233–41). Mathematical language is used in science because it has a capacity to 'bring whatever is there to the surface – to light', but mathematical language can also do the reverse; it is in this sense a pure language, and the beauty or elegance of it, and the danger of it, is that it can be used to mystify or 'to preserve the numinous (dark) core of being' (Tuan 1989: 233–41).

Wren and Dyer support faiths that have fundamentally different concepts of time. Wren is portrayed as a man of the times in the eighteenth century, and claims that 'Men are weary of the Reliques of Antiquity', and are concerned now with 'Sensible Knowledge of the Experimentall Learning' and 'real Truths'; Wren claims 'This is our time . . . and we must lay its Foundacions with our own Hands', but, asks Dyer, '. . . how do we conclude what Time is our own?' (H: 55).

Dyer questions the validity of a society marking out its own time and trying to take charge of its own destiny in isolation from all the mysteries that surround it. Dyer also suggests that Wren's scientific truth is self-referring, abstracted from the real world: 'your Zeal, *I said*, is more for Experpiments than for Truth, thus you will turn Experpiments into a Truth of your own devising' (H: 147).

For Dyer, the Royal Society's emphasis on measurement and prediction leads to a quantitative time that moves beyond the scientific realm and comes to dominate time in cultural and social realms. Here, Dyer anticipates Lyotard's complaint against modernity: the loss of the differend, or gulf, between different realms. There is also a stock critique of nineteenth century Utilitarianism in this, and both point to Ackroyd's cunning anachronism – the pre-modern man anticipating modern and postmodern critiques of modernity, and having the satisfaction of seeing himself proved right. This is how Dyer objects to the application of quantitative time and empirical methods in ethical and moral judgement:

> The Mysteries must become easy and familiar, it is said, and it has now reached such a Pitch that there are those who wish to bring their mathematicall Calculations into Morality, *viz.* the Quantity of Publick Good produced by an Agent is a compound Ratio of his Benevolence and Abilities.
>
> (H: 101)

The critique against modernity continues with Dyer pointing to the gap between the reported progress of the enlightened society and the actual experience of life for ordinary people in eighteenth century London which still seems a dark and sordid affair:

> This mundus tenebrosus, this shaddowy world of Mankind, is sunk into Night; there is not a Field without its Spirits, nor a City without its Daemons, and the Lunaticks speak Prophesies while the Wise men fall into the Pitte. We are all in the Dark, one with another.
>
> (H: 101)

Although London is in the process of being rebuilt after the Plague and the Great Fire, the intended rational order in the designs for the city is only implemented in part, and as Dyer records :

> London grows more Monstrous, Straggling out of all Shape: in this Hive of Noise and Ignorance, Nat, we are tyed to the World as to a sensible Carcasse and as we cross the stinking Body we call out *What News?* or *What's a clock?*
>
> (H: 48)

Wren's vision of a society taking hold of its time, and constructing a new city based on rational thought and science is not what Dyer sees. For him, society is monstrous, expanding too fast and obsessed with time and 'news'. This darker vision of life in London is surely due in part to the emergence of trade capitalism. A shift in the form of time is crucial to this, and Dyer's reference to the clock is a small but significant pointer to a major societal shift. The growth of trade capitalism in the seventeenth century is coincident with a huge change in the consciousness of space and time. The map, the compass and the clock were essential tools in navigation and so crucial to world trade. The clock also began to appear at this time as the harbinger of the new public time, for the synchronisation of human activity such as meetings and markets, and for quantifying labour time. Behind all of this is capitalism that quickly establishes its own dynamics of quantitative time and money. Such a form of time, suggests Nigel Thrift, is absorbed into the hegemony of capitalism by the eighteenth century, and is 'sedimented into the interstices of practical consciousness' (Thrift 1980: 57).

Dyer's criticism of quantitative time implies a failure in this emerging modern, scientific and capitalist society to pay heed to the corruption, misery and deprivation among the London poor. Dyer's concept of time is odd to a modern consciousness and yet it is given a spin by Ackroyd to place it closer to conflicts in social time of the period. Wren's quantitative time on the other hand, while having an obvious function in a modern society, is seen as divisive within that society. At least this is how it appears from a postmodern perspective. When Georges Gurvitch refers to social time within a 'total social phenomenon', he means that man and society are not to be abstracted and divided. To explore social time, he suggests, is to 'reconstruct the whole in its irreducibility' (Gurvitch 1990: 67). The idea of an irreducible society wrapped in time is what Dyer imagines as:

> Mist in Humane affairs, a small thin Rain which cannot be perceeved in single Drops of this Man or that Man but which rises around them and obscures them one from another, yet it takes Form in the Fabrick of my new built Church.
>
> (H: 204)

This mist obscures but is also inclusive, and Dyer soaks his churches in the time of human affairs; unlike Wren, whose approach is to create timeless beauty through abstract mathematical concepts of harmony and order.

Dyer's faith in the power of his churches to endure and connect across historical time is upheld in the novel by the apparent projection of events and their consequences into the future. And on the other side of time, the present is to receive this as an encounter with the past. The inscription of time within the fabric of Dyer's churches involves the sacrifice and interment of the body of a boy or young man within the church itself. A series of sacrifices in the eighteenth century connects with a series of murders in the twentieth century perpetrated on their doubles. Each victim meets his fate at precisely the same place as his precursor. The detective, Hawksmoor, is unable to solve this series of murders, although (or perhaps *because*) he relies on rational scientific methodology, backed up by computers and other twentieth century technology, to reconstruct the crime scene. Ironically, his approach depends on the same time consciousness, linearity and faith in causality that Dyer, Hawksmoor's *alter ego*, is opposed to in the eighteenth century. Hawksmoor's approach is an extension of the same empirical systems that Wren enthusiastically promoted:

> On an occasion such as this, he liked to consider himself as a scientist, or even a scholar, since it was by close observation and rational deduction that he came to a proper understanding of each case; he prided himself on his acquaintance with chemistry, anatomy and even mathematics since it was these disciplines which helped him to resolve situations at which others trembled. For he knew that even during extreme events the laws of cause and effect still operated; he could fathom the mind of a murderer, for example, from a close study of the footprints which he left behind – not, it would seem, by any act of sympathy but rather from the principles of reason and method.
> (H: 152–3)

The trick played on Hawksmoor is that the 'footprints', which connoting evidence in a phenomenal world, have long since disappeared and it is only by some kind of 'sympathy', or irrational psychic communication, that he could solve the crimes. Or perhaps Hawksmoor, the modern detective, might look into himself to find the author of these atrocities. For the novel presents Dyer and Hawksmoor, murderer and detective, as two halves of a single identity, a ploy suggested by giving the twentieth century detective the name – Hawksmoor – of the real historical character who built some seven churches in and around east London in the early eighteenth century.

Hawksmoor's rational methodology is undermined here because there appears to be no *beginning* from which to start plotting the events and so solve the mystery. Hawksmoor gradually breaks down as his investigations seem to lead nowhere, and more murders come to light. He begins to ponder then on the laws of cause and effect, and the direction of time, because he seems to have an inkling (and he is right) that he is being deceived by time. He is restricted to only half the story in the text, *Hawksmoor*; the other half of the story is Dyer's and takes place hundreds of years earlier. But Hawksmoor, the fictional character, is gradually made aware of echoes and shadows reaching him from the other side of the text, and is prepared to accept these as evidence of the closing of the pattern and the end of the narrative. The pattern of murders becomes a narrative to Hawksmoor, a story, the beginning of which he has failed to understand, yet he must 'go on reading it. Just to see what happens next' (H: 126).

Although the eighteenth century architect can appear to create structures whose temporality somehow reaches across historical time, the twentieth century detective stumbles through the present dimly aware that something, far back in time and out of his grasp, is casting itself forward to meet him. Occasionally, Hawksmoor articulates the problem; for example, when his assistant finds it 'difficult to know where to begin', Hawksmoor replies 'perhaps there is no beginning, perhaps we can't look that far back' (H: 126). There is an obvious irony here as this postmodern detective fails to see what the reader can see all along. The detective only has access to half the text and is stumbling through the present, only dimly aware of the past reaching forwards to him. The tables are turned, and the detective hero is no longer going to step into the chaos of the world and put it all in order to comfort a worried audience.[6] From a postmodern perspective, the detective is trapped in the present, his access to the past conditioned by the text in which he is also trapped, and which can only reach its conclusion in his death. In postmodernity, the detective is fallible and the world – rather than becoming safer – becomes more mysterious. The detective cannot step out of the text that encloses him and has already anticipated his every move.

The present is not returned to us cleared of the unfamiliar and strange, but is made contingent with this underground side of life out of which the mysteries of the past present themselves unresolved. In his perpetual present, Hawksmoor is hostage to postmodernity's loss of historicity. He is unable to predict the past and project this forward into the future. In this, he is presented as a parody of the modern detective, all method and reason, but no insight or intuition. This is further complicated by the double figure of Hawksmoor/Dyer stretched across historical periods, as though Hawksmoor's identity is itself partly in the present and partly trapped in an inaccessible past.

Hawksmoor comes to the conclusion that there is a pattern too large for him to resolve. Beyond the quantitative time he is familiar with, he sees only 'invention'. So if he cannot solve the chain of causality because it reaches beyond the linear scale of modern rational time, it must lie in the uncharted territory of the metaphysical or be a fiction. In one sense, he is right, he is a character in a fiction, and this is a self-conscious postmodern fiction in which characters acknowledge their fictional status. In another sense, he is also right because the fiction as a whole entertains the metaphysical and the transpersonal, out of reach of rational method. Hawksmoor, as a modern detective, could never accept the 'everlasting order' proposed by Dyer, but Hawksmoor as a postmodern detective is unable to step outside Dyer's pattern as it draws him in.

Dyer's pattern is concretised in the seven churches that represent the seven spheres, each designed to a pattern in which 'every Straight line is enrich'd with a point at Infinity and every Plane with a line at Infinity' (H: 186). Hawksmoor continues to grapple with the pattern that flickers in front of him, as it appears and disappears again before he can grasp it. In his attempts to piece the pattern together, the once clear distinctions in his analytical mind between fact and fiction now become blurred:

> The event of the boy's death was not simple because it was not unique and if he traced it backwards, running the time slowly in the opposite direction (but did it have a direction?), it became no clearer. The chain of causality might extend as far back as the boy's birth, in a particular place and on a particular date, or even further into the darkness beyond that. And what of the murderer, for what sequence of events had drawn him to wander by this old church? All these events were random and yet connected, part of a pattern so large that it remained inexplicable. He might, then, have to invent a past from the evidence available – and, in that case, would not the future also be an invention?
>
> (H: 157)

As the pattern of events expands and the chain of causality extends too far, Hawksmoor considers inventing, rather than constructing, the past: a shift from reason and method to imagination and fiction. From a postmodern perspective, this is consistent with the problematisation of history in which access to the past is always to some extent an imaginative projection, an invention. Here, Hawksmoor also realises the danger of using an imaginative prediction of the past and projecting this into the future. At this point, the puzzle is too overwhelming for the detective and, to add to his problems, he begins to become aware of being manipulated. As a character in a postmodern novel, he is never far from admitting that he is himself and invention, being pulled this way and that by the author. But within the text, the detective also becomes conscious that something or someone from the past is manipulating him.

As the novel reaches its climax, Hawksmoor falls into Dyer's secret plot at the church in Black Step Lane. This church, built by Dyer in the eighteenth century on the site of the Druid temple as the conclusion to his 'everlasting Order', incorporates an effigy of Francis Bacon, who Dyer wants to punish for daring to define time. In the pattern of churches, Dyer has secreted a plot that will eventually draw Hawksmoor into this church for its conclusion, and he eventually sees Hawksmoor in a vision of futurity, coming to discover his secret: [7]

> There is also a Narrative which is hidden so that none may see it and in a retired Place have I put the effigy of Friar Bacon who made the brazen Head that spake *Time is*... This shall now suffice for a present Account, for my own History is a Patern which others may follow in the far Side of Time. And I hugg my Arms around my self and laugh, for as if in a Vision I see some one from the dark Mazes of an unknown Futurity who enters Black Step Lane and discovers what is hidden in Silence and Secresy.
>
> (H: 205)

In the conclusion, the detective Hawksmoor is drawn into the pattern constructed by Dyer, a pattern through which Dyer foresees eternity, figured in his own shadow stretching across time and space: 'I had run to the end of my Time and I was at Peace. I knelt down in front of the Light, and my Shaddowe stretched over the World' (H: 209). As Hawksmoor connects the pattern created by Dyer with the pattern of the present day murders, he imagines, or dreams, or actually does (this is deliberately ambiguous in the narrative) meet with Dyer in his church at Black Step Lane. Before the meeting, Hawksmoor has seen an image on a TV screen, an indistinct figure, like a shadow, speaking from within one of Dyer's churches. The trap begins to close, as Hawksmoor goes to the library and reads about the architect Dyer. He senses that the pattern is not yet complete, and he is impelled to go to the church at Black Step Lane where he meets with Dyer, or is it himself? As he walks to the church, his identity starts to break down – 'Am I me?' (H: 209). In the church, the already disintegrating identity of the fictional Hawksmoor merges with the fictional Dyer to produce the 'real' architect Hawksmoor.

The shape of the *Hawksmoor* chronotope is the most complex we have come to yet, as it brings together conflicting forms of time. Hawksmoor is forced to question linear time when events from the past seem to catch up with him, and Dyer proposes a trans-historical time that the novel as a whole seems to confirm. In the conclusion, Hawksmoor appears within the Dyer narrative as a vision that confirms, within the novel's own logic, that Dyer's metaphysical concept of time does endure. Dyer's criticism of the systems and models devised by the 'forward thinking' system builders of the Royal Society in the eighteenth century, might also find sympathy in postmodern critiques of time in modernity:

> They build Edifices which they call *systems* by laying their Foundacions in the Air and, when they think they are come to sollid Ground, the Building disappears and the Architects tumble down from the Clowds. Men that are fixed upon *matter, experiment, secondary causes* and the like have forgot there is such a thing in the World which they cannot see nor touch nor measure: it is the Praecipice into which they will surely fall.
>
> (H: 101)

Finding Time: Astronomy and Archaeology in *First Light*

In *First Light*, time is also problematised. As in *Hawksmoor*, the idea of a form of time reaching across historical time is conceptualised and used to bring into question forms of time based in rational and scientific thinking, and so forms of time commonly associated with modernity. Once more, the postmodern chronotope is used to rework the modern, to test its assumptions. In *Hawksmoor*, this questioning was effected by entertaining the possibility of mystical, pre-modern forms of time. In *First Light*, the postmodern chronotope connects an enduring prehistoric time with recent scientific theories from cosmology in which the direction of time is largely arbitrary and theoretically reversible. In *Hawksmoor*, human attempts to fix historical and cosmic time, and so project the past into the present and the present into futurity, are made through the physical construct of the church and, figuratively, through the cultural construct of the book.

In *First Light*, time endures (somewhat unconvincingly) through successive generations of the same family bypassing historical time. The thesis seems to be that these families have evaded historical time by remaining within the *pre-historic*, protected from history and yet projected into futurity. The vehicle for this spectacular time travel is a neolithic burial mound in Dorset. The presence of these burial mounds, or barrows and tumuli, is a noticeable feature of the landscape in this part of southern England. This region contains many neolithic burial mounds built to endure and provide *passage* into future times for their occupants. It is a landscape that certainly impressed itself on Thomas Hardy as a constant reminder of the long past impressing itself on the present, a major theme in a number of his novels.[8] This is an impression not so much of history, but of something older than history, an enduring and constant past which conflicts with the passage of time, a counterbalance to history.

In *First Light*, these sites, *outside history*, are connected with a cosmological time in which all time is contained, because this is the time (and space) of the universe from its beginning to its end. But this cosmological time is about to go into reverse as the universe is about to cease expanding – and so cease creating time and space – and begin to contract. The imminent change in the direction of cosmological time is discovered by an astronomer, and this astronomer happens to be exploring an area of the solar system with the same name as the family buried in the neolithic tomb. The plot is never quite science fiction nor realism and, unlike *Hawksmoor*, it lacks a sense of the uncanny that might shake our sense of reality. However, the novel does weave contemporary science into what might be read as a critique of the historical time of modernity. Leaving aside the plot and its unsatisfactory conclusion, *First Light* presents a typically postmodern reflection on time. Here, an archaeologist, Mark Clare, is peering into the deep past, and an astronomer, Damian Fall, is spying on the furthest reaches of the universe, only for each to find they are in fact exploring the same moment in time, a moment that is about to reoccur from the other side of time and space as the universe collapses back in on itself.

In *Hawksmoor*, an architect working in the early eighteenth century inscribes in the pattern of his churches a form of time which, projecting itself into futurity, seemed to challenge modern assumptions about linear time and history. Within the novel, the architect seems to achieve some success here as his concept of an extensive, trans-historical time and trans-personal time is vindicated. But this is contained within a fictional space–time, within a postmodern novel that does not take itself seriously enough to propose an *alternative* form of time. The play with time is unsettling perhaps and, for some, consistent with a return to pre-modern and mystical forms of time,[9] but it is not, in the end, an antithesis to modern time. This postmodern play with time is, at the same time, a postmodern play with language, with most of the clues and connections given as signs in the text: linguistic signs and echoes that travel through time. The fictional chronotope creates a representational world outside historical time, but this is not a representation of a realistic habitable world outside time. The architect is like an author, he sets out his plot, arranges his time, and installs his mysteries, paying particular attention to the structure, plot and the 'Signe' that is placed in the church 'so that he who sees the Fabrick may also see the Shaddowe of the Reality of which it is the Pattern or Figure' (H: 45). The detective here is that implied reader, tracing the plot, discerning the structure and reading the signs. But, as a modern man, he is a bad reader of the writings of non-modern societies. His insistence on linearity, cause and effect, and system, disqualify him from understanding other societies where different forms of social time have been constituted, and from understanding the time of marginalised social groups within modern society.[10]

In *First Light*, there is none of this textual play to compensate for and, in some ways, filter out, the incredibility of the plot. The novel presents itself as science fiction/realism, and yet it breaks the bounds of realism and science fiction without the release of a postmodern self-reflexivity through which it might present itself as a reflection on the processes of representation. Broadly, this novel presents itself as a realist novel with only the occasional hint of self satire. Here there are two detectives/readers, the astronomer and the archaeologist, but unlike *Hawksmoor*, there is no author of mysteries (other than Peter Ackroyd himself) and the author of the universe, herself, himself or itself.

The role of the archaeologists and astronomers is to bring the mysteries of the past *to light*, by bringing the evidence of the past to the surface (literally as well as metaphorically in the case of the archaeologists). These attempts of modern science to throw light upon the past and so illuminate the future are turned inside out in *First Light* by the endurance of a living past in the present and by a futurity which turns out to be the past in reverse, closing in on the present. But although the idea of a reversible cosmological time is theoretically possible, the novel has a major problem in trying to conceive of this as an actual occurrence within human society. Technically such an event is inconceivable, and imaginatively it proves beyond Ackroyd. A reversible cosmological time does not necessarily imply a change in direction of biological time or historical time, both of which would be extremely problematic. For one thing, life itself requires biological processes of growth and decomposition – a universal reversal here would immediately bring an end to all life on earth. It is possible to conceive of time travel even though it is technically impossible. In time travel an individual is transported into another time and space, but once there, time and space are normalised. The reversal in time is provided by a vehicle, a compartment in which life is suspended and any logic of space and time transcended. The burial mound in *First Light* is a *passage* grave that is designed to transcend death by projecting its interns into an eternal future. But this is surely to be understood in a spiritual sense, something beyond the physical continuity Ackroyd presents in this novel.

Leaving aside the many problems the novel introduces, the central chronotope of a contracting universe is an important moment to consider in the postmodern. This chronotope signals the end of history, end of modern progress, end of time, end of ideology, and the presence of apocalyptic thinking coincident with the millennium. It also signals a moment made scientifically possible, and yet beyond sensible representation. This is a postmodern moment in which science presents the ultimate unpresentability, not the end of time in some realistic catastrophe, but the end of time as a zenith whose fall reverses time. Modern development, according to Lyotard, proceeds according to its own dynamics not according to a plan or idea, and the only end point of such dynamics is the life of the sun, its only punctuation the full stop of an exploding star (Lyotard 1991: 7). So we might read in the finality of the cosmos conceived in *First Light*, representation of an encounter with that end. Unlike *Waterland*, which questions modern development as an idea of progress advancing in a straight line through history, this novel connects time and history with the cosmos and with the ultimate failure of the cosmos. The universe is unable to sustain the continuous expansion which has, from the beginning of time, produced the space and time of history and of life. Through this connection, the fate of the universe is linked to historical fate, and the time of the cosmos is reconnected with mundane historical time: a connection that modernity itself had done so much to tear apart. Indeed, in postmodernity, science seems to present ideas and metaphors more relevant to the uncertainties and mysteries of pre-modern times, than to the enlightening and rational discourses of modernity.

In *First Light*, the astronomer Damian Fall sees the past as no more than a 'succession of present moments' where each star visible in the sky today is a sign of a long passed moment in cosmological time. Each is a sign in space, moving away, yet still visible, quantifiable and legible:

> Everything on the earth existed with him, shared his time with him in an ever-receding present moment; everything was connected, but this network of invisible relations was a network of simultaneity. Damian

> had to assume that there was such a thing as the past but any evidence for it was part of the present, too. All the world had ever known was a succession of present moments. There was – there is – nothing else.
>
> (*First Light*: 134)

Damian's conception of cosmological time (perfectly sound as far as contemporary science is concerned) is not that far removed from Nicholas Dyer's in *Hawksmoor*. Both recognise a connectivity of present moments and a simultaneity that promises to spread the past before us as a pattern, a set of signs – a writing tablet in space. When Damian thinks he has observed the moment at which the universe starts to contract, the stars no longer mark successive *past* moments, but become *future* moments. Time (as we know it) collapses in on itself when the star Damian has been observing, Aldebaran, ceases to travel away from the earth, and starts to move towards it. His spectrograph registers this change of time direction, detecting emissions of shorter wavelength from the star and representing them in a colour shift from red to blue. Damian, aware of the implications this simple shift of colour, wavelength and direction, is unable to understand how he is still able to function on the earth:

> If the universe were contracting, returning to its unimaginable moment of birth, then surely it would have happened instantaneously? Once the pressures of time and space were reversed, and the universe doubled back on itself, surely this unravelling would occur outside time – would occur, in a sense, after time had ceased to exist?
>
> (FL :296)

Damian realises that he still exists, 'There was a world around him still', and it was only Aldebaran that had been 'shaken from its accustomed place' (FL: 296). Even so, his faith in the stability of the universe is unsettled, because this moment forces him to try to reconcile cosmological time with the forward moving psychological time that delineates his own existence:

> . . . the visible firmament was no more than a wave of dying energy, eddying through unimaginable spaces to some unknown destination. The universe was a structure established upon . . . established upon what? Nothing. And as he looked up he was filled with the fear of emptiness, the fear of non-being. And he became nothing.
>
> (FL :297)

Damian experiences a kind of vertigo in time, an unmappable existence in the emptiness of non-being, because being, as he understands it, is to be in a time that carries his existence forward from present to future. Cosmological time, as an inescapable property of the universe, is an absolute time, and if this comes to an end then all the forms of time constituted within society – psychological, ecological, social and historical time – are constructs without foundation.

A similar worry is presented to the archaeologist Mark Clare in *First Light*. He is startled out of his faith in future-directed linear time, and the systems theory by which he sequences excavations, when he penetrates a neolithic barrow and senses four thousand years of time suddenly contracting within the central tomb. Here are two parallel investigations of time: one aimed at the stars, and the other underground, and both are profoundly unsettling for the main characters. But by connecting the experiences of archaeologist and astronomer, an event takes shape to disturb all time–space relations, shifting individual uncertainty to general indeterminacy. The astronomer and the archaeologist both direct their attention to the same point in time: the 'unimaginable moment' when the star, Aldebaran, was formed, and prehistoric man in the guise of 'Old Barren One' was buried in a neolithic barrow. Cosmological time connects with historical time on earth when the penetration of the barrow and the removal of the coffin of the 'Old Barren One', whose shape is marked out in 'red ochre' (FL: 288, 289), coincides with the red–blue shift that marks the time–space collapse of the star, Aldebaran. Once the prehistoric remains are brought into the present, time immediately compacts, both within the valley containing the passage tomb and the passages leading to the central tumulus, and within the narrow corridor of space between the barrow and the star Aldebaran. The two investigations into time validate each other, but they also uncover what has been an extraordinary connection across time within the tomb, which continues on into the present, through the Flint family, descendants of the 'original' Mint, supposedly their neolithic ancestor. All of historical time is suddenly spread out, spatialised in the Dorset landscape, in an image of undifferentiated and unmappable present time, similar to that which Damian Fall had already seen in space, and consistent with a postmodern concept of a perpetual present.

Prior to the excavation of the barrow, Mark Clare, the archaeologist, had regarded Dorset as a 'special place':

> ... Dorset was his obsession. He believed that this place had its own sound ... It possessed an almost human presence, as if the generations of those who had dwelt upon its surface had left some faint echo ... Yes, this was a haunted place. It contained mysteries.
>
> (FL: 33)

One of the past generations who clearly left an echo in the landscapes of Dorset was Thomas Hardy, who, like Peter Ackroyd, used the many ancient remains in the region and the clear star-filled skies in his novels, to conceive of time and the relationship between cosmological time and psychological time. As Mark Clare looks up at the Dorset sky, he recalls one of Hardy's descriptions of the stars:

> The rainstorm had passed and it had become a clear, calm night – on just such a night Gabriel Oak was tending his sheep on Norcombe Hill in Thomas Hardy's *Far from the Madding Crowd*, and Hardy describes how '... the sovereign brilliance of Sirius pierced the eye with a steely glitter, the star called Capella was yellow, Aldebaran and Betelgeux shone with a fiery red' for this was a night when 'the twinkling of all the stars seemed to be but throbs of one body, timed by a common pulse'.
>
> (FL: 34)

This was another time, when the stars still seemed to represent an order and a constancy in the universe, and in Hardy's tale, this suggests a mood of harmony in human affairs as well.[11] For many societies, the night sky has been a representational space on to which human designs for the universe, and for society, have been written. In postmodernity, as astronomy and cosmology reveal ever more information about the positions and velocities of stars and planets, the more chaotic and mysterious the universe becomes. Now, the sky can no longer signify harmony and least of all constancy. As Damian Fall puts it:

> But the stars are not pulsating in quite that manner. They are rushing away from an unknown point of origin, and this planet is rushing away with them, driven on by the force of some event that created time in the same unimaginable moment as it created space.
>
> (FL: 34)

Damian Fall is aware of the chaotic nature of the universe, and also of a society's tendency to read into its design the pattern it forms of its own constellation of individual lives. And so the problem of positionality, in which the observer can never entirely divorce the figure he has hypothesised from his reading of the pattern observed, is both a scientific and a cultural problem. Damian tries to explain this to his assistant, who still believes that science can disclose absolute truths of the world:

> We really know nothing after all. We see what we want to see. In each generation the heavens become a kind of celestial map of human desires... They reflect all our recent theories about the universe, and although we no longer see the stars in the shape of gods or animals our own theories are no less fabulous.
>
> (FL: 158)

As the novel progresses, the astronomer becomes increasingly unsettled by knowledge of the lack of order and design in the universe, masked and papered over by provisional theories based on human desires. In the kind of wholesale criticism of science that gives postmodernism a bad name, he repeats a commonplace of postmodern narrative theory:

> Science is like fiction, you see. We make up stories, we sketch out narratives, we try to find some pattern beneath events. We are interested observers. And we like to go on with the story, we like to advance, we like to make progress. Even they are stories told in the dark.
>
> (FL: 159)

More specifically he refers to an aspect of quantum physics that seems to throw into question the reason and method of modern science by ignoring laws of causality, linearity and space–time:

> Do you know that in quantum physics objects simply appear and disappear? And then we see objects suddenly emerging in two places at once which, as far as I remember, was always supposed to be impossible... We see an electron at one point but then somehow it is also at another, and it has reached it by travelling in all possible trajectories at once.
>
> (FL: 160)

Within *First Light*, such reports on science are not fundamentally wrong, but they do misrepresent science as a whole by presenting particular ideas from the outer reaches of theoretical physics. Ackroyd seems to both use and question science at the same time, relying on science as a privileged form of truth to present recent scientific thinking and, at the same time, using this against mainstream scientific method and reason.

But I think we need to guard against reading such postmodern fictions as scientific fact, since this would be to confuse too much the boundaries between fiction and science. It is in the appropriation of knowledge from science and its representational possibilities in explaining the postmodern, that the novel might be more kindly assessed. As metaphors from postmodern science find their way into representational forms such as the novel, they need to be read both in the context of the science that produced them (so that the metaphorical structure they derive from can be understood) and also in the cultural context to which they are applied. For instance, placelessness might be described as a commonplace in postmodern societies, and a sense of not belonging is conveyed in the novel through a loss of the fixed points of scientific reason. This loss follows from the exaggerated, but not wholly inappropriate, emphasis on certain avenues of contemporary physics such as those that engage Damian Fall:

> The other night I was eagerly searching through a book – I do not remember why – and I came across a phrase. I can repeat it: '. . . that old sinking of the heart and longing after home'. I looked around, startled, because I have no home. My threatened reason has nowhere to rest, nowhere to go.
>
> (FL: 178)

In this example, the questioning begins within science, and science then disorientates the scientist by undermining his intellectual and perceptual equipment. This leads to the scientist's loss of belonging, and the common postmodern complaint of loss of 'home', or placelessness, a theme that we will return to in Chapter 8.

We turn now to the archaeologists, another set of scientists and detectives of a kind, who might be expected to be immune from disorientation in space, time and reason. Archaeology would seem to be one of the most grounded of sciences, literally and metaphorically, delving among the roots and origins of things. Their work starts well enough, with Mark Clare leading the excavation of the tumulus in Pilgrin Valley strictly according to archaeological procedures. To an archaeologist, time must appear like a rock face, concrete, quantifiable, strictly sequential and visible. When Mark addresses his assistants at the site, he is careful to impress on them the need to record everything strictly according to order:

> All of you must keep records of everything you see. Drawings. Notes. You know all about systems theory don't you? . . . Keep everything in sequence. Nothing must be lost, since all the data we collect here will

> pass through high level computer analysis. Our goals include total recovery, objective interpretation and comprehensive explanation. We are creating an electronic archive, because only then will we understand the real nature of this site.
>
> (FL: 37)

Mark is a methodical scientist who believes that only rigorous attention to detail and strict adherence to sequentiality will reveal the 'real nature' of things. It is this sequentiality of evidence that will enable them to reconstitute historical time from the objects they find and reconstruct the past. However, the problems posed are similar to those met by the detective in *Hawksmoor*, that is, there is either not enough evidence, or it is out of sequence, or it is not possible to project far enough backwards to 'see' the whole picture.

But in *First Light*, there is another kind of detective whose highly theoretical approach is less likely to be confounded by details. Julian Hill might be described as a postmodern archaeologist, less concerned with digging and the manual reconstruction of the past than with superficial probabilities. To modern science, he is a 'bad' scientist with a tendency for big ideas and self-promotion. He has the vision, but not the rigour, and would lead archaeology into a virtual and approximate reconstruction of the past, simulating the 'real' where the real can no longer be dug out:

> Julian Hill's lecture . . . concerned the future of archaeology. He had a vision of a time when there would be no cause for excavation at all, when soil-sounding devices would be able both to detect all the objects buried underneath the earth and to reconstruct them in three-dimensional form. The subterranean world need never be disturbed, since these three-dimensional images could be reproduced as holograms: in the museum of the future passage graves and underground chambers would float in light upon the exhibition floor, perfect simulacra of objects that remained concealed within the close-packed earth. The stone of these neolithic monuments would seem as real as the stone of the museum in which they had been created, decayed bones and pottery as solid as if they had just risen out of the earth, all the evidence of prehistory resurrected in glowing form. And nothing would actually have been touched: there would be two worlds, therefore, one buried forever in darkness and one filled with light.
>
> (FL: 81)

Unlike the other 'detective' characters in Ackroyd's novels, Julian Hill revels in the theoretical, the virtual and the unreal. He dreams of never needing to see and touch the evidence of the past. He would create another world in virtual space–time and place himself there, unconnected to any 'real' place. Where science threatens the reason of Damian Fall, leaving him 'placeless', it seems to fulfil Julian Hill's dreams, providing an illuminated if illusory and virtual place. Julian Hill is the postmodern scientist because he seems 'at home' in the placelessness and inauthenticity of postmodernity.

Practical excavation of the past is the task of Mark Clare, who, as the dig proceeds, becomes increasingly concerned about the sequencing of the finds when they start appearing in the 'wrong place', and the sense of an impenetrable mystery pervades the site. Mark begins to look rather like the detective in *Hawksmoor*, hovering over the past, unable to solve the mystery:

> Here were the remains of a culture which no one professed to understand, relics of that expanse of time which was a 'period' only in the sense that a story must have a beginning as well as a middle and an end. The disruption of the site confirmed Mark's sense that the secrets of the tumulus would remain secrets, reminders of the larger mystery from which they had so unexpectedly been rescued. They might help refine the story, but it was a story being told in the dark. The chaos which had descended on them was a reminder of that darkness.
>
> (FL: 93)

As the excavation proceeds in *First Light*, it becomes a major find, because it contains not only the expected neolithic relics, but a whole chain of relics connecting the neolithic to the present day. The tomb is no longer an isolated moment in prehistory, but the marker for a family who have continued to use and extend the burial site over time, until now, four thousand years on, it forms a great subterranean circle reaching under the Pilgrim Valley. So much historical time is concentrated in this one site, that in a world where chaos and uncertainty seem to hold sway in scientific and cultural realms, it appears like a symbol of harmony and order, and its disclosure seems to offer connection with past societies. What is discovered is something like the church in *Hawksmoor*, in that time is inscribed in it, and a concept of enduring time social time is communicated through it. When Mark Clare enters the tomb, he senses this:

> In this enclosed space he sensed the closeness of worship but it was not just the worship of ancestors but, rather, the worship of time itself. The passage of time. And, yes, this was a passage grave.
>
> (FL: 185)

As in *Hawksmoor*, it is the inscription of time in the landscape, or some enduring material fabric of society like a church, that seems to be important. It as though time must be 'sedimented' in space to enable society and individuals to connect across historical time; and in postmodernity, which is perhaps a more retrospective period than the modern, it is to the spatially extended past that our attention is drawn. The tomb becomes a representational space soaked in time, which might offer a conceptual anchor point for the placeless and homeless soul Damian Fall has become. It also becomes a beacon in the novel for various marginalised social groups like New Druids, New Age travellers and old-aged hippies. Each of these groups is 'not of these times', and they are all looking for some connection with other times. But they are also looking for a different conception of time, one which offers a 'deeper and richer' sense of reality:

> They were all unemployed; they were poor; and, in a sense, they were desperate. It may be that they had come to Pilgrim Valley to be close to a world which was somehow different from the one which oppressed them and offered them no hope – as if the passage grave represented a reality deeper and richer than the one through which they were forced to move.
>
> (FL: 218)

These groups may be seeking an alternative conception of time, a flight from a present dominated by the linear time perspective of modernity and capitalism, and a time which has marginalised them. But what kind of reality can they expect to find secreted in the burial mound? There is confusion here, as in *Hawksmoor*, between a reworking or rethinking of the modern, and the promise of a 'deeper and richer' reality.

In the end, the passage grave does not represent a new beginning, but a return to a completed past and the end of all futures. There is no hope here, only a lemming-like rush towards apocalypse. The novel only offers the illusion of a deeper reality contained in the sedimentation of time in the burial mound that connects across four thousand years of historical time. This sedimentation of time seems to offer the continuity and grounding that the otherwise placeless and groundless postmodern is lacking. But in reality, the novel only further registers that absence by presenting not only a absurd connection across time, but an end of time, a collapsing of all time into the present.

The desire for grounding in the postmodern is also represented through loss of, and a desire for, family. In the novel, two figures are both desperate to find a family in which to place themselves and find continuity. One is Mark Clare's 'crippled' wife, who can see no future because she is childless and, she believes, unable to create anything new or leave anything behind. The other is Joey, the orphaned entertainer who discovers that he is related to the Mint family:

> But the discovery of his family had allowed him to see his life as part of some larger continuity and, just as he could now look backward with more confidence, so also could he look forward. The world, before, had merely been an index of his ageing; but now it seemed to him to contain the possibility of change, to be always capable of renewal.
> (FL: 222–3)

But as with the New Age travellers' search for a 'deeper and richer' reality, Joey's search for family is met with bizarre and unreal connections. The postmodern chronotope extends what might be a comforting return to family relations to an impossible and unpresentable bonding. Science, physical grounding in place and family relations, which might all provide some kind of ballast against the temporal and spatial airiness of the postmodern, are all offered within this postmodern novel but then turned into grotesque parody. Rather than finding any response to the postmodern condition, the novel seems only to find ways of recording that which has been lost. On the same theme, Ian McEwan's *The Child in Time*, is also about loss, here the loss of the child and the idea of childhood in the postmodern.

LOST TIME AND CHILDHOOD IN IAN MCEWAN'S *THE CHILD IN TIME*

In Ian McEwan's rather more human and largely realistic novel, *The Child in Time*, time is an intrinsic part of human and social being, and it is more specifically about a particular postmodern society – Britain in the 1980s. Whereas Ackroyd's novels present time as an abstract concept and play with alternative forms of historical and cosmological time, McEwan's novel is more concerned with the experience of time from individual and social perspectives.

The main character's withdrawal from time is triggered by the loss of his child, an event which seems to transpose him into the unreal time of her disappearance. As a time that continues in parallel with the real world, but without her presence to fill it, this is a lost time, a time that is only capable of marking the time since her loss. This is not a time of renewal and regeneration, but a time of stagnation, a perpetual present without future. In my reading of the novel, Stephen's fate after the loss of his child implies the fate of a postmodern society that has also lost the child in itself. This is a society that has lost what Lyotard calls that 'inhuman' that gives to adulthood its sense of being human: 'this debt to childhood . . . which we never pay off' (Lyotard 1991: 7). But in a more obvious sense, this is a society that, by losing the child, has lost its will to renew itself, and its ability to look forward.

What shakes Stephen back into time, and into the physical process of regeneration, is an 'out of time' experience in which he 'remembers' a moment between his conception and his birth. But the novel relies on a number of quirks of time and is informed, like *First Light*, by theories of non-directional time in quantum physics. On one level, this is story about how a man unlocks himself from the moment in which his child was stolen from him and re-enters procreative time. As his wife gives birth to their new child, they both reconnect with a continuous time and are part of a regenerative world again.

But on another level, the novel also suggests that British society in the 1980s also needs to stop mourning for its lost past and get on with renewing itself. The novel portrays a society that has become stagnated, trapped in the present. Within this society, a rift has developed between an adult vision of the world and the world of childhood, and the solution to the crisis would seem to lie within the social constitution of time, which somehow needs to have an idea of childhood reintegrated back into it. In the novel, however, although the government is ostensibly defining childhood and, ensuring it is included within society, it is murdered by institutionalising a regulated form of childhood designed to replicate the present society and its values. By attempting to define and standardise childhood the child is made an extension of the adult world.

Stephen and postmodern Britain are both 'lost in time', stagnated and without will to the future. Stephen feels cut off from 'biological time' – the time measured not by a mechanical clock, but by a clock that is 'sinewy like a heart' (CT: 8). His sense of time alternates between a vacant timelessness filled with alcohol and television, and the fiction that is the *missing time* of his daughter's life. After she has been snatched from him in a supermarket, she continues to exist, for Stephen, in some other world separated from him by a 'frail, semi-opaque screen', with its 'fine tissues of time and chance' (CT: 8). He feels he must keep faith with the 'biological clock' which unceasingly measures her progress because 'Without the fantasy of her continued existence he was lost, time would stop' (CT: 8).

In the society portrayed by McEwan here, which is clearly a slightly exaggerated version of Britain in the 1980s under the premiership of Margaret Thatcher, the redefinition of childhood is a major issue. We could say that Stephen's loss of a daughter awakens him, eventually, to the concept of a regenerative time, in which renewal is always possible. But, within the society portrayed here, regenerative time – the true time of childhood – is turned into a fantasy world, separate from the 'real' world, and contained within children's story books and 'The Authorised Childcare Handbook'. Stephen's own novel, 'Lemonade', which was meant to be a more or less factual account of his own early years, becomes a best seller, seized upon by children and adults alike, because it recalls a lost childhood; it restores the idea of childhood by registering its absence.

This book is to have a profound effect on another character in the novel, the right-wing politician Charles, who abandons his government post and his work on producing 'The Authorised Childcare Handbook' to indulge in a fantasy of childhood. Charles, who in a previous career had published Stephen's novel of childhood, regresses, turning away from public life to live the life of a child again. For Charles, Stephen's novel creates an ideal of childhood as an especially creative, carefree and ungoverned life, a chaotic world of innocence. But his own work for the Prime Minister has all been concerned with ordering that world. In the internal conflict that follows, this friend of Stephen's and favourite of the Prime Minister, regresses into childhood to seek that lost world denied by his adult self. But this is a conditional escape from the adult world, one entered through a fantasy suggested by Stephen's novel 'Lemonade', which, as the title suggests, might be sugary and frothy and unable to sustain him. The regression is a fantasy that ends in Charles's death.

The Prime Minister's attempt to authorise childhood in society could be read as a fictionalised account of Margaret Thatcher's attempt to purge 1980s Britain of what she considered to be the excessively liberal and degenerative trends of the 1960s. This decade of hippies, women's liberation, the pill and free love, has often been considered as one of 'youth power' – a radical shift in fashion and cultural trends towards the demands of youth. In the novel, this is the period of Charles's and Stephen's childhood and the time of the novel 'Lemonade'. For Thatcher, and by implication, the Prime Minister in *The Child in Time*, it was this decade which, through its youth culture and emphasis on personal freedom, destroyed the family and traditional values of self-reliance. She is committed then to controlling society and purging it of the unruly elements of youth. At the same time, she is committed to removing dependence on the state, and shifting responsibility to the individual and the family. Part of the Prime Minister's strategy for achieving this in the novel is to produce 'The Authorised Childcare Handbook', a government publication aimed at purging society of the non-adult or inhuman world of childhood. Childhood is being standardised and authorised, because it is seen as a threat to the order of society.

In this portrayal of 1980s British society, not only has Stephen's child been snatched away, but large groups of children have also been taken out of society and turned into 'ex-children', or 'licensed beggars' (CT: 8). The kind of childhood in which play and the imagination have free rein is being displaced by a government convinced of the need for a society of self-reliant adults. There is no room and no money for the right of the child to be a child, and 'The Authorised Childcare Handbook', cited throughout the novel, makes this clear:

> Childhood is an invention, a social construct, made possible by a society as it increased in sophistication and resource. Above all, childhood is a privilege. No child as it grows older should be allowed to forget that its parents, as embodiments of society, are the ones who grant this privilege, and do so at their own expense.
>
> (CT: 93)

The government attempts to control childhood by creating the chronotope of the child under licence, as it were. Inverting Lyotard's claim that 'the debt to childhood is one we never pay off', we are presented with a society in which childhood is granted as a privilege, a luxury. Childhood here is only offered as an inducement into a fully integrated adult world, with parents as the embodiments of that adult society, and here it is the child who owes the debt to adulthood. The control of childhood is managed through education, especially through language, and through the enforcement of clock time which synchronises childhood with the adult world:

> Make it clear to him that the clock cannot be argued with and that when it is time to leave for school, for Daddy to go to work, for Mummy to attend her duties, then these changes are as incontestable as the tides.
>
> (CT: 27)

The child has limited freedom to make his own time here, and must conform to the chronotope of the adult world dominated by the clock time that divides the day into work, rest and play. In capitalist societies, this division of time is 'incontestable', and impressing this on the child is clearly an attempt to condition the child for work.

In *The Child in Time*, the government's attempts to condition and control childhood as a formative period prior to adulthood are countered by attempts to reconstitute and re-enter childhood. The popularity among adults of Stephen's novel about childhood indicates nostalgia not only for times passed at an individual level, but also for the general loss of the child from society, figured in the particular loss of Stephen's daughter. This loss, for Stephen, forces him to reach out towards the world he imagines she inhabits. He loses a sense of his own time by trying to enter her time, and by trying to return to the moment before he lost her:

> Stephen was to make efforts to re-enter this moment, to burrow his way back through the folds between events, crawl between the covers, and reverse his decision. But time – not necessarily as it is, for who knows that, but as thought has constituted it – monomanically forbids second chances. There is no absolute time . . .
>
> (CT:14)

Charles demonstrates that it is possible to reconstitute the time of childhood as a complete chronotope, but an unreal one constituted out of a denial of adulthood and his adult self. It seems that it is possible to move from the chronotope of childhood to that of adulthood by denying the childhood out of which the adult grew and defined himself. The arrow of time here is again one that protects the ideology of development, and the tragic end to Charles's regression suggests that reversing the process is not feasible. Stephen is less radical in his attempts to escape the chronotope of adulthood, and his attempts appear to have positive results. In the conclusion to the novel, Stephen and his wife are at last able to contemplate the regenerative time the birth of their baby brings, and the future once more opens out before them. Now they feel able to 'rejoin' the world – it is as if they are on the threshold of time, 'before the beginning of time', and have rediscovered the future again (CT: 220). The child brings with it not only a new life, but also, it would seem, a new time.

Stephen's return to the future is achieved through a personal reconstitution of time that involves a disordering of linearity. The attempt to turn the clock back or to regress cannot work, because the clock continues to run from that point and so eventually takes him back to the point of regression. Neither can denial work because Stephen is unable to forget the loss of his daughter. The breakthrough seems to be two 'out of time' experiences which shake him out of his highly linear concept of time. The moment that is most difficult to explain is Stephen's 'memory' of the day his parents decided whether he should be born or aborted. If Stephen can remember a moment before he is born, then commonsensical linear time cannot explain it. He solicits the help of Thelma, a theoretical physicist and the wife of Charles, who suggests that it might be possible, one day, to describe this kind of experience mathematically, if relativity, which describes a causal and continuous world, and quantum theories, which describe a non-causal discontinuous world, could be unified. Because then:

> Different kinds of time, not simply the linear, sequential time of commonsense, could be projected through consciousness from the higher common ground, from which consciousness itself would be a function, a limited case which in turn would be inseparable from the matter which was its subject, or the space within which it occurred . . .
> (CT: 119)

This does not explain Stephen's 'unplaced' memory but, using the non-linear time of quantum physics, it does suggest the possibility of it being explained, and does not rule out a rational explanation for a seemingly irrational event. This might presumably offer some hope to Stephen who is haunted by a particular sequence of events, and is unable to project himself beyond the memory of the loss of his daughter. He needs to reconnect with the present, and imagine himself in time, moving forwards with it, rather than being locked into a continuous and barren past.

In his futureless frame of mind, Stephen finds contentment in a landscape that seems to signify timelessness. In this chronotope, time, or rather timelessness, is spatialised and represented as monotony and lack of direction: 'All sense of progress, and therefore all sense of time, disappeared. The trees on the far side did not come closer. . . . the disappearance of any real sense of a destination, suited him' (CT: 52). By way of contrast, Stephen imagines his wife 'transforming herself', as she walks purposefully 'through the symmetrical pines, reassessing her past, their past, shuffling priorities, making arrangements for a new future' (CT: 54). He envies her what he believes to be that aspect of the feminine that provides 'Such faith in endless mutability, in re-making yourself as you came to understand more, or changed your version' (CT: 54). Stephen wonders if there is a fundamental difference here in the way men and women approach time. Women it seems are more able to adjust and adapt to events, to change direction, to remake themselves if necessary, while men get stuck in a particular track: 'Past a certain age, men froze into place, they tended to believe that, even in adversity, they were somehow at one with their fates' (CT: 54).

For Stephen it is the shock of further events that eventually reconnects him with the present, and this is also perceived as a shift in the consciousness of time from its simple linear and sequential form. As he tries to avoid running his car into an overturned truck, he finds that time has slowed down:

> Now, in this slowing of time, there was a sense of a fresh beginning. He had entered a much later period in which all the terms and conditions had changed. So these were the new rules, and he experienced something like awe, as though he were walking alone into a great city on a newly discovered planet.
>
> (CT: 94)

This represents a significant shift in Stephen's time horizon since marching across the wheat field, and he can now reassess the 'out of time' experience in the pub on the other side of that field. This pub, The Bell, is where his parents met to determine his fate some forty years earlier, and Stephen finds himself suddenly confronted with this time and this place charged with significance but somehow dissociated from his biological time, outside the linearity of his own existence:

> Stephen stood on the edge of a minor road in Kent on a wet day in mid-June, attempting to connect the place and its day with a memory, a dream, a film, a forgotten childhood visit. He wanted a connection which might begin a process of explanation and allay his fear. But the call of the place, its knowingness, the longing it evinced, the rootless significance, all this made it seem quite certain, even before he could tell himself why, that the loudness – this was the word he fixed on – of this

> particular location had its origins outside his own existence... The day he now inhabited was not the day he had woken into...
>
> (CT: 57)

This is a similar chronotope to the non-linear chronotopes found in *Hawksmoor* and *First Light*, where a concept of absolute linear time is also problematised. But rather than problematising social time and historical time, this chronotope is more concerned with reconstituting the time of personal experience. The introduction of non-linear time from quantum physics is used to map phenomenal experience. As in Ackroyd's novels, place seems capable of simultaneously organising multiple forms of time, and of carrying the past into the present across historical time. But although The Bell triggers Stephen's out of place memory, the subject of the memory itself has no home – its disembodied voice is that of an embryo, before birth and so *before* history, it is of a time before time:

> His eyes grew large and round and lidless with desperate, protesting innocence, his knees rose under him and touched his chin, his fingers were scaly flippers, gills beat time, urgent hopeless strokes through the salty ocean that engulfed the treetops and surged between their roots; and for all the crying, calling sounds he thought were his own, he formed a single thought: he had nowhere to go, no moment which could embody him, he was not expected, no destination or time could be named; for while he moved forward violently, he was immobile, he was hurtling round a fixed point.
>
> (CT: 60)

For a moment, Stephen seems to become this unborn child, out of time, and floating in a timeless, placeless, void. But when he awakes from this dream, he finds himself at Julie's cottage, which was his original destination when he set out across the wheat field. They make love there, and he realises that this moment is somehow connected with the one earlier: 'Obscurely, he sensed a line of argument was being continued... the two moments were undeniably bound, they held in common the innocent longing they provoked, the desire to belong' (CT: 63). Rather than regress, Stephen has in a sense experienced rebirth and begun again the voyage towards belonging. And this *voyage in* coincides with the conception of Julie and Stephen's new child, completing a complex cycle of loss and renewal, displacement and belonging. Stephen's displaced memory shows him how he must have called himself into being, into time, and now it seems that a new child is calling itself into being – this is the child 'in time' that mirrors the stolen child taken out of time. And it is the new child in time that leads Stephen's recuperation, placing him back in time: 'Time was redeemed, time assumed purpose all over again . . .' (CT: 64).

The embodiment in time of Stephen and his new child satisfies a desire for belonging which somehow redeems the past and connects it to the present and future. Stephen finds himself back 'in time', through the family ties that connect him in time and the process of regeneration which creates new time. The novel also seems to suggest that postmodern British society is in hiatus, suffering from lack of belonging and from the loss of a future time perspective, and that this is because it has lost the power to regenerate itself. Britain in the 1980s is depicted as a society with the child removed from it, so it has become an adult world, producing new adults in the same mould, afraid to let a new generation define itself and create a new time for itself. The lack of a sense of belonging, which Stephen refers to when he is searching for the moment that will embody him and redeem time for him, is a kind of placelessness. But this is a temporal problem as well as a spatial one, and in social terms, lack of belonging can also refer to the failure for society to place itself in time, to place itself in history. But the answer, in my reading of this novel, is not to regress, to re-enter history at some predetermined point and engage in a fantasy of reliving the past, but to find some way of moving outside history, to reconstitute time itself and create new beginnings. But this is not an ideological recreation based on some idea of the future, so the revolution is not explicitly political. Rather this is a revolution in the nature of time itself, imagined through the chronotope of non-directional time.

In Conclusion – The Social Politics of Non-directional Time

Social time provides the embeddedness, stratification and synchronisation necessary for placement and order in society (Lewis and Weigart 1990). To the individual, social time is important as a prevalent order enfolding and giving shape to psychological time, and extending psychological time into some larger context. It seems to me that as well as the problematisation of historical time in the postmodern novel, which has received considerable attention in this work and elsewhere, we also need to pay attention to the problematisation of social time. If the postmodern novel imaginatively reconstitutes social time as well as historical and historiographic time, it is the *form* of social time itself that needs investigating. Especially as it is through this form of time that western societies can be seen to embed, stratify and synchronise themselves both within and with respect to other societies.

The perspectives of social time in the West in the twentieth century were formed largely by the demands of industrial capitalism and modernity. But this linear and future-directed time perspective is associated with a modern ideology of development and progress that the postmodern as a whole brings into question. The postmodern explores the past, not to find meaning for the present and guides to the future, but to trouble the present with conflicting evidence about the content and the form of the past. As to the content of the past, the postmodern regards it as continuing to exist in the present and it cannot therefore be regarded as closed and finalised. As regards the form of the past, here the postmodern questions the very concept of linearity by which the past stays behind the present and the future remains ahead. This is both a problematisation of the social constitution of time in modernity, and a response to the history of modernity whose high point is marked, many say, by both the end of ideology and by rampant capitalism. The question that many ask is whether postmodern theories and practices offer a path through the ends of modernity, or whether they are too implicated in and subject to the temporal and spatial disorientation of the times.

In my readings of this selection of postmodern novels, it seems to me that a creative approach to history and to forms of social time is being practised, and if this does not envision futures as such, this is not necessarily important, nor is it to be expected. Indeed, I think we would be more suspicious of postmodern novels which did offer utopian visions of a postmodern future, or a return to the modern. It is enough for the moment to find that postmodern cultural practices engage in trying to unravel and rework the past and displace the present as a rational consequence of an already written past. And that in doing so, they consider alternative forms of social time and most importantly make no attempt to revere and preserve the past. As Yi-Fu Tuan points out, an obsession with history and preserving the past is not the sign of a 'truly rooted community', at ease with itself. Although a rooted community might enshrine and monumentalise the past, attempts to preserve the relics and forms of the past is a sign of a society fearful and uncertain of the future, and unsure of its roots (Tuan 1977: 198). On the contrary then, if the postmodern novel is prepared to dispense with and play with the relics and forms of the past, this suggests it might be the product of a society confident, without fear for the future and certain of its roots.[12]

In *Hawksmoor* and *First Light*, by Peter Ackroyd, and *The Child in Time*, by Ian McEwan, 'violations' of space–time occur which cannot be accounted for in realistic terms. Science is used metaphorically rather than literally, and it is transposed into the social and cultural spheres to help us conceive of the multiplicity and non-directionality of social time. In postmodernity, particularly, which is a period in which history seems to have stalled, society does not seem able to place itself in a continuum of time that connects it with the past and the future. In the novels we have explored here, there are several attempts by society and individuals to create time, and to embed themselves in a time that travels in both (or many) directions. These novels all suggest that British postmodern society needs to regenerate itself, and to do this it must have a conception of time in which it can place itself, but this need not be a return to a future-directed linear form of time. Indeed, perhaps a society can only ever be at ease with itself if it is capable of creating space and time by regenerating itself, while at the same time, keeping paths open into the past.

But beyond the theoretical constitution of a British social time we must begin to consider now a more global, multicultural situation. Increasingly in Britain and elsewhere it is not simply a matter of society as a whole conceiving of itself in time, but of heterogeneous social groups vying to 'sediment' conflicting conceptions of time in the same physical location. There have always been different conceptions of social time constituted by different societies, but these differently constituted times were usually more geographically and historically distinct. In *Hawksmoor*, two different conceptions of time divide society in eighteenth century London as the city moves into the modern age, but this is mainly a transitional problem. In the late twentieth century, different constitutions of social time are brought together in the same place and at the same time, particularly following post-colonial migrations, but also as a result of postmodern mobility and lack of belonging. This contributes to a multiplicity within place and to conflict between different groups trying to 'sediment' their particular form of social time in the same place.

The next chapter examines postmodern novels that explore multiplicity of time and space from a post-colonial perspective.

CHAPTER 7

Post-colonial Island Chronotopes:
Michel Tournier, *Friday, or The Other Island*
J. M. Coetzee, *Foe*
Caryl Phillips, *Cambridge*
Marina Warner, *Indigo: Or, Mapping the Waters*

POSTMODERN PLACELESSNESS AND POST-COLONIALISM

So far, the postmodern novels covered in this work are set within European and American shores, and so from a post-colonial perspective are limited to rethinking history and reworking modernity from a *centrist* position. This chapter widens the field by including postmodern novels, which although always pegged to the colonial centre, look outwards to, and inwards from, the islands and problematic shores of the Caribbean.[1] Here, the postmodern chronotope is not only concerned with problematising reality, as framed by tradition and modernity, but is also used specifically to problematise a colonialist reality articulated in representations of the Caribbean and centre–periphery relations.

The postmodern chronotope is involved in mapping the changing shape of the post-colonial world in the context of postmodernity, and it takes postmodernist strategies into a reworking of colonialist histories and other forms of colonialist representation. There is some conflict here and there is pressure on the chronotope in both temporal and spatial dimensions. Firstly, the emergence of post-colonial nation states independent from the motherland must compete with the globalising forces of postmodernity with their tendency to erase national boundaries. Secondly, in the temporal dimension, a postmodern problematisation of history makes it difficult for new national identities to emerge forged from rediscovered and homogenous native histories.

Turning this on its head, post-colonialism might be relied upon to provide resistance to postmodern globalisation by reasserting ethnic and racial difference as a geographical and cultural divide over and above (or more likely underneath) the postmodern. Post-colonialism is an important element in a dialectics of local/global not always accounted for in accounts of globalisation. This dialectics is crucial to mapping the postmodern world and helping to account for its shifting boundaries and multiple topographies. The old boundaries of modern nation states no longer give an accurate picture of the political and economic world, nor of the world of experience (if indeed they ever did). Pressures on the boundaries of the nation state come from two directions. Firstly, there is an obvious weakening of national boundaries from globalisation mainly driven by the economic forces of capitalism supported, in neo-imperialist fashion, by the power blocs of the west. What makes this globalisation postmodern is that it is *transmitted* through media and cultural production that is itself at the leading edge of the tide of post-industrial capitalism. In a world dominated by information and image, we might say 'the medium is the message is the business'. In this respect, TV advertising, fashion, MTV, the internet, McDonalds, Disneyland, mobile phones and so on are both *signifier* and *technique* of postmodern globalisation.

But there are contrary forces, and in the late twentieth century, while globalisation rolls out, another process of re-differentiation has been taking place, namely the reassertion of the ethnic and racial divides that the modern nation state had suppressed. At one level, the world is amalgamating into three or four huge power blocks dominated by the US; and underneath, thousands of enclaves, cantons, districts and regions are getting more autonomy. One of the least bloody examples of this was the recent devolution of Scotland from the United Kingdom, a devolution made possible largely by a weakening of UK sovereignty through membership of the European Community. But devolution and the gathering of geographically dispersed ethnic, racial and social groups can also be assisted by the same new technologies that enable and transmit globalisation. A more positive effect of the new technologies of communications in postmodernity is that ethnic, racial and social groups are no longer necessarily confined to geographical boundaries. Although such technologies transmit globalisation, it also becomes possible to transcend the geographical and to gather and meet in virtual worlds. Social being, and even to some extent, human being, is thus partly removed from the terrestrial. Somewhere between reality and fantasy, 'terminal users' place themselves in virtual worlds and, within the limits of 'virtual' experience, select other roles and environments to inhabit.

Post-colonial situations have ensured that racial and ethnic groups become more geographically dispersed, largely through post-colonial migrations of the post-colonised to the motherland of the post-coloniser. At a superficial level, disparate racial and ethnic groups share the same geographical space and, through several generations, might even begin to share the same histories, but there is not an even process of assimilation. Dispersed ethnic groups, especially when they are from ex-colonies, are often confined economically to certain areas – ghettoised – while others wheel and deal above, below and around them in postmodern global space. Doreen Massey refers to this uneven access to global space as the 'power-geometry' of space (Massey 1993: 61). A study of the literature of conflict within post-colonised communities in postmodern Britain, a conflict between assimilation and the reassertion of difference, is clearly called for, but there is no space for this in the present study.[2]

This chapter is concerned with the other end of the problem, with how the post-colonial nation emerges in postmodernity and seeks to define itself against colonialist representations of it. The problem is one of defeating, or appropriating and subverting, previous realist representations in which the colonised and her country are defined out of and subordinate to the colonial centre. To a lesser extent, it is concerned with reattachment to displaced and silenced histories and traditions, but this process of *recuperation* is complicated by its necessarily fictional basis and with its reinvention of mythologies. As we have already seen, the postmodern chronotope is often used against realist representations that rely on linearity and continuous time–space.

In post-colonial literatures, the postmodern chronotope can be used to equal effect to disrupt colonialist representation. The question remains, of course, once realist representation itself is ruled out, as a tool of the coloniser, what form of representation can help reconstruct a new identity for the post-colonised? The answer is perhaps to be found in the common postmodern loophole that nothing is ever entirely one thing or another. Postmodern novels frequently make use of realist form as well as shaking the frames that produce such reality. For example, Marina Warner's *Indigo* weaves fantasy, fictionalised history, myth and realism into a powerful political novel very much concerned with the identity and future of a real place and its people.

Today's multicultural and post-colonial societies are an integral part of postmodernity. Postmodernism may have emerged from white, male academics in the US, but postmodernity is a global phenomenon, almost by definition. In this context, traditional definitions of 'authentic' and 'organic' place rising out of tradition, lived experience and history, clearly will not do. So, unless we are to reach extinction in continuous struggles for space, tribe against tribe for the same patch of earth, we need to construct for ourselves a more accommodating, more flexible and more progressive concept of social space (and time). This would be a space–time that could reach back and forth through various histories and encompass different sociological times. The role of the postmodern novel in conceiving of such space–times within representational space is important here, because as we saw earlier, representational space is an intrinsic part of the production of social space and the building of place.[3] In which case, the towns, cities and countries of the future might be a mishmash of styles and traditions, non-exclusive and rejecting modern aesthetics of abstract unity and form. The same could be said for the postmodern novel.

Postmodern globalisation will inevitably lead to a condition of placelessness where society loses that sense of belonging customarily found in traditional constructions of place. In postmodernity, this is not only a geographical problem, but also an historical one, with society losing sense of its place in history as well. A truly rooted sense of place, in which social groups are knitted into a shared history within a shared locale, is becoming a thing of the past. We have already seen that in postmodern novels such as *Waterland*, history no longer provides structures for society to place itself in and build futures on. On the other hand, from the previous chapter on the novels of Ackroyd and McEwan, there emerges a compulsion to try to 'sediment' time, through its inscription in monuments, churches, texts and other representational sites. We can probably assume that a desire for society to construct sites of some kind that connect across history is a constant, but the approach is necessarily different in different societies at different times. In postmodernity, a desire to connect with the past and reach across history is often attempted without what the moderns would call 'a sense of history'. So, sites, in which the past has been secreted as an underground time capsule, will thrust themselves into the present, without history. We have just seen an instance of this in Julian's vision of archaeology in *First Light*, with the past reproduced alongside the present as simulacra. The postmodern chronotope reaches into the past without sequence, without historicity – the phenomenal past appears as the shock of the old, almost as spectacle.

This chapter examines postmodern placelessness (in the temporal and spatial sense) in the context of a particular post-colonial situation, specifically that of the Caribbean. But this is also an examination of post-colonial lack of belonging and problematic identity in a postmodern context. In a post-colonial context, placelessness is firstly a questioning device to re-examine the histories with which, and on which, colonial places like the Caribbean have previously been constructed, by and for Europe. In the postmodern chronotope of the novel, it is possible to contain the multiple conflicting histories that lie behind these colonial constructions, and to imagine new post-colonial constructions in which separate geographical places like Britain and the Caribbean are linked by multiple but overlapping histories. This might undermine a traditional sense of rooted place on either side of the centre–periphery divide, but as this is already happening because of postmodernity, and as such rootedness often leads to exclusion, elitism, and then racism, perhaps, in some instances, we should not mourn its passing. We move on in this chapter to an idea of place that is not cemented in traditional historical narrative, but is stretched across multiple histories and geographies. Furthermore, this complex sense of place is made forcibly contingent with the contemporary, not to anchor the present, but to set it in a sea of flux – to convey a sense of what Doreen Massey calls a 'progressive sense of place' (Massey 1993: 61). For this process, we could use the subtitle of Marina Warner's novel *Indigo: Or, Mapping the Waters*.

THE OLD NEW WORLD – THE CARIBBEAN BY AND FOR EUROPE

Colonialist discourse produced a cultural map of the Caribbean and the American colonies and incorporated its islands within an *imago mundi* centred in Europe. This east-in-the-west that Vespucci christened the 'New World' performed a role as Europe's other, but this negative mirror image soon turned into the objective reality of jealously guarded insular possessions. Crucially, this New World, unlike the culturally and economically superior east-in-the-east that Marco Polo had presented to European audiences, was empty and primitive and ripe for domination.[4]

The portrayal of the Caribbean island in Daniel Defoe's *Robinson Crusoe* is typical of the colonialist discourse that articulates the empty place, the almost-nowhere place, the place without history and without culture, save the savage customs, borrowed from mythical reports of the East, of cannibalism and idolatry. What is not borrowed from reports of the East, is the childlike innocence and feminine passivity of a race apparently prepared to accept domination. This colonialist discourse was never present in Polo's earlier orientalism. In Marco Polo's *Travels* (Latham 1958), and in *The Travels of Sir John Mandeville* (Moseley 1983), both widely available in Europe in the fifteenth and sixteenth centuries, the East is a place of immense riches and diversity. Early exploration of the Americas was a huge disappointment to Europe seeking to expand venture capitalism through trade. The viability of the Americas was dependent on slavery, so a colonialist discourse in which slavery might be regarded as not only possible but, rather perversely, Christian and benevolent, was extremely helpful.

Robinson Crusoe is designed to appeal to the European imagination. The Caribbean here is not a real place but a place designed for European delectation, a 'not-Europe' that differentiates civilised Europe from nature and barbarism. As Tzvetan Todorov reminds us, ever since Amerigo Vespucci seduced European readers with salacious accounts of the New World as a female object of desire, Europeans have exploited the Caribbean imaginatively as well as materially (Todorov 1994: 50). There is no attempt by European writers to present a real Caribbean, rather it is used as material for constructing what Jon Stratton refers to as 'colonial Other', turning the Caribbean into a site of difference at the periphery of colonial Europe (Stratton 1990: 136–9). The Caribbean is mainly represented in terms of its difference from Europe, so where Europe had lack, the Caribbean had plenty; where

Europe was civilised, the Caribbean was savage; and where Europe was cultivated, the Caribbean was natural. For Stratton, the extraordinary success in Europe of Daniel Defoe's *Robinson Crusoe* was because it 'helped organise aspects of the discourse of exploration and colonialism in a way that made sense of it for literate Europeans' (Stratton 1990: 155). The centrality of this text in colonialist discourse makes it an obvious target for post-colonial revisions and postmodern disruptions, and it is these that are the subject of this chapter.

The Caribbean had a 'special place' in the European imagination because it marked the first frontier between the Old World of Europe and the New World of America. Beyond here was the promise, initially of untold and untoiled for gold and riches, which proved mainly unfulfilled, and then of deserted and open spaces, virgin land in which self and society might impose itself. But this space of the New World proved to be an ambiguous space – full but empty, pure but in need of redemption. It is in this ambiguous space that European literature begins to stage first encounters between native Carib Indians and European explorers; and later between transported African slaves and European planters, traders and administrators – the colonisers.

In island stories like *Robinson Crusoe* and *The Tempest* there are first encounters between people from different worlds, and in a sense from different times as well. The New World is often depicted here populated by savages whose cannibalistic culture is 'sub-human'. In this monstrous grotesque, European Christianity finds its other, with its emphasis on the naked body and bodily functions including the ultimate crime against humanity, the eating of human flesh. The Christian, on the other hand, hides his flesh and depravity from the world by clothes and faith. There is a dichotomous relationship, then, between the naked savage and the spiritually and physically covered-up European. The gulf is so wide that assimilation seems impossible, and so civilising Friday is only a gesture that reaffirms Crusoe's superiority, not a genuine attempt to make him equal.

The colonialist import of the gulf between native and European is obvious, and what makes this all the more divisive is the fact that it is largely based on supporting myth, and contrary to actual experience of first encounters.[5] The European Caribbean presents a history of the world as one of uneven evolution, with the New World lagging behind in some primitive era, disconnected from the 'real' history of development in Europe. And to support the myth, Europe re-invokes antiquity and the conflict between the civilising order and the barbarians. In the classical world of antiquity, Europe found an iconography through which to translate and elevate its own barbarous actions of genocide and slavery.[6] Europeans exported more than the practical tools of colonisation to the Caribbean, they also exported a Christian and classical mythology to displace native systems of belief. The casting away of Crusoe is a defining moment marking the de-peopling and de-mythologising of native space in the Caribbean, the beginning of its mastery by external forces, and its re-peopling with slaves, lackeys and colonial adventurers. All of which culminates in Crusoe's self-proclaimed sovereignty over his island state, his imperial and sovereign gaze makes him master of all he surveys.

A critical factor in this process, and one at the heart of the present work, is the role of emergent modern concepts of space and time through which the New World is appropriated into the maps and histories of Europe. The concept of island space seems to be fundamental to this process, or at least as far as literature's involvement in this process is concerned. As well as constituting the margins of the New World, the Caribbean is also an island geography, and island space has special significance in the European imagination and especially the British imagination. Britain has always had a sense of itself as an island detached from the European continent. In English literature, the island is often an abstraction of English society projected into fictional space – a little world beyond place and time, in which certain aspects of that society can be emphasised, idealised or satirised.

But the chronotope of a displaced or dislocated English society is not entirely one of non-place, because we find (in island stories such as *The Tempest*, *Utopia*, *Robinson Crusoe*, and *Gulliver's Travels*) references to the New World, links to Europe, and to the time of exploration and colonisation of the Caribbean. However, these island stories do not seem to say a great deal about exploration and colonisation itself, and Jon Stratton's claim that *Robinson Crusoe* was so popular because it organised 'aspects of the discourse of exploration and colonisation' to Europeans, seems rather unlikely, unless by this he means that it purged and simplified the discourse by transforming it from one of greed, piracy and tyranny into the noble struggle and moral duty of one man/nation to dominate another. More to the point of the present work, *Robinson Crusoe* and other island stories help organise colonial discourse by massively simplifying the spatial complexities of colonisation. The desert island promises sovereignty and control at the expense of community. On Crusoe's island, what society exists is so stratified as to offer virtually no social interaction. Crusoe's presence on the island functions as the 'just' exercise of power. He is an exemplar for the colonial administrator who, despite being presented with absolute power, is somehow able to remain uncorrupted. As well as signifying the space of colonialist power, the desert island also promises separation and integrity, a clear and distinct mapping of the self as a kind of psychological purification, removed from the bother of debts, the guilt of abandoning family, and other baggage of the past. In the postmodern novels that revisit Defoe's island story, the island is no longer a distinct unified space, but is shot through with contradictory spaces and temporal and spatial connections.

The idea of island space as ego and delineated order, surrounded by a sea of unconsciousness, alterity and disorder, is a common theme in literature. But there is a paradox in the separation, because each individuated soul also wants to be part of a larger whole. John Donne, who was himself involved in trade with the New World in the early seventeenth century and who frequently draws on geographical imagery of the New World in his writing, presents this paradox in *Meditation*:

> No Man is an *Iland*, intire of it selfe; every man is a peece of the *Continent*, a part of the *maine*; if a *Clod* bee washed away by the *Sea*, *Europe* is the lesse, as well as if a *Promontorie* were, as well as if a *Mannor* of thy *friends*, or of *thine owne* were . . .
> (Donne 1967: ll. 35–9)

During the seventeenth and eighteenth centuries, Britain was busily connecting itself economically as well as imaginatively to the rest of the world, establishing interdependence beyond its own shores. The creation of this global economic space in some ways runs counter to the emergence at the same time of fiercely protected private space within the individualistic bourgeois culture of Europe. Ian Watt has argued that the emergence of the novel form in England in the eighteenth century is in some way connected with attempts to bridge this private space to a widening public and economic space. Although essentially a solitary and individualistic experience in its production and reception, the novel inserts a representational space between private and public space, enabling the two to be bridged and re-imagined. The rise of an individualistic culture as background to the rise of the English novel is a major theme in Ian Watt's influential study *The Rise of the Novel*, and *Robinson Crusoe* is one of his primary texts (Watt 1957; Watt 1969: 39).

This may seem to be straying from the point in a discussion of post-coloniality and the postmodern novel, but it is necessary to appreciate the use of space and time in literature of this period – such as *Robinson Crusoe* – and its links with colonial discourse. This is important background to the deconstructive moves and other forms of questioning in postmodern novels engaged in post-colonial discourse. Daniel Defoe's classic tale of man and island is perhaps both a representation of the conflicts of private and public space in bourgeois culture, as Watt suggests, and a pivotal text in a colonialist discourse, as Stratton suggests. Either way, English literature together with the notebooks of explorers, the accounts of plantation owners and the diaries of travellers, turned the Caribbean into a discursive site rather than a realistic site. This discourse is entirely one-sided because not until the twentieth century has there been much of an attempt to incorporate native Caribbean and African perspectives. So complete was the process of European colonisation, that it is hard to find native voices that have their origins in native culture. Finding the 'real' Caribbean still seems to be largely dependent on a European imagination, or a Caribbean-European hybrid imagination, like that of Caryl Phillips, whose work is discussed later in this chapter.

REPRESENTING POST-COLONIALITY IN POSTMODERN FORM

The postmodern novels covered in this chapter recognise and try to redress the myopic representation of Caribbean history and identity in which natives are generally regarded as 'other'. Where early modern fictions such as *The Tempest* and *Robinson Crusoe* portray a native culture that is mostly dumb or silent, postmodern fictions, such as those explored here, give voice to previously marginalised and silenced histories. In some respects this project is anthropological – to find and record the native voices of an authentic history of the 'real' Caribbean, and to displace the imaginative terrain constructed from within European discourse. But this project is fraught with the problems of recovering native history, and of separating truth from fiction within existent written history.

The history of the 'native' Caribbean is so wrapped up in British and other European colonial history that extricating it requires a certain unravelling of history. The Caribbean was colonised as surely by writing as by material means, and European literature was complicit in the representational colonisation. The dominant forms of this literature, which include the novel and travel literature, have particular narrative forms and also particular conceptions of space and time, all of which would have seemed 'normal' and familiar to European audiences. But native Caribs in the seventeenth and eighteenth century would have constituted their own, and probably very different, conceptions of space and time, and different forms of narrative (if only because it would have been oral and not written). As James Duncan has argued, a key aspect of the colonisation process is the replacement of native representational forms and belief systems, with those of the colonisers (Duncan 1989: 185–201). So, in *Robinson Crusoe*, when Friday fails to comprehend Crusoe's lessons with their European bias of use-value, hierarchy, and cultivation, Friday is depicted as a native lacking values, rather than a native with native values.

The postmodern post-colonial novel challenges the realist form which dominates colonial representations of the Caribbean and the values of order, sequence and structure it inculcates. Postmodern narrative technique subverts the determinism and causality of realist form by juxtaposing realist accounts of events with magical or metaphysical accounts. Where realist form helped fix the Caribbean within European colonial history and helped incorporate it within Europe's nation-building and Empire-building narratives, postmodern form, in this post-colonial context, disturbs these settled and placeable relationships using non-realist forms such as fantasy. A key strategy here is to invert the implied authority of the coloniser's realism over the native's magic.

Postmodern narrative also unsettles European colonial history by introducing multiple viewpoints and multiple histories, so that no one place can be anchored to a single historical chain. In the novels covered in this chapter, the history of two previously separate and distinct places – Britain and the Caribbean – are seen through multiple perspectives which 'unplace' both. Each site is prevented from becoming embedded in unequivocal 'official' history. The effect of this is not only to make Britain and the Caribbean unplaceable, but also to draw them together in shared unplaceability, so the Caribbean island becomes detached and distinct from its colonial centre. Conceptually, a reverse of colonisation occurs in these postmodern novels, with Caribbean history being imported into Britain, rather than British and European history being exported to its colonies. Colonial history comes home to roost, as it were, within post-colonial fictions that seem to bring the Caribbean island with it. In novels like *Foe*, *Cambridge*, and *Indigo* which we will look at in detail later in this chapter, Crusoe's island is no longer a detached outpost of Empire, but seems to 'hover' over the mainland, another layer within the multi-layered, multicultural space of Britain.

The postmodern novel, through its inherent intertextuality, freely mixes and imbricates 'true' and fictional accounts, testing distinctions between truth and fiction. Where it includes a post-colonial account, the postmodern novel uses this intertextuality to resist that assertion implicit in realist form, that empirical truth and rational thought constituted in European culture are superior to the magical belief systems that guide native culture. The postmodern novel also tends to highlight the silent spaces or holes in the narratives of earlier fictions to which it refers, and draws attention to the partial view of history resulting from these omissions. In *Foe*, for example, voices that might oppose the dominant white, male, European and order-loving voice of the hero of Defoe's novel, are reintroduced. So this novel tries to restore to *Robinson Crusoe* the native, black, magical, female or disorderly voices which have been excised from the original text.

In the postmodern novel, it is sometimes difficult to distinguish between technique and theme, and between form and content. For example, where the postmodern novel manipulates the indicators of space and time to enable earlier texts to be revisited and revised, this can be treated as technique, but it can also be read as an attack on a modern concept of quantifiable space and time. Exploration and colonisation in the seventeenth and eighteenth centuries employed modern representations of space and time to map, divide and exploit the New World. In several of the postmodern novels explored here, the chronotope of *Robinson Crusoe's island* is significantly extended, disrupting the cartographic clarity with which it is represented in Defoe's story. This is a process of de-differentiation acting against the cartographic clarity of modern map making that enabled exploration and colonisation. In the temporal dimension, it also acts against the standardisation of time introduced by the chronometer, that in turn helped standardise space by fixing longitudinal position.[7]

In some instances, the postmodern novel, in its manipulation of space and time within the novel's chronotopes, attempts to reassert pre-modern concepts of space and time before the map, the compass and the chronometer. It is a daring venture to imagine such a chronotope, and we need to look further back in literature to find representations of it. In *The Tempest*, written in the seventeenth century when the world was still being discovered by Europeans rather than being systematically explored, the Caribbean is portrayed as an enchanted isle connected to the rest of the world by nature and spirits, unconstrained by the quantitative space–time used in cartography. Ariel moves in a magical chronotope created by the writer/magician Prospero. In *Indigo*, Marina Warner revisits *The Tempest* and borrows this chronotope to help organise a narrative that interweaves pre-modern space and time with modern realism.

WRITING A POST-COLONIAL CARIBBEAN – THE 'NEW' NEW WORLD

The postmodern novel revisits and revises history, and in this post-colonial context it helps disclose the suppression in the colonial discourse of 'real' Caribbean geography and native Carib culture. But the postmodern post-colonial novel is more than a history lesson, it also has an imaginative purpose in recuperating key historical moments in native culture by, for instance, resuscitating – breathing new life into – first encounters between colonisers and natives. This is the route Marina Warner takes in *Indigo* and Caryl Phillips takes in *Cambridge* and *Crossing the River*.

The identity of the Caribbean is, as we have seen, the product of a European imagination that never conceived of it as a nation in its own right; this was never a nation born out of native relationships with its islands. The difficulty in the post-colonial situation, here and elsewhere, is to find some basis for an authentic native identity that is more than a mere refutation and negation of Eurocentric representations. The question is: can authentic histories, stories or myths be found from which a more creative and forward-looking sense of place might grow? There are two major problems here – first, most of the inhabitants of the Caribbean are of African descent, and have little in common with a pre-colonial Carib culture; and second, present day inhabitants of the Caribbean, including its writers and historians, can have little knowledge of what constituted Carib culture and a Carib history of place before the Europeans arrived. In the only available recorded history, European discovery is 'chapter one' in Caribbean history, as the reality of the Caribbean as a viable self-contained habitat for people with their own history and sense of place was lost as soon as the Europeans arrived in the sixteenth century. Prior to this, all is imagined territory and can only be visited through constructed fictions.

In *Indigo*, Marina Warner evokes Shakespeare's *The Tempest* to help create an imaginary island prior to European discovery. Although this imaginary island is still largely the product of a European imagination and is part of a European tradition, she uses it to speak for a lost native culture. She finds in this 'enchanted island' a counter to the age of discovery, and the rationalistic and economically dominated modern age that this ushered in. Finding in Shakespeare's island a world and a mythology opposed to Europe, she then uses this as a representational core for a Caribbean nation-building mythology. But this is not entirely an imaginative venture. *Indigo* also retrieves some of the cultural history of the Caribbean, referring to Peter Hulme's work on 'encounter narrative', while at the same time presenting a critique of colonial European narratives designed to interpret the New World for European audiences.[8] *Indigo* orchestrates narratives of first encounters and brings these into a post-colonial context through the hybridised voices of generations of mixed race families echoing back and forth between Britain and the Caribbean island.

TRANSFORMING ISLANDS

The forefather of the 'island text' in English literature is undoubtedly Defoe's *Robinson Crusoe*, even though *The Tempest* predated it by a hundred years or so. By the mid-nineteenth century there were hundreds of volumes of 'robinsonnades' which imitated or referred to Defoe's island text (Loxley 1990: 5). It seems likely that the idea in the European imagination of a deserted Caribbean island was fostered by stories of shipwrecks and island stories like *Robinson Crusoe*, where the island of the castaway is self-contained and far away from Europe. In Defoe's paradigm of the 'island story' there are links which connect Crusoe's island to mainland Europe and Africa through economic and family ties, but it is the distinctness of the island's unitary space, and its distance from the complexities of mainland life, that dominate the novel. Crusoe's island, enhanced by its tropical location, offers an escape from mainland life, a fresh start, a perfectible kingdom, and total power.

Of course if we study *Robinson Crusoe* itself, we are reminded that the island and Crusoe's adventures are carefully connected to Britain, North and West Africa, Europe and the already colonised regions of South America, but somehow this geographical placement seems insignificant beside the core of the island story. Although it seems to set the fiction in a realistic context, by explaining the causes of Crusoe's predicament and the consequences of his rescue, oddly it appears more like contrivance and clutter around the 'real' story on the island, so powerful is the island myth. In the postmodern novels that revisit *Robinson Crusoe*, the island chronotope is always reconnected in space and time with several 'mainland contexts', or rather 'mainland texts'. Here it is the mainland and the relationships between the island and the mainland that are the core of the story, not the island space itself. The island is reconnected to its colonial history, its literary context and its sociological context, where the castaway self and the individualistic tyrant are integrated back into the rest of society.

In *Robinson Crusoe*, Defoe's realist adventurer sets about turning disorderly nature into order within an island space. We might imagine that prior to Crusoe's arrival, the uncharted native space of the island was at one with the sea around it. But Crusoe transforms it, erasing its native and natural context. Crusoe turns the island space from the newly conceived 'nothing' into a fortress of European order. The sea, now in opposition to Crusoe's fortress, represents the disorder of natural and native elements that threaten his imposed order. He has no control over the sea, and fears the liminal space at the shoreline. In the postmodern novels that revisit *Robinson Crusoe*, this perceived opposition between island space and sea is deconstructed. In *Foe* and *Friday* in particular, the threat presented by the sea is textual, as a disorderly narrative impinges on the centred structure formed by the authority of Crusoe's insular narrative. But this sea of disorder not only disrupts and erodes Crusoe's patriarchal and colonial order, it is also inserts a (feminine) space of creativity and fecundity. In *Foe* and *Indigo*, the sea redeems the sterility and barrenness of Crusoe's island fortress.

This chapter examines a number of postmodern re-presentations of key 'source' texts – *The Tempest*, and *Robinson Crusoe* – in the light of post-colonial repositioning and focusing on use of the postmodern chronotope to disorganise the temporal and spatial dimensions of the island text. The organisation and disorganisation of island space might be arranged as follows:

- **Enchanted islands,** *The Tempest*: Shakespeare's island is at something of a crossroads. As a narrative for explaining the New World to Europeans, it associates the unknown and uncharted with magic and the imagination. The time is still one of discovery.

- **Cultivated islands,** *Robinson Crusoe*: Defoe's island is ordered. Crusoe dominates its native elements, transforming it into a unified and rationalised space, set in a sea chaos and unpredictability. The time is not one of discovery now, but of a scientifically mapped and rational order. It is 'modern' space, purged of the magic of the unknown.

- **Transcendental islands,** *Friday, or The Other Island*: in the postmodern, the island space is less clearly defined and more ambiguous once more. On Tournier's island, chance and mysticism begin to take over from the order of science and Providence. The island chronotope is violently divided into two mutually exclusive worlds, one corresponding loosely with Defoe's representation, and the other its binary opposite.

- **Paper islands,** *Foe*: In Coetzee's island space, the difference implied in Tournier's double island space explodes into multiple island spaces, each associated with a text that signifies another text, and so on. This could be regarded as the post-structuralist response to Tournier's structuralist island.[9]

- **Translated islands,** *Cambridge*: Phillips' island space is produced initially in an English, colonising narrative, and then translated by an islander, although he too is translated, having been initially 'written' in African, and then converted to English.

- **Recovered islands,** *Indigo: Or, Mapping the Waters*: Warner's island space covers colonial history with a mythological and magical time, letting the 'true' island space emerge through its creation myths that transcend history and interpenetrate the contemporary.

REWRITING THE CARIBBEAN, PART 1 – MICHEL TOURNIER, *FRIDAY, OR THE OTHER ISLAND*

The remote location of Defoe's island in *Robinson Crusoe* removes the castaway from European society at home, and from Europe's outposts in the New World colonies. It is a site that presents a personal challenge to Crusoe, but also to the values instilled in him, which are rooted in eighteenth century Puritanism and colonialism. When Crusoe imposes his will on the island, it is consistent with the will of his Christian God, because it is Providence that guides the narrative guaranteeing Crusoe's material and spiritual rewards. With the authority of God invested in him, he rules the island for Europe and rules out the indigenous native culture personified in Friday.

In Tournier's *Friday* a similar situation confronts the castaway, but the outcome is very different. Here, Robinson discovers another side to himself, who, in cahoots with Friday, flouts Christian and colonialist ethics by failing to cultivate, convert, and exploit the island. In *Robinson Crusoe*, chance brings Crusoe to the island, but from then on Providence guides him. In *Friday*, chance continues to play a hand, as the narrative follows the tarot reading given to Robinson in the moments before his shipwreck. With Providence now ruled out, Friday and Robinson enjoy the lazy, anarchic regime which seems to be the island's 'natural' state.

Robinson escapes the strictures of a colonialist and Puritan ethos based on hard work, which he imposed on the island, by contriving to ignore clock-time and the division of time and space into tasks and schedules. It is the failure of Robinson's water clock that leads to his escape from this self-imposed regime, and this is then followed by an eruption that brings another version of the island to the surface. This alternative island matches Robinson's new-found desires, and releases Robinson and Friday from purposeless toil.

Robinson seems to lose faith in the colonial enterprise within the sensual and exotic atmosphere of Speranza, and he senses another person within, trying to displace the European coloniser in him:

> ... he was beginning to feel more and more often that the cultivation of the island was a meaningless enterprise. It was at these moments that a new man seemed to be coming to life within him, wholly alien to the practical administrator. The two men did not yet coexist in him; they came by turns, each excluding the other ...
>
> (*Friday*: 119)

Robinson's other self eventually displaces the 'practical administrator', but not before the island space itself has undergone a similar division. The island is not a two-dimensional space here, but is an organic whole, only one face of which has surrendered to the cultivation and civilisation of the European coloniser. Beneath this superficial island, lies the 'real' Speranza, to which Friday has always had access, and which is cast as the natural and 'native' space of the 'other island'. It is as though two islands are now mapped on to the geographically construed island space, each corresponding to one of the possible worlds Robinson might belong to. One island space represents the quantifiable economic chronotope of a European coloniser, and the other seems to represent a timeless reality closer to that of Friday's native culture. But although the novel is called *Friday*, this is not Friday's story; it is another version of the Robinson Crusoe account. The natural side to the island refers to a European concept of nature projected on to the Caribbean island, so this is a European representation of the natural, not a native one.

In *Robinson Crusoe*, the island is a 'realistic' material space, a space that Crusoe makes his own, a unity of nowhere, a utopia. This unitary space, circumscribed out of the chaos all around it, is where Crusoe constructs his world through the outward projection of his will and determination. By his conversion of this space to his ideology, through his will and the hand of Providence, Crusoe puts down his mark and claims incontestable sovereignty over a land of heathens. There is only one view of the island in *Robinson Crusoe*, and only one map, because there is only one point of view. Crusoe never seems to be in any doubt about his claim to the island, or his primacy over the savages. Any doubts about his plight, his meaningless existence, and his projects, are answered by recourse to Providence and God's will, giving Crusoe access to an all-seeing external authority which confirms the existence of himself and the island space as two separate and distinct entities.

In *Friday*, this external authority is removed and the castaway and the island merge into a subjective unity which has no perspective, or context.

> But in Speranza there is only one viewpoint, my own, deprived of all context. And this shedding of context was not completed in a day. At first, and as it were instinctively, I projected possible observers-parameters-onto hilltops or behind rocks or into the branches of trees. The island was thus charted by a network of interpolations and extrapolations that lent it different aspects and rendered it meaningful. . . I became aware of this function – with many others – only when I found it dying within me. Today the process is complete. My vision of the island is reduced to that of my own eyes, and what I do not see of it is to me a total unknown. Everywhere I am not total darkness reigns.
>
> (F: 54–5)

Without an external viewpoint Robinson cannot make a cartographic representation of the island, or its place in the world and his own place within it. Robinson's world is reduced to what he can see, and to what is happening at the time. The chronotope of the modern world of chronometer and cartography is undermined by this perspective.

Friday is never dominated by Robinson here, and even before Robinson's transcendence, redemption or 'going native', Friday is never convinced by European values. Significantly, Friday does not just mimic Robinson here, as Defoe's Friday does, but engages with Robinson, eventually subverting his transported values:

> All that his master ordered was right, all that he forbade was wrong. It was good to toil night and day for the functioning of an elaborate system that served no purpose; it was bad to eat more than the portion allotted to him by his master. It was good to be a soldier when his master was a general, a choirboy when his master prayed, a builder's labourer when he built, a farm labourer when he farmed, a herdsman when he herded, a beater when he hunted, a paddler when he travelled by water, a bedside attendant when he was sick, an operator of the fan, and a killer of flies. it was wrong to smoke a pipe, to go naked, or to hide when there was work to be done.
>
> (F:140)

Whenever Robinson is not present, however, Friday behaves as he will, and according to the chronotope of his Speranza. Clearly, the native here only responds to the presence of the coloniser's power, not to his value system. And as Robinson's other self emerges, he too recognises that the regime he has imposed seems 'out of place'. He becomes aware then of the tension and superficiality in the artificial order of the 'Charter', the 'Penal Code', and the rigidly observed time schedule governed by the measure of the water clock. This artificially imposed chronotope, he comes to regard as a 'strait jacket of conventions and prescriptions'. (F: 79).

The 'other island' within Robinson's colony begins to assert itself as his doubts grow about the cultivated and ordered world. So when the water clock stops one day, rather than worrying about his tasks and schedule, he begins to enjoy a sense of being outside time – he slips into the chronotope of holiday. This abandonment of clock time not only affects schedules, it affects the whole island, and things begin to shed the use value Robinson had previously assigned to them as he appropriated them from nature. The chronotope of the island seems to return, outside clock time, to its natural state. It is as though Robinson's colony is a temporary imposition maintained by the colonialist's clock, and by extension the colonialist's power to impose his historical and geographical order. But for Robinson, there is nothing to fear from the native island that always existed underneath the colonial order. There are no cannibals or wild beasts; this other island, this other Robinson, is a warm, 'fraternal' place which all his labours had hitherto repressed:

> It was as though in ceasing to be related to each other according to their use – and their abuse – things had returned to their own essence, were flowering in their own right and existing simply for their own sakes. . . in a moment of inexpressible happiness Robinson seemed to discern *another island* behind the one where he had labored so long in solitude, a place more alive, warmer and more fraternal, which his mundane preoccupations had concealed from him.
>
> (F: 90)

Robinson puts aside his colonial responsibilities as governor, administrator and military commander whenever he stops the water clock, and begins to explore this 'other' island, beneath or behind the surface of the cultivated one. When Friday accidentally blows up the cultivated island, this other island comes to the surface completely displacing it. This is a place where Friday and Robinson discover unity

– an equitable society – rooted in the warm and fraternal Speranza. The new Robinson emerges then as if through metamorphosis:

> A new Robinson was sloughing off his old skin, fully prepared to accept the decay of his cultivated island, and at the heels of an unthinking guide [Friday], enter upon an unknown road.
>
> (F: 180)

The reconstructed Robinson enters a different chronotope. Having escaped the economic space–time of the colonialist, he now enters the timeless native world along an 'unknown road'. The explosion on the colony he now sees as a 'volcanic release of peace', and rather than the 'other island' being buried beneath his cultivated and colonised island, he is 'transported to that other Speranza'. This other island is outside clock time and outside cartographic space, and it is here that Robinson wishes to continue the timeless idyll he shares with Friday:

> He was still alive. He had triumphed over madness during his years of solitude. He had achieved a state of stability, or a series of states, in which he and Speranza, and then Speranza and Friday, and himself had formed a unity which endured and had brought supreme happiness. After much suffering and many fateful crises he now felt able, with Friday at his side, to defy the passage of time and, like a meteor launched frictionless in space, to continue indefinitely on his course without weariness or loss of momentum.
>
> (F: 218)

This unity between Robinson and Friday is established within the native chronotope of the island, outwith the modern chronotope of colonialism. In the unity of this native chronotope, colonialist oppositions of master/slave and man/nature appear to be resolved, while the colonialist division of time and labour is suspended. The only problem with this back to nature, anti-modern and existentialist sentiment is that it only occurs within the subject's perspective, a perspective that now encompasses the identity of the island and Friday as well. The timelessness and the unity of space perceived by Robinson are derived from his subjective mapping of the island, so the old European mind still has its imperial sway. But this cannot last. Robinson might be able to include Friday in his personal version of reality, but when a group of unreconstructed colonisers/pirates arrive on the island, Robinson realises that other realities might disrupt his world:

> Each of these men was a *possible* world, having its own coherence, its values, its sources of attraction and repulsion, its centre of gravity. And with all the differences between them, each of these possible worlds at that moment shared a vision, casual and superficial, of the island of Speranza, which caused them to act in common, and which incidentally contained a shipwrecked man called Robinson and his half-caste servant . . . And each of these possible worlds naively proclaimed itself the reality.
>
> (F: 220)

While the invaders slaughter his stock of animals, ruin his crops and steal his gold, Robinson looks on bemused and detached, realising that each man is, in a way, his own island only *superficially* mapped on to his Speranza. The unity that Robinson thought he had found on the island with himself and Friday is only mapped in his own psychological space. The visitors from Europe that plunder his island and take Friday away with them still have their eyes set on Europe.

This rewriting of *Robinson Crusoe* disrupts the cultivated island space that Defoe portrayed by describing other perspectives of it. But this rewriting depicts transcendence by the individual of a particularly ordered regime, which is recognisably colonialist but might also be a projection of European capitalist society. *Friday* shadows *Robinson Crusoe*, often reversing moves from order to disorder in Defoe's narrative, and undermining the Providence that guides Crusoe. Chance is Robinson's guide here, and the unity Robinson thinks he finds on Speranza is the result of a series of accidents. The natural island space of Speranza helps disrupt the colonialist's island, but it is not a revolutionary space, and there is no vision of a post-colonial space emerging. This island chronotope is rather an anti-modern escapist fantasy in which the individual reacts against the order, toil and tyranny of capitalist clock time.

When Friday leaves Robinson on his island, and throws in his lot with the pirates, he seems disloyal to the man that rescued him and shared the island with him. But we must remember that in this rewriting of *Robinson Crusoe*, Friday is half Negro, and not therefore a native of the New World. Unlike Defoe's Friday, he is not proximate with his own nation, and has no concept of belonging to any other nation. This Friday, unlike Defoe's Friday who is temporarily displaced, is, like the majority of slaves in the Caribbean, abjectly placeless within the colonial world, and therefore prey to colonialists and writers alike who place him and shape him as they see fit. This silence and placelessness of Friday is a theme developed in *Foe*, where author and narrator struggle to find a voice for Friday and the native Caribs and slaves for whom he is a sign.

REWRITING THE CARIBBEAN PART 2 – J. M. COETZEE, *FOE*

The title of Tournier's novel – *Friday, or The Other Island* – is misleading in that it does not, as one might expect, tell Friday's story, but tells another version of Robinson Crusoe's story. In Coetzee's novel, Friday's story still evades us, because this novel is mainly a story *about* the writing of *Robinson Crusoe*. The conceit at the centre of *Foe* is that the author-to-be of *Robinson Crusoe*, Mr Foe,[10] meets Susan Barton, a female castaway, who has a story to tell him of her experiences with an obtuse and characterless castaway and his loyal but unfathomable black slave. This story gives the reclusive and often disappearing author, Mr Foe, a number of problems. It is not, as Susan Barton presents it, a complete story but is rather a number of isolated fragments, each an island in itself. The intertext of Defoe's *Robinson Crusoe* emerges out of this metafiction as a constructed version of that part of the story related to Cruso.[11]

In Defoe's text, Robinson Crusoe becomes the central figure with his story extended across the whole, and Susan Barton's story is erased. Friday remains, but he is enclosed in Robinson Crusoe's story. The fuller picture that would include Susan Barton's search for her daughter, and Friday's brutal separation from his family and fellow slaves, has been edited down by Mr Foe to the story of a man on an island. Perhaps the idea is that Mr Foe will use the mother's search for her daughter in South America and the daughter's search for her mother in London in *Moll Flanders* and *Roxana*, two other novels by Daniel Defoe in which the protagonists are female. In *Foe*, Mr Foe wants to write Susan Barton's story of the search for her daughter, but on this she remains silent. Mr Foe thinks the story of Cruso on the island is too disconnected, and is not a whole story. The story Susan Barton wants Mr Foe to tell is of Friday but this cannot be told because Friday is unable to speak or write his story.

Foe might not tell Friday's story, but it does tell the story of the lack of Friday's story, which is a beginning. Friday's silence, and Susan Barton's attempts to fill this silence with words, inscribes the sign of

Friday, which is the sign of slavery. So, in silence, Friday is presented in real relation to his ancestry and he discloses the real relations between slaves and colonisers that are masked in the childlike mimic that is Friday in *Robinson Crusoe*. In revisiting *Robinson Crusoe* and giving it a post-colonial context, the silence that stands for Friday's history is shifted from the margins of eighteenth century fiction into the centre of twentieth century fiction. Susan Barton draws attention to this when she suggests to Mr Foe that the lack of Friday's true story is to blame for the poverty and monotony of the story she asks him to record:

> if the story seems stupid, that is only because it so doggedly holds its silence. The shadow whose lack you feel is there: it is the loss of Friday's tongue. . . . The story of Friday's tongue is a story unable to be told, or unable to be told by me. That is to say, many stories can be told of Friday's tongue, but the true story is buried within Friday, who is mute. The true story will not be heard till by art we have found a means of giving voice to Friday.
>
> (*Foe*: 117–18)

The lack of Friday's story becomes a central theme in *Foe* creating an empty space in the centre of the narrative. Susan Barton describes Friday's story as 'properly not a story, but a puzzle or hole in the narrative (I picture it as a buttonhole, carefully cross-stitched around, but empty, waiting for a button)' (*Foe*: 121). Friday's silence in all of this represents neither absence nor presence, but an expectant gap that Brenda Marshall calls 'a space, a moment which provides the need and the opportunity for Barton to speak and write within the "space" between hole and button' (Marshall 1992: 73). But what can Barton write and speak? She brings Friday to London, against his will, rather as a novelty: as a story to be told. She fails to connect Friday with his history, and his silence is no more than a puzzle, which once solved will *author* his history. If Friday remains silent, his story will remain untold, but if he does speak, his story will be taken over by an author who will shape it to his own design. In *Foe*, Friday is again the subject in someone else's story and again he is being exploited for finalcial gain, as Susan Barton comes to London to sell the story Mr Foe.

The story of Friday and Crusoe is the raw material Susan Barton wishes to capitalise on, but she fails to realise that she is just another player shaped by other (male) authors. Mr Foe will reshape her in his eighteenth century fictions, and Mr Coetzee shapes her in this twentieth century fiction. But in this postmodern text, she has an inkling that she is being manipulated, just as Hawksmoor does in Peter Ackroyd's novel. She is a 'text-enclosed' self, conscious of her fictionalisation and of the constraints put around her, not simply by this particular narrative, but by the master narratives of a culture that to some extent determine the role she can play. She asks Mr Foe 'Do we of necessity become puppets in a story whose end is invisible to us, and towards which we are marched like condemned felons?' (*Foe*: 135). In her case the answer must be 'yes', because she is contained in this chronotope that is a textual island.

She is castaway on these shores, just as Robinson Crusoe is castaway on the shores of a 'real' island. Each are constrained partly by their own actions and partly by the discourse that produces them as particular characters in a particular story. For Crusoe, this is a colonialist discourse that demands not only his survival, but his effective domination of the island chronotope. His narrative fills this chronotope as he appears to write the island and himself at once through the illusory device of realism. For Susan Barton, this is a postmodern, post-structuralist and post-colonial discourse that reverses such domination and exposes such illusion through the problematisation of narrative representation. Throughout the novel she is haunted by a textual shadow that is the role Mr Foe is constructing for her. The discourse that constrains her, demands that her story intersects with other fictions and that it makes explicit its own status as fiction.

In the story itself, Mr Foe is more interested in Susan Barton's silence about her journey through Bahia than in the silence of Friday. This is the space he would like to fill and the narrative thread he wants to follow. For Mr Foe, her island story is only an episode, a moment without context. It is without history and not a story, because it does not belong within the larger narrative required of histories and stories. Without Friday's voice, because his tongue has been cut out, without Cruso's voice, because he is dead, and without Susan Barton's history, the island chronotope is without variation and direction:

> We can bring it to life only by setting it within a larger story. By itself is no better than a waterlogged boat drifting day after day in an empty ocean till one day, humbly and without commotion, it sinks. The island lacks light and shade. It is too much the same throughout.
>
> (*Foe*: 117)

When Susan Barton is in England with Friday, her memory of life on the island with Friday and Cruso begins to merge with the present. Her sense of history as a continuing narrative that places her temporally and spatially begins to fade, and she becomes aware of life as a fragmentary experience. The chronotope that represents this experience is that of the island:

> ... the life we lead grows less and less distinct from the life we led on Cruso's island. Sometimes I wake up not knowing where I am. The world is full of islands, said Cruso once. His words ring truer every day.
> (*Foe*: 71)

As well as presenting Susan Barton's fading sense of history, this also refers back to Cruso, for whom existence on the island had no meaning. There is no hope on Cruso's barren island because it is not connected, spatially and, by implication, temporally. The world for Cruso is one of disconnection, of separation, and this is perhaps somewhat closer to the real experience of Alexander Selkirk on whose experience Defoe's story is partly based. But it is not realism that Coetzee is seeking to establish here, rather it is the processes by which fictions are shaped and constructed.

Perhaps the crucial difference between *Robinson Crusoe* and *Foe* with regard to the chronotope of the island is that, in Defoe's novel, the island is an organising chronotope, a space and time that is produced, ordered and governed by Crusoe. But in *Foe*, the island is a disorganising chronotope, problematising the particular unity represented in Defoe's representation of Crusoe, Friday and the island, and disrupting its historical and geographical continuity. In this postmodernist revision of Defoe's fiction, the world is now 'full of islands', and the narrative process for contextualising these and drawing them together into coherent experience is exposed as a fiction. *Foe* depicts the heterogeneous nature of experience and the artifice of fictional constructions that try to homogenise this experience. It lays bare the artifice, turning Cruso's island into a sterile, dislocated place, lacking other voices and context. Cruso is turned into an automaton, sense and feeling drained from him. In *Foe*, the real is represented as lack and absence, unable or unwilling to be brought to presence. Robinson's island is not a single, self-contained space here, but a hole in the fabric of history.

As with all the postmodern novels dealt with in this chapter, problematising the image of island space as a clearly delineated, self-contained and mappable entity is coupled with a postmodern problematisation of narrative representation. In this, post-structuralist approaches to language and postmodern approaches to geography share common ground, so to speak. There are other antithetical urges in the postmodern novel concerned not only with narrative representation itself, but also with questioning the tradition of literary representation. In *Foe*, it is the exotic nature of desert islands, a common feature of eighteenth century travel literature and one which Defoe's fiction exhibits, that is to be exposed:

> For readers reared on travellers' tales, the words *desert isle* may conjure up a place of soft sands and shady trees where brooks run to quench the castaway's thirst and ripe fruit falls into his hand, where no more is asked of him than to drowse the days away till a ship calls to fetch him home. But the island on which I was cast away was quite another place: a great rocky hill with a flat top, rising sharply from the sea on all sides except one, dotted with drab bushes that never flowered and never shed their leaves.
>
> (*Foe*: 7)

Here, the verdant, bountiful and feminine object of desire that became a stock representation of the south sea island in European literature and especially in Renaissance narratives of discovery, is turned into a hard, unwelcoming place.[12] This may be partly due to the shift in gender of the narrator, as this is a woman's view of the island, a view coloured perhaps by associating the cold, unfeeling and masculine Cruso with the island itself.

But returning to the novel's metafictionality and its postmodern chronotopes, we can see that the chronotope of the island is used here mainly to map fictional space–time rather than map any 'real' geographical space–time. In a sense, any resemblance the island might have to a real island is irrelevant. Within the explicitly textual world of *Foe*, the novel Mr Foe is to write is only a paper island, an island of symbols and marks on paper. This paper island is circumscribed from the various stories and characters that might have been included, but which are 'written out', erased (or rather under erasure): disconnected signifiers floating in the sea that washes around the dry land of Cruso's island. The island is the place of writing, but this sea is the place of signs, and it is into this sea of signs that a narrator, in the present, comes to seek Friday's unarticulated voice:

> His mouth opens. From inside him comes a slow stream, without breath, without interruption. it flows up through his body and out upon me; it

> passes through the cabin, through the wreck; washing the cliffs and shores of the island, it runs northward and southward to the ends of the earth. Soft and cold, dark and unending, it beats against my eyelids, against the skin of my face.
>
> (*Foe*: 157)

We have already seen how the island space in Tournier's *Friday* offers Robinson an escape from the original role cast by Defoe. He is given two possible worlds to join, and the binary structure of the island space is used to explore a duality in Robinson. In *Foe*, the island space on which Cruso is cast away is transcribed back into the representational space anchored to the house in London where Daniel Defoe is to write *Robinson Crusoe*. This island has no underlying native space, as the island in *Friday* does, because there is nothing beneath the surface of this paper island except other intertexts each deferring one to another. Each text signifies another text, as shown in the concluding section of the novel, where a recursive structure of fictional worlds is discovered, each enclosed within another like 'Chinese-box worlds' (McHale 1987: 112).

The ending(s) unravel new fictions, leaving the story of Susan Barton to be picked up by another narrator who comes into the room to discover the bodies of Mr Foe, Susan and Friday. When this new narrator comes to the body of Friday, (s)he listens to the sounds coming from his mouth:'the sounds of the island' (*Foe*: 154). The new narrator then seems to re-enter the house, now written into history with a blue plaque on its wall reading '*Daniel Defoe, Author*'. Once more in the writer's den, (s)he picks up the text of Susan Barton's story and reads, 'Dear Mr Foe, At last I could row no further' (*Foe*: 155), which is the first line of *Foe*. But then the narrator enters the story and, no longer writing to Mr Foe, returns to the scene of Susan Barton's shipwreck. In this later revision (s)he is not castaway on Cruso's island, but finds the marker left by Friday, as reported in the Susan Barton narrative (the petals scattered on the surface of the sea) and dives down into the shipwreck to find Friday.

The key to this complicated ending lies in the attempt to articulate Friday's history. Mr Foe's answer is to set Friday, who cannot speak, to writing. When Friday begins to write, he makes the letter 'O', signifying the silence, and the lack, and the nothingness that has been his place, and the place of the natives and slaves whom he represents is in colonial history. Then Mr Foe instructs Susan to teach him the letter 'A', and so begin the sequence of the alphabet. Friday must begin to write because without a voice he will always be a blank piece of paper for others to write and shape:

> Friday has no command of words and therefore no defence against being re-shaped day by day in conformity with the desires of others. I say he is a cannibal and he becomes a cannibal...
>
> (*Foe*: 121)

The process of placing Friday in history is linked to Friday's entry into language, but this is not his language, these are not his signs. Even if he does find the command of words, the novel seems to imply that this is not the end of the matter. Susan, who is literate and is given a voice, doubts whether she can any longer distinguish between text and reality, and Mr Foe himself is conscious that the relations between words and reality is tenuous. He is also apt to get lost in the maze of writing if he doesn't plant some kind of marker, some enduring signifier that he can return to and find himself again:

> In a life of writing books, I have often, believe me, been lost in the maze of doubting. The trick I have learned is to plant a sign or a marker in the ground where I stand, so that in my future wanderings I shall have something to return to, and not get worse lost than I am.
>
> (*Foe*: 136)

Friday's sign goes deeper than this; below the surface structure of words his sign reaches the utter reality of things when he scatters petals on the sea to mark the spot where the slave ship containing his people sank off Cruso's island. This is the time and place Friday might be returning to through his spinning and dancing and repetitive music. It is a chronotope that has slipped out of the web of colonialist narrative, the loophole through which he escapes the colonial world. Through this loophole Friday revisits the time before he was written into Cruso's island. This is the place to which the latter-day narrator is drawn to search out the origins of Friday's true history, or rather the origins of the speaking subject that Friday represents. From three hundred years hence, the petals mark the underwater grave of a slave ship that symbolises the death of Friday's ancestors. Friday's petals register the killing of generations of slaves, just as poppies symbolise the 'mud of Flanders, in which generations of grenadiers now lie dead, trampled in the postures of sleep' (*Foe*: 156). As the narrator descends into the imaginative space below Friday's shrine, (s)he finds 'petals floating around me like a rain of snowflakes' (*Foe*: 156). This is the reference point to which Friday's story is destined to return. The slave ship is one immutable and irrefutable reference, an enduring signifier in the story of Friday, and an incontrovertible pointer in the history of European colonisation of the Caribbean.

The narrative structure at the end of the novel slips between different times and different narrators. In the end it is self-referring, pointing back to the Susan Barton narrative as a completed text, and it refers to the house of the writer Daniel Defoe as a historical site. But lodged within these metafictional devices is this striking poetic image in which an unknown, unplaced writer finds Friday in the wreck of the slave ship. By placing this arresting image at the end of the novel, Coetzee offers a closure which moves beyond the simple narrative and history of Friday that has seemed to be the novel's trajectory. In other words, Friday's story cannot be contained in narrative, it is not a story that can be told as other stories. As in George Lamming's *In the Castle of my Skin*, memory of the time before slavery is contained in memories and dream images that fall outside narrative and are represented as poetic image. In Lamming's novel, it is Old Pa's lucid dream of the time before in Africa and of the middle passage, which he communicates to Old Ma just before she dies, that provides the narrative slip and the poetic image (Lamming 1998).

In *Foe*, the poetic image of the slave ship serves the same purpose, it connects with unwritten and unarticulated histories and stories, which are nevertheless still present, lurking and flowing beneath the master narratives of western history. These poetic images within the narrative of the novel have a disruptive effect, undermining, or at least pointing up the deficiencies of, modern linear narrative. In the postmodern novel, such disruption of narrative is more or less expected, so breaking the realist chronotopes with poetic images, anachronisms and the mixing of fact and fiction is customary. When Lamming was writing in the 1950s and 1960s he did not have the postmodern novelistic form available to him, and the result is an uneven narrative moving towards poetry, which was to become his favoured form.

In Bachelard's phenomenological approach, the poetic image has another effect, which is its reversal of the usual order of comprehending language. In the poetic image, claims Bachelard, we see the depths before we fully comprehend the words that bring us there, because the image appears in consciousness before meaning is found for the words that conjure that image. In the poetic image, he claims, we find the origin of the speaking being:

> By its novelty, a poetic image sets in motion the entire linguistic mechanism. The poetic image places us at the origin of the speaking being. . . After the initial reverberation, we are able to experience resonances, sentimental repercussions, reminders of our past. But the image has touched the depths before it stirs the surface. . . The image offered us by reading the poem now becomes really our own. It takes root in us. It has been given us by another, but we begin to have the impression that we created it. It becomes a new being in our language, expressing us by making us what it expresses; in other words, it is at once a becoming of expression, and a becoming of our being. Here expression creates being.
> (Bachelard 1969: xix)

Oddly, Coetzee chooses to present this image through words that evoke Shakespeare's *The Tempest*: 'It is huge, greater than the leviathan . . . If the kraken lurks anywhere, it lurks here, watching out of its stony hooded undersea eyes' (*Foe*: 156). This becomes for a moment the wreck in which Ariel, at Prospero's bidding, locks the ship's crew 'five fathoms deep', in a timeless sleep, while the play unfolds. But here, the sunken slave ship marks the beginning of Friday's story, rather than the resolution of courtly intrigues. It is as yet a submerged mystery: the unwritten history of Friday's Caribbean. Friday's home is outside time and outside language, and as he lies dying in Mr Foe's den in London, it is not words that come from Friday's mouth. The narrator begins to hear the 'faintest faraway roar . . . the roar of waves . . . the whine of the wind and the cry of a bird', and then, 'From his mouth, without a breath, issue the sounds of the island' (*Foe*: 154). Friday's silence has now become this 'roar'. When the last narrator visits Friday's 'home', he finds that it is 'not a place of words', but a place where 'bodies are their own signs' (*Foe*: 157).

Rewriting the Caribbean Part 3 – Caryl Phillips, *Cambridge*

We move now to a text where a Caribbean slave is given a voice, although it is not a voice that Friday could have had, because it is the voice of a *translated* slave: a man converted to English and Christian ways. In one sense his translation is so complete that he can criticise the English through their own language, using their own value systems directly to judge them. But in another sense, he always bears the mark of having been translated. As a Negro, no matter how English he becomes in manners, education and position, he is always conscious that he bears the mark of his race and so can never become a complete Englishman.

But the novel is not entirely about Cambridge, in fact most of the narrative belongs to Emily, a white European and the daughter of an absentee plantation owner. As in other novels by Phillips, multiple narrators are used to convey a refracted black consciousness. This narrative style uses a mix of black male and white female voices, and in *The Nature of Blood*, this extends to include Jewish voices. Hybridised voices explore the *in-betweenness* of being both black and European, which is Phillips own experience, but they also shift the category 'black' from an essentialist racial category, to an existential outsideness that might transcend racial difference. In *Cambridge*, the reader is invited to seek the improbable waves of empathy that connect the white daughter of a plantation owner with the black slave.

Although Emily comes to the Caribbean to visit her father's plantation, she has a secondary motive, which is to write a journal of her true experiences. She arrives with her narrative already half-written, peppered with the sentences of English novelists and pamphleteers. For much of the narrative, her voice rarely digresses from the script of received middle-class liberal opinion. She tries to maintain a distance between herself and a strange, unfamiliar Caribbean that in her writing oscillates between the picturesque and the grotesque. But gradually the novel discloses a gap between her prim and tightly written report and her wildly fluctuating emotional experience. Her self-censorship eventually comes to light, and at the end of the novel, the 'real' Emily, on the verge of a breakdown after a miscarriage, presents a very different persona.

In writing her 'true' account of the Caribbean, and her false account of herself, Emily is constrained by an English woman's education, which could not possibly have prepared her for real life in the colonies. Through Emily's shock of the unfamiliar, the novel highlights the discrepancies between actual colonial life, and its common representation at home in England. For a woman such as Emily, adjustment to the real Caribbean proves particularly traumatic, and yet in the end she appears to choose to stay there rather than return to the different constraints of life in England. It is questionable whether she is given much choice; as a woman of this period, her life is more or less determined for her by her plantation-owning father, or the man that will take his place in England if she goes through with the arranged marriage. Like the slave Cambridge, she is to be passed from one master to another, and freedom, when it is granted, is conditional.

Emily's narrative is unreliable, if only because her education prevents her from comprehending and describing her real experiences. The unreliability of Emily's account is not only significant for the story of Emily, however; it could be seen as criticism of a whole representational mode in colonialist discourse, in which objective and properly framed sentimental accounts are emphasised, but in which many truths are avoided or evaded. Emily's 'true' accounts of the colony follow the style of epistolary travel narrative and seem sincere, but she avoids telling us about experiences that have a direct bearing on the state of the plantation and colonial life in general. A sense of the real Caribbean is reported through other hard-bitten residents of the island who Emily is unwilling to trust. There is a clash between Emily's picturesque and sentimental accounts and the realism of the locals.

In the Caribbean Phillips portrays, the abolition of the slave trade brings sweeping changes to the economic and social atmosphere of the place. The islands are also becoming 'creolised' through the progeny of white masters and black mistresses, and the rigid social structure of the plantations, established in the eighteenth century to produce sugar with forced labour, is beginning to break down. The novel reports the emergence of 'free' blacks, the arrival of 'low-life' whites, and the ruin of some of the plantations leading to looting and social unrest. Petty crimes and minor insurrections among the black community are dealt with summarily and harshly, amid growing fears among the white authorities of insurrection.

An ironic distance opens up between Emily's reports, based on her expectations of the Caribbean, and these reports of the real Caribbean. Eventually a distracted Emily comes to terms with her adopted home, but her opposite number, as it were, fares less well in England. When Cambridge comes to England, he naively expects to be treated as an equal, having been educated in English language and customs. So an ironic distance opens up here as well, between the England he expected to find, and the reality of a racist society unwilling to regard him as a free Englishman. Cambridge is a victim of that 'confusion' in the 'minds of many true Englishmen' who see Cambridge not as he sees himself – 'Truly I was now an Englishman, albeit a little smudgy of complexion! Africa spoke to me only of a history I had cast aside' (*Cambridge*: 147). But although he tries to cast aside history, he is still trapped inside that history and subject to the prevalent cultural forces that disallow his freedom, as surely as they disallow Emily's freedom.

To reinforce the idea that, for Cambridge, history is a set of irons he can never cast away, Phillips has him sold back into slavery while travelling to Africa as a missionary. He is forced to reconnect with history, and is made brutally aware that his history is determined by his race, not by his will. It does not help that, as a 'virtual Englishman', he manages to foster a racist attitude to his own race. This condemns him to perpetual outsider status, not English and not African, and it only exacerbates the pain of losing what little freedom he had: 'That I, a virtual Englishman, was to be treated as base African cargo, caused me such hurtful pain as I was barely able to endure' (C: 156).

Phillips is one of a number of 'cosmopolitan' writers who set out to encompass divergent European and West Indian points of view in the postmodern novel. He is himself a cultural hybrid, born in the West Indies and brought up in Britain, and his work makes use of a double consciousness to articulate the multi-voicedness of post-colonial discourse. With this hybrid viewpoint the nature of the Caribbean island changes from being the circumscribed, undialectical space found in *Robinson Crusoe*, to a provisional space, shaped and reshaped by its connections with the rest of the world. The Caribbean island is not formed from its own native space, because it has no historical roots there. And just as Friday, without command of words, cannot help himself being shaped and reshaped, the island too, without history, is without voice and also subject to external shaping forces.

As George Lamming puts it in *In the Castle of My Skin*, the Caribbean island is a floating place, a Little England connected to the Big England, and vaguely connected to Africa, but through broken and fictionalised histories (Lamming 1998). The Caribbean island is essentially a chronotope adrift, unanchored temporally and spatially, and this floating existence is the history of a largely placeless people who have, as it were, been placed in a historical transit area, not African, not European or American. Of course, in postmodernity there is a general situation of placelessness and reduced sense of belonging in place and in history. Sometimes this is a matter of choice, leading some cosmopolitan writers to boast of an *excess* of *belonging*, because they belong to more than one place.[13] But sometimes lack of belonging is enforced and there is no amelioration in reading it simply as an abstract postmodern condition.

In *Foe*, Susan Barton claims that Friday's story would set her island story in context, and this would also place the Caribbean island in its true light, but Mr Foe insists that no island can be a story in itself. It must be set within the context of the rest of the world, giving it a geographical and historical dimension: a beginning, a middle, and an end. What has to be done, the writer claims, is to 'establish the poles, the here and the there, the now and the then – after that the words do the journeying' (*Foe*: 93). In *Cambridge*, the Caribbean island is set within its global context by trafficking in slaves from Africa, the arrivals and departures of English colonialists, and the movement of goods to world markets.

The representational space of the island is constructed mainly from the different viewpoints of the two narrators. Between them they complete the triangular passages between Britain, Africa and the Caribbean that produced the Caribbean as an adjunct to the colonial centre of Britain, and Africa as a place of slaves. As the narratives cross and weave, they do not produce a real and visitable geographical place, but something closer to an imaginative place. The Caribbean island in *Cambridge* is a place from which English plantation owners can absent themselves, a forgotten place, and a place that seems on the verge of disappearance once slavery is taken out of the economic equation. What is clear is that the future of the island is dependent on Europe, it is literally and metaphorically what England will make of it. It is in that sense no longer an island with a separate people and culture, but a translation of England, an impoverished version of the 'home' country.

As with any travel narrative, Emily's account of her journey and arrival in the Caribbean requires a translation of the unfamiliar into the familiar, and of the real into the representational. When she first sees the island she sees the 'tropical paradise' she was expecting:

> Indeed, I was beholding a tropical paradise. Our exploratory party returned with baskets of fruit, excellent milk and fresh fowl . . . I retired to my small cabin with a constitution well-watered and nourished, and a heart light with anticipatory joy at what I might witness in this new world that I had crossed the ocean to discover.
>
> (C: 18)

As she lands on the island and travels to her father's plantation house, this pictorial paradise is given some experiential depth. She is manhandled by a Negro, given an uncomfortable ride in a carriage, and suddenly becomes aware that genteel England is far away:

> This first part of my journey was over and I was breaking the last remaining link with a past that I understood. From this moment I would be entering a dark tropical unknown.
>
> (C: 22)

But Emily's poor imagination pops up one representational cliché after another out of her 'picture book' of the colonies. When she arrives at the Great House, she catches sight of 'this edifice' at the end of an 'Arcadian grove' of 'cedars and palmettos' (C: 26). The classical reference here could be imaginative interpretation by Emily or actual description of the place, as it was commonplace in colonial architecture to allude to classical narrative. In this way, Europeans might think of themselves as latter day Greeks and Romans, as carriers of civilisation to the New World.[14] In this case, it must have taken a lot of imagination to see a sugar-cane estate maintained by forced labour as pastoral. From classical narrative, Emily moves to the picturesque, where she finds the life of the West Indian slave something to be envied:

> I have never witnessed so picturesque a scene as a Negro village . . . These village gardens are decorative groves of ornament and luxury, and filled with a profusion of fruits which boast all the colours of the rainbow. . . If I were to be asked if I should enter life anew as an English labourer or a West Indian slave I should have no hesitation in opting for the latter.
>
> (C: 42)

Slowly a strain appears between Emily's received views and her experience of the island. She begins to understand the power structure of the island and the external connections that shape it, and realises that the 'tropical island' is not a unity, but is divided according to estate ownership and connected to other islands through trade. The importance of this is reflected in the prominence of the maps that decorate the Great Hall:

> . . . the walls sport many prints and maps, some of which relate to navigation, a great number being of local interest and depicting the divisions of land and breadth and extent of the estates. The most

interesting of these maps is the one which shows the trafficking islands in relation to each other.

(C: 29)

So the island in *Cambridge* is not the clearly defined and separate island space of *Robinson Crusoe*, it is divided within and connected without through the lines and forces of geopolitics. It is connected with England through a series of unhappy and ugly ties. First, the English dispatched the native Indians, making it no longer 'home' to anyone or 'nation' to anyone. Then they enslaved African labour and set it to work producing wealth for absentee owners, like Emily's father, who squanders his profits on whoring, gambling and champagne. It is hardly surprising that the place loses the picturesque and paradisiac quality noticed earlier by Emily. A more realistic view of the English-owned islands in the Caribbean comes from Mr Wilson, the usurped manager of the estate who recognises the structures of power and lack of allegiances that undermine the place:

> . . . there was little that could be called beautiful in the West Indian townships, for nobody cared. The streets were poorly laid out, the public and private buildings most clumsy wooden structures . . . neither outward appearance nor civic amenity seemed to be given any consideration.

None of the islands 'could boast anything worthy of a glance' because:

> They were the holding stations for those who simply wished to extract profit to be lavished on English gaming tables and other more domestic vices.
>
> (C: 125–6)

The islands are represented here as economic and discursive sites that happen to be located in the Caribbean. With the natives driven out, nobody is rooted to the place. As Emily notices, the slaves are 'torn from their native soil and thrust into the busy commerce of our civilized world' (C: 70). These people are placeless, partly Caribbean, partly English and partly African, but not wholly belonging anywhere. Even the dialect they use to sing of their placelessness has mixed roots, a displaced language, for a displaced people:

> If me want for go in a Ebo
> Me can't go there!

> Since dem tief me from a Guinea
> Me can't go there!
>
> If me want for go in a Congo
> Me can't go there!
> Since dem tief me from my tatter
> Me can't go there!
>
> If me want to go in a Baytown,
> Me can't go there!
> Since Massa go in a England,
> Me can't go there!
>
> (C: 71)

The island is inhabited by those not rooted in the Caribbean, and without the freedom to travel elsewhere. For the *massa*, the colonial world is becoming increasingly open, and European culture is enriched with the experience of discovery and travel. Whereas for the transported peoples of Africa, colonialism means confinement and restriction, and their culture is one of broken histories and maps of places they have been torn from.

In the novel, a distinction is made between English and French colonisation in the Caribbean that partly accounts for the loss of place and the peripheralisation of English colonies. According to McDonald, Emily's doctor, the Frenchman 'will determine that his island is his "home", which naturally results in his making a greater effort to ensure his moral and social survival' (C: 49), but the English planters look upon their stay on the island as a period of 'exile':

> They never see, or inhale the fragrance of, a *creole* rose without letting their imaginations stray through the rich gardens of fair England.
>
> (C: 50)

This may be true of the colonial planter but, for Emily, England does not hold such sweet memories. As an English*woman*, rather than an Englishman, her attachment to home is based on a different sense of her place within England. Like a character in a Victorian *Bildungsroman*, her identity is formed from her environment as much as by her individual character, and this environment is hinted at in her style of reporting. She writes in a pinched and straitened prose, suggesting the ordered chronotope of Victorian domestic life, and for her, travel to the Caribbean is an escape from this confinement:

> The truth was she was fleeing the lonely regime which fastened her into
> blackboards, corsets and stays to improve her posture.
>
> (C: 4)

Her experience in the Caribbean helps rewrite the Caribbean, but it also helps to rewrite Emily. The Caribbean impresses itself on her and gradually displaces her attachment to England. Her confinement on the island is also a kind of freedom from the confinement of England, but as with Cambridge, translation leads to lack of belonging rather than an exchange of belonging. Where Cambridge becomes a 'virtual Englishman', Emily is creolised, neither at home in England nor the Caribbean. To return to England would be to place herself again within family, society and home, so she chooses to be a native of no place. In this placelessness, her own body becomes home, for a while, to a 'little foreigner' (C:183), a foetus which is aborted. Recovering from the experience of having her own body temporarily inhabited, she can no longer conceive of returning England. She has changed, and the 'corsets and stays' that claimed her body in England, for England, will not fit her now:

> England. Emily smiled to herself. The doctor delivered the phrase as though this England was a dependable garment that one simply slipped in and out of according to one's whim. Did he not understand that people grow and change? Did he not understand that one day a discovery might be made that this country-garb is no longer of a correct measure?
>
> (C: 177)

Emily's linguistic encounter with the Caribbean, in the form of her prim English reports, gradually changes to a sensual and imaginative encounter with the place:

> The fragrance of poinsettia came wafting into the room in small eddies that caused the light in the lamp to dance in tune to the scent. She remembered. Journeying up the hill to Hawthorn Cottage with her friend. Stella. Dear Stella.
>
> (C: 184)

Emily does not return to England with a journal of her 'true' experiences to add to European narratives of the colonies, but rather enters a far less pervasive and largely hidden Creole narrative. She stays on to form a tragic unity with the island, where she has experienced the loss of her baby, the loss of her father's estate, the loss of her lover, murdered by

Cambridge, and the loss of Cambridge himself who is hanged. Emily describes her child as a 'little foreigner', and perhaps when it is aborted it signifies the expulsion of European progeny on the island. In this novel, the Caribbean island seems to drift towards a post-slavery creolised place. But in reality, the foreigners do not go away, and after slavery, colonisation was to continue for another one hundred and fifty years or so before independence came.

As Lamming's work demonstrates, there is another phase of colonialism to come in which the Caribbean island is still a little England, still tied into the fortunes of the British Empire. And the story continues, through Caryl Phillips' *Crossing the River* and *The Middle Passage*, Jean Rhys' *The Wide Sargasso Sea*, and Joan Riley's *The Unbelonging*. All of which testify to the continuing heritage of translation and displacement emanating from the *transit region* of the African diaspora – the Caribbean island colony.

The next stage in imagining and rewriting the Caribbean, as far as this chapter is concerned, is to look beyond rewriting colonial narratives, which we have concentrated on so far, to the longer history of the islands. Marina Warner's *Indigo*, offers an imaginative reconstruction of a time before colonisation, and in a sense, a time before time, the disrupted narratives, echoes and images of a chronotope before the history of the colonial Caribbean. This chronotope of native Carib history and mythologies is made contingent with two contemporary twentieth century narratives – one describing a Creole family that continues to move between the Caribbean and England, and another that attempts to assert an independence from England. The novel presents an attempt to forge a cultural and political identity for the Caribbean Island that rests in part on the continuing presence of an imagined native Carib mythology, combined with Marxist politics.

REWRITING THE CARIBBEAN PART 4 – MARINE WARNER, *INDIGO*

In *Indigo*, the colonial Caribbean is again reconstructed through multiple viewpoints and multiple chronotopes, as in the other novels in this chapter, but here, these chronotopes extend into the pre-colonial and post-colonial. This extension is not linear however, and does not proceed in an organised fashion through the periods of Caribbean history, but is organised through an extensive timelessness. This timelessness is mythopoeic, involving the reassertion of the mythical time of Sycorax. This mythical figure preceded colonisation in an enchanted island which alludes to that of Shakespeare's *The Tempest*. The mythical time of Sycorax bypasses historical time to carry her voice forward into the contemporary world of post-independence politics. Here is another example of the use of the general form of the postmodern chronotope to organise non-linear time and to de-differentiate space within the context of post-colonial revisitings.

In the organisation of the novel's chronotopes, a mythical time endures the arrivals and departures of the colonisers with their clocks, charts and the comings and goings of ships, all of which enmeshed the island of Sycorax in a modern chronotope of expansion and discovery. The time of Sycorax is outside the modern chronotope because it is a time governed by cycles of nature, in particular the turning of the tides, and the returning sun and moon. Only when foreigners arrive with their designs on the island do the islanders experience an abstract space and time that will connect their island to the modern world. In an emerging Eurocentric geopolitics, the island chronotope is overwritten by the timetables and trade routes that connect it to Africa and Europe. While the English colonisers incorporate the island of Sycorax into their maps and, at the same time, differentiate this new world from their own, the islanders prepare for the beginning of a new time. The first sign of the impending shift is when the bodies of African slaves are first washed ashore, and Sycorax and her 'cavey' fetch Dulé from the womb of one, to allow him to be born into their world:

> It was the beginning of a new world for her and her people, the start of a new time, and as yet Sycorax did not know it.
>
> (*Indigo*: 82)

Later, in this first contact between the natives and the colonisers, Ariel is shot, and Sycorax is burnt out of her hut. The chronotope of the old island world is irrevocably changed. The old chronotope, based on the cycles and rhythms of the sea and the sun, is brought to an end by a modern European chronotope based on locatable points and vectors:

> The revolving of the world came to an end, space and time collapsed into a point, and the point was there, where the tatters of Sycorax's pagne adhered to her flesh and burned her.
>
> (I: 131–2)

In the subtitle of the novel, 'Mapping the Waters', there is the suggestion that something naturally unplaceable and unfixable – water – might be fixed into a mathematical representation. Of course, in a general sense, the islands and the oceans can be incorporated in a grid of latitude and longitude and projected on to a chart, otherwise the colonisers would have difficulty ever finding the island again. But the process of incorporating Sycorax's island into a European map is not just about discovery, it is at the same time an act of appropriation which precedes the imposition of power and exploitation. The European chronotope is not just an alternative time–space, it is a time–space of domination for Sycorax's island, and a displacement of the island's culture.

During colonisation, a further turn of the screw is the displacement of the island's mythological past with the straight line of European history. This picks up the island as if colonisation is its zero time: its prehistory falls away, unwritten and unvoiced. It is this mythical prehistory that *Indigo* presents, through an imaginative reconstruction of a mythic past. Here, before Sycorax's island is mapped in the signs and symbols of cartography and chronography, there was a more mysterious language. Sycorax uses it to mark her routes and the places where her medicinal and magical plants grow. These dents and grooves represent a workable concept of space and time quite apart from the straight lines and direction of the European's historical time and cartographic space:

> Neither straight downstrokes, like the stems of letters in Kit Everard's log, nor the tripped and fledged arrows that plotted the course of the *Hopewell* on Kit's portolan, the marks reflected the concept of time and direction Sycorax shared with her people; for as yet, they did not know time as a straight line that can be interrupted, even broken, as the people did who were arriving in their archipelago, the slaves from Africa, the adventurers from Europe; they did not possess a past, for they did not see themselves poised on a journey towards triumph, perhaps, or extinction.
> (I: 121)

Unlike the foreigners, Sycorax and her people understand only an unbroken and recursive time, and the chronotope they inhabit is like a 'churn or a bowl' where the individual is separate, but also mixed in with the rest of society in a 'continuous present tense of existence' (I: 122). This chronotope of a perpetual present did not swallow the individual or 'snatch their own stories away from them', as had happened to Dulé, who was snatched from his African home and history by slave traders, and then removed from the womb of his dead mother after a shipwreck. Dulé is a 'child out of time and place' (I: 88); ripped from the womb, and from his world, he imagines his existence as a broken history, a ruptured line that would reach back to the chronotope of Africa. For the European settlers, time is progressive and space continuous, and their future is wrapped up in this modern chronotope. For Sycorax, the island chronotope is a continual presence, in which 'the past abided, rolling into a present, an ocean swelling and falling back, then returning again' (I: 95). This is interrupted by contact with the modern European chronotope. But although Dulé is born on the island, he is not a native, and existence is always *between* the island chronotope and that of Africa. He imagines a ladder 'spanning one isolated phenomenon of space–time to another' (I: 121–2), and the cyclic nature of time on Sycorax's island does not bring the past back to him, rolled into the present; rather the ocean is a constant reminder of the 'lost country', a 'place that the ocean never brought back to lay at his feet' (I: 95).

As the novel moves forward into the post-colonial period, the island remains colonised in a representational sense. The idea of the Caribbean island, its real history and its myths, are commodified as the place turns into an inauthentic vacation site for European and American tourists. The selling point of the island is that it offers an escape from the worries of modern progressive time, back to the perpetual presence of Sycorax's island. But to cater to modern tastes, and to ensure that capitalist enterprises can make some profit, the island also provides a simulation of the privilege, luxury and grandeur of a colonial period continuing on into the present. Here, there is an element of the nostalgia for the past, a continuation of the colonial within the post-colonial through a peculiar simulation of a discredited history. The past is made available, mainly as image, and yet the 'real' legacy of colonialism is also made available, as economic exploitation of the post-colonial island seems to continue in another form. Sycorax's island is still subject to the imperial forces of global capitalism, the workforce is still exploited, and the islanders are not in control of their own destiny. The means of production remains the same – capitalism from outside investment – the only difference is that the product has changed from sugar to tourism.

Through the chronotope of a continuing present, the novel brings characters descended from Sycorax, but now living in England, back to the island. But in their return, romantic and exotic notions of the island have displaced the 'real' past of Sycorax to which they belonged. Xanthe sees the island as if through European romantic fiction and inauthentic constructions of the Caribbean island, tastes which the tourist sites will surely pander to:

> ... think of the scented nights and the sapphire sea and the conches blowing through the palms! ...
> ... it's history with a big H, you can't make it happen or unhappen just as you please. The Elizabethan seadog, the dream of Eldorado, the lost paradise, this is the past that we belong to, you can't hide from it.
> (I: 278)

But Miranda is concerned with the colonial past as it has been presented to her by the black nurse and storyteller, Serafine:

> The slaves, the slaves. The sugar, the Indians who were there, the Indians who were brought there afterwards. Feeny and Feeny's parents and grandparents and ... her daughter, the one she had to leave behind. The plantations. The leg-irons and the floggings. Sugar. Sugar.
> (I: 278)

Both carry with them preconceptions, images that are part of the postcolonial reality. But neither is aware of the real political and economic issues, or the search for cultural identity within the island that is hindered in a large part by the kind of clichéd vision they each harbour. When they arrive on the island, they become involved in the 'real' destiny of the island, and experience the island's emergence into a 'real' post-colonial world. The novel presents a tension between the postcolonial world, *as it really is*, and Xanthe's and Miranda's preconceptions. But these preconceptions are not just the typical European fantasies of the Caribbean island, they are also memories, carried forward through generations and stretching back to the time of Sycorax. The postmodern chronotope allows the novel to indulge in common memories through which stories of Sycorax are brought forward into the present. Miranda and Xanthe, as Europeans of Caribbean descent, are thus implicated in the history of the 'whole tribe's existence'. This brings a rather different European presence to bear on the post-colonial situation to that of simply being the one-time colonisers. The novel is to some extent an imaginative study of what Edward Said has called the odd 'hybrid historical and cultural experiences' that constitute any culture, but post-colonial cultures especially (Said 1993). The postmodern chronotope is the form used in the novel to imagine these experiences.

When Miranda's father, Kit, returns to the island where he was born, he finds himself disorientated. As a Creole, he is partly rooted here, but he was educated in England and descended from the mixed island blood of an Arawak Indian and an English coloniser. Sight of the island does not evoke memories of home – he is not a native returning, but a person of mixed race, with a mixed history, and is therefore always an outsider, unplaceable:

> The aerial map of his birthplace unfurled and streamed in the high vault above him. He was wrapped in the presence of the islands, and yet, recognising them, all he could feel was the stab of loss. He could not know any longer what it meant to belong somewhere.
>
> (I: 292)

Kit finds a role for himself on the island as a translator, making use of his mixed race, he 'translates' the native island and its myths and legends into a 'language' foreign tourists can understand. The 'Spice of Life' Hotel, where he is employed, is testimony to the inauthentic postmodern place that the island has become. Here, the timelessness or continuous presence in the myths of Sycorax's island, which was displaced by European colonisation, re-emerges, but this time as a postmodern fiction for sale:

> This is the place of lost time if ever there was one. Island tempo, no hurry, nowhere to go, nothing to do.
>
> (I: 295)

The casino of this hotel, like one of Foucault's heterotopia[15] is an impossible space attached to a strange space and time outside the island. It is a space of lost time, disconnected from the hotel even and out of bounds to the islanders for fear of corrupting them. Kit exists on the threshold of this non-place, as both an islander and an outsider he is tolerated in the casino. His 'indigenous status' is overlooked, because he gives the place a 'tone historic and *mondain*' (I: 345). Here is another virtual Englishman who cannot escape the marker of race, but in this case it appears to work to his advantage because there is a situation in which his colour authenticates the place he inhabits, and in this strange postmodern place, such authenticity is a valued commodity.

A Marxist style coup on the island quickly sends foreign investment scurrying off in search of more fertile ground. The island now enters a crucial phase as it tries to assert itself as a new socialist republic. The 'Spice of Life' Hotel is converted into a training centre for local people. The coup appears to cut loose the island from the ties of Europe and America, returning it to something like the insular integrity Sycorax's island maintained prior to the arrival of the Europeans. In this reconfigured, recovered island, Kit finds a new role for himself (removed from the disconnected space of the hotel's casino) out in the sea, where he farms the oyster beds. Here he reconnects with the island of Sycorax, like a native returning. In his new job, he gathers the 'native' blue (indigo) oysters from the waters around the island, a symbolic returning to the bowl used by Sycorax to mix her indigo dye, and through which an image continuing presence is presented.

But just as in Hardy's novel, the native's return is never straightforward. Modern history did happen and global economics and geopolitics shape contemporary reality. So, the oysters he farms are sold into a global market place, reconnecting the island world with America and Europe. The island, it would seem, can never re-enter that time in which the ocean continued to roll in and return, the past abiding in the present.

For a moment during the coup, there is a hiatus, history is suspended and in the vacuum a new identity and direction for the island is sought. There is a conflict here between Sy Nebris's vision of the island as a 'nowhere place of idyll and romance' (I: 357), and Abdul Malik's fundamentalist demand for a new radical and separatist space. This battle echoes that staged between Sycorax, Dulé and the islanders against the first colonisers, which lives on as the imperial game of Flinders. The fundamentalists fail to create a new separatist space for the island, just as Sycorax and Dulé failed to maintain their separate space against the colonisers, but they do create a rupture in space–time and, in this gap, Sycorax is somehow evoked. Her voice is heard emanating from the waters where Xanthe has drowned, and where Kit will make his living from farming oysters. This appearance of Sycorax reinforces the idea of a 'continuous present tense', but it is not a nostalgic return to pre-colonial times. This is clearly not an option. When Sycorax speaks through the government leader, Atala Seacole, to demand a new manifesto for the island, this surely calls for a progressive sense of place that takes back control of foreign investments, but also recognises the place of the 'whole tribe's existence' within the context of the rest of the world to which it is irrevocably joined. The hybridity of the island's history and culture is now what is meant by the whole tribe's existence not the native tribe which was long ago dispatched.

Indigo portrays a post-colonial Caribbean that rejects the postmodern space of the island as a commercially-motivated nowhere place of idyll. But the creation of a new radical space by separatist fundamentals does not succeed either. There is no return to artificial timelessness or self-contained space. It is with pragmatism that Atala sets about redefining and reconstructing the space of the island, although, in the novel, this pragmatism is not without some magical intervention from Sycorax, re-awakened from her place between life and death in the waters where Xanthe has drowned. Sycorax hears Atala's calls to reconstruct the island, and looks forward now to a time when there will be no more cries to wake her, and she can at last rest quietly: 'the noises of the isle will be still and I – I shall at last come to silence' (I: 376). Sycorax, like Prospero in *The Tempest* can withdraw from the story once her 'magic' has been used to bring about the looked-for reconciliation of the island story.

Beyond the island, the novel has traced the 'whole tribe's existence' to England; although the transformation of Xanthe (Goldie), as she becomes 'mantled in pearl, layer upon layer spun about her foreign body' (I: 376), completes the 'story' of the 'fat man' and the princess turned to gold (told by Seraphine to Miranda at the start of the novel) and incorporates the story of Xanthe into the history and the mythology of the island, Miranda is left to complete her story in England. With reference to *The Tempest*, and using a plot in which Miranda is involved in a production of the same play, the novel allows Miranda to complete a complex web of relationships designed to interrelate the island and England in shared mythologies and histories.

This reconstruction and rewriting of post-colonial place, in which multiple histories connect the space of the island with England, seems to present an enlarged history of a whole tribe's existence. It also presents an enlarged geography, because the whole tribe is no longer connected to a single place, but is stretched across geographical space – 'mapping the waters'. The relationship between Miranda and the black actor playing Caliban in an English production of *The Tempest* seems to signal reconciliation and closure, but at the same time it warns against the easy reconciliation figured in Shakespeare's play:

> In the lumpy and formless place called this world, people didn't meet before the drop of the curtain and begin a happy ending together.
> (I: 393)

In the postmodern, interconnected histories and interwoven geographies disallow the use of foreign spaces as separated sites of enchantment, from which actors can withdraw to resume their usual positions. Here the magic of Prospero's isle extends into the everyday world of history and politics.

Miranda knows she is not 'living inside one of Shakespeare's sweet-tempered comedies, nor in one of his late plays with their magical reconciliations', in her world, the 'real' world at the end of the twentieth century, ' breakage and disconnection were the only possible outcome' (I: 391). The postmodern world described here by Miranda, which is also the post-colonial world, suggests a time before the straight lines of colonial history mapped the world and gave it shape. But perhaps it actually describes a more complex form which is mapped by different conceptions of space and time, and in which different histories coexist – the form of the postmodern chronotope. The end of the novel does not signal a reconciliation between the transformed daughter of the magician Prospero, and his black slave and, through this, reconciliation between coloniser and colonised, but rather it signals the beginnings of a continuing play within intertwined histories and geographies of inevitably hybridised characters:

> They had begun play. Their openings were well-tried, unadventurous. But these same familiar moves would take them in deep . . . crossing the lines, crossing the squares, far out on the board in the other's sea.
> (I: 395)

CHAPTER 8

The Trope of Placelessness:
Graham Swift, *Out of this World*
Don DeLillo, *Ratner's Star* and *The Names*

> 'What is this but a place?' he said. 'Nothing more than a place. We're both here in this place, occupying space. Everywhere is a place. All places share this quality. . . There's nowhere you can go that isn't a place. So what's the difference? . . . Think of the word "place". A sun deck with views of gorgeous mountains. A tiny dark kitchen. These share the most important of all things anything can share. They are places. The word "place" applies in both cases. In this sense, how do we distinguish between them? How do we say one is better or worse than the other? They are equal in the most absolute of ways. . .'
>
> *(Ratner's Star:* 228)

DIALECTICS OF INSIDE/OUTSIDE

A traditional distinction between space and place has been formulated by the humanist geographer Yi Fu Tuan: *place is circumscribed from the undifferentiated space that surrounds it and threatens it with its instability; space becomes place as we inhabit it, get to know it better, and endow it with value.*[1] But in the postmodern, such distinctions become problematic. This image of a differentiated and delineated place can be most clearly recognised in the form of the mediaeval city, surrounded by high walls and gates that secure it from the threat of the open and undifferentiated space outside. And in the mediaeval garden – a doubly secured space within the city walls – nature is reinvented as a temporal sanctuary, the cycle of the seasons resisting the ravages of historical time. The representational spaces of a mediaeval cosmos derive from an idea of a fixed and already completed time–space. Modernity may have defined itself against such an idea, but a mediaeval time–space was perhaps always constructed retrospectively as a nostalgic anti-modern urge for the unhistorical. The actual experience was probably never so clear cut and the physical separation of the city was certainly never a straightforward differentiation.

As Edward Relph points out, boundaries between cities and their surrounding space have always been a matter of gradual fading out, rather than a sudden shift from place to undifferentiated space: 'medieval city walls were surrounded by *Faubourgs*, and modern cities fade through suburbia, subtopia and exurbia into the countryside' (Relph 1976: 49–50). Phenomenologically speaking, it is rather a *sense* of being inside that sets place apart from space, and this sense is connected with belonging and identity; it is not necessarily conditioned by walls, which can as easily divide place as circumscribe it.

As Norberg-Schultz has written, 'to be inside is the primary intention behind the place concept; that is to be somewhere, away from what is outside' (Norberg-Schultz 1971: 25). The construction of an *inside*, as Lyndon suggests, is 'the difference between safety and danger, cosmos and chaos, enclosure and exposure, or simply here and there' (Lyndon 1962: 31–41 cited in Relph 1976: 49). But the construction of this inside is as much cultural, social and psychological as physical. A sense of being inside is not necessarily dependent on physical confinement or exclusion, and this may even work against the state of *insideness*.

On the other hand, *insideness* might be felt, as it is for the character in DeLillo's *The Names*, in the middle of a desert as well as in the intimacy of home. For Bachelard and Relph, this possibility results from an egocentric mapping and remapping of the space of experience necessary to the negotiation of physical, social and cultural boundaries. From egocentric mapping comes existential insideness and outsideness, increasingly important elements in postmodern and post-colonial being. In Bachelard's study of the 'poetics of space', which is a study of the phenomenological experience of space through poetic image and 'day dreaming', inside and outside are reversible. This reversibility is what allows us to map and remap the boundaries we encounter or imagine we encounter. As Bachelard explains, there is a 'dialectic of division' occurring at the threshold where inside meets outside (Bachelard 1969: 211). It is the very intimacy of these two states, suggests Bachelard, that makes them interchangeable, so inside and outside are 'always ready to be reversed, to exchange their hostility . . . [and then] intimate space loses its clarity, while exterior space loses its void' (Bachelard 1969: 218).

Through egocentric mapping, the individual is capable of retaining or constructing some sense of insideness, and the material condition of placelessness in postmodernity, which is the main subject of this chapter, does not mean that insideness necessarily disappears. Nor should we assume that it is necessarily a bad thing if place-bound insideness is replaced by other forms of insideness. Indeed, for some, the loss of traditional insideness derived from being bound to physical place may prove beneficial in reconstructing a complex sense of belonging to more than one place. An increasing sense of hybrid belonging is likely to result in post-colonial contexts, especially as hybrid cultural experience was already common, but hidden, under colonialism (Said 1993). And in postmodernity, the processes of globalisation inevitably work towards placelessness, through the transmission of placelessness in the media, both of which brings about a multiple sense of belonging. So differentiated places are not prerequisites for belonging and insideness, but the loss of such places does transform the cultural, social and psychological means by which they are constructed.

Since the middle of the twentieth century, commentators have noted the destruction of richly varied places and their replacement by monotonous patterns of buildings and streets. Yet in much of America, from where this placeless geography supposedly emanated, strong feelings of belonging and identity can be traced to these landscapes. It is clearly possible to belong to what appears from the outside to be a placeless geography. Furthermore, in the former Yugoslavia, for example, a richly varied geography of mediaeval towns and cities, released from the iron grip of Soviet control, has become a confusing mix of identity and belonging. Pre-Soviet ethnic and physical boundaries resurface, but demography has changed, and these boundaries no longer provide a sense of insideness or belonging for all of those caught within them. For some, place has in this case been turned inside out, they are outsiders in their own homes. There is a political danger here of regression and re-differentiation through cultural and social ties, acted out in physical spaces. As a general rule, such re-differentiation must surely be resisted as it is inappropriate to the needs of mobile, transnational and trans-ethnic postmodern societies. Quite a separate concern is that of reverting to the forms of traditional place as places for living in postmodernity. Increasingly this seems to be a popular option, and there should be no harm in echoing elements of traditional place in new urban environments. Indeed, as Richard Rogers has suggested, some aspects of mediaeval towns, with their large, 'open-minded' social spaces, may provide an appropriate architectural form for a plural postmodern society (Rogers 1999). Then the representational space of the mediaeval city is redrawn as an open and undifferentiated space, rather than as a separating and differentiating wall.

This chapter explores the construction of insideness in the context of the placeless geographies, but it also explores the way in which placelessness might be considered as a representational mode or trope in the postmodern. The trope of placelessness applies to local, global and cosmic dimensions in the novels covered in this chapter, but I will be arguing that this is not necessarily only a reflection of the historical condition of postmodern society. Because at the same time, within the chronotopes of postmodern novels, the trope of placelessness can be detected operating in tandem with postmodernist strategies to rework and question values and belief systems associated with modernity. These include, but are not limited to, certain forms of scientism and historicism, futurism and the ideology of development. Within the artistic-literary sphere, the trope of placelessness also signifies problems in representation and, more problematically, in the role and functions of language systems (linguistic and mathematical) in representation.

The intervention of the trope of placelessness in architecture, although something of an aside here, offers an illustration of some of the interesting contradictions implicit in postmodern placelessness. Postmodern architecture is commonly regarded as a reaction to the abstract and sometimes utopian architecture of modernism and particularly against the reduction, commodification and replication of this in International Style, itself a manifestation of modern placelessness.

At the same time, postmodern architecture continues to respond to similar demands for functional and economically-determined building designs. In the end, the change may be very superficial and at worst merely the continued replication of similar (postmodern) designs, but without the marriage between form and function that was one of the goals of modernist architecture. If postmodernism is without ideology, then postmodern architecture is basically a reaction to modernism without any manifesto of its own. In which case, it seems unlikely that postmodern architecture can be relied on to recreate those significant places in which societies have traditionally constructed an identity centred on shared history and shared value systems.

But turning this argument on its head, postmodern architecture can use the trope of placelessness to create a context of decontextualisation: places whose character lies in the extent and integrity of their placelessness. It is a doubling of difference in which placelessness is transmitted through the proliferation of non-places that jar with their surroundings to such an extent as to draw attention to the juxtaposition between their own surroundings and their own inauthenticity. Such attention centres on the 'real' that has been erased, but whose absence reasserts itself through the trope of placelessness. One city that enjoys this kind of identity is Hong Kong, whose double erasure, of its Chinese origins and now its colonial heritage, is constantly returned in the gap created between its newly installed placelessness and its lost contexts. The trope of placelessness, by daring to erase place and displace it with replicated non-places, brings back into being a multiple identity for Hong Kong, constituted in lost pasts and imported presents.

But not all places are like Hong Kong, and there remains the fact that in societies more traditional than this, the failure to create and maintain place through shared values and history is perceived as a problem. What is to prevent us falling into a condition of chaos and insecurity: a mass feeling of existential outsideness? And if, in the postmodern, the trope of placelessness extends into representation, how can we even begin to describe the representational places we might imagine?

In the following novels, although the trope of placelessness suggests the loss of traditional place, a sense of outsideness, and a questioning of modern systems and beliefs, I will argue that the attempt is still there to create those defences against chaos and non-differentiation, to find something to crawl inside and call home. In the novels of Graham Swift, this tends to revolve around family relations. But in the novels of Don DeLillo, placelessness is more endemic, and the creation of shelters from the chaos become more artificial, virtual and bizarre.

GRAHAM SWIFT, *OUT OF THIS WORLD* – THE HUMAN SIDE OF PLACELESSNESS

Although *Out of this World* begins with a politically motivated murder by the IRA, in my reading it is structured around three key historical moments in the twentieth century: the bombing of Nuremberg in the Second World War, the Vietnam war, and the Apollo moon landings. These are presented as milestones in the modern destruction of place and a progressively fading sense of the real. They are giant steps 'out of this world'. The resulting sense of placelessness is presented through the narratives of two differently displaced characters: a war photo-journalist, Harry, and his daughter, Sophie. Neither character is grounded or experiences a sense of belonging, so they both express what Relph refers to as 'existential outsideness'. Swift's novel concentrates on the camera and the aeroplane as instrumental in the destruction of place in the twentieth century and the ensuing placelessness of postmodernity. Using key historical moments as examples, these would seem to be the main points of attack on place described in the novel:

- place is physically destroyed by air power, e.g. the destruction of Nuremberg and Vietnam by bombing
- terrestrial and planetary boundaries that delineate place are routinely overflown and outflown by air travel and space travel
- film brings the world to the screen, first into the cinema and then into the intimacy of home. The outside is thus domesticated, brought inside, but the insideness of home is simultaneously altered by the presence of this simulated outsideness

- film tends to collapse distinctions between 'real' place and representations of place. Increasingly film legitimises reality, reversing the mimetic function of representation.

Harry's narrative is a personal account of the twentieth century from the perspective of a photo-journalist whose life has been largely influenced by the aeroplane and film. It is a record of the promises and disappointments of these two fundamental components of the modern age. Beginning just after the First World War, he recalls a growing sense of optimism on the tenth anniversary of the Armistice when he is taken up in an aeroplane for the first time. He senses the dawn of a modern age that would lift civilisation out of an old Europe with its entrenched, terrestrial boundaries, signified by the muddy trenches of the First World War. The spirit of the new age is symbolised by the transcendent possibilities of the aeroplane:

> I was being lifted up and away, out of this world, out of the age of mud, out of that brown, obscure age, into the age of air . . .
> (*Out of this World*: 208)

That brown and obscure age is also the age of photography and film in its early days, a sepia-tinted representation of the real that had not, as yet, significantly reduced the status of the real. For Harry, that now archaic piece of aeronautical history, the Argosy biplane, was 'the very stuff of the future', heralding the modern age. And, combined with the camera, the aeroplane was to offer a perspective of the world previously reserved for the gods.

Harry's father, a veteran of the First World War, pushes him forward into this new age, but remains with his feet 'still on the ground, still caught in the mud' (OW: 208). As in *Waterland*, Swift denotes historical and cultural shifts through generations of family history. He slices history into generations with each generation gap signalling changing relationships with the world. But, as in most postmodernist fiction, this is not a sequential, uniform and unproblematic historical chain. There are mysteries, contradictions, unexplained rifts and short-circuits within Swift's family sagas which disrupt the narrative, and this disruption in the grand narrative of family history is echoed in the telling of the history of the modern age. We are constantly apprised of the unreliability of historical accounts, of their provisional and often subjective nature. Swift's novels take this problematisation of history into the form of the novel, so that they are not only concerned with the particular family history, but at another level with the history of the twentieth century and with the idea of history that the twentieth century presents us with.

In *Waterland*, the family history is short-circuited by Dick's parentage, which places him across two generations, the son of his mother and his grandfather. In *Out of this World*, the disruption is across two generations, father and daughter, whose narratives connect only across the pages of the novel, and not in the world, or rather the separate worlds, the novel constructs. Both *Waterland* and *Out of this World* use the confessional mode of narration, tracing recollection through the uneven paths of guilt and repression. In this novel, the two alternating narrators, Harry and his daughter Sophie are set apart in two different worlds, one homeless in the old world, and the other equally homeless, though for different reasons, in the New World of America. In the course of the novel, Harry and Sophie never meet, but the novel brings them together through disjointed first person autobiographies juxtaposed as in an epistolary dialogue. The structure of the novel is of letters they might have written to each other, but never did.

The trope of placelessness in the novel can be read in a number of ways. The alienation of Harry and Sophie, father and daughter, from each other and from their world is partly due to the nature of Harry's work as a war photographer. The final straw for Sophie is her father's insensitivity in taking pictures of her grandfather (Harry's father) after he has been blown up in an IRA car bomb attack. On one level, the novel is the story of secrets and lies in family relations, continuing a productive strand running through most of Swift's novels, but there is also a major strand in the novel relating to different accounts of placelessness reported by the two narrators.

It is clearly significant that the successive generations of the Beech family span the twentieth century, and each generation seems to take a step further 'out of this world' in the sense that they become one step further removed from the real. Harry rationalises this as the shifting nature of the times and, from his perspective as a photographer, he maps the trajectory on to advances in the business of capturing the real in snapshots of history as it happens. For Sophie, being 'out of this world' means being out of touch with reality as a psychological condition. Her sense of outsideness is not due to material conditions of postmodernity, with its general sense of placelessness and loss of the real. Rather it is a matter of personal circumstances which she eventually seems to come to terms with. Similarly, Harry, having mapped out a postmodern conditioned by placelessness and the loss of the real, is in the end forced to face the fact that it is not his work or the state of the world in general that has cut him off from his daughter and placed him 'out of this world', rather it is his own egocentrism.

The novel presents the twentieth century as a decline from the promise of the modern age into the placelessness, and an increasing sense of unreality, but this is in some respects an excuse for the main character not to face up to his guilt and lack of responsibility. In which case, it might be argued that the trope of placelessness is used in the novel as a device for presenting two kinds of individual breakdown and trauma. In the end, I think the novel is *both* an investigation of the emotional lives of family members, to some extent traumatised by the material effects of life in the late twentieth century that includes loss of place and loss of the real, *and* it is an investigation of the history of this 'loss' or 'decline' and an account of how individuals develop strategies for coming to terms with the loss, or rather the transformation, of place and the real.

Following the history of the impact of the aeroplane (and space ship) and the camera on twentieth century experience, the Beech family mark a progressive journey away from 'the real', or rather from a modern concept of *realism*. In this case, the journey traces a postmodern reconstitution of the real, and this will be largely conditioned by placelessness. They travel from the muddy reality of Flanders in the First World War, through an airy, unplaceable futurity between the wars, to the obliteration of reality in the bombing of Germany, and towards simulated and 'Disneyfied' reality in postmodernity. It is as though the much-vaunted 'shrinking world' of the twentieth century is shadowed by an equivalent 'expanding world' constituted in image and simulation.

Air travel tends to collapse the Cartesian space with which the modern world had been mapped and experienced – through the map – as a set of terrestrial boundaries and markers. The aeroplane changes all that, as Harry discovers on his first flight in 1928:

> . . . being in a foreign country for the first time was nothing to being several thousand feet in the air, from where, in fact, one country looked much like another and the demarcations of maps and atlases seemed suddenly a sham.
>
> (OW: 206)

In the Second World War, Harry finds that the aeroplane changes the nature of war as it is no longer confined by terrestrial boundaries. The geography of western Europe was altered, not only by the devastation and disappearance of places, but also by a gradual re-assimilation of the conceptual space of Europe to account for the aeroplane. This is not to say that terrestrial borders and political boundaries tied to those borders no longer existed, as the division of Berlin was to demonstrate all too clearly, but the aeroplane nevertheless transformed the imaginative and representational space of Europe and the world. Harry finds that during bombing raids the landmarks of Europe are translated into beacons and targets, and the whole of western Europe can be traversed in a night-time journey. In a sense, Europe is unified by this but it is at the same time immediately exposed to the destructive power of aerial bombardment. There is no hiding place, for the most remote enclaves are, for the first time in history, prey to the airborne gaze.

Harry describes how aerial warfare physically destroys place, and how the pre-war concept of place in Europe is irreversibly changed by the wide-scale use of aerial photography. He analyses aerial photographs of German cities in 1945, recording the destruction after Allied bombing raids. The aerial view he experienced in 1928, in which demarcations of place seemed a sham, is now recorded on film, where the geography of western Europe is translated into the evidence of the physical destruction of some of its most prominent and historic places. On seeing Europe from the air in 1928, Harry was filled with optimism for a continent *sans frontières*. But the Second World War soon dashed this as boundaries dissolved in hostility rather than cooperation.

If modernity put pressures on the borders of Europe prior to the First World War, as Stephen Kern has argued,[2] then the development of the aeroplane as an instrument of war must have increased this pressure considerably. The role of the aeroplane as it crosses borders is to obliterate place, reducing it to nothing in massive bombing raids. Harry describes his involvement in this process as translating 'two-dimensional images, which were the records of three-dimensional facts, into one-dimensional formulae – tonnage dropped as against acreage devastated' (OW: 47).

After the war, the reconstruction of Europe led to some interesting questions of place. Should the past be reconstructed through the rebuilding of bombed towns and cities as replicas of the past, or should the past be left behind with the construction of new modern places, looking forwards to the future? Nuremberg, the old mediaeval capital of Franconia, which had progressively been laid waste until 1945, was rebuilt after the war. In the novel, Harry notices that the modern reconstruction of this 'intricate product of the centuries' is not 'real'; it has been painstakingly restored to 're-conjure a world before certain irreversible historical events had happened' (OW: 103). After this reconstruction, the main attraction for visitors to Nuremberg, according to Harry, is to experience the place as it was before the Third Reich, not to see its role in the rise and fall of Hitler's Germany:

> People go for these picturesque reconstructions, mixed with genuine remnants of the old, for the fairy-tale spires and gables. The one-time site of Nazi rallies and the scene of the War trials are of secondary interest.
>
> (OW: 103)

Swift charts the modern destruction of place here through the devastation and the upheavals of the Second World War, but he also draws attention to another contributing factor to placelessness, in which the production of place has some 'other-directedness', as Edward Relph describes it (Relph 1976: 93). In postmodernity it is quite common for landscapes to be produced for tourists, or to simulate some other place or time, creating what Relph calls 'inauthentic place' (Relph 1976: 82–95). But here, the production of inauthentic place derives from attempting to diminish recent history by retrieving Nuremberg's pre-war history. Nuremberg is not part of a modern reconstruction which looks to the future, but seems to be designed to excise the historical events of 1940–1946, taking tourists back into a pre-war fantasy, and drawing attention away from those key historical moments of the war rallies and war trials.

In post-war Nuremberg, Swift points to an example of 'inauthentic' place designed to provide an escape from particular history, into a fantasy of the past in the present. It is an exercise in post-traumatic defence against the past by a whole people, which is paralleled in Sophie's flight from the past into the 'New World' of New York. Sophie's flight is from the memory of the assassination of her grandfather by terrorists. She is also, in this escape, cutting herself off from her father who she has somehow implicated in this shadowy and borderless world of terrorism. Sophie's world is shattered when she realises that her grandfather's world has been literally and metaphorically blown away.

She had looked to the stability of the time and place her grandfather inhabited, the 'real muddy' world, for her own stability. She flies to the 'New World', to the 'land of escape, the land of sanctuary', but she realises that this idea of America is really a 'come-on, a sales-pitch' (OW: 15). She attaches herself to that fantasy of starting afresh, disconnected from history, by trading the Old World of Europe for the New World of America. But the trauma of history and memory traps her in the moment and the place that blew her world away:

> . . . it just keeps on happening. So that afterwards, when I was some place else, here in New York, three thousand miles away, it wasn't afterwards or some other place, I was still there, on the terrace at Hyfield, standing, frozen, as if I might never move again, with that strange noise in my ears, the noise of absolute silence.
>
> (OW: 109)

Sophie is aware that her dream of 'getting away from it all' in the 'New World' is no more realistic than the dreams of escape back into the 'Old World' that her husband sells to tourists:

> I'm not blind to the fact that what Joe sells every day in his Sixth Avenue office – what keeps us here in the land of the free – is just the same dream only in reverse: golden memories of the Old World. Thatched cottages and stately homes. Patchwork scenery. Sweet, green visions.
>
> (OW: 15)

The postmodern chronotope reasserts itself here when the modern dream of escaping into the future and into a New World turns back inwards. In postmodernity, there are no new worlds, only more or less real versions of the Old World, rewritten and reconstructed. And there is no escape from the world of self in which Sophie is trapped:

> But away-from-it-all is such a shifting, strange, elusive place. There isn't a point in the world where you can get away from the world, not any more, is there?
>
> (OW: 15)

This is an example of a character's personal entrapment coupled with a reflection of the condition of postmodernity. Sophie is trapped partly by her own particular trauma, but she is simultaneously trapped by a loss of transformative places in postmodernity, which would enable her escape. This feeling that secure and stable places, *authentic* places, like home, have been lost, is accompanied by the feeling that there is no escape within the world, because the world is somehow unified in its lack of place. Sophie's condition is that of existential outsideness exacerbated and partly brought on by postmodern placelessness. In postmodernity, the old demarcations disappear, and there seems to be nothing to replace that sense of belonging that existed in her grandfather's world. In Greece, Sophie notices that tourists grab photos of places as though 'They are trying to possess something that doesn't belong to them' (OW: 130). Tourists try to take hold of place, to turn the images they see into places they can own and move *inside*, but they are part of the process that turns place into surface and image. Tourism represents place as image and spectacle and so removes from place its promise of home and belonging. It turns place inside out, so that it is all surface, always there and never here.

Sophie does not experience 'insideness' in New York. She does not feel belonging there, but she also realises that no place like 'home', stable and secure, can exist for her now. As she tries to explain to her sons on their journey back to England, even her memories of home do not provide her with a place she can retreat into. The past is an unreliable place:

> . . . we will go to England. We will get the plane, just you and me, to England. . . What is it like? It's where you come from in a way, it's where you *were*, but of course you won't remember it. And maybe it's no longer the way I remember it. Or rather, the way I remember it is like it never was.
>
> (OW: 191)

As old demarcations disappear and the aeroplane brings increased mobility, a more sinister aspect of postmodern placelessness emerges, in which chaos and terror reign. It is out of this chaos that terrorists emerge to murder Sophie's grandfather. In the 1970s Harry recalls 'ominous times', in which there was:

> the sense of a new, barbarous world encroaching, a world no longer keeping to its former demarcations, former protocol. Bombs going off in airports, embassies, shopping centres, homes.
>
> (OW: 92)

The placelessness that destroys the concept of home, also provides the space in which international terrorism flourishes. Wars are waged within and across national boundaries, and there are no longer secure and circumscribed places protected from this war – there are no safe areas. Sophie's home is destroyed when her grandfather is blown up by terrorists and, in this moment, Sophie realises that she has not only lost her grandfather, but something more fundamental has been blown away, which will affect her own internal sense of place and security, and reduce everything to dangerous, undifferentiated space:

> That's when I knew it's all one territory and everywhere, everywhere can be a target and there aren't any safe, separate places any more.
> (OW: 111)

The loss of separate places does not seem to affect her father to the same extent, because he seems always to have been placeless, or rather self-contained, carrying his own shell around with him. It seems that the only place he feels that he belongs is located within the confines of self, and as a photo-journalist, this self is reduced to a pair of eyes, a disembodied lens: 'All you are is your eyes, all there is is in your eyes, your vision is you.' (OW: 121). To not belong seems to suit Harry, and this is the crucial difference between Harry and his daughter Sophie, who never accepted her father's disconnection from family and self-imposed unbelonging.

This idea of not belonging occurred to him as a child as he is sent off across Surrey to school. On the train to school he would think to himself that he belonged in no one place, but would always be between places:

> You belong nowhere. Or rather: *This* is the only place you belong – this transit region, this in-between space.
> (OW: 121)

This portability is useful to Harry as a news photographer travelling the world's trouble spots, grabbing images out of dangerous situations. To seem to exist only as a pair of eyes, ego collapsed into vision, gives Harry and his colleagues a sense of god-like presence and invulnerability:

> The camera seems to make them invisible, invulnerable, incorporeal. They are like those immortal gods and goddesses who flitted unharmed round the plain at Troy.
> (OW: 121)

After his father's death, and Sophie's flight to America, Harry gives up being a news photographer and tries to settle down, to find some piece of England which he can call his own, and belong within. But how does this roving lens of a person manage to find a home in a postmodern world where ordinary mortals struggle to achieve a sense of insideness? He buys a thatched cottage in Wiltshire, the kind of place Sophie's husband sells to American tourists as part of an 'English heritage' package. This is not a real home, not an authentic place, as Harry knows, and because Harry has spent his career operating between reality and its representation as image, he ought to be able to distinguish between the authentic and a façade:

> Picture-books aren't real. The fairy-tales all got discredited long ago, didn't they? There shouldn't be thatched cottages still, tucked away among green hills.
>
> (OW: 79)

Unlike the reconstruction of Nuremberg, and the fantasy of the New World in America, the cottage is in itself authentic. Its inauthenticity stems from its re-presentation as a site that continues to contain a traditional rural life, a past and often false history. The false history arrives through the delusion of nostalgia and through the deliberate fictions of estate agents, tour agents and other commercial interests. The cottage with its true and false histories is commodified. It evokes what Raymond Williams has called the 'enamelled world' of a rural tradition, based on pastoral or bucolic tradition, but like all traditions, highly selective and, importantly, not connected to the present day (Williams 1993: 18). The thatched cottage in an English village has now become what Jonathan Smith calls a 'deceptive text', a 'lie' in the landscape, because it no longer contains the signs and signifiers once enclosed in it. It now misrepresents, evoking a long lost way of life (Smith 1993: 81).

For Harry, the cottage and the English countryside are 'unbelievable', and he cannot understand how others manage to 'contrive that impossible trick called Where I Live' (OW: 60). This landscape is not one he can inhabit. He remains outside it, and being here, or rather being *there*, reminds him of his existential outsideness. He still inhabits only the world drawn by his own egocentric mapping, the world of self:

> I would come back to the cottage, open the front gate, walk through the picture-book façade and crawl into the tent of myself.
>
> (OW: 60)

The cottage is reduced to a façade, a film set, behind which Harry wraps himself in his own unbelonging.

FILM AND POSTMODERN PLACELESSNESS

> Film is more than twentieth century art. It's another part of the twentieth century mind. It's the world seen from inside. We've come to a certain point in the history of film. If a thing can be filmed, film is implied in the thing itself. This is where we are. the twentieth century is *on film*. It's the filmed century. You have to ask yourself if there's anything more important than the fact that we're constantly on film, constantly watching ourselves. The whole world is on film, all the time. Spy satellites, microscopic scanners, pictures of the uterus, embryos, sex, war, assassinations, everything.
>
> (*The Names*: 200)

Placelessness can be caused by the creation of inauthentic places and the marketing of illusory, dream places, as well as by the physical destruction and reconstruction of authentic place. The trope of placelessness is also used in the postmodern novel to connect with a wider discourse on the postmodern, especially relating to material, cultural and philosophical concerns for loss of direction, loss of absolutes, and loss of the real. As the character in DeLillo's novel puts it, film has been the prime medium of the late twentieth century, and the effects of film on the idea of place are significant in discussing postmodern placelessness.

Film simultaneously dislodges place from the real, synthesises it, distorts it, and disrupts it. Place does not really exist in film, certainly not as a historically grounded site that we might crawl inside and inhabit. Indeed, place turns the time–space of place into surface and inserts it into the disconnected time of the image-sequence. The *mise en scène* of movies is a selective re-presentation of place in which the frame of the camera turns place into setting, editing and erasing the real. And film is always in the *present tense*, resituating place in a perpetual present, torn out of the historical and social time within which place is constituted. Place in film is not circumscribed from the undifferentiated space around it, but is stretched and compressed, synthesised and fragmented by the movement of the camera. In TV soaps, place is important, because these are often about fictitious, but representative communities, and offer a continuous view of life in a real place, reintroducing history and insideness through film, but doing so in a simulated place. The popularity of soaps is surely something to do with this re-presentation of place as an ongoing, and virtually habitable *inside*. But TV places, like 'Brookside Close' and 'Coronation Street' in the UK, although they seem to present rooted communities, actually highlight the loss of such communities in postmodern Britain, and their popularity might be attributed to a nostalgia for that loss.[3] The failure of a soap like 'El Dorado' is perhaps attributable to the fact that it did not succeed in creating the illusion of a place that might be, or might have been, inhabited. To British audiences it was re-presentation of an already inauthentic place – the Spanish holiday village.

Oddly, although the unreal effects of film seem obvious to a late twentieth century audience suspicious of its truth claims (even when presented as 'news'), film was originally expected to introduce realism into the world. As James Duncan points out, film is underpinned by a 'mathematization of space', which 'appeared to promise a systematic means of producing a mimetic reproduction of the world' (Duncan 1993: 41). Film was expected to rid the world of suspicion and legend by providing a transparent lens on the world. Harry, in *Out of this World*, also thought the camera would be in the vanguard of the new realism:

> Ours was the age in which we would say farewell to legends, when they would fall off us like useless plumage and we would see ourselves clearly only as what we are. I thought the camera was the key to this process.
>
> (OW: 187)

The camera has allowed us to see many things more clearly, but it has *transformed* knowledge rather than qualitatively altering it. The language of recent camera technology includes terms such as remote sensing, scanning, surveillance and monitoring, suggesting windows on to the real world, but at the same time the camera creates a synthetic shadow of that real world, and this other 'real' is not quite the real thing. Society has not become as tyrannised by technology and the state control of technology as George Orwell predicted in *1984*.

Wim Wenders' movie *The End of Violence* shows that the synthetic shadow of the real is just too easy to manipulate for it to be relied on for total surveillance. It has become a standard device in recent thriller movies to place video loops in security cameras to fool security guards into thinking they are seeing the present when they are only seeing a repeated loop of past time. Film is an abstraction of the world from the world, limited by the frame and the moment, and altered imperceptibly by the presence of the camera. In a sense, the world on film has taken over as the place we inhabit, and we grow fearful of the undifferentiated space that is not on film. When an event occurs, anywhere in the world, we demand film, and lack of filmic confirmation suggests that the event may lay outside the real, in some dangerous unfilmed/unmapped land.

In *Out of this World,* Harry refers to the 'new myth of its [the world's] own authentic-synthetic photographic memory' (OW: 189). Outside this memory, lie the new darknesses, the new unexplored countries, echoing the mysterious spaces of the pre-modern world where the blanks in the Cartesian map were filled with dragons. In postmodernity, the 'here be dragons' spaces are present wherever there is no camera. As Harry suggests, the greater fear in the twentieth century is to be left out of the picture, in unpoliced badlands: 'Not to be watched. Isn't that a greater fear than the fear of being watched?' (OW: 189).

In postmodernity, the ubiquitous camera produces two forms of unknowability:

1. overload of information and a degree of complexity beyond human comprehension (total dependence on information technology to organise information);

2. proximity of fact and fiction in film, so it is no longer possible to determine whether film is a true, simulated or modified picture of reality.

Film seems to reduce the world from the depths of history to surface reality. It is as though the texture of the world has become more superficial – more film-like. Tuan suggests that 'scientists strive to stand far above their material, for a view from nowhere, in the hope that they will be able to plunge well below the surfaces of reality' (Tuan 1989: 233–41; Nagel 1986). But in film, there is a lack of such depth models, as all viewpoints are within the surface phenomena of reality, and there is no vertical orientation. This is the postmodern chronotope of superficiality.

When Sophie is returning by aeroplane to England with her sons, she considers relations between the unreality of movies, and the unreality of being 'out of this world', where for generations only birds, gods and legends existed:

> You know, a long time ago, they'd have thought what we're doing now was magic. Impossible! Out of this World! They'd have thought only gods could fly up in the sky.
>
> (OW: 202)

Her sons, however, have no romantic sense of being up among the gods, and their attention is on the mundane unreality of the in-flight movie. They take the placelessness of their world for granted, blissfully unaware that by overflying oceans and continents they are fulfilling one of man's greatest dreams. Sophie relates the experience of flying to seeing a movie, turning the real into a fiction but then confusing reality and movies: 'The real movie is out *there*, isn't it? Those clouds – look, we're *above* them! A whole ocean sliding underneath us.' (OW: 202). But her postmodern children are interested in watching the in-flight movie, not the 'real movie'. To them, and by implication their generation, the aeroplane journey as such has no romance, but is the dull passage in time, or a distance between two points, marked by so many drinks, meals and movies.

In *Out of this World*, Harry recalls the props used in post-war newsreels. These props consisted of 'inane music' and 'plum-voiced commentaries' (OW: 188), but they did separate the 'real' world from 'fake' Hollywood movies for post-war audiences. Such distinctions between the real world and the movies seem crude and arbitrary in the postmodern, where film frequently plays with these framing devices to call into question the illusory real. As Harry notes, the real and the fictional seem to have seeped into each other:

> Now, they no longer show newsreels in cinemas, but the movies you see aspire to the 'actuality' of the newsreel, while TV can never have enough 'real life' footage. So that it's no longer easy to distinguish the real from the fake, or the world on the screen from the world off it.
>
> (OW: 188)

Harry wonders at what point in the twentieth century film ceases simply to record the real world in a matter-of-fact, after-the-event way, as supposedly it did in the post-war newsreels (although, of course, these unambiguous commentaries often covered up propaganda), and somehow catch up, and overtake, reality, so that in late twentieth century society the world waits to be claimed by the camera:

> When did it happen? That imperceptible inversion. As if the camera no longer recorded but conferred reality. As if the world wanted to be claimed and possessed by the camera. To translate itself, as if afraid it might otherwise vanish.
>
> (OW: 189)

For Harry there are two moments in film history that seem to mark this inversion of film and reality: the Apollo moon landings in 1969 and the Vietnam war. Both of these TV events, he believes, turn factual records of events into showcase movies, so not only is the TV audience unsure of what is real and what is fictional any more, the 'actors' are unclear also. Astronauts are somehow missing the 'real' action, which is taking place at home on TV sets, and soldiers suffer the delusion that they are really in a movie, and might be removed from it if the cameras are turned off. In the Vietnam war, which is where Harry makes his international reputation as a photo-journalist, the camera is for the first time used to record the horror of war on an everyday basis as it happens. War is made more immediate by the camera, but is it more 'real' for that? Footage of the Vietnam war brings real suffering into the living rooms of Americans at home, and invades the privacy of those suffering and those at home. But the camera turns that reality into a kind of unreality. Harry recalls that it was common in Vietnam for a GI to cry – 'I don't like this movie. Get me out of this movie. Someone, for Crissakes, cut this SCENE!'

In the Second World War, Harry noticed that the aerial photographs of Nuremberg had a slightly unreal quality about them: 'as operations progressed, the statistics grew larger, the images more otherworldly, more crater-ridded, more lunar' (OW: 47). But he knew then the difference between images of the world that seemed 'out of this world', and images that really were 'out of this world'. When the Apollo missions transmitted TV images of the real moon back to earth, alongside images of the real earth as seen from the moon, it seems that a shift in human perception occurred. Harry notices that the cameras were specifically set up to record the first moon walk, and this event, and the first words from the moon, were rehearsed and played to camera as though the purpose of the mission was to make a movie. The idea of the camera without an eye behind it is what concerns Harry, because without the eye, where is the humanity? As the novel's motto puts it – 'What the eye sees not, the heart rues not'. After watching the TV images of the moon walk with his father, they walk outside and look up at the moon with the naked eye. Nothing seems to have changed from this viewpoint, but they know that now the moon is on film, it will never be possible to regard it in quite the same other-worldly way. The moon loses its lunar and lunatic qualities as, captured on film, it now belongs to the 'real world'.

But for many, it was the pictures of the earth from the moon that captured the imagination and seemed to create a new reality – a new perception of the world as a unified place. Harry watches the scene on TV with his father, and recognises the significance of the image:

> The earth from the moon. The ultimate photo. All of it, the whole of it, everything. Hanging in the black velvet of space. I wish I could have taken that photo. Stopped there.
>
> (OW: 14)

The image of the earth from space, viewed as it never has been before, from this omniscient, godlike position, might be compared to the view experienced by Harry on his first aeroplane trip. Both are leaps forward that give a perspective on the world previously restricted to fiction. But in 1928, the world suddenly seemed clear to Harry. This was a time when new horizons were dreamt of, within this world and beyond it in space. It was a time of futures. In the late twentieth century, the image of the earth from space seems finally to put a seal on the futurism of the early twentieth century. Harry sees this as an ending, not a beginning – a fitting full stop to a career in photography; and this single image might signify a transition from a modern, future-directed world into a postmodern, introspective world.

In the twentieth century, space has been explored with the same nationalistic fervour that accompanied the exploration of new terrestrial worlds in the fifteenth and sixteenth centuries. Russia and America vied to control this new empire in space, and the space race became an ideological conflict as well. In space, as on the earth centuries earlier, myths of monsters and gods were dispelled as the heavens were charted and given shape. Cosmology named the waste spaces of the sky, and twentieth century science moved boldly into the new 'frontier zones' out in space. In the 1950s and 1960s, at the height of the space race, America in particular was seized with the possibility of new worlds in space. Perhaps it regarded it as a continuation of the great migration west in the nineteenth century to conquer its own wide open spaces. But after the Apollo missions, which delivered the striking but somehow unreal images of space-men and the American flag on the moon, and the stunning image of the earth from the moon, the steam began to run out of the space race.

There were financial reasons of course, and scientific reasons, such as the recognition that in an expanding universe, space exploration is always peering into the darkness of what has already happened, not the lightness of the future. But there is also a link with cultural changes in the postmodern and with some sense of the fragility of the planet, a sense that the future, if there was one, was here on earth, not out in space. In postmodernity, the expansionist dreams of America, the once great frontier nation, seem to collapse in on themselves with self-doubt.. Outer space is now regarded more as a laboratory for exploring the mysteries of our own planet, rather than as a place for futuires or flights from the present.

POSTMODERN BELONGING

In *Out of this World*, it is after the Apollo missions of 1972 that Sophie tries to escape her past by fleeing to America, following in the footsteps of generations of Europeans. But in the postmodern, post-Apollo world, Sophie realises that escape is now impossible. In the postmodern there is no escape from the past, so we are encouraged to go back inwards and rework it.

America was perhaps founded on dreams of escape, and the future is implied in the New York landscape where generations of dreamers and escapees have disembarked. Place here is not grounded in history, but built upwards in 'clean, hard, soaring, futuristic lines' (OW: 16). In 1972, when Sophie arrives in New York, she realises that this impression is an 'hallucination', and that beneath this façade there is something 'crumbling, blighted decomposed. As if the skyscrapers had to sprout out of some fertile rot' (OW: 16). But Sophie is looking at modernity from her British perspective, looking for history and something organic in which place can be rooted. New York is not going to offer her the rootedness she seeks.

While Sophie is contemplating what underlies New York's skyscrapers, Harry is in England, flying over Wiltshire looking for Bronze Age sites. In British postmodern novels, especially those of Peter Ackroyd and Graham Swift, the idea of history and place existing *below the surface* and impinging on the contemporary is a common theme. In *Out of this World*, Harry turns away from photographing the flashpoints of the late twentieth century world, and tries instead to capture on film the marks of prehistory. Flying over the English countryside, he, like Sophie in New York, realises that what lies on the surface of the landscape is not necessarily to be trusted:

> I know this landscape is a lie. Skin deep. Hedgerowed, church-towered, village-strewn England. Rub the map and civilization as we know it disappears. The Bronze Age emerges . . . these vistas which we like to think of as virgin, naked countryside, the bare bosoms of hills and little pubic clumps of woodland, are all – if it has taken millennia – man-made.
>
> (OW: 194)

In *Out of this World*, film and the aeroplane contribute to a condition of postmodern placelessness in a number of ways. Here, the rural England that Harry was already suspicious of since he moved to the thatched cottage, is rubbed out leaving an older yet still man-made landscape. Rural England has an illusory quality, it has lost its hold on reality. But in the novel, the loss of place is a transatlantic phenomenon found in New York, Greece and Britain. Although place is destroyed in many ways, and the experience of home and belonging seems distant, the novel closes with strong images of human bonding.

It is here, I think, that Swift seeks to compensate for postmodern placelessness by drawing together human beings to reconstruct belonging founded in human relations rather than in physical places. In the separate, but converging narratives of Harry and Sophie, these two placeless characters begin to conceive of belonging in some conceptual space beyond their own egocentric mapping. As Sophie flies back to England, perhaps to be reconciled with her father, she draws her sons together saying: 'Let's just be together, here, above the world' (OW: 202). The family, up in the air and ungrounded, becomes a unit, wrapping itself in a portable family home.

This sense of belonging contrasts with Harry's unbelonging in the tent of himself within the Wiltshire cottage, as he continues to discern the traces of ancient history below the surface of the Wiltshire countryside. He also begins, with his new wife Jenny, to conceive of a place, and finally seems to succeed in that trick called 'where I live'. The façade of the 'picture-book cottage', which was inauthentic before, now seems to have become invested with a sense of place that Harry realises extends beyond the 'tent of himself'. What the cottage has gained, in Harry's perception, has nothing to do with history, the building itself or what it signifies, it is the prospect of the home he might make with his new wife:

> We speed back in the direction we have come and as we ascend over the apron and the tower, we see her wave, in that stubborn, clumsy way in which people wave when they cannot see if their wave is acknowledged ... And I could almost believe it, could almost be guilty of believing it: the rest of the world doesn't matter. The world revolves around that tinier and tinier figure, as it revolves round a cottage in a tiny village in Wiltshire, where she has taken up residence. That I am home, home.
> (OW: 39)

Although *Out of this World* is mostly concerned with the destruction of place in the twentieth century, it also suggests a number of re-rootings in which some concept of 'home' is rediscovered, and re-situated through human relationships and family bonding. However, this is not altogether convincing, as there is little grounding to Harry's rediscovered 'home' with Jenny in Wiltshire, and it seems unlikely that by returning home from America with her sons, Sophie will rediscover place, as it was before her grandfather was blown up. These returns to place, and of place, must be at best provisional.

However, Swift does present us with what is perhaps a particularly British way of understanding place, and postmodern placelessness. This is the association between place and history, and the continuing drive to historicise, even when history is being dismantled and disordered. While Harry relates a history of the loss of place in the twentieth century, this process of historicising begins to offer a structure in which he is able to place himself – or rather, it creates a structure which enables him to bury his history under the Wiltshire countryside. Modernity and postmodernity are historicised here, and then put into perspective in a long history stretching back to the Bronze Age.

But, as Sophie discovers, the American place is built on flights from history, rather than the sedimentation of history; on myths of vast open spaces and borderlands, rather than on enclosed domestic space; on the future rather the past. Tropes of placelessness in the American postmodern novels I am going to examine now are less concerned with historicity and home, and more concerned with projecting futures and representation. Placelessness here stems from perceived breakdown in the fundamental systems by which humanity organises and orientates itself, specifically those of language and mathematics.

AMERICAN DIMENSIONS: DON DELILLO, *RATNER'S STAR* AND *THE NAMES*

Certain forms of geographical placelessness were already manifest in the creation of modern places in America. Instant new towns and suburbs, International Style in architecture, and the replication of industrial and commercial sites are characteristic of, and contribute to, this placeless geography.[4] But although the cultural geography of North America may appear placeless, compared to some of the richly varied and historic cities of Europe, America has a sense of place that presents itself to the outside world as a strong sense of belonging.

Such belonging is not immediately associated with physical place, grounded in history, but rather more in the myths and legends of wide open spaces and borderlands. In a sense, Americanness is conditioned more by space and the opportunities suggested in undifferentiated space, than by the physical evidence of history in which European place is founded. A further component of American belonging and identity is founded in the tradition of rational, egalitarian, and progressive value systems. An American sense of place is founded therefore in the potential of open space and in the systematic and mathematised space of modernity. This sense of place defines itself against what might be termed the darkness, mysticism, and regressive and constricting values and histories that underpinned the old place, 'old Europe'. Geographical placelessness may not therefore be such a problem in America because it does not register a corresponding loss of history.

Flights from history and the erasure of history have traditionally been part of being American, or at least of being white American. The voices of Black Americans, Hispanic Americans, Asian Americans and Native Americans have only recently been heard, and for such groups history remains crucial in maintaining cultural identity. White American identity is forged from a sameness and abstract commonality which defines itself against the cultures and the histories that America's white immigrant population left behind. Placelessness and loss of historicity are thus built into mainstream American identity.

In Britain and Europe, there is a legacy of richly varied places, unplanned on the 'grand scale' of American modernist landscapes, and built up gradually and organically over several centuries. When those placeless geographies of America reach Britain and Europe, there is resistance to what seems from a European perspective to be a displacement of traditional and authentic place with inauthentic reproductions of American place. Of course the placeless geographies that we are concerned with here do not all originate in America, and it is the spread of a placelessness powered by multinational economic forces and consumerism that is the real issue, even though in Europe and Asia this is often perceived as 'Americanisation'.

Place in Britain in the twentieth century still retains its historic roots, which might offer resistance to economic globalisation and the spread of this placelessness. Postmodernism, if put into practice in urban planning and architecture, might reintroduce difference and plurality into place to counter the spread of placelessness, but there is really no evidence that such postmodernist practice resists global economic forces. Indeed, it seems more likely, as discussed earlier, that postmodernist architecture does little to counter placelessness in anything other than a very superficial fashion. In some cases, postmodernist architecture actually colludes with consumerism to produce easily replicated *kitsch*, such as the 'decorated sheds' of Las Vegas (Venturi *et al.* 1977).

We cannot expect postmodernism to assist in the creation of authentic places in which there is a sense of security and belonging for its inhabitants. Furthermore, in Britain and Europe, postmodernism can work against the historic root of place, by seeming to overemphasise, and at the same time trivialise and make more superficial, this root: commodifying history and packaging it as heritage. In an American context, postmodernism turns less against history than against the integrity of the abstract value systems that underlie the American Constitution. The physical evidence of this might be found in the subversion of the strong, futuristic lines of the skyscraper, and the symbolism contained in this urge to rise up and conquer the skies. The skyscraper still dominates the postmodern landscape, but it is often dressed down, distorted, disguised as an orange here, a telephone there, with a bit of Art Deco and a bit of Palladian, and so on. Self-doubt and self-consciousness have crept into the skyscraper and it can no longer stand as the brash and naked pointer to the future. Now it tries to cover its shame, to mask itself and the progressive futurism it symbolised.

The trope of placelessness in the novels of Don DeLillo explores the self-consciousness of American postmodern society, and in particular the self-questioning of the scientific and mathematical systems, and the sign and language systems of American modernity. In DeLillo's work, the emphasis is not on disturbing the bedrock of history, but rather on undermining the values and systems in which American identity and belonging are constituted. Nominally, these values are declared in the Constitution itself, but they extend into science, language systems, and a mode of thinking and representation, all of which are essentially modern. In the postmodern literature of Don DeLillo, the trope of placelessness is used as the mode of questioning of modern faith in, and dependence on, systems.

So DeLillo's novels are not so concerned with real places and real histories as the British novels of Swift and Ackroyd, but they also seem less concerned with individuals and 'real life'. Characterisation in DeLillo's novels often seems weak, partly because his characters speak so explicitly about issues, apparently voicing the concerns of the author figure. But DeLillo, in *The Names* and *Ratner's Star*, also describes abstract systems that mediate between humans and the real world. In these well-researched works there is often just too much background information for the novels to accommodate, and the fictional world of the characters sometimes seems rather thin. But they nevertheless share similar concerns to those of Swift for the individual and the cohesion of social groups in the chaotic and sometimes terror-stricken world of postmodernity. DeLillo's fiction clearly draws attention to the same issues of existential outsideness, and the human impulse to create 'insides' and places that might offer a refuge from the reigning chaos outside.

In *Ratner's Star*, science and mathematics are put to what seems a fairly simple test: to interpret a series of electronic pulses, assumed to represent a significant string of numbers, and therefore a message. The message is assumed to have been transmitted from deep space, and if this is the case, contact with the sender would be a step towards fixing the earth within the universe, *placing* the planet in space. To solve the enigma of the message from space, all branches of science are represented in a giant consortium of knowledge. But, in an ironic snipe at the knowledge industry, the novel has this consortium spending itself on self questioning and self justification. It is as though the message is simply a device to test the procedures of science and to expose its dependence on arbitrary sign systems.

Scientific procedure is presented as 'closed loop' systems and specialisms that are inevitably self-referring. Science and mathematics, although perfectly rational and defensible within each specialism or loop, are reduced to absurdity in attempting this grand sweep, this grand unifying theory that will produce a perfect synthetic model of the world, finally placing it in the universe. Communicating with another point in deep space will give the earth a 'fixed point' and, from here, further transmissions from earth are intended to poll responses from other planets, which will eventually lead to a grid of reference points, 'conclusively proving' the Earth's *place* in the universe.

The project designed to interpret the message is 'Field Experiment Number One': the first 'beacon in a shit-filled night' (RS: 274) as its director, Softly, describes its position in the chaos of contemporary reality to the prodigous mathematician Billy. This project is a vast self-contained and self-sufficient 'hothouse' of scientists, mathematicians and specialists. Understanding the received message itself becomes a minor task assigned to the child Billy. But finding a response that will enable a dialogue to take place between earth and the Ratnerians who transmitted the message, becomes a vast undertaking that seems to involve every branch of science, as well as some bizarre and rather alternative 'twigs'. A major component of this work is to define a 'logical language' – Logicon – but this immediately runs into a closed loop, which Softly believes can only be saved by the use of a metalanguage:

> I can't perfect the control system without a metalanguage. Logic rendering just won't work. The machine won't be able to render Logicon until I figure how to separate the language as a system of meaningless signs from the language about language.
>
> (RS: 339)

But of course the development of a metalanguage is restricted by the same closed loop and can only achieve a self-referentiality, requiring a 'meta-metalanguage' to define it. One of the scientists tries to transpose the problem into the language of Logicon by encoding the statement that explains 'proof'. But what he actually explains is that language escapes referentiality and is based on arbitrary fixes between sign systems that could never be formalised into set of rules or metalanguage which would be sensible to a remote linguistic community. In other words, dialogue is impossible across two disconnected sign systems, disconnected from each other and from any common system of reference. Logicon is doomed to a closed loop of circular logic:

> 'If the word "proof" in this context applies only to arrays of sentences that make an assertion about an object language L, then in fact the proof itself, as opposed to the word 'proof', shall be evident only in terms of the language M, or metalanguage, in which we draw necessary conclusions about the object language L, this method M also being subject to formal study through investigations carried out in M prime, or meta-metalanguage, the purpose being to preserve selectness by using only those statements that consistently refer to themselves,' Bolin said.
> (RS: 308)

The project as a whole, especially the attempt to develop Logicon although not far removed from the realms of contemporary mathematics and theoretical science, is taken to absurdity by DeLillo. DeLillo is sending up science and mathematics here, drawing attention to the 'closed loops' of scientific systems, and comparing these systems, on which modernity has placed so much faith, to alternative, mystical and metaphysical systems, which also try to make sense of the world, our place in the world, and the Earth's place in the cosmos. There is a deliberate blurring of physics and metaphysics, each trying to recover the world from chaos by constructing some overarching symmetry, or some underpinning history that places the world:

> Tiny cracks in the model are becoming evident, it seems. There is the problem of absolute velocity. There is the suspicion of matter crossing over to us from elsewhere. There is the lack of cause and effect in the behaviour of elementary particles. Certain basic components of our physical system defy precise measurement and definition. Are we dealing with physics or metaphysics? Maybe we need a fundamental reconstruction of our ideas of space and time, or space–time, or space–time sylphed . . . what we need at this stage of our perceptual development is an overarching symmetry. Something that constitutes what appears to be – even if it isn't – a totally harmonious picture of our world system.
> (RS: 49)

Postmodern placelessness in *Ratner's Star* is represented through the undermining of science and scientific reason. Placelessness has a cosmic dimension here, as attention is drawn to chaos and uncertainty. As modern science destroyed the security and stability of the ancient cosmos, so contemporary, postmodern science undermines some of those faiths of modern science founded in the myths of a rational and predictable universe. The need for some new kind of 'overarching symmetry' could as well be a call for a new religion as a call for a new scientific theory. A partial loss of faith in modern science leads, in the postmodern, to the urge to find security elsewhere. DeLillo's use of placelessness gives an almost equitable status to religions and cults as to science in creating a sens of a postmodern world slipping back into the cosmic gloom of pre-modern superstition and myth. Put another way, the logic of scientific reasoning is deconstructed by the postmodern, revealing the limitations of its truth claims. The strategy is to de-differentiate physics and metaphysics, finding in each the common mystery of numbers and sign systems.

Physics and metaphysics have a common ancestry in primitive number and sign systems. Mathematics belongs both in the shadowy world of primitive belief systems, and in the rational systems which underpin modernity:

> Number is a metaphysic, the secret source of entire cultures . . . The whole history of mathematics is subterranean, taking place beneath history itself, misunderstood, ignored, ridiculed, unread, a shadow-world scarcely perceived even by the learned . . . Existence would be sheer dread without the verifiable fictions of mathematics.
>
> (RS: 195)

The project centres on mathematics to decode of the message received from outer space. Historical approaches to the problem are explicitly excluded although, ironically, it is an historical and archaeological analysis of bat dung in a cave in Thailand that provides the solution to the mystery of the message from Ratner's Star. Mathematics is only used in the end to verify what has already been predicted. Within the development of Logicon itself, history is banned, and only binary logic is to be used:

> 'History is full of interesting things,' Softly said. 'It has no worthwhile statement to make to us, however, in our current preoccupation. We're permitted to deduce, at least at the outset, that everything is either *a* or

> non-*a*. What we're not permitted to do is say that everything is either the Great Wall of China or something else. In our present circumstances we don't even know the Great Wall exists. We've never heard of it. So let's forget about history.'
>
> (RS: 287)

The significance of the Great Wall of China is of course that this is one of the few man-made structures discernible from space, and this mark could provide a reference point for communicating with the Ratnerians. History and human geography are excluded from the project, but the occasional humanist and 'comonsensical' solution is voiced:

> Wouldn't it be almost as simple if we used an enormous topographical marking to indicate to any visual monitoring device that there's intelligent life on Earth. Somebody thought of a huge pine forest planted in Siberia in the form of a right triangle. . . Ideas like that really appeal to me. They're such human ideas. Only humans could think of ideas like that. Radio emissions are impersonal. What can you learn about a civilization from pulses and gaps? We could plant a right triangle with a square of blue spruce attached to each side. The extraterrestrials would be charmed by it. If not, we wouldn't want to know them anyway.
>
> (RS: 120)

By referring to what Tuan might regard as a 'human universal' in aesthetic terms (Tuan 1989: 233–41) this topographical marking might convey far more about cultural life and humanity on earth than a series of pulses and gaps. This is not only because it is an intrinsically human thing, directly communicating some dimension of being human to the extra-terrestrials, but also seeking a common code in aesthetics from which an understanding might develop. Of course such a sign is not a transcendental signifier, nor does it quite stand as a human universal, but it is a symbol of some aspect of humanity and it encloses meaning within itself. It is both signifier and signified, so it does not require a system of reference to give it meaning.

What is lacking in the systematic attempt to interpret the message from Ratner's Star, and to create a synthetic model of the world, is essentially one of *direction*, which requires some kind of *external reference*. This surely is paradigmatic in the postmodern condition. Through the trope of placelessness, postmodern society is presented as essentially without direction, without any external fixed points against which to map its spatial and temporal position. The postmodern chronotope extends here to the whole of human society and the place(lessness) of the earth in the universe.

This chronotope reverses the assurances of modern mapping by undermining the power of mathematics and science to fix the fundamental questions of human existence: Who are we? Where do we come from? Where are we going? Science in postmodernity is presented as increasingly esoteric, inward looking, and specialised. At the same time, history and the humanities have become discredited and these can no longer provide the grand sweeps that once gave the affairs of men and women purpose and direction. Commander Shrub bemoans this loss of history:

> 'Historical inevitability has changed since my day,' Shrub said. 'There's no longer any grand sense of sweep to the affairs of men. Where are the complex historical forces, the tides, the currents? What happened to the wide canvas on which we were supposed to play out our roles? It was simpler in my day. We could talk about the surge, the tragic pageant.'
> (RS: 128)

But *Ratner's Star* has not lost the sense of a 'grand sweep'. Although the novel refers to the loss of direction in postmodern society, within the text itself it still seems to be possible to narrate a history of events with direction and purpose. There is, in this sense, a bit of a mismatch between form and content in the novel. The story contained with the novel is quite clearly one of disorientation within American postmodern society. Where does the future lie? This might be the novel's underlying question, and the answer would seem to be that it is not out in space, but back here on earth. Softly conceived of Field Experiment Number One as a beacon in the 'shit-filled night' focusing man's attention on a common goal:

> If we're going to behave as a single people, as rational human beings who inhabit the same planet, we desperately need goals and pursuits that can unite us. Finding a way to speak to intelligent beings on another planet is one such pursuit.
> (RS: 274)

So there are two goals to this massive scientific experiment, the immediate one of interpreting and responding to a message from beings on another planet, and the indirect one to provide a sense of purpose for humankind. In the latter case, does science and mathematics here simply become another religion, a faith through which humanity comforts itself and *places* itself within the undifferentiated and chaotic night of space and time?

But the attempt to get a fix on Ratner's Star that would help place the earth in the universe and rescue it from the chaos turns in on itself. The main reason for this is that the message has actually come from earth, and it comes from *the past*. The novel divides into two sections – the 'adventures' of Field Experiment Number One, and the 'reflections' of 'Logicon Project Minus One' – and this maps the shift from modern outward-looking and forward-looking project to the postmodern backward-looking reflection through a chronotope collapsing in on itself.

The message it seems was transmitted by Ratnerians living in pre-prehistory but then undergoing a 'backwards evolution', regressing until they reached the beginning of Neanderthal man. When the Ratnerians realised they were starting to evolve backwards, they sent a message into space which contained the time of a solar eclipse in the twentieth century. That a civilisation pre-existing ours was able to predict this event either meant that they had superior knowledge of the universe and could predict events far into the future (and the past), or it meant that time itself was in reverse. The postmodern implications in the fate of the Ratnerians are again fairly obvious. The story is one of a civilisation that reached a zenith and rather than simply falling, as previous civilisations had done, this one simply reverses the process of evolution – not revolution, but de-evolution.

As Field Experiment Number One collapses in on itself, and the solar eclipse begins to track across the earth, the novel suggests the collapse of a certain kind of *place*. The collapse of the place that the western world has created for itself in modernity is due to a failure in scientific determinism. To experience postmodern placelessness here, it is only necessary to take a step outside that 'outgrown frame of logic and language' (RS: 430) that is the modern western world.

The novel suggests that modernity lost something when it put up that frame: when scientific reasoning brought humanity in from the untamed spaces of nature and the transcendental times of religion. The narrator, who seems at this point to be speaking from outside humanity or at least from outside science, claims that humankind, in attempting to frame and re-present reality, has substituted perception for a meaningless mathematical structure:

> Having dismantled the handiwork of your own perceptions in order to solve reality, you know it now as a micron flash of light-scattering matter in a structure otherwise composed of purely mathematical coordinates.
>
> (RS: 431)

This god-like presence at the end of the novel calls for a reorientation towards the earth and towards human goals. The final scene is of a hitherto obscured side of humanity: the millions of poor, starving and oppressed, who constitute two thirds of the world's population. A solar eclipse pans across the world, bringing an unexpected darkness to the earth, but there is also a strange white light that precedes the lunar shadow. Through this light, the darkness at the margins of modern society is illuminated, and another reality is revealed:

> ... the earth along the eclipse path and its outer borders of partial darkness resembles a charred immensity, children with begging bowls, men surrendered to meditation ... The blind stand begging in places that are the same, hanging wash, some goats, as places everywhere, toy stores, coloured glass, the squalor that customarily surrounds the working of miracles.
>
> (RS: 430-1)

The dialectic of inside/outside is once more evident in this move from the 'inside' of modernity, with its self-defining structures of logic and language, to the larger 'outside' where life continues to exist in the shadows and margins of this modernity. The intimate space and self-enclosing space of the modern world, encapsulated in Field Experiment Number One, 'loses its clarity', while exterior space 'loses its void' (Bachelard 1969: 218). Field Experiment Number One (and by implication the projects of modernity) not only fails in its specific goals but also fails in its larger goal of defining humanity:

> Mathematics is what the world is when we subtract our own perceptions. In your earthly study of the subject, you went beyond its natural association with the will to live and found that it contained a painless 'nonexistence', the theoretical ideal of n-space. And so you beamed into the heavens a clue to the limitations not only of (y)our science, but of human identity as well.
>
> (RS: 432)

The narrator does not suggest that we abandon the insideness of modernity, with its protective shell of science and reason, but that we take a step outside of this to rediscover the human dimension as well, and this human dimension is conditioned by limits:

> To be Outside is to know an environment infinitely less complex than the one you left. Far from wishing to revisit misery, you are nonetheless able to experience once again some of the richness of inborn limits . . .
>
> (RS: 432)

In DeLillo's other novel to be examined here, *The Names*, the dialectic of inside/outside continues, but here the characters are outsiders to begin with. In this novel, characters are conscious of the chaos of a placeless world and search for 'an inside' in which to find safety. If *Ratner's Star* is an exploration of the structures and frames constructed by science and mathematics, *The Names* is an exploration of the structures of language, of finding place in the world through naming.

The trope of placelessness is organised through the nomadic existence of the characters, most of whom experience placelessness because of their occupations, which not only remove them from their home country, America, but also expose them to the precarious transit areas of international travel. The main group of characters is involved, appropriately enough, in occupations concerned with risk analysis and security; they are qualified to assess the insecurity of being an American on the 'outside'. One attempt they make to rationalise and counter this insecurity is to *name* place. In 'one-sentence stories' they construct shared 'insides' they occasionally shelter within:

> Case had come from Nairobi with a one-sentence story. When Kampala fell to the Tanzanian forces, people greeted them with flowers and fruit and beat their own captured troops to death in the street. All these places were one-sentence stories to us. Someone would turn up, utter a sentence about foot-long lizards in his hotel room in Niamey, and this became the solid matter of the place, the means we used to fix it in our minds. The sentence was effective, overshadowing deeper fears, hesitancies, a rife disquiet. There was around us almost nothing we knew as familiar and safe. Only our hotels rising from the lees of perennial renovation. The sense of things was different in such a way that we could only register the edges of some elaborate secret. It seemed we'd lost our capacity to select, to ferret out particularity and trace it to some center which our minds could relocate in knowable surroundings.
>
> (N: 94)

Ironically, these stories are often linked to the actual dangers of being in these places, such as stories about where Americans are being killed, or where there is a high risk of planes crashing. These stories are also set within a general placelessness and loss of differentiation, which is experienced as unfamiliarity, loss of mapping, lack of centre; space that becomes filled, in the minds of these characters, with dark secrets and conspiracies. They begin to suffer the paranoia common to existential outsiders. Stories create some kind of structure or sequence, and the need for place is translated into a need for structure. Structure is provided here by language.

In the novel, Owen Brademas is an archaeologist specialising in ancient language systems, and his occupation, unlike that of the international businessmen, takes him into the origins of structures and systems, literally digging for objects that might complete a particular pattern. For Owen, the outside must have a pattern; the chaos of outside must be made safe:

> Elements falling into place. A design. A shape in the chaos of things. I suppose I find these moments precious and reassuring because they take place outside of me, outside the silent grid, because they suggest an outer state that works somewhat the way my mind does but without the relentlessness, the predeterminative quality. I feel I'm safe from myself as long as there's an accidental pattern to observe in the physical world.
> (N: 172)

The dialectic of inside and outside seems confused here. Owen recognises his inner site of egocentric mapping, but this is not where he feels safe. He needs the outside to be structured as a refuge from himself. As a boy he remembers the 'safe place' of the 'church, by a river, among cottonwoods in the shade of the long afternoons', but when his parents joined the Pentecostal church in the 'tallgrass prairie', there was 'nothing safe about this church' (N: 172–3):

> It was old, plain, set in the middle of nowhere, it leaked in wet weather, let in everything but light. A congregation of poor people and most of them spoke in tongues. This was an awesome thing to see and hear . . . The inside-outness of this sound . . . What a strangeness to the boy in his lonely wanting, his need for safety and twice-seen light.
> (N: 173)

The novel returns to this prairie in its finale, and while all around him people are speaking in tongues, Owen, or 'Orville', as he is renamed here, is 'tongue-tied'. In this 'inside-outness' of sound there is no longer any distinction between voice and language system, and where *langue* and *parole* merge, the identity of the speaker is dispersed, and the illusion of being separate from the world is broken. This is for Orville, the 'nightmare of real things, the fallen wonder of the world' (N: 339). He falls into silence in the glossolalia of the novel's 'Prairie' section, as the syntax of the narrative itself breaks down, losing the order and rules of writing. Here, DeLillo does allow form to follow content, although it is not an entirely successful experiment, as the written text never loses its power to signify. In the chaos of language that the speaking world has become for Orville, there is a drift towards silence and undifferentiated space. As the structure of outside breaks down, both linguistically and geographically, Owen/Orville is trapped. The trope of placelessness is extended here into the aporia of a post-structuralist world. Because of Owen/Orville's dependence on structure to create meaning in the world, the loss of such structure is a double loss; there is nowhere for him to go anymore, no escape from himself.

Prior to this, Owen had been literally digging for meaning in the outside world, and finding it, in limited ways, on a Greek island with James Ashton's wife Kathryn and their boy Tap. But this safely differentiated world, bounded in the clearly defined depth models of archaeology, is disturbed when his attention is drawn to a secret cult, the 'Abecedarians', who commit a series of apparently motiveless and random murders in obscure sites around the world. This cult emerges into the material placelessness in which other Americans are struggling to create the structures, or illusions of structure, that might provide some provisional sense of safety. But the cult feeds on that placelessness, concerned only with its own internal logic for survival. It is inherently anti-social, creating its order out of the chaos of postmodern society:

> Inwardness is very much the point. One mind, one madness. To be part of some unified vision. Clustered, dense. Safe from chaos and life.
> (N: 116)

The cult represents that dark side of the postmodern, in which absence, unpresentability and lack of tradition and history prevail:

> The cult's power, its psychic grip, was based on an absence of such things. No sense, no content, no historic bond, no ritual significance.
> (N: 216)

The Abecedarians are the antithesis of modern humanity, they 'mock our need to structure and classify, to build a system against the terror in our souls. They make the system equal to the terror.' (N: 308). In particular, the cult members mock the idea of language as system, devising a linguistic code for mapping the world through ritual killings that link place and victim through shared initials. The system is more or less arbitrary, it has no sense, but it creates a structure of sorts in the outside world.

Owen is drawn to this cult, because their members seem to be interested and expert in ancient language systems, especially those in which letters have shapes linking them to objects in the external world, and he hopes to find through language, an underlying pattern in the external world. He is 'gravitationally bound to the cult, as an object to a neutron star, pulled towards its collapsed mass, its density' (N: 286). But rather than adding to his knowledge of language structures, which have always been his escape from the world, the cult of Abecedarians connect Owen's make-believe world of language structures directly to the real world. Andahl, a cult member, persuades him that there is no structure in the outside world that we can escape into, because the real world and the synthetic models of the world we have made for ourselves have become one and the same:

> The world has become self-referring. You know this. This thing has seeped into the texture of the world. The world for thousands of years was our escape, was our refuge. Men hid from themselves in the world. We hid from God or death. The world was where we lived, the self was where we went mad and died. But now the world has made a self of its own. Why, how, never mind. What happens to us now that the world has a self? How do we say the simplest thing without falling into a trap? Where do we go, how do we live, who do we believe? This is my vision, a self-referring world, a world in which there is no escape.
>
> (N: 297)

The idea of self-referring systems is a common theme in DeLillo's fiction, and one that he admits to being particularly interested in.[5] The circular logic of systems that seem to provide structure to the world is a key target for postmodern thinking, and here the structure of inside/outside, of the ability of the self to orientate itself through language, is problematised. The 'dialectic of division' breaks down because inside/outside is de-differentiated. In the novel, language, through which the individual might normally place herself/himself in society, and so find a place in the world, has somehow lost its power to fix meaning outside the system that contains it. The individual therefore has no means by which to distinguish his or her voice from the language that produces it: all is placeless in a self-referring world. The postmodern placelessness presented here by DeLillo is linked to material conditions of postmodernity, such as globalisation, but added to this is a vision of a post-structuralist world in which language has slipped its anchor to the real world.

The Americans in this novel are, for the most part, existential outsiders coping with lack of belonging and home by creating little fictions that they can inhabit. Owen is drawn to the cult that seems to promise an underlying pattern in the texture of the external world, but when this pattern is exposed as a sham, Owen regresses into childhood in search of the safe places of a pre-linguistic past:

> All the land was gray. All the sky was black. No where did he see the gentle prairie of his careless days... He looked in vane [sic] for familiar signs and safe places. No where [sic] did he see what he expected.
>
> (N: 339)

Owen Brademas is driven mad by the desire to find structures to explain the world, but other characters in the novel find other ways of coping with postmodern placelessness. Frank Volterra is another kind of modern, who uses his egocentric mapping to create a place for himself wherever he might be. The rest of the world exists not in language, as it does for Owen, but as image, as space ready to be framed and organised into the chronotope of his movies:

> 'I can't surrender myself to places,' Frank said. 'I'm always separate. I'm always working at myself. I never understood the lure of fabulous places. Or the idea of losing myself in a place. The desert down there is stunning at times. Shapes and tones. But I could never be affected in it in a deeply personal way, I could never see it as an aspect of myself or vice versa. I need it for something, I want it as a frame and a background. I can't see myself letting it overwhelm me. I would never give myself up to the place or to any other place. I'm the place. I guess that's the reason. I'm the only place I need.'
>
> (N: 143)

In the desert, where Frank is to film the cult members, he recognises a quality in the space, the wilderness, and the occasional figure. He immediately makes this space American, and finds in it the essential quality of American film. American space, as defined by Frank, begins as an empty landscape, an abstract frame, and characters placed in this emptiness are forced to work out their purpose and their existence, exclusive of any already-written culture or history. American space is open and devoid of history, it is a blank space on to which Americans might impose their will. The cultural form that captures this urge is the American movie, and the classic western in particular:

> People talk about classic westerns. The classic thing has always been the space, the emptiness. The lines are drawn for us. All we have to do is insert figures, men in dusty boots, certain faces. Figures in open space have always been what film is about. American film. This is the situation. People in a wilderness, a wild and barren space. The space is the desert, the movie screen, the strip of film, however you see it. What are the people doing here? This is their existence. They're here to work out their existence. This space, this emptiness is what they have to confront. I've always loved American spaces. People at the end of a long lens. Swimming in space.
>
> (N: 198)

But the cult that Frank is to film is not American in this same sense. Frank detects something 'traditional and closed-in' about it, as though they have some secret that 'goes back' (N: 198). He requires a sense of the vertical in his film, some ancient towers, perhaps, to capture these dimensions and boundaries. But he also imagines using sound – different languages will provide a landscape differentiated by language:

> Three, four different languages. I want to make the voices part of a landscape of sound. The spoken word will be an element in the landscape.
>
> (N: 199)

Frank plans to use *differentiated* voices to make this landscape, using language to add some depth to an otherwise superficial and undifferentiated space. In this respect his attempts to map space and place are similar to those of James Ashton and his friends in the international business community, who use the names of places, and 'one-sentence' stories, to construct some kind of structure in unfamiliar and chaotic territory.

Finally we come to James Ashton and his family, who are central to the novel and who, in several ways, are at the 'heart' of the novel. We are coming to them last because I think they represent DeLillo's faint counter to the placelessness of the postmodern in their various attempts to create forms of 'insideness'. Like Swift, DeLillo uses the family unit for this purpose, and both authors present families that are geographically dispersed, but are trying to re-form.

In *Out of this World*, the reading of the novel draws together the separated characters, Harry and Sophie, to provide one kind of bridge through language. Although in the chronotope of the novel itself there is no communication between them, as their narratives do not connect directly, but there is a sense that they are being brought back together, there is some process of healing divisions.

In *The Names*, James is separated from his wife and son, who are living on a Greek island, while he flies around the world, occasionally meeting up with them in Greece. He recognises that he is the outsider in this group, and tries to find a way back in. In the 'Island' section of the novel, Kathryn tries to redefine things as she works in her trench on Owen Brademas' archaeological dig. To James, she seems to create an 'inside' for herself – her own island within an island. The physical digging in the trench is an attempt to place herself in a world that has become placeless. It is as though she is trying to find what the physical limits of her self are in the clearly defined spaces of the trench and the island. She readjusts her egocentric mapping by defining the objects in her immediate vicinity:

> She senses the completeness of her trench. It is her size, it fits. She rarely looks over the rim. The trench is enough. A five-foot block of time abstracted from the system. Sequence, order, information. All she needs of herself. Nothing more, nothing less. In its limits the trench enables her to see what's really there. It's a test device for the senses. New sight, new touch. She loves the feel of workable earth, the musky raw aroma. The trench is her medium now. It is more than the island as the island is more than the world. . . She was digging to find things, to learn.
>
> (N: 133)

While Kathryn is redefining her world through the solid matter of time and depth in her trench, she is also cutting herself off from the wider world, which she redefines as the lesser world, and in which she has a defining role as wife and mother. She is redefining herself against her previous life, and in the process excluding her husband James. James' son, Tap, is also defining his world, not by defining himself against his father, but through a world of language in which words have direct association with things. His 'novel' is an attempt to make this happen.

James recognises that the rest of his family is busily creating egocentric places for themselves which exclude him. They are no longer fitting into his world, but are creating their own, and this only adds to James' sense of placelessness in the world:

> They were the freelancers now but I couldn't shake that feeling that I was the one taking the major risk. There was nothing to come back to if I failed, no place in particular I belonged. They were my place, the only true boundaries I had. I went, I set out, as a man on a dangerous journey, feeling a grimness and will I'd never felt before.
>
> (N: 49)

The trope of placelessness here is extended into the redefinition – or undefining – of gender and family roles. James' placelessness is experienced through material placelessness in postmodernity and through the general concern for the loss of language to define the world (which extends to all the characters in the novel) but it is also conditioned by a loss of masculinity and safety in the role of 'man' in society. As with Harry in *Out of This World*, James has found that home and belonging have been dependent on family, and on the unthinking acceptance of an inside automatically constructed by this. Kathryn and Tap, like others in this novel, rely too much on egocentric mapping to create an inside that is outside family, and outside the social. Postmodern placelessness here emphasises a shift from society to the individual, and the only hope presented for a return to belonging appears to be through language.

As James Ashton climbs the hill to the Parthenon (in the section of the novel preceding Orville's capitulation into the nightmare of undifferentiated sound) he finds that the place is not as complicated or as ambiguous as he had anticipated at the beginning of the novel. The apparently crazy and bizarre juxtaposition of this monument with the noisy modern city of Athens that strikes him with such force at the beginning of the novel, no longer worries him. He had previously 'read' the Parthenon as a monument to all that humanity had rescued from the madness and chaos of the world – 'Beauty, dignity, order, proportion' (N: 3). But when he returns there at the end of the novel, he finds that the monument has been easily assimilated into the contemporary, and where Owen/Orville is plunged into a landscape of chaotic noise, James finds that (social) language is really what saves the world from chaos, and allows the past to be assimilated into the present. James had set apart the timeless and pure values of the past, monumentalised in the ruins of ancient Greece, from the undifferentiated chaos of postmodernity permeated with anonymous terror. Now he reads the monument as a very human and relevant 'cry for pity' (N: 330). The past is assimilated into the present, and each props up the other and gives meaning to it, rather than defining a course of inevitable historical decline:

> People come through the gateway, people in streams and clusters, in mass assemblies. No one seems to be alone. This is a place to enter in crowds, seek company and talk. Everyone is talking. I move past the scaffolding and walk down the steps, hearing one language after another, rich, harsh, mysterious, strong. This is what we bring to the temple, not prayer or chant or slaughtered rams. Our offering is language.
>
> (N: 331)

James had separated the Parthenon from the contemporary city. It seemed to him to symbolise the ideal traditional, circumscribed place, in which the highest values had been sedimented. These values of 'beauty, order and proportion' seemed to be corrupted by the modern city, and this juxtaposition was a constant reminder of the failure of contemporary society to create and maintain comparable places. But when James visits the Parthenon, he experiences the bustle of people passing through the place, and the noise of people talking, and he recognises that in reality, this site no longer stands for the exclusive values of an ancient regime, but has been assimilated into the contemporary. What he sees and hears here is the *social* production of space and language, as defined by Lefebvre and Bakhtin respectively. Language, as a social construct, and the everyday production of social space, are what we have to offer. These are what save us from the totalitarian and dictatorial on the one hand, and the chaotic and undifferentiated on the other.

Notes

1. Introduction and Preliminaries

1. See Chapter 3, note 5.

2. See, for example, Edward Soja, *Postmodern Geographies: The Reassertion of Space in Critical Social Theory*.

3. See David Harvey, *The Condition of Postmodernity*; Edward Soja, *Postmodern Geographies*; and Henri Lefebvre, *The Production of Space*, pp. 42, 116. Lefebvre argues for a 'history of space' and this includes not only the history of the production of space, and, under capitalism, the subsequent commodification of space, but also a history of representations of space.

4. See Jean-François Lyotard, *The Differend: Phrases in Dispute*.

5. Linda Hutcheon, *A Poetics of Postmodernism*, pp. 61–2, cited in Fredric Jameson's *Postmodernism, or The Cultural Logic of Late Capitalism*.

6. See Henri Lefebvre, *The Production of Space*, pp. 110–9 for a discussion of the history of space.

7. See Andreas Huyssen, *After the Great Divide*, p. 213. *Lanark* is an example of the postmodern text in which, as Huyssen says, 'questions of subjectivity and authorship have resurfaced with a vengeance'.

8. Tom Stoppard, *Travesties*, first performed in London in 1974. This quotation is from Act 1, p. 28.

9. For a cogent and concise account of neo-conservatism in postmodernism see Andreas Huyssen, *After the Great Divide*, pp. 199–204.

10. See, for example, Patricia Waugh, *Metafiction: The Theory and Practice of Self-Conscious Fiction* and Mark Currie ed., *Metafiction*.

11. Few authors, I am sure, would claim to be fully paid-up postmodernists. I suspect none of the novelists covered in this work would be comfortable with the label, even though their novels are frequently cited in works on postmodernist fiction.

2. Postmodernism's Spatial Turn

1. See Stephen Kern, *The Culture of Time and Space*, 33, (paraphrasing Saint Augustine, *Confessions*).

2. In Zeno's Paradox, it appears that an arrow can never reach its target because if the distance to be travelled is repeatedly divided into equal parts, the remaining

distance the arrow must travel to reach its target is always greater than zero. Hence, as Tom Stoppard would have it in *Jumpers*, if we believe in mathematics, Sebastian must have died of fright. *Jumpers,* Act I, p. 19.

3. See for example the number of titles on space and place that were published in the 1980s and 1990s – for example, *Mapping the Futures* (Bird, 1993), *The Condition of Postmodernity* (Harvey, 1990), *Place/Culture/Representation* (Duncan and Ley, 1993), *The Power of Place* (Agnew and Duncan, 1989), *Postmodern Geographies* (Soja, 1988) and, of course, the English translation of Lefebvre's *The Production of Space* (1991).

4. See Marshall Berman, *All That is Solid Melts into Air*, pp. 38–88 for a discussion of Goethe's *Faust* and the desire for development.

5. Michel Foucault. The lecture given in March 1967 was published firstly as 'Des Espaces Autres' in the French journal, *Architecture-Mouvement-Continuité* in October, 1984, and later as 'Of Other Spaces' in *Diacritics*, Spring 1986: 22–4, trans. Jay Miskowiec, from which the following extracts are taken.

6. Michel Foucault, *The Archaeology of Knowledge*, p. 182; the brackets are inserted by Lefebvre – see Lefebvre, *The Production of Space*, p. 4 for Lefebvre's critique of Foucault's use of 'space' here.

7. Radio, the telephone and the electric doorbell are all examples of technology intruding into private space. In psychology, Freud concluded that his patients suffered from a 'privatisation of older communal celebrations and religious rites', and in literature, Conrad is cited as the first modern novelist in England to draw attention to 'situations in which public codes were inapplicable'.

8. See pp. 87–90 below for a discussion of Harvey's argument on time–space compression.

9. I have taken some liberties with Lefebvre's definitions here because for my purposes here I want to emphasise literature's involvement in representational (poetic) space, and because I want to prepare for a shift from modern to postmodern sensibilities in spatial affairs. However, I don't think I've deviated too much from Lefebvre's central premise.

10. See Lefebvre, *The Production of Space*, p. 13, where he cites Fred Hoyle, *Frontiers of Astronomy*. Note that Big Bang theories ruled out Hoyle's hypothesis, but recently, since stars have been discovered that seem to predate Big Bang by 8 billion years, Hoyle's theories, for the moment, are ruled back in again – see leading article in *Scientific American* December 1994.

11. The site of the annual choir festival has particular significance for Estonians. The festival continued during Soviet occupation, but singing in local dialects was banned. In 1991, the reclaiming of Estonian independence was signalled by Estonian choirs singing in their own language. This has become known locally as the 'Singing Revolution'.

12. See footnote below to Chapter 3, no. 16, for reference to Hawking's three

'arrows of time'.

13. Inset quotations from J. Le Goff, *Time, Work and Culture in the Middle Ages* (no page number given in Harvey).

3. The Chronotope as Idea, Optic and Weltanschauung

1. See for example, Christopher Norris's critique of Lyotard's emphasis on the Kantian sublime in *The Truth about Postmodernism* pp. 15–28, and Jean-François Lyotard, *The Differend: Phrases in Dispute*.

2. The affirmative position is put by Fredric Jameson on one side and Daniel Bell on the other. See Jameson *Postmodernism,* and Bell *The Coming of Post-Industrial Society*.

3. See Thomas Hardy, *The Return of the Native*, for example, in which the chronotope of the road, where characters meet, or fail to meet, and make their entrances and exits, is entirely tied to narrative time. The road functions as a vehicle for the plot. The chronotope of the heath, by contrast, extends through historical time, through all time, and by containing all time, is unmoving, a static space on which time hardly makes a mark.

4. We might consider here a contrast between the interiorised chronotope of Mrs Dalloway's London in Virginia Woolf's *Mrs Dalloway*, and the quasi-romantic chronotopes of nature in many of the novels of D.H. Lawrence.

5. The term de-differentiation comes from Scott Lash's *Sociology of Postmodernism* p. 15, although he uses it rather more widely in his deconstructionist approach to postmodernism, suggesting that this is appropriate to a form which is designed to install instability in our experience of the real and thereby to shake our faith in reality.

6. See Michel Foucault, 'What is an Author?' and Roland Barthes, 'Death of the Author'.

7. See Hans Bertens' discussion of Lash in Bertens *The Idea of the Postmodern*, pp. 215–17.

8. The social scientist Zygmunt Bauman suggests that postmodernity is concerned with re-enchanting a world which modernity has dis-enchanted. Here, enchantment requires a certain amount of de-differentiation. See Zygmunt Bauman, *Intimations of Postmodernity*, x.

9. Albert Gleizes and Jean Metzinger, 'Cubism', in Robert L. Herbert (ed.) *Modern Artists on Art*, pp. 7–8.

10. His emphasis.

11. See for example, Charles Jencks, *The Language of Post-modern Architecture*;

Robert Venturi, Denise Scott Brown and Steven Izenour *Learning from Las Vegas*; and Jane Jacobs, *The Death and Life of Great American Cities*.

12. This is not to dismiss 'end of time' thinking or its representation in the novel – at least two of the novels, *Ratner's Star*, and *First Light*, contemplate a universe collapsing in on itself, a situation in which life on earth would be inconceivable.

13. The prophetic writings of the sixteenth century French astrologer and prophet Nostradamus are explored in the non-fiction literary work *Remember the Future: The Prophecies of Nostradamus*, which focuses on his unfulfilled predictions. The Maya people of Guatemala were guided by their Maya Calendar, and the Maya World Studies Center in Yucatan, Mexico, has made The Maya Calendar 2000 which follows this ancient tradition. Mother Shipton was an English visionary born in Knaresborough in 1488. She is said to have predicted the Spanish Armada, the Great Fire of London, and the advent of modern technology. Her prophecies were published in 1797.

14. See Mark Currie's analysis of schizophrenia and the perpetual present in postmodernity in which he draws on ideas drawn mainly from Jameson (*Postmodern Narrative Theory* pp. 96–113).

15. See Allan Pred's reply to Michael Curry's article, 'Postmodernism, Language, and the Strains of Modernism', both published in *Annals of the Association of American Geographers*, Curry in Vol. 81 (2) 1991, pp. 210–28, and Pred in Vol. 82 (2), 1992, pp. 305–19.

16. See Stephen Hawking, *A Brief History of Time*, p. 152; the three 'arrows of time' are – the thermodynamic (increasing disorder), the cosmological (the direction of the universe expanding, not contracting), and the psychological (the direction of time in which we remember the past and not the future).

4. The City in Late Capitalist Fantasy

1. See Gray's 'Index of Plagiarisms' reference to Thomas Hobbes (*Lanark*: 489).

2. See Christopher Harvie, 'Alasdair Gray and the Condition of Scotland Question', in *The Arts of Alasdair Gray*, p. 77. But note that Scotland has since achieved devolution from the British parliament in Westminster; its own parliament began to sit in 1999.

3. Cooke's brackets.

4. Randall Stevenson, *The British Novel Since the Thirties*, p. 221; here Stevenson claims that Gray, 'flaunts the illustrious pedigree of devices he derives from modernist and other writers', and suggests charges of 'narcissism', or 'self-aggrandisement' may 'occasionally be justified'. And yet he applauds the 'diversity and inventiveness' of the novel's 'means of envisaging the city', part of which is connecting it with the 'real world' of the author, and at the other end of the scale of realism, connecting it to other literary landscapes.

5. See Witschi, *Glasgow Urban Writing and Postmodernism*, pp. 48–9, for a discussion of Gaitkens' vision.

6. Although there is no direct reference to Chaucer's *House of Fame* in *Lanark*, the carrying of Lanark to Provan, and his subsequent meeting with the optimist and the pessimist (L: 468), is very like Chaucer's vision of the poet being carried by an eagle to a 'house of twigs' in which truth always has two sides. See Geoffrey Chaucer, 'The House of Fame', in *Geoffrey Chaucer: The Love Visions*, trans. Brian Stone, p. 119, ll: 2081–94.

7. See above, Chapter 3, page 90.

8. This is not to suggest that human activity isn't capable of quickly eroding and destroying a great deal more than the earth's surface, but this does not reduce geological time, it only reduces some of its more visible traces.

9. The novel refers to The Merovicnic Discontinuity which runs underneath Glasgow. In the novel, it is pressure on this fault that causes the tectonic plate to tilt and pitch Unthank into the sea. But this discontinuity is global – an imaginary subterranean line where the Oceanic crusts meet the Continental crusts. The name is often shortened to 'Moho', a term alluded to in the 'mohomes' of Unthank.

10. See above, Chapter , p. 50–1 for reference to Fred Hoyle's theory in Lefebvre's work.

11. V.S. Naipaul *The Enigma of Arrival*, cited in Gillian Tindall, *Countries of the Mind*, p. 10.

5. Spatial Historiographies

1. However, there is an argument that there is a change of emphasis in postmodernism, a change of dominant. See for example, Edward Soja, *Postmodern Geographies: The Reassertion of Space in Critical Social Theory*.

2. Andreas Huyssen, 'The Search for Tradition: Avant-Garde and Postmodernism in the 1970s', in *New German Critique* 22, pp. 23–40, cited in Linda Hutcheon, *A Poetics of Postmodernism: History, Theory, Fiction*, p.16.

3. Author's emphases and brackets.

4. See Robert M. May, 'From Newton to Chaos' in the programme notes to *Arcadia*, and Benoit B. Mandelbrot, *The Fractal Geometry of Nature*.

6. Chronotopes of Reversible Time

1. See David Lewis and Andrew Weigart, 'Structures and Meanings of Social-Time', in *The Sociology of Time*, ed. John Hassard, pp. 82–101.

The Postmodern Chronotope

2. See Pierre Bourdieu, 'Time Perspectives of the Kabyle', and Bronislaw Malinowski, 'Time-Reckoning in the Trobriands', in *The Sociology of Time*, pp. 203–237.

3. See also M. Eliade, *Cosmos and History* and A. Diamant, 'The Temporal Dimension in Models of Administration and Organisation', in D. Waldo (ed.), *Temporal Dimensions of Development Administration*.

4. See *Hawksmoor*, p. 213, where the detective senses the presence of his eighteenth century alter-ego as a shadowy image on the TV screen. See Fredric Jameson *et al.*, and Chapter 1 above for discussion of the perpetual present as a feature of the postmodern chronotope.

5. See above, Chapter 2, pp. 36–7.

6. See also Umberto Eco, *The Name of the Rose*, where another postmodern detective fails to solve the mystery, despite offering 'reason and method', and compare these with the great modern detectives like Sherlock Holmes who used reason, method, and sometimes intuition to make a chaotic and mysterious nineteenth century London safe for his middle class readers.

7. See also the short story by Jorge Loius Borges, 'Death and the Compass', in which a series of murders is committed with the sole purpose of trapping the detective who the criminal knew would be unable to resist tracing the pattern of the crimes and predicting the time and place of the next murder – which is, of course, to be that of the detective.

8. See Thomas Hardy, *The Mayor of Casterbridge*, and *The Return of the Native*, for example. In both novels, an enduring time of prehistory contained within visible features in the landscape impresses itself on the present. This long past is disconnected and yet connected; locals are not directly affected by the discovery of human remains from so long ago – 'that between them and the living there seemed to stretch a gulf too wide for even a spirit to pass' *The Mayor of Casterbridge*, p. 140.

9. I am thinking of 'New Age' followers such as those who come to visit the neolithic tombs in *First Light*, but the millennium has fostered many neo-religious groups with irrational approaches to time and space.

10. Clearly women's time would be one such alternative to that rigid linearity associated with the time of modern 'man'. See Julia Kristeva, 'Women's Time'.

11. Of course, Thomas Hardy himself knew that the cosmos only appeared to suggest order and harmony. Hardy was a keen astronomer himself, and in *Two on a Tower*, (see above, Chapter 3, p. 101–2) the astronomer refers to the stars travelling away from us and decaying.

12. This view is of course restricted to the postmodern as it is theorised in a selection of postmodern novels and could hardly be applied generally to the postmodern or postmodern culture.

7. Post-colonial Island Chronotopes

1. For the purposes of this study, I refer to an extended Caribbean that includes the islands of the West Indies and the close coastal areas of North and South America, stretching down to Bahia in the south. It is in this area that the novels in this chapter are mostly located.

2. If I were undertaking such a study I would begin with the following texts: Timothy Mo, *Sour Sweet*; Salman Rushdie, *The Satanic Verses*; Joan Riley, *The Unbelonging*; V.S. Naipaul, *The Enigma of Arrival*; Caryl Phillips, *The Nature of Blood* and *The Final Passage*.

3. See above Chapter 2, pp. 43–5.

4. See Marco Polo, *Travels*, and *The Travels of Sir John Mandeville* as key texts for defining the 'other half' of the world to mediaeval audiences and early modern explorers of the New World. To these explorers, the New World was initially a displaced East, islands in the way of the real goal of Cathay. As the New World developed as a new land, it still retained some of the mythological baggage of the earlier East, but the idea of empty space, ripe for colonisation, this was a new mythology designed to mask the genocide of native Carib Indians and native Americans elsewhere.

5. See Frank Kermode, 'Introduction' to the New Arden Shakespeare *The Tempest*, pp. xxx–xxxiv.

6. See George Kimble, *Geography in the Middle Ages*, p. 208 for evidence of this interest in the classical in seventeenth century geography.

7. The invention of the chronometer by John Harrison in the eighteenth century greatly improved navigation, enabling trading routes to be firmly established around the globe – see David S. Landes, *Revolution in Time: Clocks and the Making of the Modern World*, p. 151.

8. See Peter Hulme, *Colonial Encounters: Europe and the Native Caribbean, 1492–1797*. Marina Warner refers directly to this work in the acknowledgements to *Indigo*.

9. See Brenda K. Marshall, *Teaching the Postmodern: Fiction and Theory*, especially chapter 4. 'From Work to Text to Intertextuality: *Robinson Crusoe, Foe, Friday*', pp. 121–146.

10. Note that Daniel Defoe changed his name from Foe to Defoe.

11. Note that in *Foe*, Robinson Crusoe is renamed Cruso.

12. For an account of Vespucci's description of the New World as feminine and bountiful, see Tzvetan Todorov, 'Fictions and Truths', p. 50; See also Neil Rennie, *Far-fetched Facts: The Literature of Travel and the Idea of the South Seas*.

13. See Salmon Rushdie, *Imaginary Homelands*.

14. See Jon Stratton, *Writing Sites*, especially chapter 3, for an account of the classical episteme in articulating the colonial other.

15. See above Chapter 2 p. 41–2.

8. The Trope of Placelessness

1. See above Chapter 2, p. 55.

2. See Stephen Kern, *The Culture of Space and Time 1880–1918*. Kern argues that changes in concepts of time and space were a factor leading to the outbreak of the First World War, and influenced the way it was fought.

3. See Bill Bryson, *Notes from a Small Island*, for an amusing account of his visit to the Coronation Street studios near Manchester and the double and displaced nostalgia that he as an American could find in recollecting the experience of watching *Coronation Street*.

4. See above Chapter 2, p. 53–7.

5. See Anthony Curtis, 'An Outsider in This Society: An interview with Don DeLillo', in *Rolling Stone*, reproduced in Frank Lentricchia, 'Introducing Don DeLillo', *South Atlantic Quarterly* (1991), vol. 89 no.2, p. 61.

List of Novels

Peter Ackroyd	*Hawksmoor*	(H)
Peter Ackroyd	*First Light*	(FL)
J.M. Coetzee	*Foe*	(*Foe*)
Don DeLillo	*The Names*	(N)
Don DeLillo	*Ratner's Star*	(RS)
Alasdair Gray	*Lanark*	(L)
Ian McEwan	*The Child in Time*	(CT)
Caryl Phillips	*Cambridge*	(C)
Graham Swift	*Waterland*	(W)
Graham Swift	*Out of This World*	(OW)
Michel Tournier	*Friday, or The Other Island*	(F)
Marina Warner	*Indigo: Or, Mapping the Waters*	(I)

Note

The first reference to the novels examined in *The Postmodern Chronotope* uses the title of the novel in full. Subsequent references are made using the word or abbreviation appearing in brackets above, followed by the page number.

Bibliography

Ackroyd, Peter (1986) *Hawksmoor*, London: Abacus.
Ackroyd, Peter (1990) *First Light*, London: Abacus.
Agnew, John A. and James S. Duncan (eds) (1989) *The Power of Place; Bringing Together Geographical and Sociological Imaginations*, London: Unwin Hyman.
Ahmed, Suleiman M. (1993) Introduction to Thomas Hardy, *Two on a Tower*, Oxford: World's Classics, Oxford University Press.
Allard, Roger [1910] 'At the Paris Salon d'Automne' in Edward Fry (ed.) (1966) *Cubism*, New York.
Amis, Martin (1984) *Money: A Suicide Note*, London: Jonathan Cape.
Auster, Paul (1988) *New York Trilogy: City of Glass, Ghosts, The Locked Room*, London: Faber and Faber.
Bachelard, Gaston (1969) *The Poetics of Space*, trans. Maria Jolas, Boston, Mass.: Beacon Press.
Bakhtin, Mikhail (1981) *The Dialogic Imagination*, trans. Caryl Emerson and Michael Holquist, ed. Michael Holquist. Austin: University of Texas Press.
Barth, John (1967) 'The Literature of Exhaustion' in *The Atlantic* 220(2): 29–34.
Barth, John (1988) 'The Literature of Replenishment' in *The Atlantic* 245: 65–71.
Barthes, Roland (1988) 'Death of the Author' in Stephen Heath (trans.) *Music-Image-Text*, New York: Hill and Way.
Baudelaire, Charles [1863] 'The Painter of Modern Life' in J. Mayne (trans.) (1964) *The Painter of Modern Life and Other Essays*, London: Phaidon.
Baudrillard, Jean (1983a) 'From the Precession of Simulacra' in Paul Foss, Paul Patton and Philip Beitchman (trans.) *Simulations*, New York: Semiotext(e).
Baudrillard, Jean (1983b) 'The Ecstasy of Communication' in Hal Foster (ed.) *The Anti-Aesthetic: Essays on Postmodern Culture*, Port Townsend, Washington: Bay Press.
Bauman, Zygmunt (1992) *Intimations of Postmodernity*, London: Routledge.

Beer, Gillian (1983) *Darwin's Plots: Evolutionary Narrative in Darwin, George Eliot and Nineteenth Century Fiction*, London: Routledge.
Bell, Daniel (1973) *The Coming of Post-Industrial Society*, New York: Basic Books.
Bell, Daniel (1976) *The Cultural Contradictions of Capitalism*, London: Heinemann.
Berger, John (1974) *The Look of Things*, Harmondsworth: Penguin.
Bergson, Henri (1911) *Creative Evolution*, London: Macmillan.
Berman, Marshall (1983) *All That is Solid Melts into Air*, London: Verso.
Bertens, Hans (1995) *The Idea of the Postmodern*, London: Routledge.
Blythe, Ronald (1972) *Akenfield: Portrait of an English Village*, Harmondsworth: Penguin.
Borges, Jorge Luis [1942] 'Death and the Compass' in Norman Thomas di Giovanni (ed. and trans.) (1973) *The Aleph and Other Stories 1933–1969*, London: Pan Books.
Bourdieu, Pierre (1990) 'Time Perspectives of the Kabyle' in John Hassard (ed.) *The Sociology of Time*, Basingstoke: Macmillan.
Bryson, Bill (1995) *Notes from a Small Island*, London: Doubleday.
Calvino, Italo (1979) *Invisible Cities*, trans. William Weaver, London: Picador.
Calvino, Italo (1998) *If On a Winter's Night a Traveller*, trans. William Weaver, London: Vintage.
Carter, Angela (1991) *Wise Children*, London: Chatto and Windus.
Chaucer, Geoffrey 'The House of Fame', in Brian Stone (trans.) (1983) *Geoffrey Chaucer: The Love Visions*, Harmondsworth: Penguin.
Coetzee, J.M. (1988) *Foe*, London: Penguin.
Connor, Steven (1989) *Postmodernist Culture: An Introduction to Theories of the Contemporary*, Oxford: Blackwell.
Conrads, Ulrich (ed.) (1970) *Programmes and Manifestos on Twentieth-Century Architecture*, London: Lund Humphries.
Cooke, Philip (1990) *Back to the Future*, London: Unwin Hyman.
Currie, Mark (ed.) (1995) *Metafiction*, Harlow: Addison Wesley Longman.
Currie, Mark (1998) *Postmodern Narrative Theory*, Basingstoke: Macmillan.
Curry, Michael (1991) 'Postmodernism, Language, and the Strains of Modernism' in *Annals of the Association of American Geographers*, Vol. 81 (2).

Curtis, Anthony (1991) in Frank Lentricchia (ed.) 'Introducing Don DeLillo', *South Atlantic Quarterly* 89(2), p.61. (First published as 'An Outsider in This Society: An interview with Don DeLillo', in *Rolling Stone*, November 17, 1988.)

Deleuze, Gilles and Félix Guattari (1984) *Anti-Oedipus: Capitalism and Schizophrenia* trans. Robert Hurley, Mark Seem and Helen R. Lane, London: Athlone Press

DeLillo, Don (1987) *The Names,* London, Picador.

DeLillo, Don (1989) *Libra,* London, Picador.

DeLillo, Don (1991) *Ratner's Star,* London, Vintage.

Derrida, Jacques (1978) *Writing and Difference*, trans. Alan Bass, London: Routledge.

Diamant, A. (1970) 'The Temporal Dimension in Models of Administration and Organisation', in D. Waldo (ed.) *Temporal Dimensions of Development Administration*, Durham, N.C.: Duke University Press.

Doctorow, E.R. (1994) *Ragtime,* New York: Modern Library.

Donne, John [1633] 'Meditation', '17. Nunc lento sonitu dicunt, Morieris', in H. Gardner and T. Healy (eds) (1967) *John Donne: Selected Prose*, London: Clarendon.

Dostoyevsky, Fyodor (1972) *Notes from Underground/The Double*, trans. Jessie Coulson, Harmondsworth: Penguin.

Duncan, James (1989)'The Power of Place in Kandy, Sri Lanka: 1780–1980', in John Agnew and James Duncan (eds) *The Power of Place*, London: Unwin Hyman.

Duncan, James (1993) 'Sites of Representation: Place, Time and the Discourse of the Other', in James Duncan and David Ley (eds) *Place/Culture/Representation*, London: Routledge.

Durkheim, Emile (1915) *The Elementary Forms of Religious Life*, trans. J.W. Swain, London: Allen and Unwin.

Eagleton, Terry (1996) *The Illusions of Postmodernism*, Oxford: Blackwell.

Eco, Umberto (1984) *The Name of the Rose* trans. William Weaver, London: Pan Books.

Eliade, M. (1959) *Cosmos and History*, New York: Harper.

Eliot, George [1872](1987) *Middlemarch*, Harmondsworth: Penguin.

Farrell, J.G. (1984) *The Singapore Grip*, London: Fontana.

Featherstone, Mike (1991) *Consumer Culture and Postmodernism*, London: Sage.

Folch-Serra, M. (1990) 'Mikhail Bakhtin's Dialogical Landscape', *Environment and Planning D – Society and Space*, 8(3).

Foster, Hal (1985) *Recording: Art, Spectacle, Cultural Politics*, Port Townsend, Washington: Bay Press.

Foster, Hal (1996) *The Return of the Real: The Avant-Garde at the End of the Century,* Cambridge, Mass.: MIT Press.

Foucault, Michel (1972) *The Archaeology of Knowledge*, trans. A.M. Sheridan Smith, London: Tavistock.

Foucault, Michel (1980) 'Questions on Geography', in C. Gordon (ed.) *Power/Knowledge: Selected Interviews and Other Writings 1972–1977*, trans. Colin Gordon, Brighton: Harvester Press.

Foucault, Michel (1986) 'Of Other Spaces' in *Diacritics*, Spring, trans. Jay Miskowiec. Lecture given in March 1967 first published as 'Des Espaces Autres' in *Architecture-Mouvement-Continuité*, October 1984.

Foucault, Michel [1969] 'What is an Author?', in David Lodge (ed.) (1988) *Modern Criticism and Theory*, trans. by Joseph V. Harari, Harlow: Longman.

Francese, Joseph (1997) *Narrating Postmodern Time and Space*, New York: State University of New York Press.

Frank, Joseph (1991) *The Idea of Spatial Form*, New Brunswick: Rutgers University Press.

Gaitkens, Edward (1948) *Dance of the Apprentices*, Glasgow: William MacLellan.

Giddens, Anthony (1981) *A Contemporary Critique of Historical Materialism*, Basingstoke: Macmillan.

Giddens, Anthony (1999) 'Runaway World', BBC Reith lectures, London.

Gleizes, Albert and Jean Metzinger (1964) 'Cubism', in Robert L. Herbert (ed.) *Modern Artists on Art*, New York.

Gray, Alasdair (1991) *Lanark*, London: Pan Books.

Gould, P. and R. White (1974) *White Mental Maps*, Harmondsworth: Penguin.

Gurvitch, Georges (1964) *The Spectrum of Social Time*, Dordrecht: D.Reidel.

Gurvitch, Georges (1990) 'Varieties of Social Time' in John Hassard (ed.) *The Sociology of Time*, Basingstoke: Macmillan.

Hardy, F.E. (1928) *The Early Life of Thomas Hardy*, London: Macmillan.

Hardy, Thomas [1886](1985) *The Mayor of Casterbridge*, London: Penguin Classics.
Hardy, Thomas [1878](1985) *The Return of the Native*, Macmillan: London.
Hardy, Thomas [1882](1993) *Two on a Tower*, Oxford: World's Classics, Oxford University Press.
Harvey, David (1990a) *The Condition of Postmodernity*, Oxford: Blackwell.
Harvey, David (1990b). 'Between Space and Time: Reflections on the Geographical Imagination', *Annals of the Association of American Geographers*, 80(3).
Harvey, David (1993) 'From Space to Place and Back Again', in Jon Bird *et al.* (ed.) *Mapping the Futures: Local Cultures, Global Change*, London: Routledge.
Harvie, Christopher (1991) 'Alasdair Gray and the Condition of Scotland Question', in Robert Crawford and Thom Nairn (eds) *The Arts of Alasdair Gray*, Edinburgh: Edinburgh University Press.
Hassan, Ihab (1982) *The Dismemberment of Orpheus: Toward a Postmodern Literature*, Wisconsin: University of Wisconsin Press.
Hassard, John (ed.) (1990) 'Introduction' in *The Sociology of Time*, Basingstoke: Macmillan.
Hawking, Stephen (1988) *A Brief History of Time*, London: Bantam.
Hoyle, Fred (1955) *Frontiers of Astronomy*, New York: Harper and Brothers.
Hulme, Peter (1986) *Colonial Encounters: Europe and the Native Caribbean, 1492–1797*, London: Methuen.
Hutcheon, Linda (1988) *A Poetics of Postmodernism: History, Theory, Fiction*, London: Routledge.
Huyssen, Andreas (1981) 'The Search for Tradition: Avant-Garde and Postmodernism in the 1970s', *New German Critique* 22.
Huyssen, Andreas (1988) *After the Great Divide*, Basingstoke: Macmillan.
Jacobs, Jane (1964) *The Death and Life of Great American Cities*, Harmondsworth: Penguin.
James, William (1890) *The Principles of Psychology* London: Macmillan.
Jameson, Fredric (1988) 'Imaginary and Symbolic in Lacan' in *The Ideologies of Theory: Essays 1971–1986*, Minneapolis: University of Minnesota Press.

Jameson, Fredric (1991) *Postmodernism or, The Cultural Logic of Late Capitalism*, London: Verso.

Janowitz, Anne (1990) *England's Ruins: Poetic Purpose and the National Landscape*, Oxford: Blackwell.

Jencks, Charles (1984) *The Language of Post-modern Architecture*, New York, Rizzoli (4th ed.).

Johnson, B.S. (1973) *Aren't You Rather Young to be Writing Your Memoirs?*, London: Hutchinson.

Johnson, Mark (1987) *The Body in the Mind: The Bodily Basis of Meaning, Imagination, and Reason*, Chicago: University of Chicago Press.

Kermode, Frank (1988) Introduction, New Arden Shakespeare, *The Tempest*, London: Routledge.

Kern, Stephen (1983) *The Culture of Time and Space 1880–1918*, Cambridge, Mass.: Harvard University Press.

Kimble, George (1938) *Geography in the Middle Ages*, London: Methuen.

Kristeva, Julia (1981) 'Women's Time' from *Signs* 1, 13–35.

Lamming, George (1998) *In the Castle of my Skin*, Harlow: Addison Wesley Longman (first published 1953 by Michael Joseph.)

Landes, David S. (1983) *Revolution in Time: Clocks and the Making of the Modern World*, Cambridge, Mass.: Harvard University Press.

Lash, Scott (1989) *Sociology of Postmodernism*, London: Routledge.

Latham, Ronald (ed. and trans.) (1958) *The Travels of Marco Polo*, Harmondsworth: Penguin.

Lee, Alison (1990) *Realism and Power: Postmodern British Fiction*, London: Routledge.

Lefebvre, Henri (1991) *The Production of Space*, trans. Donald Nicholson-Smith, Oxford: Blackwell.

Le Goff, J. (1980) *Time, Work and Culture in the Middle Ages*, Chicago: University Chicago Press.

Lentricchia, F. (1991) *Introducing Don DeLillo*. London: Duke University Press.

Lewis, David and Andrew Weigart (1990) 'Structures and Meanings of Social-Time' in John Hassard (ed.) *The Sociology of Time*, Basingstoke: Macmillan.

Loxley, Diana (1990) *Problematic Shores: The Literature of Islands* Basingstoke: Macmillan.

Lyndon, D. (1962),'Towards making places', in *Landscape* 12 (3).

Lyotard, Jean-François (1983) 'Answering the Question: What is Postmodernism?' in I. Hassan and S. Hassan (eds) *Innovation/Renovation*, Wisconsin: University of Wisconsin Press.
Lyotard, Jean-François (1984) *The Postmodern Condition*, Minneapolis: University of Minnesota Press.
Lyotard, Jean-François (1988) *The Differend: Phrases in Dispute*, trans. Georges van den Abbeele, Manchester: Manchester University Press.
Lyotard, Jean-François (1991) *The Inhuman: Reflections of Time*, trans. Geoffrey Bennington and Rachel Bowlby, Cambridge: Polity Press.
McEwan, Ian (1988) *The Child in Time*, London: Picador.
McHale, Brian (1987) *Postmodernist Fiction*, London: Routledge.
Malinowski, Bronislaw (1990) 'Time-Reckoning in the Trobriands', in John Hassard (ed.) *The Sociology of Time*, Basingstoke: Macmillan.
Mandelbrot, Benoit B. (1982) *The Fractal Geometry of Nature*, San Francisco: W.H. Freeman.
Marshall, Brenda K. (1992) *Teaching the Postmodern: Fiction and Theory*, London: Routledge.
Massey, Doreen (1993) 'Power-geometry and a Progressive Sense of Place', in Jon Bird *et al.* (eds) *Mapping the Futures: Local Cultures, Global Change*, London: Routledge.
May, Robert M. (1993) 'From Newton to Chaos' in programme notes to *Arcadia* by Tom Stoppard, Royal National Theatre of Great Britain, London.
Meyer, Leonard B .(1993) 'The End of the Renaissance?', *Hudson Review* 16.
Mo, Timothy (1992) *Sour Sweet*, London: Vintage Books (first published 1982 by André Deutsch).
Morris, Jan (1992) 'Vermont' in *Locations*, Oxford: Oxford University Press.
Moseley, C.W.R.D. (ed. and trans.) (1983) *The Travels of Sir John Mandeville*, Harmondsworth: Penguin.
Nagel, T. (1986) *The View from Nowhere*, Oxford: Oxford University Press.
Naipaul, V.S. (1987) *The Enigma of Arrival*, London: Viking.
Norberg-Schultz, C. (1971) *Existence, Space and Architecture*, New York: Praeger.
Norris, Christopher (1993) *The Truth About Postmodernism*, Oxford: Blackwell.
Phillips, Caryl (1985) *The Final Passage*, London: Faber and Faber.

Phillips, Caryl (1992) *Cambridge*, London: Picador.
Phillips, Caryl (1997) *The Nature of Blood*, London: Faber and Faber.
Picasso, Pablo [1923] 'Statements to Marius de Zayas' in Edward Fry (ed.) (1966) *Cubism,* New York.
Pound, Ezra (1934) *Make it New*, London: Faber.
Pred, Allan (1992) in *Annals of the Association of American Geographers*, 82(2).
Raban, Jonathan (1974) *Soft City,* London: Hamish Hamilton.
Relph, Edward (1976) *Place and Placelessness,* London: Pion.
Rennie, Neil (1995) *Far-fetched Facts: the Literature of Travel and the Idea of the South Seas*, Oxford: Clarendon Press.
Riley, Joan (1985) *The Unbelonging*, London: The Women's Press.
Rogers, Richard (1999) *Complete Works*, London: Phaidon Press.
Ross, K. (1988) *The Emergence of Social Space*, Minneapolis: University of Minnesota Press.
Rushdie, Salman (1988) *The Satanic Verses,* Harmondsworth: Penguin.
Rushdie, Salman (1992) *Imaginary Homelands,* Harmondsworth: Penguin.
Said, Edward (1993) *Culture and Imperialism,* London: Chatto and Windus
Self, Will (1994) 'A Short History of the English Novel' in *Grey Area*, London: Bloomsbury.
Smith, Jonathan (1993) 'The Lie that Blinds: Destabilizing the Text of Landscape', in James Duncan and David Ley (eds) *Place/Culture/Representation*, London: Routledge.
Smith, Neil and Cindi Katz (1993) 'Grounding Metaphor: Towards a Spatialized Politics', in Michael Keith and Steve Pile (eds) *Place and the Politics of Identity*, London: Routledge.
Soja, Edward (1988) *Postmodern Geographies: The Reassertion of Space in Critical Social Theory*, London: Verso.
Spanos, William V. (1972) 'The Detective and the Boundary: Some Notes on the Postmodern Literary Imagination' *Boundary 2*, 1: 147–168.
Stevenson, Randall (1986) *The British Novel Since the Thirties*, London: B.T. Batsford.
Stoppard, Tom (1975) *Travesties*, London: Faber and Faber.
Stoppard, Tom (1986) *Jumpers*, London: Faber and Faber, revised edition.
Stoppard, Tom (1993) *Arcadia*, London: Faber and Faber.

Stratton, Jon (1990) *Writing Sites: A Genealogy of the Postmodern World*, Hemel Hempstead: Harvester Wheatsheaf.
Swift, Graham (1984) *Waterland*, London: Picador.
Swift, Graham (1988) *Out of this World*, Harmonsworth: Penguin.
Thomson, James [1857] in A. Ridler (1963) (ed.) *Poems and Some Letters of James Thomson*, Carbondale: Southern Illinois University Press.
Thrift, Nigel (1980) *Owner's Time and Our Time: The Making of a Capitalist Time Consciousness, 1300–1880*, Melbourne: Australian National University.
Tindall, Gillian (1991) *Countries of the Mind*, London: Hogarth Press.
Todorov, Tzvetan (1994) 'Fictions and Truths', in Robert M. Polhemus and Roger B. Henkle (eds) *Critical Reconstructions*, trans. Jennifer Curtiss Gage, Stanford: Stanford University Press.
Tournier, Michel (1969) *Friday, or The Other Island*, trans. Norman Denny, New York: Doubleday.
Tuan, Yi-Fu (1977) *Space and Place: The Perspective of Experience*, London: Edward Arnold.
Tuan, Yi-Fu (1989) 'Surface Phenomena and Aesthetic Experience' in *Annals of the Association of American Geographers*, 79(2).
Tuan, Yi-Fu (1993) *Passing Strange and Wonderful*, NewYork: Island Press.
Versluys, Kristiann (ed.) (1992) *Neo-realism in Contemporary American Fiction*, Amsterdam: Rodopi.
Venturi, Robert, Denise Scott Brown and Steven Izenour (1977) *Learning from Las Vegas: The Forgotten Symbolism of Architectural Form*, Cambridge, Mass.: MIT Press.
Walsh, Richard (1995) *Novel Arguments: Reading Innovative American Fiction*, Cambridge: Cambridge University Press.
Warner, Marina (1993) *Indigo: Or, Mapping the Waters*, London: Vintage.
Watt, Ian (1957) *The Rise of the Novel: Studies in Defoe, Richardson and Fielding*, Berkeley and Los Angeles: University of California Press.
Watt, Ian (1969) 'Individualism and the Novel', in Frank H. Ellis (ed.) *Twentieth Century Interpretations of Robinson Crusoe*, Englewood Cliffs, N.J.: Prentice-Hall.
Waugh, Patricia (1984) *Metafiction: The Theory and Practice of Self-Conscious Fiction*, London: Methuen.

Williams, Raymond (1993) *The Country and the City*, London: Hogarth.
Witschi, Beat (1991) *Glasgow Urban Writing and Postmodernism* Frankfurt am Main: Peter Lang.
Woolf, Virginia [1924] 'Mr. Bennett and Mrs. Brown', in *Collected Essays* (1971), Vol. 1, London: Hogarth Press.
Woolf, Virginia [1925](1976) *Mrs Dalloway*, London: Grafton Books (first published by Hogarth Press).

Index

1984, 283

A

Ackroyd, Peter, 15, 19, 107, 110, 223 173–218, 243, 289, 293
Adorno, Theodor, 71
Agnew, John, 90
Ahmed, Suleiman, 101
Akenfield, 157
Allard, Roger, 75
Amis, Martin, 72
Anderson, Laurie, 79
Anglo-Saxon poetry, 59
Apollo missions, 272, 286, 288
Arcadia, 171
Archaeology (in *The Names*), 302, 303, 307
  (in *First Light*), 197, 198, 200
Archaeology of Knowledge, The, 42
Architecture, postmodernist, 26, 27, 80–2
Austen, Jane, 17
Auster, Paul, 16, 72
Avant-garde(ism), 13, 70, 71, 72, 74

B

Bachelard, Gaston, 44, 248, 268, 269
Backwards evolution (in *Ratner's Star*), 299–300
Bakhtin, Mikhail, 6, 10, 12, 38, 45, 64, 67, 68, 69, 70, 100, 102, 309
Barth, John, 7
Barthes, Roland, 72
Baudelaire, Charles, 25, 36
Baudrillard, Jean, 3, 12, 56, 74, 98, 99
Beckett, Samuel, 97
Beer, Gillian, 109
Berger, John, 62
Bergson, Henri, 32, 37, 38, 40, 183
Berman, Marshall, 37, 40
Bertens, Hans, 8, 97
Big Bang theory, 105
Bildungsroman, 102, 256
Biological time, 176
Birmingham, 54
Blake, William, 116, 117, 126, 129, 132, 135
Bleak House, 39
Blythe, Ronald, 157
Bourdieu, Pierre, 177, 178
Brief History of Time, A, 178

Brookside Close (television series), 283
Byron, Lord, 59

C

Calvino, Italo, 18, 19, 24, 64, 67, 72, 79, 110, 111, 112
Cambridge, 20, 219–66
Caribbean (as colonialist construction), 224–8
Carter, Angela, 73–4
Chaos (theory), 84, 88, 105, 106, 179
Chaucer, Geoffrey, 131
Child in Time, The, 20, 173–218
Christo, 78
Chronotope(s), 5, 6, 10, 12, 65–70, 100
Cinema, *see* Film
City of Dreadful Night, The, 133
Clock time, 176, 238
Clocks, 60
Coetzee, J.M., 20, 219–66
Colonial history, 229, 230, 233, 235, 246, 266
Condition of Postmodernity, The, 7, 88
Connor, Steven, 8, 35, 80, 98
Conrads, Ulrich, 80
Cooke, Philip, 120, 121, 123, 124
Coronation Street (television series), 283
Cosmological time, 176
Creolisation (in *Cambridge*), 251, 258
Crossing the River, 231, 258
Cubism, 36, 75–7
Culture of Time and Space, The, 31, 40
Currie, Mark, 8, 85, 86, 87

D

Dance of the Apprentices, 127
Dante, 68, 69, 116, 117, 126, 131
Darwinism, 101, 102, 103, 108, 109, 113
Darwin's Plots, 109
De-differentiation, 4, 18, 20, 72–4
DeLillo, Don, 15, 20, 21, 39, 267–309
Defoe, Daniel, 224, 225, 227, 228, 230, 232, 233, 234, 235, 237, 240, 241,
Deleuze, Gilles, 85
Demoiselles d'Avignon, Les, 76
Derrida, Jacques, 85
Des Espaces Autres, 42
Dialogism, 45–6, 80, 156
Dickens, Charles, 39, 102, 118
Differend, 12, 23

331

Digital culture, 98–100
Disneyfication, 56, 92, 94
Divine Comedy, 68, 131
Doctorow, E.R., 4, 18
Donne, John, 227
Dostoyevsky, Fyodor, 37, 52, 67, 69
Duchamp, Marcel, 71
Duncan, James, 90, 229, 283
Durkheim, Emile, 32
Dystopia, 16, 133, 136, 137, 140

E

Eagleton, Terry, 11, 27
Ecological time, 175
Ecstasy of Communication, The, 98
Edinburgh, 136, 143
Einstein, Albert, 19, 32, 75, 104
Eliot, George, 5, 102
Eliot, T.S., 63
End of Violence, The, 283

F

Far from the Madding Crowd (in *First Light*), 201
Farrell, J.G., 146–9
Featherstone, Mike, 77
Film, 3, 36, 41, 57, 74, 75, 76, 77, 85, 142, 272, 273, 276, 282–8, 305, 306
First Light, 19, 107, 173–218, 223
Flaubert, Gustave, 63
Florence, 43
Foe, 20, 219–66
Folch-Serra, M., 69
Forms of Time and Chronotope in the Novel, 64
Foucault, Michel, 7, 8, 35, 36, 41, 42, 43, 50, 72, 108, 110, 121, 263
Francese, Joseph, 8
Frank, Joseph, 62, 63, 64, 113
Friday, or The Other Island, 20, 219–66
Full Monty, The, 119

G

Gaitkens, Edward, 127
Gaskell, Elizabeth, 118
Geographical imagination (in Waterland), 150–3, 158–65
Geological time, 175

Geopolitics, 149, 159, 167–8, 255, 259, 264
Giddens, Anthony, 11, 38, 87
Glasgow, 15, 16, 17, 72, 115–43, 145, 158
Gleizes, Albert, 75
Globalisation, 1, 2, 12, 16, 34, 87, 88, 115, 220–1
Gould, P., 60
Grand Tour, The, 58, 59
Gray, Alasdair, 15, 17, 72, 115–43, 145, 155, 173
Gropius, Walter, 80
Guattari, Félix, 85
Gulliver's Travels, 226
Gurvitch, Georges, 178, 190

H

Haacke, Hans, 76, 78
Hamlet, 57
Hardy, Thomas, 17, 68, 101, 102, 103, 133, 160, 195, 201, 264
Harvey, David 7, 12, 33, 36, 47, 60, 85, 87, 88, 89, 91, 93
Hassan, Ihab, 25, 97
Hassard, John, 177, 178
Haussmann, 37, 47
Hawking, Stephen, 84, 101, 103, 106, 178
Hawksmoor, 19, 107, 110, 173–218
Heisenberg, Werner, 57, 103, 106, 180
Heterotopia, 41, 42, 55, 117, 118, 125, 142, 263
Historical time, 176
Historiography (in *The Singapore Grip*), 146–50
History and narrative, 17, 109–13, 146–9, 152, 179
Hobbes, Thomas, 118
Hong Kong, 27, 271
House of Fame, The, 131
Hoyle, Fred, 50, 140
Hulme, Peter, 232
Hutcheon, Linda, 8, 14, 35, 154, 155, 156, 157, 171
Huxley, Aldous, 105
Huyssen, Andreas, 8, 13, 22, 71
Hybridity, hybridisation, 265, 266
Hyperspace, 106, 132

I

If On a Winter's Night a Traveller, 24, 72, 79
Imagism, 63
Imago-mundi, 44, 224
In the Castle of my Skin, 248, 252
Inauthentic place, 277
Indigo: Or, Mapping the Waters, 20, 219–66
Information technology, 98–100
Insideness, 268–70, 272, 279, 281, 283, 300, 307
International Style, 26, 80, 271, 291
Invisible Cities, 18, 19, 64, 67, 110–13
Izenour, Steven, 26

J

Jacobs, Jane, 80
James, William, 37, 183
Jameson, Fredric, 8, 9, 10, 11, 12, 13, 14, 18, 35, 76, 77, 78, 80, 85, 89, 90, 91, 99, 132
Janowitz, Anne, 59
Jenks, Charles, 26, 27, 80
Johnson, B.S., 105
Johnson, Mark, 60, 61
Joyce, James, 32, 37, 63, 104

K

Kant, Immanuel, 95, 96
Katz, Cindi, 90
Keats, John, 59
Kermode, Frank, 64, 113
Kern, Stephen, 31, 36, 38, 40, 44, 80, 104, 276
Kronberg Castle, Denmark, 57
Kublai Khan
(in *Invisible Cities*) 19, 111, 112

L

Lacan, 85
Lamming, George, 248, 252, 258
Lanark, 15, 16, 17, 72, 115–43, 145, 155, 158, 162, 173
Landes, David, 60
Langland, William, 68
Laplace, Maquis de, 101, 103, 104
Las Vegas, 292
Lash, Scott, 72, 77, 78
Latham, Ronald, 224
Le Corbusier, Henri, 80, 90
Lee, Alison, 8
Lefebvre, Henri, 7, 8, 13, 15, 37, 42, 43, 44, 45, 47, 49, 50, 51, 52, 53, 55, 62, 91, 106, 112, 113, 123, 140, 149, 155, 309
Leonardo da Vinci, 71
Leviathan, 118
Lewis, David, 215
Lewis, Wyndham, 38
Ley, David, 90
Libra, 39
Lloyd Wright, Frank, 80
Localism, 15, 121–2, 123, 157
London, 46, 47, 133, 134, 136, 145, 154 (see also *Hawksmoor*)
Los Angeles, 34, 90
Loxley, Diana, 232
Lyndon, D., 268
Lyotard, Jean-François, 9, 23, 24, 25, 95, 96, 121, 188, 198, 208, 210

M

Maclean, Bruce, 79
Madame Bovary, 63
Malinowski, Bronislaw, 177, 178
Marco Polo, 19, 224
(in *Invisible Cities*), 19, 111, 112
Marshall, Brenda, 84, 85, 242
Massey, Doreen, 89, 221, 223
Maya, the, 83
McEwan, Ian, 20, 173–218, 223
McHale, Brian, 8, 35, 79, 94, 95, 246
Meditation, 227
Metzinger, Jean, 75
Meyer, Leonard B., 97
Middle Passsage, The, 258
Middlemarch, 5, 17
Midsummer Night's Dream, A (in *Wise Children*), 73, 74
Miller, Henry, 97
Milton, John, 131
Moll Flanders, 241
Mona Lisa, 71
Money, 72
Monroe, Marilyn, 71
Morris, Jan, 56
Moseley, C.W.R.D., 224
Mother Shipton, 83

Mr Bennett and Mrs Brown, 104
Munch, Edward, 18

N
Nagel, T., 284
Naipaul, V.S., 142
Names, The, 20, 39, 267–309
Nature of Blood, The, 250
New Labour, 23
New Lanark 140, 143
New World, 224
New York Trilogy, 16, 17, 72
New York, 27, 133
Newsreels (in *Out of This World*), 285–6
Non-directional time, 19, 105, 107, 110, 174, 179, 208, 215
Norberg-Schultz, C., 61, 268
Norris, Christopher, 11, 23, 96
Nostradamus, 83
Notes from Underground, 37, 52
Novel Arguments: Reading Innovative American Fiction, 7
Nuremberg, as inauthentic place, 277

O
Olson, Charles, 97
Orwell, George, 105, 283
Out of this World, 20, 267–309
Ovid, 131
Owen, Robert, 140

P
Painter of Modern Life, The, 25
Paradise Lost, 131
Paris, 37, 47, 133, 136, 145, 154
Phillips, Caryl, 20, 219–66
  as cosmopolitan writer, 252
Photography, *see* Film
Picasso, Pablo, 75, 76
Piers Plowman, 68
Pirandello, Luigi, 79
Place and Placelessness, 92
Placelessness, 12, 15, 20, 21, 33, 34, 40, 56, 91, 92–5, 118, 119, 121, 138, 164
Poetics of Space, The, 44, 248, 249, 268
Post-colonial discourse, 228, 243, 252
Post-colonialism, centre–periphery relations, 219
Postmodern detective, 179, 192, 193

Postmodern geographies, 90–5
Postmodern metafiction, 79
Postmodernist architecture, 26, 27, 80–2
Post-structuralism, 15, 25, 54, 55, 72, 85, 105, 234, 243, 244, 245, 303, 305
Pound, Ezra, 63
Poundbury (pseudo place), 94
Production of Space, The, 7, 42, 43, 44
Prophesy, 40, 51, 82–5, 113, 151
Proust, Marcel, 32
Pseudo place, 27, 33, 56, 92, 94, 121, 149
Psychological time, 176

R
Raban, Jonathan, 53
Ragtime, 14, 18, 149
Ratner's Star, 21, 267–309
Recontextualisation, 86
Relph, Edward, 56, 90, 92, 93, 94, 268, 272, 277
Representational space(s), 34, 43, 44, 48–54, 55, 56, 57, 61, 62, 64, 76, 91, 116, 124, 131, 133, 145, 158
Return of the Native, The, 103
Rhys, Jean, 258
Riley, Joan, 258
Rise of the Novel, The, 228
Robbe-Grillet, Alain, 105
Robinson Crusoe, 20, 224, 225, 226, 228, 229, 230, 232, 233, 234, 235, 236, 240, 241, 242, 243, 246, 252, 255
Rogers, Richard, 270
Rome, 58, 59
Roxana, 241
Ruin, The, 59

S
Said, Edward, 262, 263, 269
Saint Augustine, 31
Schizophrenia, metaphor of, 85–7
Science and fiction, 100–4
Science fiction, 105, 117, 197
Science and metaphor, 107–9
Scott Brown, Denise, 26
Selkirk, Alexander, 244
Scream, The, 18
Self, Will, 72
Shakespeare, William, 59, 73, 116, 232,

234, 249, 259, 266
see also *Hamlet*; *Midsummer Night's Dream, A*; *Tempest, The*
Sheffield, 119
Shelley, Percy Bysshe, 59
Simulacra, 3, 14, 23, 53, 56, 57, 76, 84, 99, 121, 137, 223
Singapore Grip, The, 146–9
Six Characters in Search of an Author, 79
Smith, Jonathan, 281
Smith, Neil, 90
Social space, analysis of, 42–51
Social time, 32, 176
  in *The Child in Time*, 215–7
Sociology of Postmodernism, 77
Soja, Edward, 34, 38, 90
Spanos, William, 97
Spatial form, 40, 62–4, 69, 75
Spatial Form in Modern Literature, 63
Spatial metaphor, 60, 61
Spatial turn, 7, 35, 37, 42
Spatialisation, 8, 10, 12, 35, 40–51, 55, 62, 64, 97, 113, 151
Stoppard, Tom, 22, 171
Stratton, Jon, 35, 59, 224, 225, 226, 228
Swift, Graham, 15, 17, 20, 21, 86, 145–72, 267–309

T
Tallinn (Estonia), 56
Television 'soap operas', 283
Tempest, The, 20, 225, 226, 228, 231, 232, 234, 249, 259, 265
Theory of Relativity, 19, 32, 75, 103, 104
Thermodynamic time, 176
Thomson, James, 133, 134
Thrift, Nigel, 183, 189
Time, different forms of, 175–7
Time–space compression, 7, 87–90
Time–space distanciation, 38–9
Todorov, Tzvetan, 224
Tournier, Michel, 20, 219–66
Travels of Sir John Mandeville, The, 224
Travels, Marco Polo, 19, 224
Travesties, 22
Trollope, Anthony, 17
Tuan, Yi-Fu, 55, 57, 58, 138, 182, 188, 216, 267, 284, 297
Two on a Tower, 101

U
Ulysses, 63, 104
Unbelonging, The, 258
Uncertainty Principle, 103, 106–7
Utopia, 226

V
Venice (in *Invisible Cities*), 110, 111, 180
Venturi, Robert, 26, 80, 292
Vermont, 56
Versluys, Kristiann, 8
Victorian novel(s), 5, 102, 109, 256
Vietnam, 272, 286
Virgil, 131

W, Z
Walsh, Richard, 7
Wanderer, The, 59
Warhol, Andy, 71
Warner, Marina, 20, 219–66
Waterland, 17, 86, 145–72, 177, 178, 179, 198, 222, 273, 274
Watt, Ian, 227
Weigart, Andrew, 215
Wells, H.G., 116
Weltanschauung, 4, 12, 65, 66, 67
Wenders, Wim, 283
Westin Bonaventure Hotel, 18, 90, 132
White, R., 60
Wide Sargasso Sea, The, 258
Williams, Raymond, 133, 134, 157, 281
Wise Children, 73–4
Witschi, Beat, 126, 127, 142
Woolf, Virginia, 32, 37, 104
Zero time, 58

OHIO UNIVERSITY LIBRARY

Please return this book as soon as you have finished with it. In order to avoid a fine it must be returned by the latest date stamped below. All books are subject to recall after two weeks or immediately if needed for reserve.

DEC 1 5 2001
SEP 1 5 2001
JUN 1 6 2003
JUN 0 3 2003

CF